SHAPERS
OF THE
GREAT DEBATE
ON THE
GREAT SOCIETY

SHAPERS
—— OF THE ——
GREAT DEBATE
—— ON THE ——
GREAT SOCIETY

A BIOGRAPHICAL DICTIONARY

Lawson Bowling

Shapers of the Great American Debates, Number 5
Peter B. Levy, Series Editor

GREENWOOD PRESS
Westport, Connecticut • London

Library of Congress Cataloging-in-Publication Data

Bowling, Lawson, 1954–
    Shapers of the great debate on the Great Society : a biographical dictionary /
Lawson Bowling.
        p. cm.—(Shapers of the great American debates, ISSN 1099–2693 ; no. 5)
    Includes bibliographical references and index.
    ISBN 0–313–31434–9 (alk. paper)
    1. United States—Politics and government—1963–1969—Dictionaries.
    2. United States—History—1961–1969—Biography—Dictionaries.   3. United
States—Social policy—Dictionaries.   4. Politicians—United States—Biography—
Dictionaries.   5. Social reformers—United States—Biography—Dictionaries.
    6. Intellectuals—United States—Biography—Dictionaries.   I. Title.   II. Series.
    E846.B63   2005
    973.923'092'2—dc22   2004017980

British Library Cataloguing in Publication Data is available.

Library of Congress Catalog Card Number: 2004017980
ISBN: 0–313–31434–9
ISSN: 1099–2693

First published in 2005

Greenwood Press, 88 Post Road West, Westport, CT 06881
An imprint of Greenwood Publishing Group, Inc.
www.greenwood.com

Printed in the United States of America

The paper used in this book complies with the
Permanent Paper Standard issued by the National
Information Standards Organization (Z39.48–1984).

10 9 8 7 6 5 4 3 2 1

IN MEMORIAM

GREGG REIDY

October 12, 1975–September 11, 2001

Son of Tom and Mary
Son of Mater Dei
Son of Manhattanville

Beloved Friend to All

CONTENTS

CHALLENGING THE GREAT SOCIETY

BOTH FOR AND AGAINST

SERIES FOREWORD

American history has been shaped by numerous debates over issues far ranging in content and time. Debates over the right, or lack thereof, to take the land of the Native Americans, and the proper place and role of women, sparked by Roger Williams and Anne Hutchinson, respectively, marked the earliest years of the Massachusetts Bay Colony. Debates over slavery, the nature and size of the federal government, the emergence of big business, and the rights of labor and immigrants were central to the Republic in the nineteenth century and, in some cases, remain alive today. World War I, World War II, and the Vietnam War sparked debates that tore at the body politic. Even the Revolution involved a debate over whether America should be America or remain part of Great Britain. And the Civil War, considered by many the central event in American history, was the outgrowth of a long debate that found no peaceful resolution.

This series, *Shapers of the Great American Debates*, will examine many of these debates—from those between Native Americans and European settlers to those between "natives" and "newcomers." Each volume will focus on a particular issue, concentrating on those men and women who *shaped* the debates. The authors will pay special attention to fleshing out the life histories of the shapers, considering the relationship between biography or personal history and policy or philosophy. Each volume will begin with an introductory overview, include approximately twenty biographies of ten to fifteen pages, an appendix that briefly describes other key figures, a bibliographical essay, and a subject index. Unlike works that emphasize end results, the books in this series will devote equal attention to both sides, to the "winners" and the "losers." This will lead to a more complete understanding of the richness and complexity of America's past than is afforded by works that examine only the victors.

Taken together, the books in this series remind us of the many ways that class, race, ethnicity, gender, and region have divided rather than united the inhabitants of the United States of America. Each study reminds us of the frequency and variety of debates in America, a reflection of the diversity of the nation and its democratic credo. One even wonders if a similar series could be developed for many other nations or if the diversity of America and its tradition of free expression have given rise to more debates than elsewhere.

Although many Americans have sought to crush the expression of opposing views by invoking the imperative of patriotism, more often than not Americans have respected the rights of others to voice their opinions. Every four years, Americans have voted for a president and peacefully respected the results, demonstrating their faith in the process that institutionalizes political debate. More recently, candidates for the presidency have faced off in televised debates that often mark the climax of their campaigns. Americans not only look forward to these debates, but they would probably punish anyone who sought to avoid them. Put another way, debates are central to America's political culture, especially those that deal with key issues and involve the most prominent members of society.

Each volume in the series is written by an expert. While I offered my share of editorial suggestions, overall I relied on the author's expertise when it came to determining the most sensible way to organize and present each work. As a result, some of the volumes follow a chronological structure; others clump their material thematically; still others are separated into two sections, one pro and one con. All of the works are written with the needs of college and advanced high school students in mind. They should prove valuable both as sources for research papers and as supplemental texts in both general and specialized courses. The general public should also find the works an attractive means of learning more about many of the most important figures and equally as many seminal issues in American history.

Peter B. Levy
Associate Professor
Department of History
York College

INTRODUCTION

Lyndon Johnson, the "accidental president," had quite a year in 1964. In January, in his State of the Union address, he declared "war on poverty"; some months later, at the conclusion of the academic year in Ann Arbor, Michigan, he outlined his idealistic vision for a "Great Society" in his commencement address before some 80,000 at the University of Michigan's "Big House" football stadium. And in November, the Democratic party, political liberalism, and Johnson himself scored their greatest modern electoral victory, putting the Great Society concept in a position to move from graduation-day idealistic rhetoric to embodied reality. The Great Society program was Lyndon Johnson's attempt to create a second New Deal, one as wide-ranging as the first, which LBJ as a young Democratic party congressman had directly experienced and now, as president, sought to emulate.

The generalizations contained in the speech that popularized the phrase itself were nearly boundless in their scope, which leads to a question of definition: what, exactly, was the Great Society? What lay behind it? Where did it come from, where did it go, and why did it become so controversial? And finally, there is the angle of approach offered here: who made it happen, and who opposed it? To which must be added: and why did they? The *Shapers of the Great American Debates* series takes a fundamentally biographical approach to history, following the dictum that people make history in the circumstances they find themselves in, in this case the upheaval of the 1960s.

The central Great Society debates of the 1960s took place philosophically, politically, and programmatically. Its two great issues, which were intertwined, were race and poverty. Other components of President Johnson's grand vision, though they got their start in the 1960s, only came into their own at later dates. Environmentalism, an updated version of a long-standing concern formerly known as conservation, hit its stride in the 1970s, with the establishment of the Environmental Protection Agency and the first popular celebration of Earth Day on April 22, 1970. Significant controversies over federal support for "the arts" belong to a much later age. These important phenomena, which had their beginnings in the Great Society era, will not be treated here.

The most recurring general question throughout the United States' national history has been the role and place of the federal government in the political system versus that of states and localities, and the Great Society had to consider this question over and over. One of the oddest facts about the Great Society was its origin at a time of relative "noncrisis." The nation was macroeconomically strong, and the Cold War, the successor to World War II as a unifying force, was enjoying one of its periodic thaws, though involvement in Vietnam was growing.

There had been, however—since the mid-1950s, at least—one domestic issue that kept steadily rising in prominence: civil rights, which had philosophical, political, and programmatic dimensions, but which also could be boiled down to a simple and recurring question: what should the federal government do? More and more people said, "More." Martin Luther King, Jr., of course, had become "the" spokesman for civil rights in the minds of everyone. In the long run, nearly everyone would come to favor the lion's share of civil rights and take for granted matters formerly deemed controversial, even unthinkable ("affirmative action" as implemented only became controversial at a much later date). The Great Society's civil rights efforts constitute one of its most significant legacies.

The other central matter of the Great Society, poverty, was not so obviously on the public mind in the 1950s–early 1960s age of American celebration, new suburbanization, and continually rising affluence. In this case, elites needed to be themselves moved before they might attempt to move a nation. Author Michael Harrington's *The Other America* justly deserves its reputation as one of only a handful of books that has ever seriously and directly influenced public policy. As civil rights consciousness had increased, so, he hoped, would a consciousness demanding a "national," "total" commitment to the elimination of poverty—"in our time"—directed by government leaders in the nation's capital. President Lyndon Baines Johnson, the Great Society's founder and most important force, brought this kind of mentality to another commencement address he delivered, this one in 1965 at Washington's historically black Howard University, when he called for equality not as a "theory" but as a "fact." With the political majorities gained in the congressional elections of 1964, plus the old master of Capitol Hill himself at the wheel, Great Society measures were being generated so as to keep up momentum by building on the successes of Johnson's first full years as president. Memories of the New Deal's bursts of federal government assertiveness in the fabled two "hundred days" periods of 1933 and 1935 danced in the heads of encouraged political liberals and fearful political conservatives. To Great Society proponents, far more could and should be done, under the leadership of the national government, to solve the problem of poverty.

The programmatic, implementation dimension of the Great Society story soon became central. *How*, exactly, was the federal government to guarantee civil rights? Regarding political and what might be called personal rights (nondiscrimination in public services, public accommodations, and employment practices), federal laws could be, and were, drafted. The Voting Rights Act of 1965, which involved direct federal supervision of electoral practices, beginning with voter registration, was soon understood to be a concrete and immediate achievement. In the Great Society's other main realm, the poverty question, things proved, in general, to be far more complicated. The creation of Medicare, under the guidance of longtime government bureaucrat par excellence Wilbur Cohen and congressional insider Wilbur Mills, stood out in 1965, linking itself to the Social Security tradition of treating the elderly as the special case they so often were, with elderly former President Harry Truman participating in the signing ceremony. Federal aid to precollege education, something long talked about but only modestly enacted before the Great Society, was another significant milestone; also related to education was the creation of the Great Society's most popular program, Head Start. Far more controversial and questioned were Great Society efforts at urban renewal and at community organizing of the poor themselves, under the auspices of the new Office of Economic Opportunity (OEO), led by the indefatigable Sargent Shriver.

Given American's long tradition of antistatism and its decentralized federal system of government, opposition existed to the Great Society approach to things long before anyone ever heard the term. In the Great Society era, of course, in the United States' tradition of modern political conservatism, this opposition was embodied principally in the Republican party, which had by assigned role as well as by conviction opposed the New Deal spirit if not always the actual legislation. President Dwight D. Eisenhower's "modern, dynamic conservatism" of the 1950s, seeking acceptance of at least some of the New Deal/Fair Deal's notions of a federal welfare state, however, had led to rumblings on the right, taking intellectual form in the person of William F. Buckley, Jr., and his new mid-1950s opinion journal, *National Review*. Then, in 1960, Arizona U.S. Senator Barry Goldwater became the incarnation of the opposition to a more powerful federal government and all its works, and the founder of a new conservative political movement. As the 1964 election results suggested, the mid-1960s was hardly the opposition's hour, though sometimes, as in the case of U.S. Senator Everett Dirksen of Illinois, a Republican conservative might play a significant Great Society role.

The great debates over the Great Society involved some household names, beginning of course with the president himself, and some public servants known only to those who followed politics, such as presidential speechwriter and coiner of the phrase "Great Society" Richard Goodwin, and top presidential advisor Joseph Califano. More typical of the moment's politics was old-line union stalwart Walter Reuther, leader of the United Automobile Workers (UAW), who made the most of the opportunity to build a more social-democratic United States, offering both general political support and direct advice and leadership regarding "urban development."

The Great Society's moment did not last long, as predicted by its chief sponsor, President Johnson. The political radicalization of an element of the rising generation, as seen in New Leftist Tom Hayden and black radical Stokely Carmichael, for instance, led to severe criticisms of antipoverty programs as almost hopelessly inadequate and ineffective, from the impatient vantage point of those with rising expectations. Established leaders of the Democratic party, such as Chicago Mayor/boss Richard Daley and party regular Congresswoman Edith Green, soon could not abide what the Great Society antipoverty warriors were up to and moved to rein them in. South Carolina U.S. Senator Strom Thurmond made his move to the Republican party, presaging a southern political realignment of truly historic proportions. In a more intellectual realm, Harvard University professor Edward Banfield's 1970 book, *The Unheavenly City*, was a bomb dropped on the whole Great Society urban antipoverty effort and provoked intense debate. Along the same lines, and both earlier and later, Daniel Patrick Moynihan, sometime government servant and an early Great Society antipoverty intellectual, found his advice regarding "national action" for the "Negro family" most unwelcome, proclaimed a "maximum feasible misunderstanding" at the heart of the antipoverty program in practice, and wound up as a domestic advisor to new president Richard Nixon. And of course there were the external forces of social unrest, brought home vividly thanks to the now-ubiquitous television, and the increasingly important and challenged American involvement in Vietnam.

The people here profiled represent insiders and outsiders, with a strong political stress, given the nature of the Great Society as a governmentally based effort. Their life journeys, of course, shaped their views on the philosophical, political, and programmatic dimensions that came up during the heyday of the Great Society, and they sometimes interacted with each other. In some cases, participants in the great debates over the Great Society cannot easily be labeled as "pro" or "con" the Great Society program. Thus the biographies will appear in three sections, including those put into the last category, "Both For and Against."

The Great Society's civil rights debate was forced on the nation by the activities of those who struggled in the Deep South either to keep or to abolish the segregation system. The Great Society's poverty debate was set off by the large ambitions of Lyndon Johnson, building on stirrings that had only just begun. The Great Society's special moment, in which much was done and many things were created or at least tried, went away far too rapidly for its partisans and is sometimes said to have been repudiated, but it did permanently change the United States, making some things new, leaving lasting legacies, but also engendering opposition that would go on to create new political currents of its own.

BUILDING A GREAT SOCIETY

MICHAEL HARRINGTON
(1928–1989)

One of the many clichés to come out of the 1960s was the claim that in the media age, everyone would now get to be famous for fifteen minutes. Michael Harrington, from the early 1950s until his death in 1989, toiled long years in the relatively obscure vineyards of extreme left-wing politics in the United States, mostly in the New York City area, promoting in a variety of ways the usually thankless effort to define the vicinity of the "left wing of the possible" in U.S. national politics. Sadly, some of his admirers and friends felt, there was, ultimately, not as much to show for it all as there should have been.

However, his several decades as a nearly full-time political activist for what proved to be the hopeless cause of creating an American socialism worthy of that tradition's name were briefly interrupted in the early 1960s with the publication of a very short book, *The Other America* (1962), which brought him, for a few years at least, not only a modicum of fame but also actual access to the corridors, meeting rooms, and internal debates of official power, as well as long-lasting name recognition. His timing, for once, proved to be perfect; his vehicle, a simple, easy-to-read-in-one-sitting, humanized report and meditation on the realities of poverty in the supposedly affluent United States of the late 1950s and early 1960s, struck a chord and has continued to be cited, if increasingly less often read. He became tagged as the man who had "discovered" poverty, at least for the educated reading public and those politically beholden to them. Hence the War on Poverty, centerpiece of President Johnson's Great Society, became inexorably associated with Harrington's journalistic piece. "Poverty" never went away after the spotlight was suddenly shone on it for the first time since the Great Depression, though the discussion as to what actually to do about it has not only continued, but has also gone all over the place, far beyond the confines briefly laid out by Harrington in the book that made him famous. As for Michael Harrington himself, circa the early 1960s, what ought to be done about U.S. poverty was, in a way, simple enough: the federal government should abolish it. That the federal government could accomplish this feat was not to be doubted. That being the case, the question arose: why did poverty continue to exist in a country whose material achievements and popular consumerism were so frequently celebrated, especially in the Cold War setting where this was supposed to demonstrate and remind people that American capitalism, as some put it, delivered the goods? Harrington's first priority in *The Other America* was to demonstrate that it was not true that the United States was a land of plenty for all. But beyond that task lay an ancient, grander vision of what a "great" society might actually consist of, since, for Michael Harrington, man did not live by bread alone.

Michael Harrington was a rather unusual version of a common enough type, the ex–Roman Catholic, in that he continued to love and admire the Church in many ways, never slandering it at all. But even when facing his early death from cancer, he felt obliged to reject repeated entreaties from some of his friends to at least see a priest. On his own personal road to Damascus, the light that had once shone, the voice that had thundered, was that of modern socialism. Not, of course, communism; that god had obviously been tried and found grotesquely wanting, as also came to be the case, for Harrington, with the God of the Bible in any remotely dogmatic sense. The Church's preferential option for the poor, its vision of the beloved community, the New Jerusalem/Heavenly City come down to Earth, however, remained the raison d'être of Michael Harrington's being and the cause to which he devoted his life, despite his loss of faith.

Born February 24, 1928, Harrington entered this world in St. Louis, Missouri, a city with a strong, large, highly organized Roman Catholic community. As the only child of a lawyer and civically active homemaker, he enjoyed a solid middle-class upbringing in a comfortable home and was formed by private, Catholic schools, first in his parish, St. Rose of Lima; then at age eight with the Marianist Fathers at Chaminade College Preparatory School; and finally at St. Louis University High School. He spoke well of his intellectually rigorous Jesuit education throughout his life, with its stress on the importance of philosophical reasoning and ideas and its moral and intellectual seriousness; as an adult, he recalled, "From the time I was a little kid the Church said your life is not something you are supposed to fritter away; your life is in trust to something more important than yourself" (Isserman 2000, 25). His principal activities in high school were the *Sodality*, the school paper (which he edited during his senior year), and the debate team, a highly organized, prestigious activity in those days. His formation naturally included the Catholic social texts such as Pope Leo XIII's 1891 encyclical *Rerum Novarum*, which while opposing socialism was anything but a treatise on behalf of a laissez-faire, libertarian vision of state and society. Politics were a frequent topic of discussion at home during these momentous years of the 1940s, and Michael was a participant.

Harrington made the unusual choice to go east for college, to Worcester, Massachusetts, where the Jesuit order ran a small liberal arts school, the College of the Holy Cross, which had few midwestern students. In college he began exhibiting small signs of rebellion, for instance against his family's Democratic partisan identity; he called himself a Republican and for a while claimed Ohio's conservative senator Robert Taft, "Mr. Republican," as his political hero. He discovered the extensive writings of the inimitable G. K. Chesterton, the prolific British convert to Catholicism, whose love of paradox Harrington found appealing. His Catholicism, in an all-Catholic environment, apparently remained strong and socially aware; in his salutatory address for his 1947 graduation, he declared, "The very foundation of democracy demands that we see our fellow man with the eyes of faith. The wealth or poverty of his fellow citizen, his color or his creed—these cannot be the determining norm of the true democrat. He is committed to the truth that every man has a moral worth and dignity . . . which comes from the fact that every man belongs to God" (Isserman 2000, 38).

In 1947 everything began to change. He went down the road from Worcester to New Haven and a very different sort of place, Yale University Law School. In just a few years, William F. Buckley, Jr., would portray the atmosphere of the nation's third-oldest institution of higher learning as atheistic, morally relativistic, and collectivist. Less stressed in Buckley's *God and Man at Yale* (1951) was how old-style New England, Puritan Protestant Yale was culturally in those days. Harrington, with a sort of Catholic ghetto background, found few Catholics at the Yale Law School, and even fewer seriously intellectually formed or grounded ones (as was Buckley, whom Harrington did not know then but with whom he would later appear in many debating forums). The Law School faculty was riddled with New Deal–oriented professors such as William O. Douglas, Eugene Rostow, Abe Fortas, and Thurman Arnold, who instinctively disliked big business (an alien world to them and also to Harrington) and who imagined themselves as the appropriate leaders for society. Harrington's Catholic, neo-Scholastic philosophical grounding was challenged, and soon overwhelmed in his mind, by the worldview of "legal realism," with its foundational moral relativism, but also its pragmatic, hopeful attitude toward Enlightenment-driven improvement. So challenged, he read, listened, thought, and evolved toward a socialistic conceptualization of the good society. Given his strong Jesuit education, he soon found law school relatively easy, and, rather bored by the curriculum, increasingly adopted a get-by attitude, preferring to spend his time on wide-ranging, private reading. He lasted in law school one year, to the dismay of his parents. Again, he was rebelling, though still in a respectable way. He headed back to the Midwest, to the University of Chicago to study English.

Chicago was, and still is, an unusually intellectually oriented university. Harrington loved his year there, in the shadow of Robert Maynard Hutchins, the father of Chicago's distinctiveness. Befitting the university's religious origins, the atmosphere combined intellectual and ethical seriousness. Here Harrington seems to have lost whatever was left of his faith, and as if to signal a change of life, began using "Mike" rather than "Ed" as his preferred name. Upon receiving the M.A., a distinctly nonpractical degree, he, for lack of much else to do, returned home to St. Louis, at loose ends, searching for some direction.

Here, in 1949, in the space of just a few days he experienced what he later reported in his memoir, *Fragments of the Century*, as an epiphany. Employed on a temporary basis by the St. Louis Board of Education in its division of pupil welfare, he had his "road to Damascus. Suddenly the abstract and statistical and aesthetic outrages I had reacted to at Yale and Chicago became real and personal and insistent" (Harrington 1977, 66). Somehow, seeing deprivation directly moved him in a new way. It did not, however, as had been the case with St. Paul, immediately grant him direction. He did not continue his brief work in the schools, remaining at loose ends for a few months, and then decided to try returning to New York, attracted by the bohemian demimonde of Greenwich Village, an attraction he would never entirely give up, even in the last phase of his life in one of New York City's northern suburbs, Larchmont. He got by in Manhattan on small writing jobs, read, and hung out in Village bars. In May 1950 he returned to St. Louis, expecting a draft call, but as it continued to fail to materialize, Harrington followed his heart back to New York, this time to stay, in January 1951.

His personal reading over the previous six months, including such spiritual and philosophical writers as Jaspers, Pascal, Kierkegaard, and Dostoevsky, guided him to take the leap of faith back toward his childhood faith. A current of modern Catholic thought, "personalism," a sort of Catholic variant of the then extremely fashionable existentialism (itself strongly condemned by Holy Mother Church's Magisterium), appealed to him. Another Damacus experience hit him in the Village, and he went to confession at the neighborhood parish, Our Lady of Pompei. Nearby he found the St. Joseph House of Hospitality on Chrystie Street, run by an unusual figure, Dorothy Day, cofounder of the Catholic Worker movement, which sought to function as a sort of Catholic version of the Salvation Army without the mandatory chapel attendance requirement. Its radical commitment to serving the immediate needs of the poor while being "fools for Christ" appealed immensely to Harrington and gave him the home he had been searching for. He became a full-fledged member of the community and a daily communicant.

It did not take long for Harrington's journalistic talents to be employed by the organization, and he became a major writer for its paper, *The Catholic Worker*. For the June 1952 issue, he contributed an article entitled

"Poverty—U.S.A." Quoting census reports, Harrington demonstrated that, public impressions and mainstream political discourse to the contrary notwithstanding, poverty remained widespread in the country. A few had a great deal, most had some, and many very little. In passing, he offered a perennial boilerplate comment of leftist economic analysis, "It goes without saying that the incomes structure just described must be changed." But the Catholic, personalist view remained central to Harrington's immediate answer to the question, "What is to be done?" His answer was, "The reaction to this poverty should be partly one of calculation, of how can it be eradicated, but it must also be of the Beatitudes, of hunger and thirst for Justice, of love and grief for what goes on before our eyes" (Isserman 2000, 78–79).

Those whom Harrington was encountering, and their difficulties, would have challenged the faith of St. Francis: an urban underclass, substance abusers, the mentally disturbed, those without families. While he continued to interact directly with the people at the bottom, most of Harrington's work was in the spreading of the word. He began to make connections to the world of public debate, both oral and written. In November 1952, for instance, Day sent him to the University of Vermont (she herself had been invited) to debate William F. Buckley, Jr., on the topic, "Is our educational system leading us down the road to socialism?" Harrington, in response to *God and Man at Yale* for *The Catholic Worker*, had accused Buckley of promoting laissez-faire in contradiction to church teaching. The debate, of course, settled nothing, but it did establish a long-standing relationship; Harrington and Buckley would meet on many occasions in debate and also conversation on Buckley's later television program, *Firing Line*. Additionally, Harrington got to know John Cogley, a former Catholic Worker who, under the pressures of World War II, had broken with the movement over its pacifism. After the war he had joined *Commonweal*, the liberal, lay Catholic magazine of opinion, becoming its executive editor. Cogley invited Harrington to write for *Commonweal*, which he continued to do long after he had become a confirmed nonbeliever. *Commonweal*'s circulation, like that of all the opinion magazines, was relatively small, but its reach and influence far outstretched that of *The Catholic Worker*.

The Catholic Worker movement made sense for a saint, but Harrington, like most people, turned out not to be one. It hardly took very long to see that this unusual group, founded in the depths of the Depression, was not going to become a mass movement transforming society. Early in 1952, Harrington, manning a picket line of the Spanish consulate, met a man who introduced him to the world of American socialism that was to be his final home— Bogdan Denitch, a veteran of the Young People's Socialist League (YPSL). Denitch befriended Harrington, giving him much literature to read, and before long Harrington joined YPSL. By the end of 1952, Harrington had left Catholic Worker housing, and his final break with Catholicism had been made (though he continued to maintain cordial ties with Day and others).

Given Harrington's centrality to socialist activism in the 1960s and 1970s, this final Damascus experience was his most significant one. Given its formative impact on many makers of the 1960s, and the amount that has been written about it, YPSL was an almost preposterously tiny organization in 1952, with a total of 134 members—in the entire country! The "country" of American socialism by the time of Harrington's formal entry into it was located in only a few places, most notably New York, with its enormous foreign-born and foreign-background population. Factionalism to a degree that would shock a specialist on fourth-century heresies was rampant, usually centering on the issue of how socialists should view the Soviet Union. Harrington's YPSL period was short-lived, as he was "expelled," a favored word in this faction-ridden world, for consorting with certain leftist groups. In 1954, he joined a new organization, the Young Socialist League, becoming the tiny group's chairman in 1955 and frequently writing for its barely circulated newspaper.

Having found his true home at last, Harrington thrived on political work, writing, speaking, and traveling frequently—all of which continued until his death. He was a classic post–World War II public intellectual, with interests ranging all over the place, who churned out essays on various topics seemingly effortlessly and repeatedly. The reason is clear enough: he had found a lasting reason to live, a cause to which to devote himself in which he could really, permanently believe, something more important than himself. Completing his move beyond the Catholic intellectual ghetto, he contributed to the original issues of both the *Village Voice* and the socialist intellectual quarterly *Dissent*, both founded in 1955. Among the most important connections he made were those with the Fund for the Republic, then under the leadership of former University of Chicago president Robert Hutchins, which began funding research and writing by Harrington and continued to support him for years.

By the late 1950s, then, Harrington was well situated to play a significant role in the emergent New Left, an intellectual product of the further discrediting of Soviet Communism after the denunciation of Stalin and the invasion of Hungary; in the United States, where the evils of the U.S.S.R. were hardly news, the stirrings of the modern civil rights movement were even more important for social activists. Harrington, with his non–New York upbringing, was certainly one activist who was well aware of the profound marginalization of his societal critique, his political compatriots, and their often seemingly futile activities. During a fall 1958 campus speaking tour, he convinced himself that the reported stirrings of a new activism were real; the following summer, he made his first trip to Europe, where he met with New Leftists and socialists who possessed real power. He also spent a day in East Berlin, still routinely accessible because the infamous wall, which he found repellant, had not yet been constructed. He returned to the United States and began working on an article for *Commentary*, suggested to him in late 1958 by one of the magazine's editors, on a new subject, for him: poverty in the United States.

In 1958 a John Kenneth Galbraith treatise on the contemporary United States, *The Affluent Society*, had attracted significant attention among the literate public, its title quickly becoming a buzzword. Galbraith did note in passing that there were "pockets" of poverty remaining, such as Appalachia. Some journalistic and political follow-ups questioned the fullness of the description; in this setting, Harrington made his first foray into a subject that suddenly, if briefly, became the topic of the day: "Our Fifty Million Poor," published in *Commentary* in July 1959. Two points stand out in Harrington's essay: his employment of a concept, the "culture of poverty," which Harrington had adopted from a study of Mexican poverty written by anthropologist Oscar Lewis; and his use of the term "comprehensive," destined to become one of the most favored in the War on Poverty. Harrington called for a "comprehensive assault on poverty" in the United States: "Housing, schools, medical care, labor standards, communal institutions must be combined in a broad planned program if any of these measures is to have real impact on poverty." Here was the conceptual spirit of the War on Poverty *avant la lettre* in a single sentence. A talismanic word for the left, "planning," was also included. Soon afterward, in a mid-1960 *Commonweal* essay, Harrington for the first time in print used the phrase his book was to make famous in its title: *The Other America*. His definition of the term here, however, did not refer to the poor, as was to be the case in his famous 1962 book; rather, here he employed it to refer to his imagined potential community of a better United States, one in touch with its democratic roots, ideas, and values—in other words, a great society, as opposed to the materialistic, mass culture that seemed to be gathering strength in the age of television.

The 1960 presidential campaign hardly focused on poverty, but the subject did get some important attention. The Kennedy campaign, whose West Virginia primary victory was crucial to the candidate's success, was full of people who professed to be, and usually actually were, shocked at the poverty they found in the Mountaineer State, and many of these people soon found themselves high-ranking federal officials. Harrington, in Los Angeles for the 1960 Democratic National Convention to participate in a march protesting the party platform, complained to a CBS Television news reporter about the party's timidity on the civil rights question. There he met and talked extensively to Martin Luther King, Jr., coming away convinced that King was a socialist in everything but name. Candidate Kennedy in his campaign occasionally addressed Harrington's new issue of interest, stating that the "war against poverty and degradation is not yet over" (Isserman 2000, 191). Shortly after the election, on Thanksgiving Friday, CBS broadcast the documentary *Harvest of Shame*, whose purpose was to raise consciousness of the poor conditions under which migrant farm workers labored.

The fall of 1960 found Michael Harrington working as an editor of *New America*, a new, small-circulation, biweekly publication of the small, noninfluential Socialist party, which failed to either run or endorse a presidential candidate for the first time in the twentieth century. In an editorial in its first issue, Harrington described a strategy of political realignment as the appropriate agenda for the left: push civil rights so as to drive out of the Democratic party "Southern racists and certain other corruptive elements" as a precondition for the revival of meaningful socialism politics in the United States as well as "meaningful and progressive social welfare, labor, and civil rights legislation"—in other words, the essence of what would soon come to be called the Great Society (Isserman 2000, 188).

In August 1960, *Commentary* published a second article by Harrington on the poverty question, "Slums, Old and New," whose conceptual base was again the culture of poverty thesis. Slums were not new, but contemporary ones were worse than those of the classical immigrant age at the turn of the previous century, with their stronger family structure, specifically meaning more male breadwinners present. To break the "slum psychology," Harrington suggested smaller public housing units, scattered among solid neighborhoods, rather than the then-dominant urban tower projects. Contacted by various publishers who expressed interest in contracting him to write a book on poverty, he did not take it seriously until approached by Herbert Roseman, a friend and leftist economist. Betty Bartelme, an editor at Macmillan who had known Harrington in his Catholic Worker phase, linked him with an editor who offered him an advance of $500, a lot of money then, and especially a lot to Harrington. He used this money, plus funds from the Fund for the Republic, to travel and investigate, publishing bits and pieces of his findings in various small-circulation publications, while continuing to edit *New America*. Harrington was becoming a familiar name to a small, growing group of campus-based activists, the emerging New Left; Tom Hayden in 1961 called Harrington one of three "over-thirty" influentials on the rising generation (the other two were sociologist C. Wright Mills and veteran socialist politico Norman Thomas).

Harrington was hardly surprised to find that JFK's "war" on poverty was a nonstarter. A couple of modest proposals—the 1961 Area Redevelopment Act, a sort of tax-break-oriented enterprise-zone concept; and 1962's Manpower Development and Training Act, an idea coming out of the then-fashionable phantom "automation" threat—failed to impress. In an effort to influence public opinion, in March 1962, Michael Harrington's *The Other America* was published, with only 186 pages divided into nine chapters. Easy to read, matter-of-fact in tone, surprisingly emotionally flat, nonpolemical, based on the culture of poverty thesis, and aimed at the mainstream (after a little consideration, he decided to avoid the use of the word "socialist") audience, the book made Harrington's reputation with a far broader public. The basic idea of the book was that there was plenty of

poverty left in the country, more than the reader might think, somewhere between 40 and 50 million; that large numbers of the poor were fundamentally
passive, apathetic people who were unlikely to move out of their disadvanta-
geous position due to the culture of poverty (Harrington did not actually
employ this phrase) they inhabited; that lack of money kept the cycle going;
that many elderly people lived in appalling conditions due to this lack of
funds coupled with no family members able or willing to help; that this situation obtained because the poor were largely "invisible" to the broader community, this invisibility being corrected by the portraits in the present
narrative; and, the conclusion of the book, that a "war on poverty" led by
the federal government was, rather obviously, the only viable solution to this
morally unacceptable situation. That, rather than any radical reorganization
of society, was the implicit recommendation. It was stressed that a *national*
approach had to be the name of the game. "Planning," as mentioned earlier,
was a talismanic word, and predictably it was ill-defined.

"Best sellers" in the United States are, of course, read by a very small percentage of the population, but it is undeniable that Harrington's book was
widely influential among the small group who most counted politically. It
became a "proof text" underlying the Great Society's War on Poverty that
was actually declared by the president of the United States early in 1964 and
that then began to be fought just a few years after Harrington's book was
published. It gave poverty a human face to the reading public. It was anec-
dotal rather than analytical; for example, even the approximation of the
number of people in question proved virtually impossible, even with a generous approach to the question, simply because even as basic an issue as
what constituted "poverty" proved impossible for warring parties to agree
on, though to some extent, all sides would probably admit, as was said in the
1960s of pornography, you knew it when you saw it.

Harrington, whose lack of pretension was always one of his most appealing characteristics, would have been the last person to have palmed himself
off as an "expert" on poverty in any serious way. But that was not really the
point. Rather, he was a witness to the difficult lives of real people, whom he
portrayed as anything but saints; given his direct experience in working with
such people, he could hardly have done that. He sought to embody what he
took to be simple decency when it came to the poverty question. The point
was that there was a lot of poverty remaining in the wealthy, rather self-
satisfied United States of the early 1960s; in a hopeful vein, the stance was
taken that if only more people's consciousness were to be raised, they would
demand that more be done about it. In the context of the growing civil rights
movement especially, that this meant the federal government was hardly
worth saying—that was automatic. Candidate John F. Kennedy had promised to "get this country moving again," and many had professed themselves
inspired. The country needed to get moving on the issue of deprivation
amidst the abundance of the so-called affluent society.

Harrington received a boost in early 1963 when a large-circulation magazine, *The New Yorker*, published an unusually long (nearly fifty pages) discussion of his book by Dwight Macdonald, who had gotten to know Harrington in New York. Macdonald, while somewhat critical of the analytical and economic weaknesses of *The Other America*, nevertheless strongly stressed the bigger point that something major ought to be done about the scandal of unnecessary poverty amidst plenty. President Kennedy is reported to have read either the book itself or Macdonald's review; it is clear that influential people inside and close to the White House did digest these two readings. Kennedy asked his economic advisor Walter Heller to obtain some data on poverty for him. Gradually, some planning proceeded, behind the scenes, deep in the bowels of the federal establishment, but nothing major seemed to be in the cards until the tragedy in Dallas suddenly produced a new president who turned out to be enthusiastically committed to the general mentality represented by Harrington's book.

Harrington made enough money from *The Other America*, which continued to sell moderately well for a serious book and was soon reprinted, to allow him to visit Europe in the fall of 1963, where he met with such rising socialist politicians as Britain's Harold Wilson and Willy Brandt of West Germany at the Eighth Congress of the Socialist International in Amsterdam. He visited Warsaw, discovering that the communist media there had hailed his book as proof of capitalist decadence in the United States. Harrington found the atmosphere appalling and left with his hard-line anticommunism reinforced. Returning to New York late in the year, he found that his fame had continued to increase steadily.

When Lyndon Johnson used his State of the Union address in January 1964 to declare the War on Poverty, Harrington was a natural choice from which ABC radio sought commentary. On January 23, Harrington went to Georgetown University in the nation's capital to speak at a Conference on Poverty in Plenty, where he complained of what he saw as the severe limitations of Johnson's apparent proposal to spend "only" a billion or so federal dollars on new antipoverty initiatives.

In this atmosphere, but only very briefly as it was to turn out, Harrington became a Washington insider. On February 1, 1964, President Johnson appointed Sargent Shriver, founding director of the Peace Corps and the husband of President Kennedy's sister Eunice, his man in charge of formulating a plan for the War on Poverty. Shriver asked his Peace Corps colleague Frank Mankiewicz to search for people, and one of the names he mentioned to Shriver was Harrington. That Shriver had never heard of Harrington is a useful reminder of the still-limited nature, to that point, of Harrington's personal fame as well as the narrow consciousness of the newly discovered problem of poverty, including among the allegedly intellectually oriented Kennedy circle. Informed of who Harrington was, Shriver asked that he be brought in, and the men had lunch the next day, where Harrington stressed his belief that small amounts of increased spending would have little if any effect. Still, Harrington was now "in." Beginning on February 4, for twelve days what was soon called the President's Task Force in the War against Poverty held planning meetings at Shriver's Peace Corps office in Washington. Harrington found himself surrounded by such powerful individuals as Heller, presidential assistant and speechwriter Richard Goodwin, Secretary of Labor Willard Wirtz, and others.

He also found himself surrounded by representatives of the various federal agencies, bureaucracies, and programs that were, each in its own way, devoted to the alleviation of this, that, or the other want. It became immediately apparent to Harrington that turf protection was at the top of their agendas. Harrington, given a unique opportunity, nevertheless continued to participate in discussions, writing memoranda in collaboration with longtime activist comrade Paul Jacobs. He favored, of course, such traditional New Deal–type approaches to poverty as public works projects (Johnson showed absolutely no interest whatsoever in such things), but he also very much wanted to find something special, something truly new, something that would provide vision, go beyond the present setup, and signal a new strategy. Some of those who participated complained that Harrington was quite weak when it came to actual proposals, but this was hardly surprising, given that in no serious way was Harrington a true "expert" on antipoverty programs, and had never claimed to be.

By far the most famous new idea to emerge from the task force was the ill-fated "community action" concept whose favored buzzwords were "empowerment" (a term that was destined to have a long life and a broad political-rhetorical appeal across the ideological spectrum) and "maximum feasible participation" on the part of poor people themselves. As much as Harrington desired something dramatic and new, he was from day one a prophetic skeptic. He asked what turned out to be the right questions: "Is it possible for governments to finance the self organization of the poor? Isn't it true that when you have a governmental program to organize the poor on their own behalf that, if it is successful, the first thing those people are going to do is hold a rent strike? The second thing they're going to do is send a committee to their local Congressman, and the third thing they're going to do is picket the Mayor. Can you expect, given the political structure of this country, governmental funds being used to overthrow governments?" (Isserman 2000, 214). Congresswoman Edith Green of Oregon, who in a few years would lead the effort to torpedo what was left of "maximum feasible participation," could hardly have said it better.

Harrington's days as a Washington insider proved extremely brief. Though Congress did pass a bill in August 1964 creating the Office of Economic Opportunity and appropriating some $800 million for its activities, Harrington was not even invited to the White House for the signing ceremony, a type of event loved dearly by President Johnson. He thus resumed his outsider's role as a prophet, but now one with a higher visibility. His speeches on campuses continued, and attracted large audiences of hundreds. His book was often found in the possession of participants in the 1964 Deep South voter registration effort organized and led by college students that came to be known as the Freedom Summer. Back in hometown St. Louis in November 1964, he called in a speech for $100 *billion* to be spent over ten years on the war. That same month, he assumed the chairmanship of the League for Industrial Democracy (LID), a venerable if largely moribund leftist organization whose purpose had evolved over the course of the twentieth century into consciousness raising and education for socialist-collectivist ideas. LID's conflicts with its newly renamed youth organization, the infinitely more famous Students for a Democratic Society, soon came to exemplify the split between old and new lefts. Harrington's newly established status was declaimed, in a particularly grotesque example of the political journalism of the day, when Jack Newfield declared him to have been "knighted by Arthur Schlesinger Jr. [a historian and former aide to President Kennedy] as 'the only responsible radical in America' " (Isserman 2000, 219).

Harrington's direct involvement in the great cause cresting in the early 1960s, civil rights, was modest though obviously quite real. He had a little to do with some of the planning for the Freedom Summer, though given his age he was not present during it. From 1964 forward he was a part of Martin Luther King, Jr.'s informal "research committee," which gathered occasionally to consider the movement's strategic vision. In the spring of 1965, he was one of many who participated in the march to the Alabama state capitol in Montgomery and heard Martin Luther King, Jr., speak there. In the fall of 1965, he attended planning sessions for the White House Conference on Civil Rights proposed for the following spring. It was, of course, a given that Harrington supported the civil rights movement in toto. But he was always known as the poverty man. At the planning conference, he was pleased to hear veteran unionist and socialist A. Philip Randolph call for "tens of billions" of dollars in federal spending, and in response was one of those who came up with a proposed "A. Philip Randolph Freedom Budget" along these lines—a proposal totally ignored by the politically realistic White House. King asked Harrington to write him a manifesto for the proposed Poor People's Campaign of 1968, saying to him, "You know, we didn't even know we were poor until we read your book" (Isserman 2000, 280).

The Vietnam issue had appeared by 1965 and began to fracture the liberal left. Harrington's anticommunism tempered his antiwar feeling and activity far longer than was the case of many so situated on the left wing of the political spectrum. Ever favoring "the left wing of the possible," he supported Humphrey in 1968 even while being elected chairman of the miniscule Socialist party that same year. Harrington also spent the late 1960s continuing to write books, which were far less read or influential than *The Other America*, and suffering from exhaustion and anxiety attacks when preparing to speak. Long after the wars of the 1960s had subsided, Harrington would continue his work, creating and re-creating various leftist organizations, remaining loyal to the term "socialist" to the end. In a review of Harrington's failed effort to "explaining everything," the hard-to-follow 1965 tome *The Accidental Century*, conservative writer M. Stanton Evans, while crediting Harrington for being honest enough actually to call himself a "socialist," deemed him significantly ignorant and out of touch with his native country: "Mr. Harrington is, in truth, a kind of European in our midst," a man who held a "literary" view of capitalism—"distant, truncated, sometimes illuminating for its very strangeness, but thoroughly alien in both idiom and aspiration to the whole point and purpose of the American experiment" (quoted in Isserman 2000, 253). Along these lines, self-described socialist and card-carrying New York intellectual Daniel Bell, in 1973, wrote to *Dissent* editor Irving Howe, "Mike Harrington [was] on the Shriver antipoverty task force, but if Mike could come out of his closet he would have to admit that he had no program, and that his fallback was always, spend more money. And that is not the answer." Despite Bell's observation, under President Nixon's administration (during which Congress remained Democratic), many Great Society programs continued to grow.

Richard Nixon's landslide reelection in 1972 signaled the definitive repudiation of the idea that tens of billions of new federal dollars would soon be flowing to combating poverty (though many other Great Society creations would continue and grow). The next day, Nixon made famous the phrase, "throwing money at problems," his characterization of the Great Society mentality. Harrington's reply, of sorts, to both Bell and Nixon was found in a 1973 article defending the welfare state, wherein he articulated anew his continued faith in a cardinal principle of socialism, opposing "preference for the unplanned, and even the irrational, as opposed to conscious government policy" (Isserman 2000, 308). This Enlightenment belief in politicized planning was foundational. But *Dissent* had a circulation of a few thousand. His 1984 Reagan-era polemic, *The New American Poverty*, had limited impact. The poverty debate, however, very much continued, and as the man who "discovered" poverty, Harrington could take some considerable credit for that—but he would have been the first to register objection to many of the paths that the debate took.

LYNDON JOHNSON
(1908–1973)

It is safe to say that without Lyndon Baines Johnson, there would never have been anything even remotely like the Great Society federal initiative of the 1960s. With all due respect to the many others who also helped to make an embodied reality out of an implicitly bland, even throwaway, political slogan, he truly was the *fons et origo* of it all. As an accidental president, Johnson was suddenly and tragically put in a position of unparalleled power and influence, the presidency of the United States of America. Once the immediate shock of President Kennedy's sudden murder had at least stabilized in both his and the country's minds, and the ceremonies of those incredible four days of November 1963 had been completed, the new reality became inescapable: Lyndon Johnson, consummate Washington political insider for a full generation, now sat at the pinnacle of the American political system, in an office for which he had for some time, and, rather pathetically and certainly unsuccessfully, run for during 1960. Thoroughly known to the D.C. political community of whom he was a pillar and a half, he was a much vaguer figure outside in the country at large. To the unknowing he might have appeared as the stereotypical tall Texan, able (almost) to avoid looking silly in a cowboy hat and boots, yet he was thoroughly a creature of Washington, and, with his New Deal and World War II background, along with his awareness of the seamy underside of so-called local control and home rule in his native state as well as elsewhere, a believer: a believer in Washington, and in Washington's capability to do good, a lot of good. The assassination suddenly and radically changed his life; he proved to be quite prepared. Who he was and what would he now do with the awesome responsibility that Providence had suddenly dumped into his lap were surely unknowns to the large majority of the public at large. The answer would prove simple enough: everything he could. For Lyndon Johnson was a thoroughly political individual. Politics was his vocation, his life, nearly his sole interest. The first small quote of newspaper-headline size that he provided the people was a simple one: "Let us continue," implying unfinished business, most obviously the rising, now unavoidable issue of civil rights. But merely continuing along a path blazed by others was not the vision of LBJ, as rhetoric and events were to prove. What did Johnson want to do with the presidency? Just about everything, it turned out. Prior to the Dallas tragedy, as a political realist, Johnson must have seriously doubted that, presuming the reelection of John F. Kennedy in 1964, the odds even remotely favored his succeeding to the presidency via the election of 1968—he would be viewed by many as too old, and besides, historical experience seemed to show that vice presidents did not fare well when attempting to succeed their bosses (Martin Van Buren having been the last to turn the trick, in the 1836 election). Johnson could hardly be blamed, then, for at least half-sensing by the early evening of November 22, 1963, that his was a rendezvous with destiny. As he later explicitly was to state in an important address to Congress, he meant to make the most of it. Not known, and for good reason, as a great political communicator, he on the other hand was very well-known within the capital for knowing the Washington political system from the inside like nobody else; what resulted—the Great Society—showed it. The Great Society enjoyed its shining hour in the aftermath of the great liberal political victory of 1964, and Johnson was a very busy man, knowing too well that the magical moment would likely not last. He was right, yet he kept fighting to the end. The way it all turned out would make the postpresidential LBJ a sympathetic, even tragic figure in the last couple of years of his life, a life that was to be shockingly short after his virtually forced retirement from the White House. His legacies were huge, his impact enormous, but he died deeply dissatisfied and hurt.

Like a lot of American politicians, at least those who can with any plausibility get away with it, Johnson liked to "play poor" with regard to his background. Sympathetic later biographers have done their best to go along with this, but the modern-day log cabin claim cannot withstand scrutiny when applied to a man from a town, small and provincial though it was, named after his own family, which had included officeholders at a state level (his maternal grandfather had served as secretary of state for Texas and also been a member of the legislature). His mother Rebekah had attended Baylor in a day when only a tiny fraction of the population had had the college experience, and his father was a community leader and sometime duly elected member of the Texas Legislature. Thanks to his father's position, Lyndon Johnson was early exposed to the legislative process and seemed to take to it the way other children find an affinity for a musical instrument or a sport. "I loved going with my father to the legislature," Johnson recalled in retirement. "I would sit in the gallery for hours watching all the activity on the floor and then would wander around the halls trying to figure out what was going on. The only thing I loved more was going with him on the trail during his campaigns for re-election" (Kearns 1976, 36). He regularly attended the then very popular outdoor political events that were in the tradition of the Lincoln-Douglas debates, that is, important community social gatherings woven into the fabric of the year's cycle, sessions not to be missed. Upon graduating from high school in May 1924, Johnson drifted to California, spending the second of his two years there working at a job obtained through relatives, but returned to Johnson City in 1926. In February 1927, still seeking direction, he determined to give college a try at nearby San Marcos College, which he knew a little about because his grandmother had worked there. At San Marcos he excelled both academically and socially. San Marcos' principal mission was to produce schoolteachers for the area, and it was common in those days for persons who had not yet completed their degrees to dive into teaching. Thanks to the college president, Johnson obtained for school year 1928–29 a position as principal/teacher at Welhausen Ward Elementary School in the small city of Cotulla, three-fourths of whose residents were of Mexican background, most of whom spoke only Spanish. Johnson never forgot the direct experience of compelling need he found there. He plunged into the situation with great energy, setting up many beyond-the-classroom activities for the children and spending his own money to supplement their educational and cultural activities. After completing his degree, he spent the next fifteen months in Houston, teaching at Sam Houston High. But he had no difficulty deciding he was not destined for a teaching career.

His first direct exposure to national politics came about on account of the coincidence that the 1928 Democratic National Convention was held in Houston. He entered the proceedings as a member of the press, representing the college paper, and got his first look at Franklin D. Roosevelt, who nominated Al Smith for president. His break came in the summer of 1930, when, giving an impromptu speech at a local political gathering that he had regularly attended with his father as a child, the candidate for the state senate on whose behalf Johnson spoke was impressed enough to ask him to manage his campaign, which he did. Willy Hopkins was elected and later proved to be the one who suggested LBJ's name to Congressman Richard Kleberg (the inheritor of Texas' legendary King Ranch) in 1931, recently tapped in a special election as a new U.S. representative. Johnson's interview in Corpus Christi went well, and he was hired as the congressman's legislative secretary. In two weeks, he was taking the train to Washington for the first time.

He never really looked back, for in Washington he found his place. Of course he knew that ordinarily all politics is local, and that those representatives who do not stay in touch with their constituents rarely politically survive to tell the tale. To outside observers he always seemed quintessentially Texan, which of course in important ways he was. But it did not take Johnson long to become a true figure of Washington, which was to be his real home, physically and spiritually, for his adult life and for the span of his long career as a professional officeholder. As a congressional staff member, Johnson, who had had the political bug from childhood, thrived and soon stood out. He did his homework, reading the papers, the *Congressional Record*, and related materials. He made himself available as a congressional messenger and thus got to know the older men of Congress. Significant figures of the Texas delegation such as Sam Rayburn and Wright Patman had known his father in the Texas Legislature and were thus prepared to like him and help him; he immediately justified their positive inclinations. In handling routine constituent work for Congressman Kleberg, Johnson began making contacts with important and often wealthy Texas citizens.

Johnson's general ambitions led him in June 1935 to seek the job as director of the Texas National Youth Administration, which he obtained; at age twenty-six, he was the youngest NYA state director in the nation. The long hours of his workdays did not bother him at all, for he had already become highly, highly focused on his work. Soon many in the loop called him hands-down the best state NYA head in the country, apparently because he worked the hardest; a "doer" in office, he would always prefer the same type. His next big break came in February 1937 when Texas Congressman James P. Buchanan died. At once, he knew his chance had come for election to the U.S. Congress, and as an Austin resident he lived in the Tenth District, which also included Johnson City. At this time, Texas members of Congress as a group had the longest tenure of service of any state delegation, so one had to move boldly. Johnson was not known even to political leaders in the district and was only twenty-eight years old, but thanks to Congressman Kleberg, he had some good, and well-off, connections. Running as a down-the-line supporter of FDR's New Deal, even including his plan to add U.S. Supreme Court members so as to prevent that body from putting further roadblocks in the New Deal's way, Johnson, after heavy personal campaigning, won the seat by plurality in a crowded field. Shortly thereafter, Johnson was invited to meet the president when he visited Galveston. Word got around fast that Roosevelt favored Johnson, and Johnson made the most of the relationship; the Tenth Congressional District got more than its share of the plentiful dollars expended in the plethora of New Deal programs. Roosevelt appreciated having a reliable New Dealer from a state largely dominated by conservative Democrats.

As early as 1940, Johnson was tapped for a national leadership post, that of chairman of the overall Democratic Congressional Campaign Committee, wherein he further enhanced his reputation and influence among the professional pols. Yet, given the large size of the House of Representatives, a man of Johnson's tremendous ambition unsurprisingly coveted a seat in the much more exclusive Senate. He therefore naturally ran when a death produced a special election in 1941, losing to Texas's governor by some 1,300 votes out of 600,000 cast in an utterly dubious count of the sort not unknown in the state's politics; he was never to lose an election again. With the United States' entry into World War II, Johnson, a member of the naval reserves, received a leave of absence from his congressional duties and was assigned various noncombat tasks before returning to Capitol Hill in mid-1942 in response to a general request by FDR to all members of Congress that they take up their elected posts.

Plenty of Texas Democrats had long been opposed to the New Deal well before Roosevelt's death in April 1945; given that Texas was utterly a one-party state, part of its Solid South, Confederate legacy, all shades of political philosophy had long had to coexist under an essentially meaningless "Democratic" label. So-called Regulars knew that a New Dealer like Johnson was no old-time, Jeffersonian, states'-rights Democrat. As for Johnson, he demonstrated his political astuteness in shifting with the times. In the postwar Truman era, Johnson loudly opposed civil rights proposals and also voted in favor of the Taft-Hartley Act, anathema to organized labor (a marginal force in Texas politics) yet popular enough on Capitol Hill to be passed over President Truman's veto. In the "New Deal" sense, Johnson remained a firm believer in obtaining federal money for local projects of various sorts, especially infrastructure, traditionally the most popular and least controversial form of federal spending, or veterans' benefits; of course, the popularity of that stance was widespread among members of Congress regardless of party label and often of political philosophy as well.

There could be no doubt after his near-miss in 1941 that Johnson intended again to seek elevation to the U.S. Senate at the earliest available opportunity. On November 3, 1948, at the age of forty-four, he earned the ironic nickname "Landslide Lyndon" in winning the Texas Senate election by 87 votes out of the 900,000 cast over another Texas governor with a strongly conservative, limited-government philosophy, thanks to a count even more unbelievably dubious than that by which he had been defeated just a few years before. This narrow victory confirmed Johnson's analysis of the conservative state of Texas politics in the post–New Deal era.

Traditionally, many new senators have been veterans of the Washington scene and of the House of Representatives, but Johnson was unusually knowledgeable and well-connected, even by historical standards, for a freshman senator. As a senator he ingratiated himself with the inner sanctum there, especially bachelor Richard Russell of Georgia, who came to regard Johnson as family; Johnson had a sure hand with small personal touches that indicated respect and cemented loyalty over the long haul. Yet Johnson avoided the southern caucus, preferring not to be subsumed under a label that would likely preclude any shot he might have, someday, at the presidency, an unspoken but real dream. Demonstrating independence and a national orientation, Johnson became a mentor to youthful Hubert Humphrey, freshman senator from Minnesota, whose outspoken liberalism, especially regarding civil rights, had immediately made him anathema to the southern-dominated Senate Democratic establishment. As usual, he worked as hard as anyone physically could, consumed with the job.

LBJ's high ambitions got a third big break when, in short order, two senior Democrats who had served as party leader and assistant leader were both defeated in 1950; Johnson was eager to take on a job that few wanted, assistant leader. Then in 1952 the new party leader was also defeated, and so it worked out that, only three years into his Senate career, he was chosen leader of the Democrats, now the minority party, on January 3, 1953. As leader he became intensely knowledgeable about the longtime players in the Senate club, gaining intelligence that would serve him well when fate suddenly elevated him to the presidency. Johnson had no particular ideological image, in keeping with the consensus spirit of the times; he always liked to say that he favored results, and sought the mainstream as circumstances allowed. With Dwight Eisenhower, a man who worried a great deal about excessive federal power, as president, nothing remotely along the lines of a Great Society was in the works.

As a professional officeholder, Johnson held to the maxim of the trade that politics is the art of the possible. Many accused him of having become conservative; Johnson felt he simply did what he had to do, given the mood of the time, and that his liberal critics were ill-informed and unrealistic. In retirement he complained about those he termed "emotional liberals" who "believed in controversy and could never reconcile themselves with anyone who believed in achievement," who saw "the words 'compromise' and 'betrayal'" as "exactly the same," and who "cared less about delivering results than they did about the purity of their route to a nonexistent accomplishment" (Kearns 1976, 149). When the occasion presented itself, Johnson promoted the expansion of federal spending and programs even in the 1950s in such areas as public housing funding and, to a limited but real extent, increased federal aid to precollege education under the shadow of the post-Sputnik hysteria (which Johnson helped encourage); his 1955 speech at Whitney, Texas, filled with a laundry list of big government proposals, short by his own later Great Society standards but long for the mid-1950s, he characteristically entitled "A Program with a Heart" (Schulman 1955, 47).

When it came to the rising civil rights question, Johnson demonstrated his liberalism, by white southern standards of the day, by refusing to sign the "Southern Manifesto" protesting the U.S. Supreme Court's *Brown v. the Board of Education (1954)* decision, one of only a handful of southern solos to do so. He played a key role in making the 1957 Civil Rights Act happen, working out the various compromises that made the first civil rights bill since Reconstruction a reality; to critics of the bill, Johnson replied that he had gotten all that could be gotten at that time, while immediately asserting that the next step, and then the next, would come as soon as practicable.

Johnson was most interested in the Democratic presidential nomination of 1960, but hesitated to campaign actively for it; in part, he suspected that a "Southerner"—for that was how, he knew, he was viewed by many—was out of the running before the running started. His name was often mentioned in the political gossip of the day, and it was known that he was more than willing, but by the time he went public with his candidacy, John F. Kennedy had captured that mysterious media phenomenon of momentum, and LBJ got nowhere. Kennedy's selection of Johnson as his running mate was based on a traditional ticket-balancing, southern strategy that succeeded; JFK carried just enough of the old Confederacy to prevail in the electoral college. Johnson's willingness to give up his well-established power in the Senate for the usually meaningless vice presidency demonstrated that his ambitions were as yet far from satisfied.

Despite Johnson's best efforts, the vice presidential slot that he filled remained relatively inconsequential. Johnson was given the chairmanship of the President's Committee on Equal Employment Opportunity and used the position to prod seekers after government contracts actively to promote equal opportunity. Included in the president's circle of advisors, Johnson argued for a more forceful stance on civil rights. Among his many overseas travels was a fateful 1961 visit to Vietnam, which solidified his prejudice that the United States had to take the lead there as elsewhere; Johnson was never one to advocate a diminished federal government role in anything, any time, any place.

November 22, 1963, is a date indelibly engraved in the memories of those Americans (and many others) then alive. Television was, of course, monopolized by the tragic national event of John F. Kennedy's murder and the ceremonials that followed, including the activities of the new president. Behind the scenes, Johnson was forced to begin the task of establishing a new presidency, his own. On November 23, he met at the Executive Office Building with economist Walter Heller of the Council of Economic Advisors, who briefed him on the current state of an internal initiative not quite a year old concerning poverty. It had reached the state of a none-too-successful-to-date task force that had considered some experimental pilot projects. Johnson responded with an enthusiastic interest that surprised Heller: "That's my kind of program. Go ahead. Give it the highest priority. Push ahead full tilt" (Johnson 1971, 71). Johnson made it clear that he wanted specifics, things that he could present to Congress at the start of the next session in January. Johnson was moving on various exploratory fronts; on November 25th, he received a requested memorandum regarding the question of federally sponsored health insurance for senior citizens, a question that had been bouncing around and about Congress since the days of Truman, and he met with civil rights leaders, promising with sincerity that he was indeed committed to the passage of President Kennedy's civil rights bill, which had been introduced into Congress the previous June. He contacted members of Congress, notably Everett Dirksen, Republican Senate minority leader, whom he viewed especially as key to the prospects for passing the long-delayed civil rights bill.

Johnson's address to Congress on November 27 produced a simple phrase that was oft-quoted, "Let us continue," and the new president, fifty-five years old and as experienced a Washington hand as there was, naturally felt it necessary to cover all the obvious bases at least a little bit, such as foreign policy (including Vietnam) and the Kennedy proposal to reduce tax rates. He briefly mentioned many others topics, including federal aid to education, and spoke vaguely about the ancient American efforts to overcome poverty. When he got to civil rights, he was more specific, insisting that "no memorial oration or eulogy could more eloquently honor President Kennedy's memory than the earliest possible passage of the civil rights bill. . . . We have talked long enough in this country about equal rights. We have talked for one hundred years or more. It is time now to write the next chapter, and to write it in the books of law" (*Public Papers* 1963–64, vol. I, 9). On several occasions, he referred to his career as member of the very body he was directly addressing, noting that for "32 years Capitol Hill has been my home" (9). He reminded listeners before him that he had "in 1957, and again in 1960" worked for civil rights legislation, and praised Congress as an institution for its "capacity and . . . ability . . . to act—to act wisely, to act vigorously, to act speedily when the need arises" (9–10). Of course, Johnson was well aware of other proclivities and traditions within Congress, too. But if there was any part of the world he knew in his bones, better even than his native area of Texas, it was Capitol Hill. He intended to make the most of this deep knowledge, and he soon did.

In the remaining weeks of 1963, the poverty task force initiated by Walter Heller in June of that year was far more under the gun than it had been while Kennedy still lived. The varieties of "poverty" in a nation as vast as the United States were clear enough; what would a "national program" mean? Think locally, fund and coordinate federally, became the idea. Heller's proposal to LBJ of December 20, 1963, dubbed the Community Action Program, called for ten demonstration projects, evenly split between urban and rural areas, all stressing coordination of the various piles of federal dollars available locally, plus an executive branch committee at cabinet level to keep the thing focused, moving, developing, and growing. Local government involvement was presumed. Meeting with Johnson at his Texas ranch, Heller found the ambitious president underwhelmed; he wanted something as big as Texas, that would gather attention, that he would be able to make a big speech, or two or three, about, that would not "disappear" into the federal bureaucracy without much public notice. The federal government had money; any local group that had ideas, Johnson demanded, could create a community action program and get some. Why wait? The pressure was still on and, given the clock, even intensified: full speed ahead in "planning" the proposal, and only a few weeks were left before Johnson wanted to make a splash with a proposal-laden State of the Union address, to be followed by a legislative package to launch what would soon be known as the War on Poverty, centerpiece of the Great Society.

Relatively few Americans on the morning of January 8, 1964, would have named "poverty" as a top problem facing the United States. But in his State of the Union address, President Johnson famously stated, "This administration today, here and now, declares unconditional war on poverty in America." Perhaps he had his idol FDR in mind, who had declared war on the Depression in his 1933 inaugural address. The circumstances could hardly have been more different, but were they more or less auspicious for Johnson's New Deal–style approach to public questions? The lack of a crisis atmosphere in 1964 meant that Johnson's task was to move a nation, but much more specifically also to move Congress, something he had supreme and well-justified confidence in his ability to do. In late March, Johnson spoke to Richard Goodwin, a former Kennedy aide who was to be for a time LBJ's most important speechwriter about his vision of the political situation: "I loved Jack Kennedy, just like you, but he never really understood the Congress. I do. And I'm going to pass all those bills you cared about. It's a once-in-a-lifetime opportunity, for you, for me, for the country. . . . I'm going to get my War on Poverty. Of course, we can't have it all in one gulp. We'll have to make some concessions, make a few compromises—that's the only way to get anything. But that's this year. I have to get elected, and I don't want to scare people off. Next year we'll do even more, and the year after, until we have all the programs. But no compromises on civil rights. I'm not going to bend an inch, this year or next. These civil rightsers are going to have to wear sneakers to keep up with me" (Goodwin 1988, 257).

If there were no "crisis" in the air regarding poverty, the same could not be said when it came to civil rights. And the two questions were, of course, connected though also distinct. Over the course of the next few weeks, planning for specific proposals for the "war" moved rapidly, under presidential pressure, led by LBJ appointee Sargent Shriver, a brother-in-law of the Kennedys. Johnson kept close tabs on the effort, providing guidance as to what he did not like (public works projects) and what he did (a stress on youth and skill development). A bill was sent to Congress on March 16 accompanied by Johnson's pumped-up rhetoric, which was already becoming familiar to the politically attentive. A "total victory" in the "war" was demanded, and a strong moral admonition was included in the message, because in the current prosperous situation of modern America, "we have the power to strike away the barriers to full participation in our society. Having the power, we have the duty" (Unger 1996, 85). The bill landed in the House of Representatives' standing committee on Education and Labor, dominated by northern advocates of large federal programs and chaired by mercurial Congressman Adam Clayton Powell of New York. As the weeks followed, a parade of witnesses from the administration and elsewhere testified to the unending need for federal money and their faith in its capacity to improve people's lives. That would be one major front for Johnson in 1964.

With regard to the other front, the civil rights bill, the old Kennedy proposal from the previous summer had already, as fully expected, easily passed the House of Representatives in early February. Johnson knew that the real struggle would come in the Senate, on account of its peculiar rules permitting "unlimited" debate in ordinary circumstances; ending such "debate," which was usually a mere roadblock tactic, required a high standard: two-thirds of the Senate. The circumstances were ideal to get the bill over the hump. Johnson and the Republicans' leader, Dirksen, not only were long-time professional colleagues but also were genuinely quite fond of each other, often socialized, and were on the same wavelength personally if not quite philosophically. If Johnson could get Dirksen behind civil rights, it would pass; in fact, he had to, given the large number of anti–civil rights southern Democrats in the Senate. Whatever it took—pork-barrel federal dollars for Illinois, public and private praise, the right to name presidential appointees—Johnson would provide and was an old hand at doing so. Things of this sort collectively amount to what had long been called the "treatment," the very essence of insider political horse trading of the very old and established school. In early May, Dirksen and Attorney General Robert Kennedy began serious discussion as to what amendments (minor, it turned out) would be necessary in order to gain Dirksen's support. On June 10, 1964, the Republican leader from the Land of Lincoln came out in favor of a bill Johnson could accept, and the Civil Rights Act of 1964, which forever altered the social landscape of the United States, resulted just a few weeks later. The record-setting three-month-long filibuster ended with the June 10 adoption of cloture, and the historic bill was signed into law by President Johnson in July. It banned discrimination on account of race, color, national origin, creed, and sex in employment practices and public accommodations. The consensus behind it was great and only got bigger as generations came to be born who had never experienced, and could barely conceptualize, the kind of open, enforced-by-law segregation that not only had prevailed but also had been seen as embedded and virtually unchangeable. The "civil rights" principles of the 1964 act were to be the most widely accepted and applauded of all the acts that collectively constituted Johnson's desire to build a "Great Society" in the modern United States.

Johnson, like Dirksen, knew that basic civil rights of the sort legally guaranteed in the 1964 law were indeed ideas whose time had come, and as the master legislator he knew how to get it through. But his ambitions were far greater, of course, and not merely confined to the already-declared, though not yet implemented (let alone legislated), "war" on poverty. In early April, now chief speechwriter Richard Goodwin, presidential aide Bill Moyers, and LBJ got together at the White House swimming pool; the president spoke of his desire for a "Johnson program" that would go well beyond Kennedy's, with the objective of taking on—and solving—all (yes, all) of the country's problems under the aegis of the federal government. Still operating in a Democratic party tradition of sloganeering (which it turned out was to die with him), Johnson wanted a successor to New Deal, Fair Deal, and New Frontier, and Goodwin was the one who had already supplied the winner, "Great Society," a term that was actually already beginning to be used in some press reports. An east-coast, Ivy League–educated liberal, Goodwin, like Johnson, entertained great hopes for the many good things that could be accomplished were there only the will and the federal dollars. It was also hoped that the economic growth, stimulated by President Kennedy's tax cuts, which were enacted under Johnson, might be further stimulated by government spending associated with Great Society programs. It became Goodwin's assignment to produce, as a sort of extended follow-up to the "war declaration" speech of January, the announcement of the Great Society; the occasion was the 1964 commencement exercises in Ann Arbor for the University of Michigan. Here it was to be demonstrated that the "domestic agenda" of the president was literally—quite literally—boundless. Evil triumphed because good men did nothing; evil included sins of omission as well as commission; having the power, we had the duty to build the New Jerusalem—not by government alone, but with the federal government clearly, unambiguously taking the lead. Mastery would replace drift.

As Richard Goodwin recalled in his memoir, his speech came from a desk "strewn with reports, recommendations, memos containing a multitude of proposals, programs, suggested laws, and executive actions," the products of the task forces that were a feature of the Kennedy administration and that became even more important during LBJ's tenure. But the overall objective of the speech was "not to produce a catalog of specific projects, but a concept, an assertion of purpose, a vision . . . that went beyond the liberal tradition of the New Deal" (Goodwin 1988, 272). As Johnson so well understood, "The country was alive with change: ideas and anger, intellectual protest and physical rebellion. Without this ferment the formulation of the Great Society would not have been possible, not even conceivable" (272–73).

Johnson, and not just for partisan reasons, had been one of the severe critics of the alleged drift of the Eisenhower administration and had been a loud crisis-mongering voice after the launch of Sputnik. The ensuing hyperbole culminated, in Washington terms, with Eisenhower's presidential commission on "national goals" with its "search for a national purpose." Now, at Michigan Stadium, appropriately enough the nation's largest, Johnson would launch his "big" idea. Some 80,000 appeared on the morning of May 22, 1964, and applauded often (twenty-nine times, according to a count that Johnson requested be made) during the speech's half hour or so. After a glance at the United States' pioneering past appropriate to an audience at Michigan, "the champions of the West," Johnson, as per normal in a commencement address, looked to the future with a challenge: "In your time we have the opportunity to move not only toward the rich society and the powerful society, but upward to the Great Society" (*Public Papers* 1963–64, vol. 1, 704). Such a society would rest on "abundance and liberty for all" and would demand "an end to poverty and racial injustice, to which we are totally committed in our time" (704). Tellingly, Johnson immediately went on: "But that is just the beginning" (704).

High-sounding, idealistic generalities then flowed rapidly: leisure time, back-to-nature, potential artistic expression, hunger for community, "a destiny where the meaning of our lives matches the marvelous products of our labor" (*Public Papers* 1963–64, vol. 1, 704). Three specifics then followed: cities, countryside, and classrooms. Urban difficulties, focusing on transportation infrastructure and housing demand, loomed, along with the more obvious "decay of the centers" and the ideologically charged notion of the "despoiling of the suburbs." Pollution threatened to turn "America the beautiful" into "an ugly America." Education, clearly Johnson's favorite topic, faced continuing growth in number of customers and hence increasing financial challenges and needs: "Poverty must not be a bar to learning, and learning must offer an escape from poverty" (706). After gently reminding his listeners of their extraordinary privilege, Johnson closed with a classic "call and response" derived from the southern preaching tradition, seeking pledges from the candidates for degrees to "join in the battle" for equality, universal affluence, and the building of a Great Society wherein "the demands of morality, and the needs of the spirit, can be realized in the life of the Nation" (706). Of course, the people "said Amen" to each call. The possible existence of naysayers, "timid souls," was acknowledged and quickly dismissed. "We have the power. . . . But we need your will, your labor, your hearts" (706). Johnson was happy as the speech went down well by all accounts.

At least since Theodore Roosevelt, the possibilities for presidents to make use of their bully pulpits has been well recognized. Given his ambitions, Johnson of course tried, but oratory was no particular gift of his, nor did he have delusions about himself in this matter. Rather, getting it through Congress, whatever "it" might be, was his gift. With a mastery of the legislative process unparalleled in the history of the high office he held, and a goal to "out-Roosevelt Roosevelt" when it came to domestic legislation, Johnson was well poised to make the rhetorical the real. Civil rights and the War on Poverty, while only parts of the whole, held center stage in the summer of 1964. Civil rights was an established, familiar issue; warring on poverty was a new creation. The antipoverty bill had continued to make its way through the congressional process in the spring and summer, supported by such elements of the liberal coalition as big-city mayors and labor unions. The House Committee on Education and Labor completed its hearings on April 28, and Democratic members conferred with Sargent Shriver and his aides over the course of the next two weeks, often working into the night. Republicans were excluded and the vote to report the bill out (to the full House for consideration) was along party lines. Hearings of the Senate Select Committee on poverty, which proved to be brief, only began in the middle of June, with such luminaries as Robert Kennedy speaking with hopeful praise while Barry Goldwater warned of sure difficulties in implementation. A Senate version of the bill was approved in committee by a 13–2 vote, with moderate and liberal Republican support. Johnson gave Hubert Humphrey the task of rounding up Senate votes, but of course the chief executive was active himself. Besides his own well-known "treatment," he drafted business leaders to contact unsure senators. Passage was not really in doubt, but the bigger the margin, the better. On July 23rd, the Senate approved a bill the administration was happy with; a third of Republican members voted yea. The final version of the Economic Opportunity Act of 1964 passed the House by a vote of 226–185, the Senate 61–35. It was signed into law on the morning of August 20 on steps overlooking the White House Rose Garden, with Johnson calling it "a new day of opportunity" for the poor (Unger 1996, 100). The law created such to-be-famous War on Poverty efforts as the Office of Economic Opportunity, the Job Corps, "community action," and Volunteers in Service to America (VISTA). From this law eventually would come Head Start and federally funded Legal Services. It would fall to Sargent Shriver to try to actualize the words on paper.

By this time, the presidential race of 1964 was in place, and, as Republican Barry Goldwater put it, Americans were offered a choice, not an echo. Everything broke Johnson's way as he added almost the entire center of American politics to his solid base on the left, and the results—the greatest Democratic landslide since the Depression era—allowed the Texan who hoped to out-Roosevelt Roosevelt to dare to dream that his Ann Arbor vision of a Great Society would not prove to be hyperbole after all. Johnson could genuinely cry "mandate," having won forty-four states and 61.1 percent of the popular vote, and congressional Democratic majorities surged to levels unseen since Johnson's first days in the House. Well before Election Day, presidential aide Bill Moyers was guiding the next set of task forces toward the production of a gaggle of new proposals in such areas as education, the environment, and urban affairs.

With majorities like these, Johnson's major task in the Eighty-ninth Congress was to make as *many* proposals as possible, sure in the knowledge that the numbers meant their passage was near certain. Dealing with Congress was LBJ's speciality, but the margins were so great that that would not even matter that much for many God, motherhood, and apple-pie sounding proposals—and Johnson found it easy, with a little help from his numerous task forces, to come up with quite a few of them, as his Ann Arbor speech had suggested. Just to make sure, Johnson had the committee structure altered a bit to make it harder for determined minorities to delay or even bottle up proposals. In particular cases, veteran congressional members would have to be dealt with, the most obvious and significant example being

Wilbur Mills, longtime chairman of the House Ways and Means committee, and health care for the elderly, which he and his colleagues had been seriously grappling with for years. Another ancient issue dear to LBJ's heart, federal aid to precollegiate education, having long been in waiting, similarly found that its hour had come.

It is striking how such difficult and complex questions suddenly broke through the traditional congressional logjam, all at once it seemed. With a truer "mandate" than most elections produce, a drive master of the Capitol Hill game at the helm, and the partisan numbers, it was almost inevitable, and it happened. Former schoolteacher Johnson delivered a "special" message on education to Congress on January 12, 1965, requesting an appropriation of $1.5 billion, two-thirds of which would go to elementary and secondary schools, targeted to school districts with high poverty rates. Improved educational attainment would reduce poverty, neatly fitting in with the "wartime" spirit, and there was certainty that these good things could be bought. The Elementary and Secondary Education Act was written so as to encourage local government spending on education, "rewarding" bigger spending districts with even more federal money, and included the possibility of money for nonpublic schools, necessary to get supporters of the parochial schools on board. House hearings lasted less than two weeks in late January and featured a parade of "witnesses" salivating at the prospects of "free" dollars. Senate hearings, if they could be called that, went equally smoothly, and what presidential assistant Lawrence O'Brien called "the cornerstone to the entire Administration legislative program for the Eighty-ninth Congress" was signed into law on April 11. Johnson went to Texas for the ceremony, held in his former one-room schoolhouse a mile from his ranch, with some of his former pupils plus his own elementary schoolteacher present for photo ops (Unger 1996, 124, 127). Free money proved addicting, and would eventually provide leverage to help get recalcitrant southern school districts to get into line regarding integration. As Johnson well understood, once the principle of federal aid to K–12 education was established, there would be no turning back, despite loose talk of conservative trends in future years. However, the tradition of "categorical," as opposed to general, grants continued; the dream of some that the federal government might provide some percentage of all school revenues across the board would remain unrealized in the twentieth century.

Johnson's second great signing ceremony of 1965 took place on July 30th in Independence, Missouri, held in the auditorium of the presidential library of former president Harry Truman, who had first proposed something like Medicare in the late 1940s and who graced the ceremony with his presence. Like civil rights, Medicare was an idea whose time had come; in part, demographics lay behind its shining hour, as there were simply more elderly and more of them were living longer. Cost mattered little to Johnson—the important thing was to establish the new program—but he knew that the details on financing mattered a great deal to the chairman of the House Ways and Means Committee. Medicare's birth, all understood, depended on Wilbur Mills, and Johnson had been working on him since 1964, through such intermediaries as Lawrence O'Brien and, most importantly, experienced aide Wilbur Cohen, but also on his own. Lightning struck on March 2, 1965, when Mills "announced" himself and his terms. Such was Mills's reputation and prestige that the bill voted out of his committee was approved by the full House on April 8, 1965, after only a day of debate. Senate debate that summer was similarly brief—three days—and the bill passed easily. The inclusion of federally funded health entitlements for the poor, Medicaid, is another sign of the spirit of the times of the War on Poverty's birth. With regard to problems, holes, and shortcomings in the Medicare setup, Johnson was of good cheer; more could always be added later to the institutional structure established.

The third great signing ceremony of 1965, of the Voting Rights Act, took place on August 6 in the Capitol rotunda, was every bit as significant as the other two of that year, and was equal in stature to the 1964 Civil Rights Act in its effect on the United States. The "power" of the federal government to ensure that the right to vote was not being withheld on account of race or color dated to the Reconstruction-era Fifteenth Amendment, whose potentially significant second clause, affirming congressional power to ensure the stated right by appropriate legislation, had been a dead letter for generations. While a significant minority of black Southerners were already voting at the dawn of 1965, it was also the case, and more widely known than ever thanks to the civil rights movement and media coverage, that in many parts of the South the right was far from being a reality. On January 2, 1965, Martin Luther King, Jr., was invited to Selma, Alabama, to breathe life into a stalled voter registration effort. The dramatic march from Selma to Montgomery, Alabama's capital city, site of the famed bus boycott of the mid-1950s and the birthplace of the Confederacy, provided some violence, compelling television news, and increased political demands for congressional action. Johnson's Texas background made him intimately familiar with the sometime machinations of local election officials with regard to who did and did not vote, and he knew that the issue of voting and the federal power to ensure its vindication was as clear as anything could be.

The president had mentioned the question of the right to vote in his State of the Union message, but now with the nation's attention fixed on the happenings in Alabama, he addressed a joint session of Congress during prime time on March 15 and began by comparing Selma to Lexington, Concord, and Appomattox in its historical significance. Quoting the now-familiar civil rights anthem, inspired by the Book of Revelation, Johnson promised, "And we . . . shall . . . overcome." It proved to be almost easy, the 1964 story redux, with Johnson's relationship with Republican leader Dirksen again important in ensuring bipartisan support. The easily demonstrated and gross abuse of literacy tests doomed this time-hallowed device. Consensus on the basics was such that Johnson's careful proposal, reflecting deep experience and knowledge of election chicanery and the convoluted history of creative devices used to disenfranchise citizens that would have seemed almost comic had it not been real and very much contemporary to Johnson's career, actually came out even stronger in its final form. The Voting Rights Act succeeded in settling a question that had been kicking around for nearly a century, and the tone of southern politics changed with a rapidity that was, to the historically minded, astonishing and that made what had been mainstream white supremacy rhetoric and actions that survived even into the 1960s suddenly appear as if from an ancient, forgotten age.

1965 was the high point of the Great Society, and this would be the case were its only fruits the three landmarks just discussed. But, given the situation, the reality is that many more bills of significance were enacted in 1965 and also in the second session of the Eighty-ninth Congress in 1966. Even to list them would take a good while; regular national business continued, meaning that not all legislation enacted that year had much to do with the Great Society idea (the significant reform of immigration law, for instance) or were terribly controversial (more federal money for this or that favored cause, such as pollution or "the arts and humanities," and the creation of a couple of new cabinet-level departments), given the strong activist majority in Congress. Doubters would have their day, but not quite yet. Perhaps it was the riot in Los Angeles, literally days after the signing ceremony for the Voting Rights Act, that provided the first big sign of potential trouble; only the locals had known the name "Watts," but now everybody did. But even this first sign of what would prove to be years of consecutive "long, hot summers" could easily be taken—and was—as only more evidence that even more, in fact far more, federal activity was needed to address, and solve, neglected social ills.

That previous June, LBJ had delivered what was perhaps his most well-received speech ever, the commencement address at Howard University in the nation's capital city. Lauding the voting rights bill that was sure to pass Congress soon, he quoted Churchill: the law marked "not the end. It is not even the beginning of the end. But it is, perhaps, the end of the beginning" (*Public Papers* 1965, vol. II, 636). In the most quoted lines from the speech, Johnson made clear that the Great Society programs, just getting started, would need to continue developing, for "you do not take a person who, for years, has been hobbled by chains and liberate him, bring him up to the starting line of a race and then say, 'you are free to compete with all the others,' and still justly believe that you have been completely fair. . . . We seek not just freedom but opportunity. We seek not just legal equity but human ability, not just equality as a right and a theory but equality as a fact and equality as a result" (636). He went on to make clear that while poverty disproportionately "trapped" black Americans, it also—of course—affected white Americans, too (in a reference to his brief first career, Johnson also referred to Mexican Americans as victims of "prejudice, distaste, or condescension") (638). No, the president warned, there were no simple, easy answers; but after listing such items as jobs, "decent" homes, improved welfare and social programs, as well as an "understanding heart by all Americans," Johnson threw down the gauntlet: "To all of these fronts—and a dozen more—I will dedicate the expanding efforts of the Johnson administration" (639). The Great Society was just beginning.

Watts seems to have, briefly, immobilized Johnson, who did not return calls to his aide Joseph Califano for the only time ever, forcing Califano to make presidential-type decisions regarding U.S. Army support for the California National Guard. After about twenty-four hours, Johnson did call, depressed, fearing a backlash. But he regained his bearings quickly, telephoning national black leaders to encourage them to issue statements condemning violence (they did), and in a few weeks set into motion another task force mandated to—rapidly—come up with an "urban" proposal (ultimately to be known as the "Model Cities" program). As Califano recalled, "Johnson lived his presidency in a race against time. He could never get his programs to and through congress fast enough; once they were passed, we could never get them in operation as rapidly as he ordered" (Califano 1991, 61). Especially when it came to anything connected with civil rights, Johnson was "at his most demanding. He knew it was essential to arouse the oppressed, and that, once aroused, their clock ticked impatiently"—as shown in Watts and, as it would soon unfold, many other cities during the forthcoming long, hot summers (62). "I began to grasp how acutely Johnson feared that the reforms to which he had dedicated his presidency were in mortal danger, not only from those who opposed but from those he was trying to help" (61–62).

And of course it continued—the Eighty-ninth Congress still had a second session ahead of it in 1966 before most of its members would face the electorate that fall. Johnson, as ever, was very busy, and had been. His urban task force, thrown together at the suggestion of United Automobile Workers Union president Walter Reuther at a September White House meeting, had been given Air Force jet transportation for its five weekends of secret meetings, which began in mid-October and culminated in a draft report on December 16th, recommending pilot programs as "demonstration projects." This was to be the direct reply to "Watts" and the next centerpiece of the expanding War on Poverty. Much legislation of a general nature not especially related to the central concerns of the Great Society was enacted by a Congress still quite sympathetic to the general notion of federal action to solve problems of all sorts (for instance, bills intended to reduce water pollution and improve automobile safety). But a perusal of any list of legislative highlights of that year fails to turn up any new *successful* Great Society initiatives.

Much of the civil rights and War on Poverty "action" was, instead, out in the field, where LBJ could have limited direct effects at best. The actual implementation of legislation had to begin. With regard to voting rights, the success story unfolded as registration figures steadily, often spectacularly, increased. But when it came to war news, be it from Vietnam, which increasingly occupied the president's time, or the antipoverty brigades, there was not much good news to be had. Reports from the Office of Economic Opportunity revealed much difficulty indeed regarding the to-be-famous catchphrase "maximum feasible participation," viewed by many local political establishments, once they figured out what it meant at all, as direct threats to their power and influence. The Job Corps suffered from negative publicity due to the conduct of some of its recruits. At Howard, Johnson had promised a big White House Conference for the fall of 1965 to be called "To Fulfill These Rights," a kind of open-session task force gathering of experts who, presumably, would lay out and discuss the next stage of Great Society antipoverty and antidiscrimination initiatives. But the release of the so-called Moynihan Report (Moynihan 1965), with its discussion of the black family, led the administration to engage in a tactical retreat, delaying movement, and the June 1966 gathering was a gigantic nothing dominated by (successful) administration efforts at damage control. President Johnson did successfully struggle to enact the Great Society Model Cities program with a classic collection of Johnson-treatment activities aimed at winning over the necessary swing votes in the late summer of 1966, but it was destined to become one of the poster children of the critics who denounced the "failed" War on Poverty. A close student of the Great Society summarized the second session of the Eighty-ninth Congress, and the country at large, as "disappointment. With each passing month confusion, worry, fatigue, and anger would come to dominate public discourse and eat away at the broad middle-class consensus of the year before" (Unger 1996, 199). Increased complaints were heard from liberals (whose constituencies, unlike Johnson's, were parochial).

The 1966 midterm elections, held in the wake of another riotous summer and negative publicity critical of the War on Poverty, were on the surface a disaster for the Great Society, with a wide swing toward the Republicans. The Senate remained liberal, including many liberal Republicans, some of them newly elected, while in the House, the ancient conservative coalition of southern Democrats and Republicans had risen yet again. "New" initiatives proved much harder, if not downright impossible, even to formulate, let alone imagine getting through Congress. More and more, Vietnam was a scar that Johnson bore. The partisan opposition, under Representative Melvin Laird (R-WI), produced a manifesto organized around the principle later known as "revenue sharing," an updated version of states' rights and responsibilities under the principle of federalism but with no taint of white supremacy; it would prove to be a very significant wave of the future of the rest of the century. An open housing bill, passed in the wake of the assassination of Martin Luther King, Jr., in 1968, did establish a national principle of nondiscrimination in housing that was both new and strongly controversial, but proved much, much harder to enforce than, say, a ban on white-only lunch counters.

When 1968 began, Johnson intended to seek reelection. It proved to be *l'année terrible*, beginning with the U.S.S. *Pueblo*'s seizure by North Korea, which was quickly overshadowed by what came to be known as "Tet," the only Vietnamese word the American public ever learned. To the general public, this uprising, despite its military failure, made a mockery of the claim that Johnson's Vietnam policy was working. When it became obvious that he could only have the nomination if he fought hard for it, and that there were no guarantees, Johnson decided to make the stunning announcement, on March 31, that he would not seek another term as president. He remained unwilling to accept defeat in Vietnam, and held off doing anything dramatically one-sided designed to end that conflict. He supported his vice president, Hubert Humphrey, for the Democratic nomination but was hardly in a position to do him much good on the campaign trail. If one puts the George Wallace and Nixon presidential vote of 1968 together and counts the combined result as a repudiation of the Johnson administration, which was represented in the election by Vice President Humphrey, and then recalls the Johnson landslide of only four years before, the swing is extraordinary.

Johnson's instincts had been sound: there turned out to be, as he feared, a brief, shining moment in which to enact as much "Great Society" as possible. He would have preferred a much larger window of opportunity, but it was not to be. However, as that ultimate creature of Washington well understood, once things got in the federal register, they were hard to get out. The Great Society accomplished a great deal and made many changes. The 1970s saw a continuing federal presence in virtually aspects of American life that is directly attributable to Johnson's Great Society initiatives. The very terms of the debate changed. It would take a long time before a serious political reaction could set in, one committed to a truly different path, and even after the 1980s and 1990s, reports of its successes could easily be exaggerated. Johnson had a largely unhappy, brief retirement in Texas, producing the usual middling presidential memoir, and died at his ranch of a heart attack on January 22, 1973.

WILBUR COHEN
(1913–1987)

The 1912 Progressive Party platform complained of the existence of an "invisible government," beyond the vision and scope of ordinary citizens, who in their innocence looked upon their elected representatives to be those who in fact wielded the real political power of society. The Progressives had in mind special-interest lobbyists entertaining officeholders and whispering to them in cloakrooms filled with smoke. The preferred vision of the Progressives in their most ideal form was of a well-regulated society disproportionately in the hands of the properly certified experts of various fields, disinterestedly managing the complex intricacies of society in a balanced, holistic way on behalf of the general welfare.

Wilbur Cohen led two public lives: the lesser as a policy-making, results-oriented academic figure, the far greater as a government employee (he arrived in Washington in 1934) whose career was primarily spent in the Social Security Administration but capped out with his brief tenure as Lyndon Johnson's last secretary of health, education and welfare. He might well have come about as close as is humanly possible to personifying the Progressive-era ideal of the humane, public-spirited professional civil servant: completely honest, selfless, devoted to the public welfare, hopeful, and optimistic that at least progress could be made in dealing with social ills. Cohen was seen as reliable and trustworthy, easy to get along with, and respectful of the political system and the officeholders it produced. He was fluid in writing, able to produce a coherent memorandum in short order, and scientific in approach.

Appropriately enough, his formative years, including college, were in Wisconsin, the state with perhaps the strongest "Progressive" tradition in the sense of this chapter's first paragraph; when Cohen first went to Washington to work with the incipient Social Security program, there were so *many* Wisconsinites already engaged that friends feared they might not be able to find him a slot. His name never became known to the wider public, even to those who can reasonably be said to follow public affairs in a responsible citizen-like way—Joseph Califano termed him "a quintessential Washington insider"—but to those in the know, he justly earned his eventual moniker: "Mr. Social Security." He was also a man with an agenda—the orderly expansion of a general welfare state of the type seen in Western Europe, the central concept of which was *entitlement*, as rapidly and completely as possible, within the confines of the American political system—and he was relentless in fighting for this aim, in which he had a deep, unquestioning faith. In this he was perfectly in tune with the mainstream of the Great Society. Yet, as an experienced realist who dealt with politics as they were, he was generally unsympathetic to some of its more daring, radical fringes.

Wilbur Cohen was at the heart of the planning and lobbying efforts of the Johnson administration to get Congress to create welfare programs across the board, including Medicare—his greatest impact on the Great Society came in the areas of Medicaid, Social Security expansion, and federal aid to education, the last of which reflected his intellectual renewal during the years he spent in the late 1950s out of Washington at the University of Michigan's social work school. To insiders, it became well-known that nobody *knew* more than Wilbur Cohen did about such matters, and as a longtime Washington player, he fundamentally possessed the same sort of view of the world, the country, and the political system as did Lyndon Johnson, the Great Society's author. As the chief proponent of Society Security over the long term, he was a central advocate of the obfuscating shell game that enabled the program to enjoy enormous, almost unquestioning popularity, at least until worrisome demographic trends and the rise of a more financially informed generation who lacked Depression-era memories and whose individualism was more pronounced than ever.

The Depression era formed the worldview of Wilbur Cohen and of an entire generation, casting a great shadow that never left them. His parents ran small grocery stores in Milwaukee, where Cohen was born on June 10, 1913, in an apartment above their current store. The family background was East Central European Jewish, part of the great migration of the late nineteenth century, and his upbringing was modestly religious in conventional ways (e.g., he was bar mitzvahed in 1926). This did not stick, however; he married a Texas Baptist in a nondenominational private ceremony and did not raise his children as Jews religiously, though, given the name "Cohen," he did discuss with them what they might think about saying if anyone were to ask them about being Jewish. While he could sense anti-Semitism over the course of his career from time to time, he found it subtle and even debatable most of the time, and was far more struck with how little there was and how it seemed not to stand in his way at all. Neither his neighborhoods nor his public schooling were predominantly Jewish, but, rather, were more of the urban ethnic melting pot variety. At Lincoln High School, from which he was graduated in 1930, he ranked in the top 10 percent and was elected student council president. Attracted to the University of Wisconsin by its still fairly new Experimental College, he matriculated at Madison in the fall of 1930 with interests in economics and political science. Half of the forty-two students in his class (all male) were from either Chicago or New York.

As a student in the Ex-College, Cohen proved more attracted to the New Deal approach of dealing with the Great Depression than to the more radical ideas circulating as the economic doldrums continued, despite associating with more radical friends. After two years, he was required to declare a major, and he chose labor economics, an area in which Wisconsin had a strong reputation, especially due to the department's leading light, John R. Commons. Commons, whose influence continued by way of a couple of his disciples in the junior faculty, Selig Perlman and Edwin Witte (all of whom served as Cohen's chief intellectual mentors and inspirations), was at the end of his long and productive career, in which he had worked closely with the state legislature at the other end of State Street on the real-world application of his studies' conclusions. Cohen spent considerable time following current events via newspapers, and it seemed clear that he was never going back to Milwaukee to the grocery business once his last summer vacation tour in that setting had been completed.

A couple of months after graduation in 1934, at age twenty-one, thanks to connections that his professors had, Cohen made his first trip east in order to take a temporary job doing technical analysis with the President's Cabinet Committee on Economic Security, created that summer with the mandate from President Franklin D. Roosevelt to help create the first general national social insurance for the United States. His former professor Edwin Witte was his head man in this job. Cohen prepared studies of social insurance systems in several European countries, and also of the then-popular, now-forgotten Townsend Plan for "revolving old-age pensions," which Cohen judged unlikely to pass Congress and unconstitutional even if it did. As a single man with no disposable income, not to mention one possessing a scholarly temperament, he found he loved the work and did it well. The job continued into 1935, when Social Security became law. At once the new Social Security Board hired him as a staff member; he would remain for the next two decades. Also in 1936, a presidential election year, Cohen was part of a group who funneled data to Democrats to assist them in defending Social Security against partisan Republican attacks (Berkowitz 1995, 41). In 1937, Cohen was named the associate economic analyst to the chairman of the Social Security Board, and its chief technical advisor; he was clearly "the" staff man. He got out of the office a lot, explaining Social Security to state officials, dealing with members of Congress and their staffs, and getting to know the ways of Capitol Hill.

The basic Social Security Act of 1935 was to be amended many times in the ensuing decades, and Cohen was at the center of these changes, first in 1939, when Cohen was constantly at the side of the board's head, even for executive sessions of key congressional committees. He consistently favored the expansion of Social Security's programs. In the mid-1940s, with an eye on parallel developments in Britain, Cohen and others began formulating proposals to add health care benefits to the Social Security world. He became a member of a group of bureaucratic insiders who called themselves "the apparatus," who shared a liberal, welfare-state, *entitlement* philosophy and who worked to advance it whenever possible. Elizabeth Wickenden, who for decades shifted among a variety of private and governmental positions in the welfare area, became his longtime top ally. In 1947, for instance, Cohen became a member of an Advisory Council on Social Security authorized by the Senate Finance Committee, whose 1948 reports recommended extending the social insurance concept on the grounds that it would reduce the likelihood of dependency; the amendments of 1950, enacted by the new Democratic Congress, were heavily influenced by Cohen via these reports and significantly expanded Social Security spending.

Of course, during the 1940s, there were public distractions from the welfare state ideal due to the pressures of wartime (even Cohen briefly worked on war-related matters) and the tense international atmosphere that immediately developed in the postwar era. Furthermore, the Republican Congress elected in 1946 made a couple of minor attempts to roll back the extent of Social Security's mandatory reach, which naturally forced Cohen and likeminded allies to play defense. On another front, Cohen coauthored a collection of essays, *Readings in Social Security* (1948), which added to his reputation as an expert. The collection was balanced and professional but, on the whole, also clearly favorable to the notion of increasingly developing an extended entitlement system to handle various social problems.

Cohen's career continued on this path in the early 1950s, and he became known to congressional insiders both as a knowledgeable, reliable provider of data and also a source of suggestions for workable compromises; this became most apparent for the first time in the 1952 amendments. With the coming of the new Eisenhower administration, Cohen experienced a period of uncertainty, but his professional manner, years of experience, and contacts with members of Congress paid off for him and for the program he believed in. Representative Carl Curtis, a Republican from Nebraska, headed an effort to expose what he regarded as Social Security's intellectual incoherence—that it was presented to the public as insurance while in reality it was nothing of the sort. Cohen actively worked to discredit the congressman's efforts, as well as to ensure that the membership of a new task force organized under the direction of Eisenhower appointee Oveta Culp Hobby was stacked with people who were sympathetic to the entitlement point of view and who shared the simple political wisdom that Social Security was here to stay. Any consideration of the possible radical restructuring of Social Security was quickly superseded by the more politically palatable discussion of how to increase payouts. Upon the April 10, 1953, retirement of Arthur Altmeyer, the original Social Security commissioner, Cohen's job status suddenly looked shaky. He accepted a position as director of statistical research in the Social Security Administration and toughed out the process whereby the questioning of Social Security by some within the new Republican administration, the first since Hoover to control both Congress and the presidency, was shortly overcome by the general support for the basics of the system, seen as too politically popular and entrenched to be touched. This moment was also many years before any impending demographic challenges to Society Security's setup became apparent.

But with the political winds having shifted, Wilbur Cohen began to consider alternatives. Realizing that the Eisenhower administration was not likely to be moving any further in the direction of significantly expanding Social Security any time soon, specifically with regard to the question of disability insurance, Cohen proved responsive to an offer from a friend at the University of Michigan's social work school. In January 1956, he began his career in Ann Arbor as a tenured professor of welfare administration. His teaching was well received, and his writing of the late 1950s reflected his practical, nontheoretical orientation. He remained politically connected; for instance, he had much to do with the drafting of the 1956 Democratic party platform statement on health and Social Security, and he attended the convention. His continuing contacts with Capitol Hill Democrats, especially Georgia U.S. Senator Walter George of the Finance Committee, were crucial in the enactment, despite the lack of enthusiasm of the Eisenhower administration, of disability insurance in the summer of 1956. In 1958, Democratic Arkansas Congressman Wilbur Mills of the Ways and Means Committee and Oklahoma U.S. Senator Robert Kerr made extensive use of their contacts with Cohen in Congress' consideration of social security extensions that year. Cohen also remained in contact with politically sympathetic congressional Republicans, too, such as New Jersey Congressman Robert Kean, long a beneficiary of Cohen's insider knowledge and analysis. When Nelson Rockefeller, a Republican, began putting together his late-1950s task force to produce a report on the nation's future, Cohen was included right from the start and contributed to its deliberations.

Housed within a school of social work, Cohen increasingly adopted the social work, provision-of-services view of welfare, in contrast to his older focusing on the provision of money to those who had little in his Social Security days. In this view, derivative of the Progressive-era tradition, social service professionals, who were experts on welfare, armed with scientific knowledge, should guide citizens in need of help. Juvenile delinquency had suddenly become a popular topic of concern, and Cohen, among many others, used this as a springboard for the advocacy of expanded services provided, as entitlements, by government agencies; as he said in a speech in Madison in 1957, "We need more schools, more roads, more hospital beds, and more housing. We want more teachers, more doctors, nurses, social workers" (Berkowitz 1995, 110). Children were stressed as the most deserving beneficiaries of such services, delivered scientifically by professionals who had been trained and credentialed. Naturally, the federal treasury was looked toward to help finance these services. Specifically, perhaps his major overall goal was a national health insurance system underneath the Social Security system umbrella.

It always seemed unlikely that Cohen, who was not a professional academic, would remain on campus; rather, he was more like a member of a government in exile, waiting for the restoration of the Democrats. In the late 1950s, he developed increasing contacts with Massachusetts U.S. Senator John F. Kennedy, even providing drafts of speeches for him, so by 1960 there was no question which Democrat he favored for the nomination. After the election, it seemed utterly obvious to all that Cohen would join the new administration. He chaired a transition team task force on Health and Social Security and wound up being named assistant secretary for legislation in the Department of Health, Education, and Welfare, the third highest official in that department. He was back in the center of the Washington loop.

Cohen's second coming to Washington, some quarter century after his original arrival, came under the auspices of a "New Frontier" rather than a "New Deal." Equally vacuous slogans, they nevertheless did indicate, especially in comparison to their immediate predecessors, changes in attitude and orientation toward activist federal government—Kennedy had promised to get the country moving again. But the circumstances differed greatly, as Cohen well knew, in 1961 as compared to 1935. There was no domestic sense of crisis whatsoever, and the Republicans had actually gained seats in the 1960 congressional election. Kennedy lacked any "mandate." But he *did* have a desire to create some sense of "movement." The two secretaries under whom Cohen served during Kennedy's administration, and the undersecretary directly above him, did not even approach his understanding of Congress or the issues of public welfare, nor did they possess his administrative talent, as their records in office bore out. In the spring of 1961, at his Senate confirmation hearing, Cohen's old nemesis, Republican Representative Carl Curtis, accurately enough, complained that Cohen's incrementalist approach to entitlements was directed toward a clear end: a general entitlement to health care across the board. But, given the Democrats' control of Congress and Cohen's stellar reputation, he was confirmed.

Reflecting his recent academic phase, his new interest was welfare reform. His objectives fit his traditional aim from his Social Security period—more federal money for more people in need, as much and as many as politically feasible—and also, from his Ann Arbor experience, to provide services linked to the Aid to Families with Dependent Children program designed to help get people off welfare (growth possibilities in this area of services were practically unlimited). Cohen was right at the center of the 1962 laws that were enacted along these lines, which, modest as they were, were welcomed across the political spectrum, given their emphasis on what Kennedy called "rehabilitation instead of relief" (little if anything changed as a result of the bill, and Cohen eventually looked back on it as a "dismal, 100% failure"; see Berkowitz 1995, 153).

Wilbur Cohen worked for the Department of Health, Education, and Welfare (HEW), and thus he participated in discussions concerning all sorts of issues, from mental retardation to the contentious question of federal aid to elementary and secondary education, which was mixed up with both religious and civil rights questions. Cohen's bias in favor of education as central to the answer to all things was quintessentially American, and that it would be better if more money were spent on it—and federal money, of course—rang true for him. Significant and continuing efforts by Cohen and others to move in this direction, however, foundered in the face of familiar and traditional arguments (the tradition of local control of schools, aid to religious schools, and school integration) during the Kennedy administration until its very closing days.

But Social Security, broadly defined, was Wilbur Cohen's true bailiwick, where he had built up years of experience and credibility among various constituencies. His interest in what came to be known as Medicare—the principle of direct federal involvement in the health care of the elderly—was his greatest contribution of the early 1960s. The American Medical Association had long labeled the idea "socialized medicine," counting on the bogeyman term "socialism" to help its cause. The AMA's legislative lobbying operation was quite familiar with Cohen and had actually opposed his nomination as assistant secretary in 1961. For his part, Cohen, as ever, was professional and moderate in his dealings with the physicians' organization, denying any intention to make doctors government salaried employees and, following his general inclination, assuring them that in fact he favored all sorts of federal grants, monies, and scholarships for them (Berkowitz 1995, 166). Cohen had provided specific proposals to Senator Kennedy before his election as president, and in February 1961 had come up with a new Medicare bill for the consideration of HEW Secretary Abraham Ribicoff. A variety of other proposals from outside the department were also circulating, and Cohen, naturally, was in communication with many of their authors and supporters; inconclusive hearings in the summer and a cautious Kennedy meant nothing changed in this old argument. Cohen never gave up and always took the long view. He once told his son Chris, "Politics is not like an athletic event. There is always a tomorrow when you must try to get support from someone who has opposed you today" (166).

It was also important to be clear as to *who* the critical people were in a given situation. Cohen possessed the sort of inside expertise regarding members of Congress that Lyndon Johnson had (Johnson's skills were not at all being put to use during the Kennedy administration). Wilbur Mills was probably more important than any other single individual when it came to Medicare, but also when it came to many other issues as well. Cohen's immediate superior and fellow Wisconsinite, HEW Undersecretary Ivan Nestingen, grew extremely frustrated with the congressional logjam and, disillusioned with Cohen's inside game, came to favor an outside public relations effort to create pressure on Congress, banking on the Medicare concept's general popularity. As to the seemingly all-powerful Mills, Cohen believed the Arkansan to be in essence reasonable and rational, if somewhat cautious, whereas others, like Nestingen, took a dimmer view of the congressional lifer and suspected that Cohen had been "captured" by the permanent elements of the Washington political system and had developed perhaps too much of a bureaucratic mind. Nestingen eventually left government service in 1965 in a fashion rumored not to be voluntary; no Medicare consensus developed during the days of the Kennedy presidency.

As a sincere admirer of John F. Kennedy, Cohen was strongly affected by his murder. Yet on November 25, only three days after the tragedy, Cohen delivered, upon request, a memorandum to the new president on the Medicare question. Cohen proved to be a key player inside the new administration on many Great Society issues. The general spirit of the Great Society, of course, was entirely Cohen's own approach to things, and in the two specific cases of federal aid to education and Medicare, he had as much to do as anyone, save for the president himself, with the successful outcomes to these ancient struggles. Though he had not known LBJ particularly well, and as a Kennedy man might have been thought of as suspect by the new president, no friction at all developed; not only were the two men on the same philosophical wavelength, but there was also a personal connection: Elizabeth Wickenden, Cohen's longtime colleague, confidante, and soulmate in the struggle to build an American welfare state, had married a Texan back in the 1930s and had known LBJ both politically and socially from that time onward. Years before, she had instructed Johnson as to Cohen's knowledge and virtues in the Social Security area. Though Johnson put the usual pressures on Cohen that he did on all his close aides, such as calling him at all hours, Cohen thrived on work and felt he was treated better than most.

Johnson quickly saw Cohen as key to helping bring to completion some of Kennedy's legislative programs, which could be presented as a sort of memorial to the departed president. On December 10, 1963, the bill granting general federal aid to higher education, on which Cohen had expended much time and energy, cleared Congress in its final form—a landmark, but one that only whetted the appetites of both Johnson and Cohen, who shared the belief in education so prevalent in the United States. With the principle of general federal aid, unrelated to defense (as had been the case in the post-Sputnik National Defense Education Act), to education now established in postwar times, the follow-throughs would be much easier.

In his January 1964 State of the Union address, Johnson famously declared "war" on poverty. Shortly after the assassination, Johnson had been briefed by Walter Heller, another Wisconsin graduate and a member of the President's Council of Economic Advisers, as to the antipoverty initiative that had been slowly gathering force in the Kennedy administration. Given an enthusiastic green light by the new president, Heller proceeded via a task force to produce legislative proposals that had been gestating before Kennedy's death. Heller had requested that HEW contribute to this effort, and Cohen had been more than happy to oblige. By and large, what Cohen and company recommended to Heller in a memorandum of November 19th was "more"—more welfare-type provisions of the sort HEW already either had or projected and desired. A hundred flowers were trying to bloom, some of the income variety, some rehabilitative/social service provision—but none of them could really be considered a truly new departure.

The most celebrated Great Society new departure, the ill-fated Community Action Programs, began to bubble out of the Council of Economic Advisers' task force, whose economists derided HEW's proposals as the same old "garbage." While Cohen had indeed become more interested in the rehabilitative notions of social services during his recent academic years at the Michigan social work school, his older orientation, income provision, had hardly disappeared. Cohen and others at HEW were skeptical of the notion of "community action" right from the start. But Heller, who made the call in setting the tone of the task force report, ultimately sided with community action proponents. Cohen also lost the bureaucratic "war" over where the new antipoverty effort would be located on the organizational chart of the government. Trained in the school of institutional economics at Wisconsin, longtime player of the institutional political game, respectful of institutions, experienced insider, and historically aware, Cohen preferred using established channels, bureaucracies, and organizations as a base on which to build new, improved programs to deal with age-old questions of the sort that he and other old hands had been grappling with for decades. The notion that for a truly new approach to break out, the best setup would be for it to be based in a freestanding agency so as to avoid being "captured" by a self-interested bureaucracy was far from instinctive to him; too experienced to be unaware of bureaucratic and other political infighting, he nonetheless knew from years of experience that he was hardly alone in actually personifying the disinterested public servant who put the greater good first.

He lost: the Office of Economic Opportunity wound up as a new, independent agency rather than one within the confines of the Department of Health, Education, and Welfare. Nevertheless, many quite traditional, "more" proposals were bound to be at least complementary to the new idea of community action, and Cohen was an enthusiastic Great Society warrior to be sure. But he did not play much of a role in early 1964 in terms of the actual content of the first big antipoverty bill, whose five titles attempted to offer something for everybody, including community action, job training, money separately targeted at both urban and rural areas, and more. Congress approved it with very minor changes and modest debate; the Senate did not even hold any hearings. Cohen was somewhat skeptical at this creation, telling an associate in May 1964, "The anti-poverty bill has been all messed up" (Berkowitz 1995, 201). He feared it was being grossly oversold given its modest funding and the truly experimental nature of much of its efforts, which meant that outcomes were highly uncertain. Furthermore, he felt, little consensus had actually been achieved within Congress.

The approval, however, did show that the country had entered a political moment in which a War on Poverty led by a federal government seeking the creation of a Great Society, a term Johnson began using that spring and soon made the centerpiece of his Ann Arbor commencement address, was intrinsically appealing. Johnson, who always thought big but counted his cards carefully, had put his focus on this bill for 1964, along with the epochal Civil Rights Act; for 1965, federal aid to education was to receive the full-court treatment. With civil rights more than ever on the books as well as a coming reality (there had by now even been some integration in Mississippi), a major phobia that had held up federal aid to education for years—that it would encourage integration—suddenly seemed much weaker, as civil rights were more of a legal reality. That being the case, why not go for the federal money, a time-honored tradition in Congress, especially when it was for education?

Additionally, the 1964 elections provided a rare moment in American politics: very large Democratic majorities in both houses of Congress (along with an extremely activist Democratic president), so large that even with the continuing influence of more conservative southern Democrats, the numbers were there to make another breakthrough in the construction of a federal-level welfare state system. Cohen, a longtime and enthusiastic backer of federal aid to education in general, hardly had to be drafted for Johnson's 1965 effort, which was to tie federal aid to education with the War on Poverty by targeting the new dollars toward children living in poverty. Though Cohen favored something much broader, in the spirit of his well-established theory of incrementalism, he had little trouble going along with Johnson's approach. Cohen participated in the Education Task Force formed after the 1964 vote and headed by John Gardner, a longtime specialist in educational issues, who in 1965 became secretary of HEW. The task force was hardly starting from ground zero; its ideas had been circulating for years. Only, and crucially, the political situation had changed.

Lyndon Johnson, of all people, understood the meaning of the 1964 landslide politically. Besides the bolstered electoral strength of liberals and liberalism, the always-significant center of American politics may be said to have moved, at least for the moment, left. Cohen was one of many important administration figures who, in the wake of the electoral victory, was told by the president to press on in the preparation for new education legislation, to be ready for introduction in January 1965. Speed was of the essence; the historical moment had to seized before, possibly, the wheel might turn in another direction. Cohen, whose memories, like Johnson's, went back to the heyday of the New Deal, fully comprehended this; one of his own underlings later recalled in an interview, "Wilbur Cohen recognized this singular moment in history. Several times during 1965 he told me to push the people I was working with as hard as I could, whether they protested or not; that we were to work any day, any hour, to do whatever was necessary to pass the legislation" (Berkowitz 1995, 206).

The long and hard days of the first six months of 1965, spent on the phone, on Capitol Hill, in endless meetings often twelve hours in length, were for Cohen and those like him well worth it—they represented investment in ensuring the dramatic fulfillment of dreams of a generation, in the ultimate (for then—as ever, there would always be a next step) form of the Elementary and Secondary Education Act of 1965. Cohen well understood that once such a law existed, and the money started being handed out, there would be no turning back; rather, the next incremental move, whatever that might turn out to be, would become what ensued for the agenda of constructing the strongest possible American welfare state. College students and their families of later generations would hardly be able to imagine that there had ever been a time when financing postsecondary education had *not* involved applying for federal aid, federally guaranteed loans, and so on.

Wilbur Cohen had not been a recognized expert in the field of education—Social Security was his baby. But he and others understood the expression "Social Security" broadly, by no means restricting it to the mere provisions of pensions for retired people. Years before Johnson ever made the expression "Great Society" a household word, Cohen had favored the creation of an entitlement to national health insurance for senior citizens connected to the Social Security apparatus. The question of the provision of medical care had many obstacles to clear, as history had shown: the American Medical Association for one, and within Congress, political power brokers, most importantly Wilbur Mills of Arkansas, longtime chairman of the House Ways and Means Committee. The "conversion" of Mills from a cautious critic to head supporter of Medicare was the key factor in accounting for its enactment in 1965.

Cohen and Mills had known each other for years, of course, and Mills, as did so many, thought highly of Cohen, a respect that was very much reciprocated. Cohen was involved in the actual writing of the Medicare bill, not caring who got the credit as long as the larger project was advanced. Many meetings took place between the two men throughout 1964, with Cohen obtaining much information for Mills about not only the provision of health insurance for retired people but also the possibilities—and costs—of the same federal provision for the indigent. Cohen prepared more than a dozen variations, with estimates, for Mills's consideration. The 1964 effort died, however, in June, largely due to the American Medical Association's objections. The Medicare cause at this point was picked up on Capitol Hill by Connecticut U.S. Senator Abraham Ribicoff, the former HEW secretary under Kennedy, who got several other interested senators to become involved. On September 2, 1964, the Senate passed its version of a House bill that significantly increased social security benefits, always a favorite in election years, but also with an amendment including a Medicare scheme. Cohen provided the specific base proposal and also sat in with the senators during key discussions that eventually produced this outcome. With his historical sense, Cohen fully understood the significance of the fact that one of the two houses of Congress had passed a bill creating Medicare.

With his political awareness, Cohen also knew that Wilbur Mills was not yet ready to agree to this Medicare plan—in fact, Cohen had firmly believed this even as he advised the senators as to the exact wording of the bill that did pass on September 2. On September 10, Cohen met with Mills for two hours. As Cohen had predicted, after careful consideration in August, Mills would not accept any proffered compromises during the House-Senate conference meetings, and, with the election around the corner, the issue died for 1964. Shortly after the results were tabulated, President Johnson told Cohen that he wanted Medicare to be the top priority—among, of course, many other thing, including education—for the new Congress, and that Cohen was to be "the" point man for the effort from the administration. By November 24, Cohen had a summary version of *another* version of a draft bill, proving yet again that the production of such key documents was one of Cohen's greatest strengths.

The process that unfolded in 1965 and culminated in the enactment of Medicare (and Medicaid) in August of that year ran parallel to many other Great Society initiatives, in which Wilbur Cohen was also heavily involved, especially the federal aid to education proposal. Close tabs were kept on every syllable that came out of the mouth of the powerful, respected Wilbur Mills; to make the medical establishment more favorably disposed, piles and piles of money were included; interested groups, public and private, were met with. From the moment the 1964 elections produced such a large Democratic congressional majority, Cohen proceeded in the belief that, this time, the process would culminate in the actual enactment of Medicare in some form—for real. Others, including Mills, were similarly oriented. During the 1965 hearings of Mills's committee, which began in January, Cohen regularly attended both open and executive sessions (which lasted for weeks), wrote volumes of memoranda, opposed various alternatives that suggested a voluntary element, and downplayed concerns about costs that in later years would threaten to overwhelm the system that eventually did emerge. When suddenly in a March 2 meeting of HEW health experts with

Mills, the Arkansas congressman announced his considered judgment as to the plan he favored, out of all the proposals that had taken substantial form (in essence, Mills went for hospitalization covered by federal money, certain doctors' services only, and significant entitlements for the indigent), Cohen found himself with basically *a single day* to produce a bill that would meet Mills's conceptualization.

Cohen's entire career had led him to this night. Well prepared for it, he lived up to his moment. He explained Mills's idea to lawyers and technical experts, who spent the evening and into the next morning grinding out the numbers, while Cohen produced a memo for President Johnson arguing that Mills's bill well answered various objections, successfully balanced various interests, and would be politically unassailable. The rest of March saw the Ways and Means Committee go through the bill that Cohen and company had produced, line by line; the agreed-upon House and Senate version passed on July 28, 1965. Many, many specific items were included in the law besides the breakthrough creations of Medicare and Medicaid, but the numerous other elements built on existing federal commitments; it was Medicare and Medicaid that were truly new, historic Great Society departures. Medicare as a general concept was an old one—visibly demonstrated in the decision to hold an elaborate signing ceremony in Independence, Missouri, in the presence of former President Harry S Truman. Doctors who may have feared a loss of income and power soon discovered that nothing of the sort was built into the structure; they got even richer and remained as powerful as ever.

The Medicare story was Cohen's high-water mark in the Great Society's moment. In April he had been named undersecretary of HEW, assuming his new duties on June 1, meaning that the various new programs of the War on Poverty fell under his purview, as well as many other matters that were receiving new emphasis (for instance, he spent significant time during 1965 on pollution, an issue truly out of his area of expertise). About 150 programs were now under the HEW umbrella. As John Gardner preferred to spend his time looking at the big picture and creating a public image, the real administrative work fell to the willing Cohen, who quite enjoyed it. Medicare had to get off the ground, a process involving a thousand details, and Cohen had much to do with its reasonably smooth launch, including using the program to promote, without fanfare, the integration of many health care facilities in the South. He also administered the money going to elementary and secondary schools from the federal government under the new Elementary and Secondary Education Act and defended it in the ensuing budgetary fights of the following fiscal years, despite the fact that much of the new spending was not being very carefully thought out. Despite the new bureaucratic responsibilities, Cohen remained on call to the president, who, for instance, dispatched him to Chicago to help begin the process of settling down Mayor Richard Daley, whose ire had been raised when a politically inexperienced

Office of Education commissioner had announced the cutting off of federal funds to Chicago schools because of their segregation (a decision that, unsurprisingly, was quickly overturned). And when it came to the process whereby the administration planned its budget requests for the next congressional session, Cohen was always there proposing new benefits and more entitlements—all incrementally done, of course. But Cohen, experienced Washington hand, though ever hopeful, could read the shifting political winds of the late 1960s. With the departure of John Gardner, Wilbur Cohen became acting HEW secretary on March 4th, and then permanent secretary on May 16, 1968. But the timing and new context were suddenly all bad, the Great Society's moment having quickly ended. Cohen soldiered on, well aware as an old hand of the ups and downs of the political cycle. The work of implementation and administration remained time-consuming and stimulating, but for now the Johnson administration was so politically weakened from Vietnam and the backlash to the increased social disorder that new initiatives were off the table, for now; anyway, the president, having announced he would not seek reelection, was a lame duck.

With the coming of the new Republican administration of Richard Nixon, Cohen returned to Ann Arbor, this time to the School of Education as dean. In 1979, he went to Austin to become a professor at the Lyndon Baines Johnson School of Public Affairs, University of Texas, and never really retired. He remained in contact with some members of Congress and politically active, but the times were different. Sometimes called "The Man Who Built Medicare," he died while traveling in Seoul, South Korea, on May 17, 1987. A month later, a memorial gathering took place in his memory in the House of Representatives Committee Room, with tributes from Joseph Califano, U.S. Senator Edward Kennedy, John Gardner, and others.

RICHARD GOODWIN
(1931–)

Among the many remarkable things about the rhetoric of Abraham Lincoln is that he wrote his own speeches. In the twentieth century, however, presidential staffs grew to include not only a large number of aides, assistants, advisors, and eventually handlers, but also speechwriters. Richard Goodwin was one of the many "Harvards," as Lyndon Johnson called them, who as young graduates of prestigious, elite institutions of higher learning entered, often via the old boys' network of academic privilege that in many cases they had earned through intellectual merit rather than birth, the orbit of U.S. Senator and then President John F. Kennedy. The mythmakers of the Kennedy administration who gave it the name "Camelot" have frequently spoken of a "generation" of "youth" who were bedazzled by the wealthy, bright, telegenic young president who provided such a contrast both to his predecessor, then the oldest president in history, and his physically older and drabber successor; by this, they mean in the main a highly educated, credentialed elite, often people who, after excelling academically, were starting out and who were looking for some role and place in society.

Not all of Kennedy's men fit such a stereotype, as seen in his longtime aide, prominent biographical mythmaker and keeper of the flame, and best-known speechwriter, Ted Sorensen of the University of Nebraska. Richard Goodwin, however, more closely fit the dominant stereotype of the Kennedy New Frontiersman type. His remarkable memoir, *Remembering America: A Voice from the Sixties* (1988), from the very different vantage point of the Reaganesque late 1980s, provides a compelling window both on his own experience and on a particular moment of youthful idealism as experienced by a certain sector of the American population. Unquestionably, Richard Goodwin had been a believer in the promise of the United States in the 1960s. It fell to him to put many of the most significant and influential words in Lyndon Johnson's mouth at critical moments of the dawning and political implementation of the Great Society, words that received heavy play in a pre–cable television nation that had only three networks and that was then more centered on national politics, given Cold War dramatics and especially the enormity of the highly televised civil rights movement. Presidents had the bully pulpit, and some of their speeches were designed, in the words of political scientist Roger Hilsman, to move a nation; Goodwin explained well in his memoir, "A speech is not a literary composition. It is an event, designed not to please the exegetes of language, but to move men to action or alliance" (1988, 327).

For Goodwin, being alive in the early 1960s was a heady, promising experience. As Lyndon Johnson, master of the intricacies of Capitol Hill, was not especially renowned for his public speech-making skills, Goodwin's role was that much more important—if the right words could be chosen, they could substantially contribute to the conceptualization and shaping of the broad public debate, especially in a world where, when the president spoke to the nation, it was the only show on television. The term "Great Society" itself, the response to the Selma situation, and the 1965 Howard University commencement address all came from Goodwin. As was the case for many liberal idealists who carried over from the Kennedy era into the Johnson one, Vietnam proved a terrible stumbling block for Goodwin and took him out of the administration at a relatively early point. If things did not turn out nearly as well as hoped, there were still many important achievements, made possible in part due to Goodwin's substantive as well as rhetorical contributions toward the shaping of the Great Society debate, especially as seen from the perspective of a later generation when the entire tone of public debate seemed almost alien from the spirit that had animated Goodwin in the 1960s.

Richard Goodwin, born December 7, 1931, came of age in the 1940s in a Jewish neighborhood of greater Boston, Brookline, after a brief period in Maryland where, decades later, he recorded in his memoir that he had been frequently harassed and sometimes beaten up (Goodwin 1988, 15). He matriculated at nearby Tufts University in Medford, Massachusetts, where his outstanding academic record (summa cum laude, class of 1953) earned him a full scholarship to the Harvard University Law School, which he took up after a year of military service, even though that was not required given his graduate school acceptance. He graduated first in his law class of 500, served as an editor of the law review, and next spent a term in Washington as a clerk to U.S. Supreme Court Justice Felix Frankfurter, then in the later, more conservative phase of his long career. As Goodwin recalled it, "I, whose still inchoate politics were to mature into 'Kennedy liberalism' and, later, to far more radical, if nameless form, was becoming an institutional conservative" (37). This made sense for one who had done well by American's open-to-achievement institutional structure and who very early found places within that structure. In the spring of 1959, lacking any clear direction as to what to do with his law degree, he was referred to the House Subcommittee on Legislative Oversight, becoming involved in the "quiz show scandals" then occupying the attention of moralists as well as the general public. That fall, he took a job in the office of Senator John F. Kennedy. It did not take him long to fall under the charismatic senator's spell.

"To me," Goodwin recalled, "Kennedy represented a new generation of believers. The elders were politicians rooted in the past, out of touch with the reawakened aspirations of the nation" (1988, 76). The 1960 election result naturally put Goodwin into the new administration, where he circulated from job to job over the course of its thousand days. First off he was assigned to help put together various task forces populated by experts—"the best people"—to come up with policy recommendations for the new president, who had vowed in the campaign to get the country moving again. Latin America soon became Goodwin's focus, especially the Cuban question. As an insider, he soon sharply increased his awareness of the enormous obstacles faced by any president who sought to make an impact: "The president does not rule America. He does not even lead it, except within limits defined by the society itself" (143). In the fall of 1961 he was shifted, not at his initiative, to the State Department, where he found himself with entirely too much time on his hands. Seeking to be closer to where the action was, Goodwin at his own initiative visited Sargent Shriver, director of the new, highly idealistic Peace Corps, and talked Shriver into giving him an office there and treating him as a personal assistant; eventually, Kennedy found out about Goodwin's "straying" and okayed it. Goodwin was happier here, as he "became aware of, felt part of, the liberating forces outside government that were working to change America" (219). In the fall of 1963, however, the president requested that Goodwin return to the White House to become his special consultant on the arts.

Richard Goodwin barely knew Lyndon Johnson at all and full expected to be looking for work after the assassination of November 22, 1963. His image of Johnson was of a Texas conservative, skilled but unscrupulous political manipulator, Senate boss, and close confidante and associate of old-line southern segregationist U.S. Senator Richard Russell of Georgia. Even more ignorant of Johnson was Robert F. Kennedy, who, in an obtuse comment, especially coming from a child of such privilege, said to Goodwin, "What does he know about people who've got no jobs or are undereducated? He's got no feeling for people who are hungry. It's up to us" (1988, 243). Apparently these "Harvards" had paid little attention to Johnson up to this point. That would soon change radically.

Ironically, it was Goodwin's Latin American expertise that led Johnson to seek him out early in 1964, when a small incident in Panama brought the two together; the initial meeting went excellently, Johnson taking Goodwin's advice and asking him to write it up for him. It was Goodwin's first introduction to that Washington legend of the 1950s and 1960s, the Johnson treatment, "that capacity for manipulation and seduction bred by his extraordinary intuition of other men—their ambitions, needs, weaknesses, pride—which was the foundation, the inward core of his political mastery." Within a day or two, presidential assistant Jack Valenti asked Goodwin to write a speech for Johnson. In preparation, Goodwin followed the speechwriter's cardinal rule of reading through his subject's prior speeches: "Speechwriters cannot make a man something he is not. . . . [I]t will not ring right, will always come out a little off-center." Goodwin quickly determined that a Johnson speech would need to be written in "simple, straightforward, unadorned language" (Goodwin 1988, 253). Valenti was very pleased, and Goodwin was offered a position on the speech-writing staff.

As indicated in his self-directed move into the Peace Corps realm, Richard Goodwin was quite taken by the growing movements for domestic social change, most obviously civil rights. What role might he, whom fate had placed amazingly close to the center of political power, play in advancing the long-deferred dream of real equality? In late March 1964, the president himself summoned his new speechwriter and again gave him a masterful Johnson treatment, hitting just the right buttons. As Goodwin recalled it, Johnson said to him, "I need you. I need you more than Kennedy ever did. And you need me. I loved Jack Kennedy, just like you, but he never really understood the Congress. I do. And I'm going to pass all those bills you care about. It's a once-in-a-lifetime opportunity, for you, for me, for the country . . ." The man had met his moment—not only Johnson, but also Richard Goodwin, who had been searching for just the right slot. "You're going to be my voice, my alter ego," Johnson expounded. "What the man in the street wants is not a big debate on fundamental issues. He wants a little medical care, a rug on the floor, a picture on the wall, a little music in the house, and a place to take Molly and the grandchildren when he retires." Johnson, the experienced political realist and successful candidate and officeholder, explained his vision: "I'm going to get my War on Poverty. Of course, we can't have it all in one gulp. We'll have to make some concessions, make a few compromises—that's the only way to get anything. But that's this year. I have to get elected, and I don't want to scare people off. Next year we'll do even more, and the year after, until we have all the programs." Johnson the wheeler-dealer? Yes, but not entirely, not in all respects: "But no compromises on civil rights. I'm not going to bend an inch, this year or next. Those civil rightsers are going to have to wear sneakers to keep up with me." Johnson was well aware of how he was viewed by the Kennedy crowd, those who didn't really know him: "Those Harvards think that a politician from Texas doesn't care about Negroes. In the Senate I did the best I could. But I had to be careful. I couldn't get too far ahead of my voters." But Johnson's situation had changed: "Now I represent the whole country, and I have the power." Johnson's vision was as expansive as any New Deal–legacy liberal's could be: "I'm sick of all the people who talk about the things we can't do. Hell, we're the richest country in the world, the most powerful. We can do it all, if we're not too greedy. . . . We can do it if we believe it" (Goodwin 1988, 257).

It would be Goodwin's all-important task to, as Johnson had put it, become his voice, select the words that would move a nation toward what it could be, to fulfill the unfinished business of the New Deal and in fact of the Reconstruction era. And Johnson meant it all; Goodwin observed the president as he communicated with national leaders who in their own right could help shape the debate, such as Walter Reuther of the automobile workers' union, or New York's Republican Governor Nelson Rockefeller. And, of course, he was continually after members of Congress, "whose individual predilections and desires seemed as familiar to Johnson as the scores of Verdi or Puccini were to Toscanini" (Goodwin 1988, 265).

Shortly after the above conversation, in early April 1964, Goodwin's "arrival" as Johnson's most important speechwriter was confirmed when presidential aide Bill Moyers, who became one of Goodwin's close friends, told him to meet him and Johnson at the presidential swimming pool; "From that day until I left the White House in late 1965, I was to draft every major presidential address" (Goodwin 1988, 267). In Johnson's system, Goodwin was now an insider at the highest level. He attended cabinet meetings and National Security Council sessions, saw the president all the time, and participated in formal and informal discussions of policy making. This regular contact would provide depth of understanding to the speechwriter as he sought to form the words and make the arguments on behalf of the administration that were addressed to the general public. The president spoke often along the lines of his March conversation with Goodwin, about political realities and the United States' potential. Johnson explained the role that Senate Republican Leader Everett Dirksen, a good friend of many years' standing, would play in the all-important 1964 Civil Rights Act: "He's not going to have his party blamed for standing in the way, not in an election year. That's one issue I won't compromise. And he knows it" (269). Johnson was reinforcing to Goodwin the need for uncompromising language when addressing the civil rights question. Regarding the idea that took shape in 1965 as Medicare, Johnson opined, "The doctors will come around when they see they'll still get rich"—as they certainly did (269).

The Johnson treatment worked on Goodwin as it did on so many. Trained as a lawyer, his natural instincts were often skeptical; hearing Johnson indulge in typical officeholders' hyperbole upon signing a tax-rate cut, Goodwin noted, "I never believed that the massive American economy had been launched into even higher orbit by such a tiny nudge from the Treasury" (Goodwin 1988, 265). Economics were not dear to Goodwin's heart in any serious sense, anyway. But the civil rights revolution, national health insurance, and a federally funded War on Poverty—these questions did move the speechwriter, and listening to the nation's most powerful politician speak of his determination to make them happen, Goodwin responded: "I was beginning to believe that, perhaps, probably, almost certainly, this was the time and Johnson the leader who could move us, move an entire country, toward some distant vision—vaguely defined, inchoate, but rooted in an ideal as old as the country" (271).

Johnson gave Moyers and Goodwin a charge: "Now, boys, you let me finish the Kennedy program. You start to put together a Johnson program, and don't worry about whether it's too radical or if Congress is ready for it. That's my job." The "assignment" from the president "within two months would enter public life as the Great Society"—the phrase itself, which had been earlier employed by Goodwin in one of the many routine, little-noticed speeches that presidential speechwriters prepare and presidents deliver, had caught Johnson's eye, and he had begun to use it enough so as to see it picked up by some of the reporters. Soon it was decided to use the occasion of the May 22nd commencement address at the University of Michigan as the rhetorical pad for the launching of the Great Society campaign. Goodwin gathered together the many reports, proposals, suggestions, and actual efforts to date to his cluttered desk, seeking not so much particular proposals as a "vision" of a better society. The outlining, much less realization, of such a vision was only conceivable due to the externalities: "The country was alive with change: ideas and anger, intellectual protest and physical rebellion. Without this ferment the formulation of the Great Society would not have been possible, not even conceivable" (Goodwin 1988, 273).

Johnson was looking to his speechwriter, his "voice," for something different, less confined to a particular set of grievances, but rather some sort of statement of "national purpose," an idea that began kicking around intellectual circles in the wake of the 1957 Soviet launching of Sputnik and that had taken form in President Eisenhower's Commission on National Goals, whose 1960 product, *Goals for Americans*, had laid out to some degree a kind of program for Kennedy's New Frontier. In the speech, though, Johnson hoped to declare an almost prophetic statement that would bind American citizens together in a new way in a sort of "great experiment." Key was a new view of the role of the federal government in leading the way, justified by the all-too-obvious shortcomings of society and their radical contrast with the affluence of that society, meaning the means did exist to alleviate many, perhaps all, of the society's material difficulties. "I could not have written about a Great Society," Goodwin recalled in his memoir, "without believing it both worthy and possible. . . . I believed that government, acting as the agent of a collective will, could change the circumstances of our daily life—our cities and environment, the quality of education, the restoration of 'power to the people'" (Goodwin 1988, 275, 277). Bill Moyers loved the speech, and LBJ, who went over it twice with care, approved it virtually as written.

With the unwitting assistance of Barry Goldwater, Lyndon Johnson in 1964 was able to co-opt the center of American political discourse and present his call for a greatly expanded federal government as a well-meaning exercise in harnessing applied social science for the betterment of all the people of the United States. Goodwin's Great Society speech in Ann Arbor succeeded brilliantly in coming off as the essence of reasonableness, rationality, even modernity, evoking a vision that bordered on the spiritual. The "happiness of our people" was the purpose of our national existence, said the president in only his second sentence. It quickly turned out to mean that that happiness was conceived far more as a *collective* than an individual one. Reflecting the basic assumption of the catchphrase associated with John Kenneth Galbraith's late-1950s classic, *The Affluent Society* (1958), now that abundance existed for the many, "we" next needed to determine the elevation of "our" life and the advancement of the "quality" of "our" civilization. The alternative was mentioned negatively as "unbridled growth," suggesting that "we"—the speaker and the graduates of a moderately elite university— would collectively determine the "bridling" of a growth that was said to threaten values and visions of a better tomorrow. The remarkable economic prosperity of the contemporary United States made it clear enough that an end to poverty should be demanded, given that it was blatantly unnecessary. Similarly, with a greater awareness of the evil of institutionalized white supremacy, brought about by the modern electronic media, an end to this "racial injustice" was something to be achieved "in our time," and something to which the president pledged his full commitment. Given his legislative agenda for 1964, these were well-known themes to the educated audience assembled at the Michigan football stadium.

Much of what followed had an environmental theme, somewhat disjointedly mixed with a call for urban renewal. Eighty percent of Americans, Goodwin's speech correctly predicted, would be living in "urban areas" by the early twenty-first century—but at present one witnessed the "decay of the centers and the despoiling of the suburbs . . . breed[ing] loneliness and boredom and indifference" (*Public Papers* 1963–64, vol. 1, 704–5). By now it was clear that the Great Society was reaching far beyond material betterment. Goodwin was projecting onto the people of the United States characteristics alleged to be associated with modernity and urbanity, traditionally summarized in the term "ennui"—boredom. Why Goodwin imagined Americans in such a way is hard to fathom; as for his snobbish-sounding disdain for the postwar suburbs, this theme that had characterized such classic 1950s popular diatribes as John Keats's *The Crack in the Picture Window*, he apparently had not had time to digest the necessary corrective to this found in Herbert Gans's *The Levittowners*, which exhibited a far stronger understanding of the new, upwardly mobile suburbanites who gave every sign of being neither lonely nor bored nor indifferent. Nor did they give much sign of looking toward the federal government in order to discover "the meaning of [their] lives."

Urban renewal had been a theme of the politics of the 1950s, and by this term downtown redevelopment was usually meant. This entirely predated the Great Society, which built on it. Richard Goodwin, a product of a much older urban United States, was not well attuned to the growing forms of "urban" living that were developing, seeing them as "despoiling" suburbanization—but they were the wave of the future. The "urban" locale of the large majority of Americans would increasingly be a *suburban* one in fact. But at Ann Arbor, President Johnson spoke, in Goodwin's words, as if large numbers of Americans would, upon the reconstruction of downtown areas, not only spend more time there but also actually move there to live.

The sections on pollution were, naturally, more easily resonant with larger populations, and tended to be understood along the continuum that featured God and motherhood. Here the point about affluence making possible concrete improvements was especially strong, as agreement to a significant degree on the benefits of cleaner air, water, and so on was more easily come by; eventually, at the margin, disputes would break out over the degree to which a cleanliness next to godliness was economically feasible, but that debate was almost entirely a post–Great Society phenomenon. It would be the Nixon administration, building on Johnson's, that established the federal bureaucracy in charge of pollution, the Environmental Protection Agency. Still, even in 1964, Goodwin's rhetoric well indicated the borderline pantheism of an influential sector of society, the highly educated who were not strongly rooted in traditional, institutional religion and who wound up at least seeking and often achieving spiritual nirvana via nature, something they of course shared with large numbers of traditional campers, hikers, hunters, and anglers.

The third and final theme of Johnson's Great Society speech concerned the favored child of all American aspiration toward societal improvement, education. Goodwin himself, of course, was the embodiment of the effects of educational opportunity, and naturally a believer. Education, inadequately funded as it was, faced the increasing demographic challenges of the so-called baby boom generation, many of whom were soon to hit college age but who might not attend due to financial shortage. Classrooms were overcrowded in many places, teacher pay was too low, and too many teachers lacked the proper credentials for the subjects they were attempting to instruct. Traditionally, the federal government had virtually nothing to do with the funding of public education in the United States, which was a state and local prerogative. A breakthrough had come in 1958 with the passage of the National Defense Education Act, justified by the "emergency" created in the wake of the Sputnik launching by the Soviet Union, but it was targeted on limited areas, especially science and mathematics, and depended on the justification of "national security" rather than general principle. In the Great Society, however, quaint expressions like "states' rights," which in the civil rights era were strongly and properly associated with the ideology of white supremacist demagogues, were dated in the extreme. The affluent United States could not pretend that it lacked the material resources to do what needed to be done—"So we must give every child a place to sit and a teacher to learn from." "Poverty," Goodwin's words read, "must not be a bar to learning, and learning must offer an escape from poverty." Johnson would make a point of going to the one-room schoolhouse he had attended in Texas for the signing ceremony of the law authorizing general federal aid to elementary and secondary education. Sticking with school but moving again into the more spiritual realm, Johnson expressed the disdain of some for the activities of the many in calling for an educational system that, moving beyond the three R's, included in its agenda "preparing youth to enjoy their hours of leisure as well as their hours of labor" (*Public Papers 1963–64*, vol. 1, 705–6).

Was such an expansive vision conceivable, or more of a dream? Goodwin inserted a cautionary note as the speech moved toward its conclusion: "I do not pretend that we have the answer." How could such a large agenda even begin to be realized? At the federal level, something Goodwin had been involved with from his first days in the Kennedy administration was the familiar way to go; Johnson promised "to assemble the best thought" for "a series of White House conferences and meetings on the cities, natural beauty, the quality of education, and on other emerging challenges" so as to "begin to set our course toward the Great Society." It would turn out that White House domestic affairs advisor Joseph Califano would play the biggest role in the assembling of many such groups over the next few years. Then, in another bow to the American tradition of fear of a powerful central government, Goodwin had Johnson say, "The solution does not rest on a massive program in Washington, nor . . . on the strained resources of local authority. They require us to create new concepts of cooperation, a creative federalism, between the national capital and the leaders of local communities" (*Public Papers 1963–64*, vol. 1, 706). And though some critics, especially later ones, might doubt the sincerity of these remarks, the record of Johnson himself as well as of the task forces as they did meet over the next few years would demonstrate that this was indeed the Great Society vision, reflecting Johnson the politician's solid understanding of the way things operated in the United States.

Goodwin's Great Society speech ended with Johnson employing the traditional call-and-response structure of evangelical Protestantism in a series of questions beginning, "Will you join?" Again, the contrast was drawn between joining up in the Great Society crusade and being condemned to mere "material progress" or to "a soulless wealth." And Johnson insisted in the last few lines of his remarks that the affluent society meant that "we have the power to shape the civilization that we want" (*Public Papers 1963–64*, vol. 1, 704–7).

The speech was widely lauded, enough so to make even the cautious Johnson celebrate with Goodwin and others. He told his speechwriter and other aides, "I'm a dreamer, always have been. My mother taught me that unless you had a dream, your life wouldn't amount to a hill of beans. . . . You boys are dreamers, too. . . . We've got a pretty good start." Johnson promised to take care of the politics; Goodwin was to keep writing the uplifting public speeches. The president was as good as his word; as Goodwin recalled the next few months, "It seemed that whenever we began the labor of designing new messages and laws, we were interrupted by a summons to a signing ceremony for those previously submitted" (Goodwin 1988, 285). Goodwin's words were not being written in vain, but were playing a role in the moving of a nation. The key was to "get the laws on the books, get things moving. The work of purification could come later" (285–86).

The 1964 elections were a dream for the Great Society visionaries; not only did Johnson earn the greatest mandate of any post-FDR Democrat, but his congressional majorities were swollen to New Deal levels as well. It was a high point for the believers, including Goodwin: "There was no talk of the 'limits of liberalism,' only the spacious vision of a Great Society, founded on the extension of opportunity. . . . I believed it, believed that it was possible, that we had the resources and skills if we knew how to use them, wanted to use them. Nor was I alone" (Goodwin 1988, 307).

By early 1965, Goodwin was downright astonished at what had been accomplished despite the well-known "deadlock of democracy" that activist-minded political scientists had grown accustomed to complaining about, and *in advance of* the greatly increased Great Society–friendly congressional majorities produced by the 1964 landslide. He remarked to his comrade Bill Moyers, "We're running out of laws. He's passing everything, and ther'll be nothing left, unless we get some new ideas." Moyers, with an expansiveness perhaps reflecting his own Texas background, assured him that there was plenty more where that came from, that there was no shortage of new problems, new issues. "And where there's a problem, there's going to be an answer." Goodwin, congenitally more skeptical, allowed himself to be carried along, and in retrospect believed that history bore out the validity of the attitude: "That case of mind, call it what you will—romantic illusion, fighting spirit, Panglossian optimism—is the carrier of the energy and will necessary to any progress, to even a modest, partial resolution of public distress" (Goodwin 1988, 288).

The winter of 1965 proved exhilarating for Goodwin and the other Great Society believers. Johnson was in a hurry, personally recalling FDR's 1936 mandate, which was followed by a loss of political power the very next year in the spent energy of the court-packing plan. The civil rights movement had shifted from a focus on public accommodations to that of securing the right to vote, and momentum was clearly on its side. One of the Second Reconstruction's most dramatic and destined to be iconic moments came at Selma, Alabama, the launching pad for a proposed march to the Alabama State Capitol at Montgomery, on Sunday, March 7, quickly known to the movement as Bloody Sunday. The Selma police department did nothing to prevent the march from setting out due to their mistaken belief that Governor George Wallace had ensured that the Alabama State Police would not interfere with the march, which at the moment of Sunday morning was technically illegal (Wallace's order would fairly soon—but not in time—be overturned by federal judge Frank Johnson, on March 17, and the march would eventually take place). At the Edmund Pettis Bridge, named for a Confederate general, the state police read through a bullhorn the order to the 600 or so marchers to turn back and gave them two minutes to obey. They did not, and the troopers advanced with clubs and tear gas. Seventy were hospitalized (Patterson 1996, 580–81). The incident was filmed and repeatedly shown on national television, and public pressure very suddenly was greatly increased to get Congress to do something about voting rights.

On Sunday, March 14, President Johnson called congressional leaders to the White House in search of an invitation to address Congress on the voting rights issue, which was readily issued. Early on the morning of March 15, Richard Goodwin was asked to write the speech. It was a dramatic moment; like millions of others, Goodwin had seen, thanks to television, "the mingled, swiftly mutating images tumbling through my mind—black bodies on the Pettis Bridge . . . the fear of my youth and the horrified terror of adult experience at the approach of muscular men whose faces were contorted by bigotry" (Goodwin 1988, 327). With this emotional orientation, shared by everyone he knew and by enormous numbers of Americans who were looking to the president for some kind of response, the burden of history weighed heavily on Goodwin: "By the purest chance, an accident of time and place, I had been given an opportunity to strike back, not from bravery bred of vulnerability, but from the crenellated ramparts of great power. I could, that is, if my craft was equal to my passion" (327). It helped that the issue could not be clearer: "There was no other side. Only justice—upheld or denied." As always, the speech needed to be "pure Johnson." And since Goodwin had now been at the president's side with great regularity for more than a year, the speechwriter had perfected his knowledge of Johnson's "view . . . his manner of expression, patterns of reasoning, the natural cadences of his speech" (327–28). At 3:00 PM that afternoon, Johnson called Goodwin and asked that he include a reference to his early teaching experiences with Mexican Americans in Cotulla, Texas—and Goodwin knew exactly what Johnson meant.

The line that would resonate, then and later, from this address was the president's employment of the civil rights movement's refrain. First he identified the collective power of all Americans as embodied in the federal government—"There is no Negro problem. There is no southern problem. There is no northern problem. There is only an American problem. And we are met here tonight as Americans to solve the problem"—and his intention to use it (*Public Papers* 1965, vol. 1, 282). Then, he identified himself, his power as president, and his well-known political power, demonstrated the previous year in the success of the Civil Rights Act and strengthened by the 1964 landslide, with the cause and with its moral justification: "Their cause must be our cause too. It is not just Negroes, but it is all of us, who must overcome the crippling legacy of bigotry and injustice" (284). Anyone familiar with the civil rights struggle to that date, as millions were, would have immediately noticed the use of the word "overcome." But before a listener could stop to think about the word, the president, with deliberate pauses, reinforced the meaning of the word: "And we . . . shall . . . overcome" (284). The "anthem of the civil rights movement," inspired by the beatific vision as recorded in the second chapter of the Book of Revelation, took form as a spiritual in the nineteenth century and was given prominence at the 1963 March on Washington and everywhere else where civil rights marchers needed inspiration and solidarity in song.

The line was effective with its audience, live and via television, including with the speechwriter who had crafted it: "I felt it too—the urge toward tears which is not the edge of grief or of some simple pleasure, but some more profoundly human need to be a part of something greater and more noble than oneself" (Goodwin 1988, 334). And there was something greater at work here than voting rights, as important as that question was; Johnson continued, "All Americans must have the privileges of citizenship . . . to exercise these privileges takes much more than just legal rights. It requires a trained mind and a healthy body . . . a decent home, and the chance to find a job, and the opportunity to escape from the clutches of poverty" (335). Echoing Franklin D. Roosevelt's 1944 campaign talk of an "Economic Bill of Rights," Goodwin sought by this passage to show that "the entire Great Society was a civil rights program," whose purpose was to "open the gates of opportunity . . . to give all our people, black and white, the help they need to walk through those gates" (335). Two days after the speech, the Voting Rights Act was introduced into Congress; after the traditional filibuster and cloture vote, it was signed into law on August 6th.

Well before that date, Goodwin made his last great contribution to the great debate over the Great Society. In early May, Lyndon Johnson called him into his office, there for the first time expressing thanks for his voting rights speech. Then, picking up on the more expansive point about how voting fit into the bigger picture of genuine citizenship, Johnson told his speechwriter, "It's only the tail on the pig, when we ought to be going for the whole hog. . . . The problem's not just civil rights. Hell, what good are rights if you don't have a decent home or someone to take care of you when you're sick?" Then, with no particular guidance, Johnson asked Goodwin to "see what you can do" (Goodwin 1988, 342). Goodwin did; speaking with Bill Moyers and Jack Valenti, he determined to use Johnson's scheduled June 5th commencement address at Washington's Howard University, traditionally the nation's most prestigious historically black university, as the forum.

There were many issues to think about. What did abstract terms like "equality" and "opportunity" mean to a Great Society visionary? Goodwin knew that when Johnson talked of his vision to his speechwriter in private, he "meant it. The grandiosity of expression, the asserting of ambitions beyond the reach of any mortal" (Goodwin 1988, 336) were real to him; could not the nation be moved at least closer to the realization—and not just rhetorically—of a great, or at least much greater, society? Late in the afternoon of June 4th, Goodwin began composing the speech, then gave it to Moyers, Valenti, and Daniel Patrick Moynihan for a look before presenting it to Johnson the next morning. The president approved it, and Goodwin then suggested it be run by some prominent leaders, such as Martin Luther King, Jr., Roy Wilkins, A. Philip Randolph, and Whitney Young. All liked it. Goodwin himself was among the thousands of people who heard the president speak his words at Howard.

The Howard University Commencement Address of 1965 became, in a way, the most significant of the oft-quoted words penned by Richard Goodwin on behalf of the Great Society. This is because it dealt with an issue that, unlike legally mandated segregation, remained alive into the twenty-first century—the general question of what could or should be done to help overcome the historical legacy of institutionalized white supremacy, especially of the de facto, more ambiguous sort. Goodwin's words provided an intellectual and moral base argument, often to be quoted in the generation to follow, for what came to be known as affirmative action. Johnson spoke of the "revolution of the Negro American" then being made, with the voting rights bill just over the horizon; however, as noted earlier, quoting Winston Churchill's words about World War II's D-Day, the president noted that its passage would not mark the end: "It is not even the beginning of the end. But it is, perhaps, the end of the beginning" (*Public Papers* 1965, vol. 2, 636).

The "beginning" was freedom—something even Barry Goldwater, a strong ideological opponent of the Great Society, could agree with. The divide between Johnsonian liberalism and Goldwater conservatism was now drawn: "But freedom is not enough. You do not wipe away the scars of centuries by saying: Now you are free to go where you want, and do as you desire, and choose the leaders you please." Then, invoking a sports metaphor (compared to most modern presidents, Johnson was strikingly uninterested in sports), Johnson delivered the words that would be most cited in future debates on affirmative action as they unfolded years after the Great Society, and that Goodwin himself chose to include in his memoir: "You do not take a person who, for years, has been hobbled by chains and liberate him, bring him up to the starting line of a race and then say, 'you are free to compete with all the others,' and still justly believe that you have been completely fair." Yes, opening the gates of opportunity was step one; but everyone "must have the ability to walk through these gates" (*Public Papers* 1965, vol. 2, 636).

Johnson then issued a clarion call that was also destined to be oft-quoted, but that was even more controversial in the long run to many who pondered its meaning: "We seek not just legal equity but human ability, not just equality as a right and a theory but equality as a fact and equality as a result" (*Public Papers* 1965, vol. 2, 636). Goodwin's words went on to explain what he meant, referring to the environment in which people grew up and its many effects on their developments and opportunities. Johnson, following the tradition of the well-worn American commencement address genre, praised the Howard class of 1965, but soon noted that it was a minority within a minority, that its achievements did not reflect the lives of most black Americans. He cited many statistics to document this indisputable claim, and also the enormous gaps between white and black America taken as gross entities.

Many blacks—and many whites, too, Johnson immediately noted in an aside—were "trapped" in poverty. The national government was, however, acting in a new way: "We are trying to attack these evils through our poverty program, through our education program, through our medical care and our other health programs, and a dozen more of the Great Society programs that are aimed at the root causes of this poverty" (*Public Papers* 1965, vol. 2, 637). "Root causes" referred to the environmentalist theory of poverty as a "culture" into which many were born and in which they were socialized in a fashion that ill-prepared them to advance in the modern, competitive United States; the Great Society represented enlightened intervention in this cycle.

Johnson insisted that "Negro poverty is not white poverty," despite many obvious similarities. Yes, other groups in the United States had faced poverty and prejudice, and there were things to be learned; notwithstanding the new federal initiatives of the Great Society, blacks were going to "have to rely mostly upon [their] own efforts. But [they] just can not do it alone." The president was on a rhetorical roll and proceeded to make several highly debatable and even flat-out wrong points that would be argued about by social scientists and others for decades to come: the other immigrants "did not have the heritage of centuries to overcome. . . . they did not have a cultural tradition which had been twisted and battered by endless years of hatred and hopelessness, nor were they excluded . . . because of race or color" (*Public Papers* 1965, vol. 2, 638).

Johnson then tread into the realm that would become known as the "Moynihan thesis," referring to the hugely greater likelihood of black children as compared to others to grow up in fatherless households. In another controversial, mindset-revealing statement, the president held the nation's majority race accountable for the "breakdown of the Negro family structure": "For this, most of all, white America must accept responsibility." In response to this situation, which would tremendously worsen in the generation ahead, Johnson said that "we" had to "work to strengthen the family, to create conditions under which most parents will stay together" (*Public Papers* 1965, vol. 2, 639).

Admittedly, Johnson noted that there was "no single easy answer to all of these problems." The already-mentioned Great Society was alluded to again, with the promise that it would continue to develop and expand as the centerpiece of the Johnson administration. The president announced the summoning of a conference full of experts to the White House for the fall, which he named "To Fulfill These Rights," an allusion to the Truman-era civil rights report, "To Secure These Rights," a phrase taken from the Declaration of Independence (*Public Papers* 1965, vol. 1, 639).

Richard Goodwin, who heard his words delivered by the world's most powerful citizen, could still believe in the promise of the Great Society on that day. Momentum was still with the administration, which had its huge congressional majorities and many friends and supporters in the national news media and other influential places. Critics were either morally discredited segregationists with their dubious associates or rejected libertarians, not yet into fashion, of the Goldwater sort.

But, suddenly, there was Vietnam. Other problems arose, too, especially civil disturbances, but for Goodwin himself and his own role, there was Vietnam. Increasingly in the summer of 1965, Johnson was spending precious time on that growing conflict. Goodwin even came to believe that Johnson had developed mental illness (Goodwin 1988, 403). He decided it was time to leave the White House. Johnson had told him that he could do both Vietnam and the Great Society, but Goodwin quickly concluded that "in the real world of fiercely clashing interests, the war became a weapon for those who, as the price of their support of Vietnam, demanded a reduction, a virtual abandonment of liberal reform" (417). In his memoir, Goodwin quoted Arkansas Congressman Wilbur Mills, that man who was most responsible for a Great Society centerpiece, Medicare, but who overall was a skeptic and then some regarding the more expansive notions of the Great Society's War on Poverty as laid out in the Howard University speech, speaking from the floor of the House of Representatives: "The Administration simply must choose between guns and butter" (418).

Johnson tried to keep Goodwin, but soon realized his speechwriter's determination to leave, and so made a Johnsonian deal, accepting his resignation in August in exchange for a promise to draft the 1966 State of the Union address, a promise that Goodwin fulfilled. Goodwin wrote Johnson, "You have broadened my horizons to include Texas, the land, and the America from which you come. Beginning in ignorance, I have ended in respect and affection" (Goodwin 1988, 422). In reply, Johnson praised Goodwin's skills in writing and his role: "It has also been a blessing for the country—for within the high councils of government you have articulated with great force and persuasion man's hunger for justice and his hopes for a better life" (422–23). Goodwin never saw Johnson again.

Goodwin moved to a think tank at Connecticut's Wesleyan University but returned to political speech writing in 1968 on behalf of first Robert F. Kennedy, then Eugene McCarthy, and finally Edmund Muskie. His opposition to the war in Vietnam was a strong motivator for his renewed high-level political activism. In 1975 he married historian Doris Kearns, who Johnson had hired to assist him in the preparation of his presidential memoir and who later wrote her own, well-received book on Johnson. Goodwin wrote several books, most significantly his 1988 memoir of his White House years, but later efforts to move the nation in a politically leftward direction had little discernible impact. He successfully moved into motion pictures, coproducing *A Passage to India* and writing the screenplay for the Academy Award–nominated motion picture *Quiz Show*, based on the late-1950s television scandal, while also coproducing this picture. He also became a modestly successful playwright.

WALTER REUTHER
(1907–1970)

Walter Reuther, like a number of influential Americans of the mid-twentieth century, was a great admirer of Sweden. He visited that country many times during the twenty or so summers in which, at the height of his influence as the most-respected American labor union leader, he went to Europe, usually briefing the U.S. State Department upon his return on his findings there, and tremendously enjoyed the near-royal treatment he received there (and also in other European countries). Regarding the various available sociopolitical models of economically developed modernity, United Automobile Workers (UAW) President Reuther was well within the Cold War's consensus, categorically rejecting Soviet communism (he had spent some pleasant times there, over in what some saw as the future, in the 1930s but ultimately concluded that no, it did *not* work); as an American, he of course had to live within the United States' version of social organization, even while trying to improve it and expand it in a social democratic direction. But as for himself, the fact was that Reuther was greatly impressed with the "Swedish model" as a real, existing example of the oft-desired "third way" between the "extremes" represented by the other two, capitalism and communism. Besides its corporatist, government-directed, institutionalized national collective-bargaining system, tinted with a strong egalitarian tone and also committed to a centrally directed, politicized process of national "planning" regarding investment decisions affecting the country's economic future, Swedish society was also characterized by what Reuther and those who shared his politics viewed as perhaps the world's most advanced welfare state provisions, beside which the anemic American version looked positively pathetic. At the center of the appealing Swedish social-democratic model was the extremely powerful Swedish trade union movement, with an influence that U.S. unions could only dream of. If Sweden may be said to have represented the Promised Land to Reuther, then it could be added that its Great Commission to the American labor leader who continually returned to it for inspiration was clear enough: "Go and do likewise."

Reuther's Swedish connection was very real, existing at the highest levels. Arne Geijer, a chairman of the Confederation of Swedish Trade Unions, became one of Reuther's close friends, and he regularly communicated with Swedish Prime Minister Tage Erlander and his secretary Olaf Palme, a future prime minister himself whose senior thesis, written while attending Kenyon College in Ohio, had been on Reuther's United Automobile Workers union and had lavishly praised its longtime president. Geijer had once asked Reuther why American unions did not describe themselves as "socialist." His reply rested on two points: first, the historical background of the United States differed greatly from Sweden's; second, what's in a name? Whatever particular term one might or might not be use, Reuther explained, "Our basic aims are similar" (Lichtenstein 1995, 338). It was a question of national nomenclature—Reuther spoke "American." In a 1953 speech to the Detroit Economic Club, for instance, Reuther stated, "Certainly I am not a socialist. There was a time that I belonged to the Socialist party for about a year. . . . I joined the Socialist party in 1932 during all the unemployment because I felt that it might be a better way of doing things. I have learned a lot since 1932" (Boyle 1995, 79).

Reuther attended summer conferences in Sweden from 1963 to 1965, held at the Swedish prime minister's country estate, whose attendees included representatives of various left-wing, social-democratic European political movements in Europe, about which Reuther personally briefed Democratic Presidents Kennedy and Johnson. This access to power in the 1960s showed that Reuther had come a long way indeed from his radical past. George Romney, a Republican and former automobile company executive who served as governor of Michigan in the 1960s, was one of many who once upon a time had "charged" Reuther with the "crime" of being a socialist; in 1945, for instance, while with the Automobile Manufacturers' Association, Romney had warned, "Walter Reuther is the most dangerous man in Detroit because no one is more skillful in bringing about the revolution without seeming to disturb the existing forms of society" (Lichtenstein 1995, vii). Given the American situation, whose development Reuther, given his decades of frontline fighting in the labor-management wars, understood as well as anyone, the early to mid-1960s presented a golden and gigantic opportunity to bring Swedish enlightenment, with the necessary "American" adjustments, of course, to the United States, and the name that opportunity took was the Great Society, whose very expression had first been introduced, not incidentally, in Reuther's own state of Michigan, home of his United Automobile Workers.

As it happened, at the Great Society's "moment," American unions were highly influential, especially within the Democratic party, whose control of the federal government following the 1964 Johnson landslide was the strongest it had been since the welfare-state-building New Deal days of the 1930s Great Depression. The UAW was by far the most politically influential labor union by any and every measure: it sent more delegates to Democratic conventions than any other, its monetary and manpower contributions to political campaigns ranked first in the House of Labor, and its lobbying setup in Washington was the strongest and best connected in the labor union world. And given that the automobile business, including its tertiary industries, employed something like one of every six Americans in the labor force, the fact that the UAW had organized and still controlled this labor force, and thus could potentially shut down this core section of the economy, gave it tremendous power, especially in comparison to other labor organizations (Boyle 1995, 3). Walter Reuther, UAW president from 1946 until his sudden death in a plane crash on May 9, 1970, was not only an enthusiastic cheerleader for the Great Society, both generally and particularly; he was also at the center of planning for it to an unprecedented degree for a labor union leader. Walter Reuther was, from the point of view of other Americans who similarly admired the Swedish model, the kind of unionist they dreamed of: incorruptible, intellectually oriented, clean living, articulate, and politically astute. Reuther gave the Great Society his all, and the resources of his union, too. He saw Lyndon Johnson as a new Franklin D. Roosevelt, and the Great Society as a new New Deal, despite the vastly different circumstances in which the two reform movements arose. When trouble came to Johnson, Reuther stood by him, to the end.

Walter Reuther came out of an immigrant, working-class area of Wheeling, West Virginia, where he was born on September 1, 1907, the second of five children, to German immigrants Valentine and Anna. His father was a committed and active trade unionist and socialist who read books and newspapers articulating ideas that were represented in the political arena by sometime presidential candidate Eugene Debs, for whom he campaigned several times; his mother ensured that her children received religious instruction through confirmation at the local Zion Lutheran Church. The combination of these influences created in the children strong moral and social consciousnesses. Walter left school at age fifteen, then a common enough occurrence, to go to work; within a year, having confirmed the mechanical aptitude he had exhibited in high school, he was offered and took an apprenticeship in the tool and die department of a local company, Wheeling Corrugating. He did well and was rewarded with pay increases; confidently, Reuther decided to leave in February 1927, one year before the completion of his apprenticeship program, attracted to Detroit by reports of what the Ford Motor Company was offering toolmakers: significantly higher pay than he could gain in Wheeling, and a regular five-day workweek. In the automobile industry, skilled workers were in high demand. Arriving on a Saturday, Reuther secured a job the following Monday at the Briggs Manufacturing Company, a maker of automobile body parts for Ford and Chrysler. In April, Reuther moved to Ford, where he remained for five and a half years, first at the Highland Park facility, then at mammoth River Rouge, the world's largest manufacturing facility, in which some 75,000 employees labored.

Reuther's skill made him a "labor aristocrat," well paid and working in reasonably pleasant conditions, soon the leader of several dozen workers, employed at the heart of the greatest mass-production industry of the twentieth century. He soon demonstrated ambition by enrolling in the company-founded high school, Fordson, where he completed his formal education. Younger brother Victor, who would spend years at his brother's side in the upper echelons of the UAW, joined Walter in Detroit in 1930.

Given their upbringing, along with the severe economic downturn that just kept heading south, the Reuthers became active in the local Socialist party, participating in such left-wing organizations as the League for Industrial Democracy and working for the 1932 presidential campaign of socialist candidate Norman Thomas. By that year, of course, the Great Depression had earned its name; nobody could argue any longer that what was going on was just another temporary downturn in the business cycle, with prosperity's return just around the corner. Employment at the car companies dropped 50 percent, but the Reuthers were among the fortunate who kept their job. The Reuther brothers began studying economics and sociology at Detroit City College (later Wayne State University).

In 1931 Walter Reuther joined the Auto Workers Union, a group not recognized by arch-individualist Henry Ford, self-made company founder, but closely tied to the local communist organization. Reuther's final workday at Ford was September 30, 1932; he claimed he was fired for his political activity, though company records do not support this (Lichtenstein 1995, 33). Encouraged by a friend who had gone to work in the intriguing social experiment on the other side of the world, the Soviet Union, Walter and his brother Victor decided to travel to Europe, heading first for Germany to see relatives, then moving on to the Union of Soviet Socialist Republics to work (as skilled workers, they were in demand), at least for a while, before returning home via Asia. They departed Detroit in January 1933, and once in Europe spent nine months visiting various countries, observing the rise of Nazi totalitarianism in Germany (Hitler having become chancellor that year), and meeting with various socialist groups and individuals over the course of their travels. On November 15, they arrived in Moscow, and soon found their way to the "American Village" at the mammoth Gorky Auto Works, directly modeled after River Rouge and still under construction, joining some 100 Americans, about half of the total foreign contingent who supplemented some 30,000 Soviets (37). Here the Reuthers were impressed by the many organized communal activities, including what seemed to be the "proletarian democracy" practiced by the workers; they also found the factory unbelievably inefficiently administered. They left for Asia in June 1935, as planned, taking with them positive views of Soviet conditions and efforts, though they found the level of industrial organization woefully below that of Detroit.

Back in Detroit in the fall of 1935, the Reuthers threw themselves full force into the increased agitation for union organization that was sweeping the industrialized areas of the nation in wake of the recently passed National Labor Relations Act. Walter Reuther heard John L. Lewis, the mineworkers' union leader, call for industry-wide (as opposed to the traditional by-particular-craft) organization in the mass-production industries at the American Federation of Labor (AFL) convention held at Atlantic City in October. Soon Lewis would be one of the leading figures in the creation of the new Committee for Industrial Organization (CIO), originally formed within the confines of the AFL, but soon to break off from its older, more traditional parent, pushing its new industry-wide gospel in a more militant fashion, and existing independently as the independent Congress of Industrial Organizations until its reintegration in the mid-1950s with the AFL to form the AFL-CIO. The CIO proved important to the automobile unionizing struggle that consumed the energies of Walter Reuther in the late 1930s. Reuther regularly attended various meetings, giving lectures on his European experiences in the Midwest, in Ontario, and at the Brookwood Labor College in Katonah, New York, where his brother Roy was teaching. Brookwood would help educate many of the founding generation of leaders of the new mass-production industries. Walter obtained membership in the numerically small United Automobile Workers Local 86 (the union had yet to obtain recognition from any of the automobile manufacturers) at General Motors' Ternstedt auto parts plant on the west side of Detroit, and then immediately became a delegate to the Wayne County Central Labor Council. The inchoate desire for unionization seemed clearly to be in the air, but successful organization continued to prove elusive. People like Reuther, with their Socialist party background (Reuther officially rejoined the party in 1936), were, predictably, disproportionately involved in the organizing efforts that ensued and wound up transforming labor relations in the automobile industry, and beyond, over the course of the next few years.

Reuther came out of the 1936 UAW convention in South Bend, Indiana, which he attended as an official delegate, with a renewed commitment and better focused strategy for organizing automobile workers; he also was chosen for the leadership position of the executive board member for Michigan. Soon the heroic days of union organizing unfolded, their centerpiece being the short-lived, long-remembered, highly effective, and strongly controversial sit-down strikes, with Reuther at the center of the drama and increasingly at its forefront, exercising leadership and gaining much publicity and credibility, especially when he, by now president of the small but soon to be large West Side Local 174, was one of a group of unionists attacked by antiunion Ford Motor Company Service Department personnel in the May 26, 1937, "Battle of the Overpass," as it became known in union lore. GM and the other automobile companies became organized, that is, the UAW became the official bargaining unit for the businesses' mass-production employees.

After failing, along with other members of a "labor slate," to win election to city office in Detroit later that year, in 1938 Reuther's political ambitions turned and developed within the union movement. At the national UAW convention in Cleveland, Reuther was named director of the General Motors Department for the whole union; by this point GM, under the leadership of managerial genius Alfred P. Sloan, Jr., had been dominating the automobile industry for some time, producing twice as many cars a year as Ford and Chrysler combined. In 1940 Reuther was elected to the vice presidency of the UAW, its third highest office (and was reelected in 1944). In terms of partisan politics, given the role of the New Deal in establishing the framework within which the UAW was able to achieve the all-important, fundamental status of recognition, Reuther edged toward the mainstream, leaving the Socialist party in 1938 to support Democratic Governor Frank Murphy, thereby rewarding him for his refusal to deploy the Michigan National Guard in support of either General Motors or the union-hostile city government of Flint during the most publicized and influential of the sit-down strikes. Reuther was rapidly drifting in the direction of being fully, clearly anticommunist, his disillusionment largely a product of numerous unhappy factional fights within the union, as indicated in his sponsorship at the August 1940 St. Louis UAW convention of a resolution barring from union office anyone who held membership in any group loyal to a "foreign government" or who belonged to organizations declared "illegal" by the U.S. government (Boyle 1995, 22). In that same year the UAW achieved a landmark, company-wide contract with GM under its new president, Charles E. Wilson, a man more accepting than his predecessors of the union concept with whom Walter Reuther developed a mutually respectful relationship. While management's prerogatives remained strong, Reuther's stature as the man most responsible for the breakthrough—organizing the nation's greatest industrial concern—was at its highest point yet. He was among those who saw to it that the UAW endorsed Franklin D. Roosevelt for an unprecedented third presidential term.

During World War II, Reuther's fame grew. Serious consideration was given to his proposed conversion of Detroit's factories from automobile to airplane production under a trinitarian, corporatist power structure whose three "persons" would be business management, the federal government, and the labor union, though nothing came of it in the end. The war brought Reuther far greater contacts with Washington figures, including Texas Congressman Lyndon Johnson—with whom he got along very well, even spending the night at his Washington residence on several occasions—and First Lady Eleanor Roosevelt (Lichtenstein 1995, 171). His interests during the war varied and included such social issues as civil rights, housing construction, and architecture (he was a very active home carpenter), but overall he became the most intrigued by the possibilities of employing the federal government, which had just successfully mobilized the nation in the greatest war effort in history, in a new national project: completing and advancing the New Deal by constructing a modern industrial and welfare state in the United States. Near the end of the war, he proposed the creation of federal regulatory and planning boards to direct the postwar economy's evolution. His interest in this political direction was reinforced by the near-total failure of the strike he led against GM on November 21, 1945, which had to be given up after 113 days. Bread-and-butter issues could still be worked out in collective bargaining, but a broader social reconstruction, Reuther believed, would have to involve the national government. Despite the strike's failure, at the UAW convention held the following March in Atlantic City, Reuther was narrowly elected UAW president, a position he was to hold for the rest of his life.

Walter Reuther came out of the World War II period an established national leader of a strong labor union movement that was usually closely allied with the nation's dominant political party; appropriately, he made the cover of *Time* in late 1945 and continued to receive predominantly favorable coverage in prominent media outlets. The war period, far lengthier than that of World War I for the United States, had inevitably created within the nation a collective consciousness and common purpose to an unprecedented degree; the rapidly unfolding Cold War that almost immediately ensued guaranteed a significant continuation of that mentality. The war had shown yet again what the federal government was capable of doing, if and when it took the lead on behalf of the entire society. As far as Reuther was concerned, the collaboration he had seen during the war of big government, big industry, and the newest kid on the block, big labor, should continue into the postwar period, together planning the next stage in society's ever-upward development. Veteran journalist John Chamberlain summarized Reuther's vision for the postwar United States in the December 1945 issue of the business monthly *Fortune*: "He believes that labor's political and economic power must be brought to bear for one great purpose: to gain for labor—and thus, he believes, for the consumer—a true partnership in the U.S. productive machine" (Lichtenstein 1995, 237). However, significant elements in government, not insignificant elements in the labor union movement itself (which, in any event, was very far indeed from representing all those in the United States who worked for a living), and the overwhelming majority of the captains of industry held opinions about Reuther's vision that ranged from slight interest to vehement opposition. Big business as a whole, very much including the automobile companies, insisted on their "right to manage" in a free-enterprise system.

Despite the surprise election of Harry Truman as president in 1948, along with the return of a Democratic majority to Congress, Reuther's imagined postwar United States failed to emerge. Controversies within the union over communism, gaining and subsequently securing for himself the UAW presidency, and of course regular union business occupied much of Reuther's time in the late 1940s; he also led the successful fight to remove any trace of communist influence inside the UAW. But Reuther did not withdraw from external politics; he was a major force in the 1947 founding of the new liberal pressure group Americans for Democratic Action (itself a renaming and, it was hoped, revitalization of an organization begun in 1941), an influential group through the Great Society years, and also worked to meld unions with local and state Democratic party organizations, perhaps most successfully in Michigan. In May 1950, a major five-year contract with General Motors, dubbed the "Treaty of Detroit," put the UAW president back on the cover of *Time*, underscoring Reuther's prestige in the wider community, even while signaling the labor leader's acceptance of the prevailing realities of the economic setup—managerial perogative—for now. The agenda for future negotiations with the automobile companies included "welfare" benefits such as medical insurance, leave policies, vacations, and so on—the sort of things that in Europe were across-the-population, legally established entitlements determined in the political realm. In keeping with his long-established and cosmopolitan values, Reuther continued to favor such an approach. But it simply was not politically possible at the time, and with the coming of the Eisenhower administration and the era of apparent national consensus around the prevailing status quo, this situation prevailed throughout the 1950s. Reuther believed that the continuing establishment of welfare-type benefits as part of labor contracts—not simply pay increases—could, if only incrementally, move the United States in the right direction; "pattern bargaining" was the term given to the idea that what one big union gained from a particular big business, another would then use as a new standard in its own ensuing bargaining phase. In time, companies might even decide that government participation in providing such social benefits could reduce financial pressures on them, and hence become more favorably disposed toward such notions; this did, in fact, eventually occur to some degree in the areas of retirement pensions and unemployment compensation payments.

Overall, however, what those who favored increased activism by the federal government called the "deadlock of democracy" continued; even the 1958 midterm election Democratic surge, which greatly increased the number of liberals in Congress, produced nothing at all. This was disappointing, yet by this point Reuther was a firmer believer than ever in the value of the inside game of mainstream politics. His wagon remained firmly hitched to the Democratic star. He maintained positive relations with the strongest Democratic congressional leader, Texas U.S. Senator Lyndon Johnson, although he was disappointed that Kennedy chose the majority leader from a state where unions were weak as his running mate in 1960.

After the 1960 presidential election result, when the fundamental political setup began to change, when John F. Kennedy's "New Frontier" promised to try to "get the country moving again," and when the civil rights movement started to attract mass attention, Reuther was more than ready. By then he had taken enough trips to Sweden and other socialist-style welfare states in Europe to enable him to produce a set of *Selected Papers* in 1961 in twelve languages, suggesting he was a sort of American labor union philosopher-king. He remained by far the most respected American labor union leader in the world, and, given the corruption of any number of union leaders within the United States, the most respected representative of "big labor" in the nation.

Reuther, like many among the mainstream left, had high hopes for President Kennedy; despite the latter's lackluster Senate career, the Massachusetts senator had at least rhetorically moved somewhat to the left during the presidential primary season. Also like many others, Reuther felt during his private meetings with Kennedy that the president treated him seriously and respectfully. He had many contacts in high places within the administration, especially Secretary of Labor Willard Wirtz, another admirer of the Swedish corporatist outlook, and former University of Minnesota economics professor, Walter Heller, Kennedy's chairman of the Council of Economic Advisers who had a strong Keynesian view of economic policy. Naturally, Reuther especially enjoyed JFK's 1962 conflict with the steel industry, in which the president successfully "jawboned" back down the companies' announced price increases, giving management a black eye in the process. The UAW president felt himself to be enjoying his greatest access to, if not real influence with, a president ever, even if his talk of economic "planning" seemed to be falling on deaf ears.

Though as time went by Walter Reuther became somewhat more critical of, and impatient with, Kennedy, more often he tended to blame the failure of the left's vision to advance, not only in the realm of economics but also (more obviously) in the area of civil rights, on forces in Congress, especially the powerful, numerous, and well-positioned conservative southern Democrats. As a natural believer in intergroup cooperation—the UAW's headquarters was called Solidarity House—and a man experienced in picketing, sit-down striking, and mass movements against entrenched power, Walter Reuther supported the postwar civil rights movement from its beginnings, as did the UAW, more than any other union (Lichtenstein 1995, 370). Reuther had been on the board of the NAACP, whose locals had supported the UAW organizing efforts back in the 1930s, and the UAW was in on the ground floor of the creation, in 1950, of a long-lasting coalition of groups that eventually took the name Leadership Conference on Civil Rights (Boyle 1995, 109). As his biographer Nelson Lichtenstein wrote, "Reuther was at heart a moralist whose chest still burned with a passion for social justice and a disdain for those motivated merely by personal gain and greed" (365). The union's publications favorably treated the Freedom Riders, and Reuther himself in the summer of 1961, and participated in a forum designed to give them and their cause favorable publicity (Levy 1994, 17). He invited Martin Luther King, Jr., to give the keynote address at the UAW's twenty-fifth anniversary dinner in 1961, where King paid tribute to the 1930s sit-down strikes as the inspiration for the contemporary sit-ins (Lichtenstein 1995, 378). Reuther used substantial UAW money from its strike fund to bail out jailed civil rights protesters in Birmingham, Alabama, writing on behalf of their struggle in a UAW publication, "What is needed in the present crises is not half-way and half-hearted measures but action bold and adequate to square American democracy's performance with its promise of full citizenship and equal opportunities for all Americans" (quoted in Levy 1994, 18).

Reuther was happy to offer critical organizational and financial support to the March on Washington of August 28, 1963, at which he spoke, though of course his remarks were immediately overshadowed by Martin Luther King, Jr.'s "I Have a Dream" speech. That the march was officially termed a "March for Jobs and Freedom" is indicative of the centrality of labor unions to the effort to turn out people, and the UAW was easily the greatest contributor to the organization required to pull the event off and make it the success it was. On June 13, 1963, Reuther and others had met in the morning with President Kennedy, urging him to include employment practices in his forthcoming civil rights legislative proposal; he had then participated in a working lunch with others interested in civil rights, including Martin Luther King, Jr., to discuss approaches to lobbying the civil rights bill through Congress as well as the forthcoming march. A kind of dress rehearsal took place the next day in Detroit, where a group of black ministers had organized a "Walk to Freedom" that turned out very well, with well over 100,000 people marching down Woodward Avenue to Cadillac Square; Reuther and King participated, with King delivering in Cobo Hall essentially the same "I Have a Dream" speech that would be heard by a far wider audience a few weeks later when it was delivered from the steps of the Lincoln Memorial.

Reuther and the UAW contributed mightily to the historic day's success, bringing some 5,000 automobile workers to Washington and distributing thousands of signs, stressing the link between civil rights and the union movement, for marchers to hold up, emblazoned with such slogans as "Civil Rights Plus Full Employment Equals Freedom" and "FEPC [Fair Employment Practices Commission], Equal Rights and Jobs NOW" (Boyle 1995, 177; Lichtenstein 1995, 387). Reuther was also called upon by Kennedy administration officials to put pressure on John Lewis of the Student Nonviolent Coordinating Committee to "soften" his militant speech, which threatened to provoke the withdrawal of some participants in the demonstration, and successfully did so. With his union perspective, Reuther, as well as the AFL-CIO, wanted employment discrimination to be part of President Kennedy's civil rights proposal, and despite serious opposition from within the administration, the unionists succeeded in having such provisions added to the bill favorably reported out of the House Judiciary Committee in late October (Lichtenstein 1995, 387–88).

On November 23, 1963, Walter Reuther, who had come to Washington to pay his respects to the slain president and his family, received a telephone call from the new president, Lyndon Johnson, who was no stranger to him. Reuther soon learned that he was one of many who had received such a call, which asked for continuing support and also for suggestions as to national priorities; Reuther quickly sent off his list, with civil rights at the top. In December, Johnson again telephoned him, seeking suggestions for the upcoming State of the Union address slated for January 8, 1964. Reuther had prepared and sent to the White House a six-page memorandum, "An Economy of Opportunity," filled with long-standing UAW ideas. Some, such as "democratic economic planning," were ignored, but others, such as the need to create the "economy of opportunity" and "a massive national effort to provide a better life for America's submerged third," were influential in the wording of Johnson's speech, the Great Society's opening salvo wherein the War on Poverty was declared.

Johnson kept calling Reuther with flattering regularity over the course of the next two years, giving him a direct access that the union leader had never experienced under previous presidents and continually reinforcing the labor leader's sense that he was at the center of things. The UAW president was in a position to help get the War on Poverty off the ground, and did so. In April 1964 he asked the UAW executive board to appropriate $100,000 to create the Citizens' Crusade against Poverty (CCAP), the institutional expression of his "coalition of conscience" idea; those who had been mobilized in the civil rights movement were to "couple the civil rights struggle with the poverty struggle. . . . This would permit us to implement the federal program and supplement it with private action" (quoted in Boyle 1995, 190). With the UAW money approved by the board, Reuther announced that his new group would be available to offer guidance to the new Community Action Programs (CAPs) to be formed under the proposed Office of Economic Opportunity (which it did, creating four centers to develop and educate leaders on how to obtain and make use of the available poverty program dollars; see Boyle 1995, 215). Before the 1960s were over, the UAW had given the CCAP half a million dollars. The link was underscored when Johnson appointed a close Reuther UAW associate, Jack Conway, deputy director of OEO to head the CAP initiative; Conway naturally made use of many UAW people as his programs developed (Lichtenstein 1995, 390). Reuther put together a founding meeting of CCAP in June 1964, held at Washington and attracting representatives of 125 groups, some old-line (the National Council of Churches, the AFL-CIO) and some of more recent vintage (the Students for a Democratic Society, the Student Nonviolent Coordinating Committee). He viewed the "war" as just beginning and, given his social-democratic vision, naturally hoped it would bloom to full flower. In a magazine article that appeared under his byline in August 1964, Reuther employed the "war" figure: "In war, we have been capable of a high degree of unity of purpose. . . . We must find the common ground of unity and purpose that we require to accomplish the complex tasks of peace, as we found it under the pressure of war" (quoted in Boyle 1995, 188).

At the 1964 Democratic National Convention, Walter Reuther was a key player, more at the center of things than ever. He had invited leaders of the organized new student left, the Students for a Democratic Society, for which his union had provided the seed money and even the facility, its Port Huron, Michigan, summer camp, to attend the convention, encouraging them to go "part of the way with LBJ" (a takeoff on one of Johnson's 1964 slogans, "All the way with LBJ"), promising to continue supporting their organizing projects with UAW money, and seeking, with success, to get them involved with both his new CCAP and also the soon-to-come CAPs. On account of the prominent involvement of UAW people, Reuther, with his years of negotiating, was also repeatedly urged by President Johnson to "settle" the fight over which of two delegations would represent Mississippi—the old-line, all-white segregationists, composed of the actual officeholders and political powerholders of the state, or the new, civil rights–inspired, black-led and integrated (though overwhelmingly black) Mississippi Freedom Democratic Party (MFDP), whose challenge the automobile union had been backing— Joseph Rauh, one of Reuther's closest UAW associates for decades, was the MFDP's chief legal representative in the delegation credentials fight. Johnson, who saw the possibility of a genuine landslide sweeping in the most liberal Congress since the New Deal era (which would actually be realized), did not want anything to threaten this possibility, with its bigger implications; he also feared a potential "white backlash." On several occasions in the summer of 1964, Johnson had asked Reuther to "take care" of the situation; by August, the president was telling Reuther that the vice presidential nomination of Senator Hubert Humphrey, a pro–labor union liberal from Minnesota whom Reuther and other unionists had long viewed as an ideal future president, depended on the credentials challenge being ended (Lichtenstein 1995, 393). The day after the August 22 dramatic testimony of MFDP activist Fannie Lou Hamer, Reuther, at Johnson's direct request, left his negotiations with the Chrysler Corporation and flew to Atlantic City to bring the challenge to a swift conclusion. Reuther met with Johnson officials and played his hardball role, along with Humphrey and old-line civil rights activist and experienced political coalition-builder Bayard Rustin. The Johnson compromise, which would give the Freedom Democrats two seats alongside the regulars, presuming the old-liners pledged never again to bring a segregated delegation to the national convention, was announced as "done" by the credentials committee even as Reuther was conducting forceful discussion with MFDP leaders, as well as Martin Luther King, Jr. In the end, no one was officially to represent Mississippi, as the regulars went home and the challengers were banned. Reuther, a longtime negotiator who knew that one won some, lost some, and compromised nearly all the time, had proven his loyalty to Johnson, gaining many enemies among the activists in the process, and Humphrey was given the vice presidential nomination. The episode was long-remembered, and bitterly so. Attorney Joseph Rauh, in retrospect, called it "the greatest mistake of his life" (395).

With the Johnson landslide of 1964 bringing in the largest Democratic majorities in Congress since the 1930s, Reuther felt vindicated in his decision to stay close to the president, whose Civil Rights Act of 1964, including the union-sponsored fair employment section, and Economic Opportunity Act would now, he hoped, prove to be but a prelude to the enactment of many, many more Great Society initiatives. One such 1965 landmark, the Voting Rights Act, resulted in part from the continuing televised drama in the South. In March, Walter Reuther went to Selma, Alabama, for the memorial service of a slain northern civil rights activist, James Reeb, and shortly thereafter led a large UAW contingent who, joining many others, prominent and otherwise, marched from Selma to Montgomery, Alabama, with Martin Luther King, Jr., in the spring, highlighting the continued denial of constitutionally protected voting rights and used by Johnson as a springboard for the proposed Voting Rights Act, which took effect in August and brought major changes to Deep South politics in a very short time, though Reuther's hopes that black voting would lead to a southern political culture friendly to his social-democratic notions proved wildly wide of the mark.

To Reuther, the American South, hardly a hotbed of labor unionism, was almost, though not quite, another country. He was a Detroiter, and so the "urban crisis" of the 1960s quite naturally constituted for him the challenge that hit closest to home. He had long been a proponent of "urban renewal" and a seeker of federal dollars and financial leveraging to help make it happen. In the spring of 1965, Reuther was hopeful and optimistic about the Great Society's prospects, telling the UAW executive board that the country was "in the midst of a great revolutionary change of forces and people" (quoted in Boyle 1995, 201). Accordingly, he successfully lobbied Johnson to support what he described as an "urban TVA," hoping to wake up the echoes of the New Deal in Johnson's mind. This Demonstration Cities renewal initiative (which eventually took the name Model Cities when opponents charged that radical "demonstrations" threatening violence were being rewarded), Reuther hoped, would provide opportunities for interesting social experimentation. Johnson asked him to make a formal presentation of the idea at the White House on May 20, 1965, which went well, and so Reuther played a role in recruiting the eight members of the task force, of which he was one, that met in the fall to shape the proposal (203). To be ready once the legislation was enacted, Reuther organized and became chairman of the Metropolitan Detroit Citizens' Redevelopment Authority, whose aim would be to rebuild the inner city "so that people now living in a slum can move into neighborhoods worthy of citizens of the Great Society" (quoted in Lichtenstein 1995, 403). Again, he put UAW money into the project. Reuther spent his fall weekends in Washington, meeting with his fellow task force members, and was credited by one of the president's aides with having supplied "the vision, drive, and sometimes mere rhetoric that kept us moving" (quoted in Boyle 1995, 204). At the union's annual convention in May 1966, held in Long Beach, California, Reuther presented the president of the United States with the UAW's Social Justice Award.

In face of the rising tide of questions over the administration's policy in Vietnam, Walter Reuther continued to see himself a loyal Johnson man. Johnson and his Great Society got it from both sides: some on the left, who criticized him for spending money on a fool's errand in Vietnam and mocked the Great Society's funding level, while some on the right, who expressed unending skepticism about the efficacy of Great Society initiatives and insisted that the war be given spending priority. Walter Reuther, who believed, with justice, that the political center of gravity had (for the moment) shifted to the left, saw himself in the middle. He found the increasingly harsh criticism of the president inaccurate, in fact ludicrous and offensive, telling fellow union leaders in 1966, "I have known him a long time. . . . I do not share the view that Lyndon Johnson doesn't care about the problems of the poor, or about the problems of our minority groups. . . . I think that basically, he is a man of compassion" (quoted in Lichtenstein 1995, 405). However, he and other UAW officials complained loudly, publicly, and continually in 1966 about the underfunding of the Great Society, to the point that Johnson became personally irritated with him (Boyle 1995, 224).

The July 1967 Detroit riot, usually considered the country's worst of the hundreds that occurred in the 1960s, naturally enough hit Reuther straight in his chest, but only served to reinforce his continuing beliefs, in the face of increasingly heard expressions like "white backlash" and "black power," of the necessity of biracial coalition building and liberal, mainstream politics. If the center (which, again, he saw as having shifted left) did not hold, what and who would fill it? Since by 1967 the federal money for Great Society initiatives had dried up in the wake of increased war spending and the changed political climate brought on by televised rioting and the ensuing 1966 midterm congressional elections, Walter Reuther became a central player in the Detroit Establishment's response to the riot, the New Detroit Committee, whose objective was nothing less than the rebuilding of Detroit. Reuther's influence was seen in New Detroit's significant emphasis on low-income housing, but meetings revealed the rise of black militancy as well as white backlash. Despite spending some $10 million in only two years, New Detroit's impact was seen as disappointingly minimal.

In 1968, the climatic year of the 1960s, Reuther, in the wake of the assassination of Martin Luther King, Jr., put the UAW's human and financial resources behind the chief attempt to bring back the suddenly faded Great Society, King's Poor People's Campaign, which, carried on by his heirs in the civil rights movement, wound up symbolically bringing the Great Society's War on Poverty to a dispiriting, whimpering end. Liberated from his tie to Johnson by the president's withdrawal from the 1968 presidential campaign, Reuther began becoming more antiwar, a position far more natural to his lifelong worldview anyway. He fought hard and, eventually, with success to get union workers to support Hubert Humphrey for president over George Wallace and Richard Nixon, whose election definitively sealed the doom of the Great Society, though it by no means overturned all of its many institutional changes. Walter Reuther was killed in a plane crash in Michigan on May 9, 1970. No subsequent union leader in the next generation was able even to approximate his role or influence; no Great Society "moment" appeared again.

JOSEPH CALIFANO
(1931–)

Executives are only as good as their top aides. Given the kinds of pressures under which American presidents operate, this is especially the case regarding the chief executive of the United States. And if that president is an activist, a man on a mission, a man with an enormous, ever-expanding, even boundless agenda, the people directly behind and with him matter a great deal. Barring scandal, such individuals are ordinarily known only to hardcore political junkies who, taking the long view, follow the developing careers of White House assistants who may, in time, advance in the Washington political scene, just as far greater numbers of people follow college athletes apprenticing for professional sports. In July 1965, at the age of thirty-four, Joseph Califano, an attorney and political activist from New York, joined Lyndon Johnson's presidential staff, and for the next three and a half years, as he recorded, "I worked with him day and night—and he used every waking minute of his presidency" (Califano 1991, 9). Johnson became so anxious to keep in contact with Califano that he even had a telephone installed in Califano's office bathroom. Of all Johnson's aides, Califano made the biggest impact on the administration's busy agenda. In the middle of virtually everything during the high tide of the Great Society's historical moment, Califano was called by some the "deputy president for domestic affairs."

Joseph Califano personified a generation of educated, upwardly mobile, urban, Roman Catholic Democratic party activists. Raised in Brooklyn, where he was born on May 15, 1931, he graduated from the College of the Holy Cross in Worcester, Massachusetts, in 1952, proceeding eastward thereafter to the Harvard Law School, which awarded him a LLB in 1955. His Jesuit education at Holy Cross stuck; he remained an active, practicing Catholic who was still contributing articles to Catholic publications at the dawn of the twenty-first century. Roman Catholic education at midcentury was quite distinctive, and the Church's social teaching stressed corporate responsibility for social welfare, in accordance with the traditional favoring of a strongly organized state. Califano, of course, made many contacts at Harvard, exemplified by his roommate, John McGillicuddy, who became a prominent New York bank president. Three years in the judge advocate general's office of the U.S. Navy exposed him to government service. However, after his military tour of duty he moved back to New York and joined the high-toned law firm headed by former New York governor and frequent presidential contender Thomas Dewey. His political career was inspired by his reading in February 1960 of James MacGregor Burns's campaign biography of John F. Kennedy, which attracted him to his fellow northeastern Catholic. Califano volunteered to campaign door-to-door on the Lower East Side of Manhattan and appeared on behalf of JFK in debates sponsored by Democratic "reform clubs," then ascending in influence and promising, like Kennedy himself, a new and better era in politics. Upon Kennedy's narrow election, Califano was one of a swarm of youthful, ambitious lawyers who sought a position in the upcoming administration. He wrote Cyrus Vance, who had been designated general counsel of the Department of Defense, to make him aware of his interest in obtaining a job, and thus soon became one of new Defense Secretary Robert McNamara's "whiz kids," sharing their mentality that anything was possible, that a new, Augustan age might be dawning led by the best and brightest of the nation determined to get the country moving again.

Califano remained ensconced within the Pentagon establishment, close to Secretary McNamara as his special assistant, until November 4, 1964, when suddenly presidential aide McGeorge Bundy called him and requested that he meet him and fellow aide Bill Moyers at the White House at eleven o'clock that morning, for the purpose of discussing the possibility of Califano's joining the White House staff. At that point he had once shaken President Johnson's hand, briefly exchanging words, but that was all. At the meeting it was proposed that Califano might handle Latin America, or help in recruiting talent, but as it turned out, Secretary McNamara, upon learning of the attempted raid on his talent, insisted on his need to keep Califano at the Pentagon.

This status quo obtained until July 8, 1965, when Jack Valenti, a Johnson special assistant, informed Califano that Johnson wanted him on his personal staff, then in the process of being reshuffled. Moyers was becoming press secretary, and Johnson wanted Califano to take Moyers's old job as principal domestic advisor, whose duties were described to him in his interview as preparing legislation, dealing with emerging crises, and being a general-utility infielder. Back in the Pentagon that afternoon, Califano received a call from the White House asking him to come to dinner that night for the purpose of meeting the chairmen of the current Great Society "task forces," highly influential groups that, having been organized around issues, were then mandated to concoct legislative proposals to deal with them, and functioned as idea incubators. Califano, who had plans with a visitor from out of the country, politely declined; five minutes later, Bill Moyers telephoned again, ordering him to attend the dinner.

Here Califano found himself in the company of a group composed primarily of academics and their close fellow travelers, highly confident that they, the best brains of the country, could continue formulating solid answers to national problems along the lines of the progressive agenda of the Great Society. The Great Society at this point seemed to be off to a creditable start indeed, with far, far more to come, it was hoped, given the nation's enormous challenges and problems, to which sufficient attention was finally being paid. Johnson briefly introduced Califano to the group as a staff member, but did not speak directly to him until the close of the meeting, when he invited him to his Texas ranch for the weekend. And so Califano found himself on a Lear jet that Saturday, on his way to receiving his first taste of the famous, so-called Johnson treatment. As so many others had discovered, Califano learned that Johnson's *imperium* ruled; schedules were made at his whim, eating was irregular, and everyone went along with it. Califano spent his time mostly participating in recreational activities, concluding the weekend by meeting LBJ on Monday at the museum in Johnson City dedicated the previous May to the town's most famous citizen. Johnson's parting words, as Califano recalled them, were revealing about the president's insecurities: "What you learned on the streets of Brooklyn will be a mean sight more helpful to your President than anything you learned at Harvard" (Califano 1991, 24). Califano's childhood neighborhood had been split about evenly between Italians and Jews, and had also included a 10 percent minority of blacks, which gave him a certain perspective regarding the potential difficulties of intergroup relations when it came to educational or housing integration.

Mid-1965 was a critical moment in the history of the Johnson administration, for the long-delayed Vietnam matter had reached the moment of decision. Johnson had great fears about the threat to the momentum of the Great Society program that Vietnam embodied; given the centrality of the domestic agenda to Johnson's conception of his destined role in American history, his selection of Califano represented a critical choice. As chief domestic advisor, Califano was in charge of the all-important grunt work for those things that LBJ by far cared the most about. Johnson himself, as a deeply experienced politico with strong Washington ties, was the most sensitive of all to the dangers the Great Society might face should the Vietnam situation prove more difficult than hoped. Califano would be the point man whose general mission was to keep the Great Society's momentum going. On July 26, 1965, Joseph Califano officially joined the White House staff; two days later, Johnson announced the fateful buildup of U.S. combat troops in South Vietnam. But in the same speech, Johnson spoke quite openly of his fears that the war might, somehow, derail his Great Society domestic vision.

The final weekend in July found Califano making his second visit to the LBJ Ranch, where Johnson became a little more specific as to the exact work he wanted Califano to do. Meeting beside the swimming pool, Johnson laid out his legislative priorities; amidst "lots of programs," Johnson named two specific ones—the consolidation of federal agencies involving transportation into a single, unified department, and the passage of a law outlawing most forms of discrimination in housing transactions (known as "fair" or "open" housing). The first, an example of government reorganization so as to improve efficiency, was not really a part of the Great Society program at all, a reminder that regular government business did continue to go on during the Johnson administration, quite independent of the Great Society effort. The second priority, however, was a straight civil rights measure, specifically focusing on one of the central areas of Great Society concern. Johnson then mentioned a third priority for Califano's concern, far vaguer yet tremendously illustrative of the Great Society's bigger spirit: LBJ told his new top domestic man that he wanted to "rebuild American cities."

Having laid out this agenda, Johnson inquired, "Now, can you do that? Can you do all these things?" Subjected to the Johnson treatment, inevitably Califano answered affirmatively, "not having the faintest idea how, but electrified by his energy." But that night, as he lay in bed at the ranch, Califano "realized that in our conversations in the pool and throughout the weekend, Johnson had not mentioned, or even alluded to, any limit to the push for Great Society programs" (Califano 1991, 51–52). There it was: limitlessness. Johnson was far too experienced a politician not to be aware of the many obstacles and difficulties posed by the American political system, and frequently exhibited to Califano and others a hardheaded realism. But Johnson's dream of a Great Society, outlined at Ann Arbor in 1964, still shone brightly a year later.

In order even to approximate such grandiosity as "rebuilding the cities," however that might be defined, ideas as to how to begin accomplishing such a thing were necessarily required. One of Califano's principal responsibilities became seeking out and developing such ideas. Given the structure of American intellectual life, broadly defined, the likeliest (but by no means exclusive) place to find them was on the campuses of the incubators of such things: the great research universities. In the spring of 1966, Johnson was already beginning to think about his next State of the Union address, in which he intended to follow his established pattern of outlining the next set of proposals to keep the Great Society's momentum going. Johnson ordered Califano to undertake a talent and idea search of the nation's colleges, stressing that he was to be sure to look all over the country, not just on the two coasts, seeking out the "finest minds in the country . . . without regard to politics. You let these intellectuals get me the ideas. I'll worry about the politics." Johnson often reiterated his clear line of demarcation as to who was to do what; he felt he knew his place, if others did not necessarily seem to know theirs. "The trouble with the Democratic party," Johnson complained more than once to Califano, "is that all the intellectuals want to be politicians and all the politicians want to be intellectuals" (Califano 1991, 113).

The president, as had been the case in his conversation with Califano that previous summer at the Johnson ranch, was still vague as to what new proposals he might like, tossing off expressions like "a program for the cities" or "something to help the Negro male and his family." Books still in manuscript might be consulted, or reports of government commissions. In response to Johnson's mandate, with aides accompanying him, Califano spent much of his first few months with LBJ visiting colleges and discussing ideas with dozens of scholars and experts, the outcome of which was a briefing book of ideas three inches thick. Besides college figures such as Yale University President Kingman Brewster or Harvard University economics professor John Kenneth Galbraith, other individuals of note from a variety of areas were consulted, including Nobel Prize–winning novelist John Steinbeck, international economist Barbara Ward, United Automobile Workers President Walter Reuther, and Dean Acheson, who had served as President Truman's secretary of state. Upon discovering that Vice President Hubert Humphrey had been included on the task force on urban affairs, Johnson instructed Califano to remove him and to silence him from even commenting publicly on "a Marshall plan or demonsration plan or any other plan for the cities" (Califano 1991, 114). Califano complied, and so Hubert Humphrey never again had anything directly to do with the preparation of legislative programs.

Besides traveling, discussing, and compiling, Califano was also assembling task forces during the summer and fall on a myriad of topics. These groups, which Johnson had been employing before Califano joined his staff, were mandated to develop legislative proposals. Those for 1966 were focused on a multitude of Great Society topics, including job training, income maintenance, education, public assistance, urban housing, urban affairs in general, health care, and civil rights; other task forces dealt with more traditional public issues not specifically identified with the Great Society moniker such as foreign policy and pollution. The president was kept apprised as the task forces proceeded with their work.

All of this activity climaxed on December 29, 1965, at the ranch in Texas, where Califano presented Johnson with a briefing book outlining possible new programs entitled *The Great Society—A Second Year Legislative Program*. All sorts of things were included, including many traditional and not particularly controversial proposals: new national parks including a national trail system and scenic roadways, and the promotion of historical preservation efforts. Regarding health, Johnson saw and approved such initiatives as "comprehensive health planning" for localities and a new committee on mental retardation; regarding education, taxpayer-funded breakfasts and an expansion of similarly funded lunches, plus summer programs for disadvantaged children. Much of this was at the time mainstream, business that needed to be done to be sure, but not especially ground-breaking.

Johnson, of course, hoped for something more than just the usual, and Califano had provided something for him: the Demonstration Cities program. LBJ's eyes "lit up" when he examined proposals that envisioned the transformation of slums over the course of five to ten years, to be achieved "with a total approach—new homes, schools, parks, community centers and open centers"; the provision of health care for residents; and the improvement of their transportation facilities and their police departments, the proceeding heavenly city to be brought about via federal tax dollars. This would be something truly new that could break new ground and even capture the imagination of idealists who sought the improvement of the "slums." It became a favorite of the president's, who deemed it, at a meeting with the Democratic congressional leadership in mid-1966, "the most important domestic measure before the Congress and to the future of the American cities" (Califano 1991, 131). Califano was responsible for the program's name, later changed to Model Cities due to the association of "demonstration" with civic protest, and it became a familiar symbol of the Great Society to the politically attentive portion of the population. Since it was in fact something new, it provided a useful symbol to friend and foe alike of what the new departure known as the Great Society actually meant.

Johnson's January 12, 1966, State of the Union address announced an array of new federal initiatives to further the creation of the Great Society. He was frequently interrupted by applause from the friendly audience, the second session of the liberal-leaning Eighty-Ninth Congress that had been produced by the 1964 Goldwater debacle. The Great Society continued in 1966 to dominate official Washington. Califano helped organize and was a key participant in the weekly breakfasts Johnson held with committee chairmen and other legislative staff. Johnson treated attendees to exhortations, complete with posterboards and cards depicting legislative organs of the Congress and major bills making their way through the Capitol Hill process, regarding strategy and tactics. Califano sat in on and participated in other meetings with congressional leaders, including such Republicans as Everett Dirksen and Gerald Ford. He helped arrange numerous face-to-face meetings and telephone calls and sometimes prepared presidential statements.

When trouble arose regarding any particular piece of Great Society legislation, Johnson expected Califano to find out what the problem was, arrange to have it fixed, and get the bill through. While the Democrats did enjoy their largest majorities in the Congress since the Depression era, the old-line seniority system was still intact, as was most of the Solid South tradition. This mean that an inordinate number of committee chairmen were southern Democrats, the large majority of whom had at least a streak of conservatism, especially when it came to anything smacking of civil rights. As a longtime creature of Congress who had served as the Democratic Senate leader for the

1950s, Johnson knew the system from the inside, better than probably any-one, certainly better than anyone who had any real power. Knowing as well that 1966 was an election year, a midterm election at that and one in which many of the huge Democratic House gains of the 1964 landslide would have to be defended, Johnson instructed Califano carefully to count heads and check with members pro, con, and somewhere in between so as to determine if controversial legislation were likely to make it through.

The Demonstration Cities idea became central to the Great Society's ur-ban vision. Originating in a proposal by automobile union leader Walter Reuther, who hoped to make his own Detroit (and a few other cities as well) examples of what a new and *comprehensive* departure might achieve in terms of rebuilding the cities, Demonstration Cities also sought, at least in part, to respond to earlier criticisms of "urban renewal," a 1950s ap-proach that, critics had increasingly come to charge, involved far more big-ticket, high-end projects accompanied by federal bulldozing and "urban removal" of "slum" populations (it was sometimes referred to as "Negro removal") than anything directly benefiting poorer residents themselves. The idea wound up in Califano's briefing book of December 1965 and set Johnson's expansive imagination running. He greatly increased the pro-posal's magnitude, envisioning six large (over 500,000 population), ten medium (250,000–500,000), and fifty small (under 250,000) "demonstra-tions" of comprehensive social planning to improve slum areas. As an ex-perienced political realist, Johnson was sure that the program had to be spread out if it were to have a chance of gaining congressional approval and sufficient funding.

Problems with the proposal soon developed. For instance, a provision of the Demonstration Cities bill required integration to be promoted in federal housing projects. John Sparkman, the 1952 Democratic vice presidential nominee and an old-line southern Democratic senator from Alabama who was the head of the Senate subcommittee to which the bill would be as-signed, of course would oppose the integration proviso, as Johnson knew, and this was an era in which committee chairmen possessed tremendous au-tocratic power and were accustomed to deploying it. Califano discovered that the next ranking Democratic member of the subcommittee, Paul Dou-glas of Illinois, was far too preoccupied with his difficult reelection cam-paign (which he would go on to lose); the *next* ranking Democrat, Edmund Muskie, replied to Califano's entreaties that there were no cities in Maine. Informed of this comment by Muskie, LBJ replied to Califano, "Well, he has one now. . . . Whatever one he wants" (Califano 1991, 132). Califano was instructed to pursue Muskie, and so arranged a meeting with him on June 22, and then, at Johnson's insistence, another one in his office in the com-pany of aide Lawrence F. O'Brien and Vice President Hubert Humphrey. Muskie, on his way to the airport for the 4th of July recess, was hardly in the mood to talk seriously. Johnson, peeved, then instructed Califano to take

O'Brien with him and pursue Muskie in Maine, where an unenthusiastic Muskie agreed to a July 6 meeting at which, after hours of work, his support was finally gained. Negotiations continued with other subcommittee members on various logrolling points, and a bill was reported out favorably by a vote of 6–4; it passed the Senate on August 19.

On the other side of the Capitol, the House committee in charge of the bill was headed by William Barrett of Pennsylvania, who was very skeptical at the outset. Califano went to work, arranging a June meeting in the office of the House speaker with Barrett, O'Brien, and Democratic House leaders. After an hour of arguing, Barrett agreed to go along with the bill if the Senate would do the honors of taking it up and working it out first. That having been accomplished, in mid-August the scene shifted to the House, which produced a bill close to the Senate's, Republicans opposing it on a party-line vote. Johnson successfully obtained the support of a number of Fortune 500 corporate leaders, who issued a statement urging the bill's passage, and Califano and his aides arranged for as much favorable support in the media as possible; for example, Califano called Joseph Pulitzer, editor and publisher of the St. Louis *Post-Dispatch*, at Johnson's direction to obtain favorable editorial treatment.

Back in the Senate, Johnson and Califano faced a new problem from liberal members, such as Abraham Ribicoff (D-Conn.) and the two New York senators, Republican Jacob Javits and Democrat Robert F. Kennedy, whom LBJ considered a personal nemesis. These senators used the opportunity to criticize the administration for not doing nearly *enough* for the cities, angering the president, who was sure that these grandstanders understood the political constraints under which Johnson operated as well as he did. By this time, the shadow of the urban disturbances that had begun rocking the nation the previous August in the Watts neighborhood of Los Angeles had been cast.

The Watts tragedy provides a dramatic example of another facet to Califano's job: helping the president get through whatever crisis might arise at a given moment. Just eight days after Califano joined Johnson's staff, the landmark Voting Rights Act of 1965 had finally passed Congress. After a night of private celebrating at the office of Senate Minority Leader Everett Dirksen, in the company of Senate Majority Leader Mike Mansfield, LBJ had spent the next day preparing for the signing ceremony, consulting Califano among others about exactly how it should be done. Live television coverage of the event on August 6th in the Capitol Rotunda found Johnson as happy as he had ever been, and his sense of the significance of the law was well borne out as the future unfolded. Almost immediately, Johnson began preparing for an anticipated conference on the bill's implementation, to be held at the White House in June 1966 under the title "To Fulfill These Rights."

On the night of August 11, word came to Washington of the breakout of disturbances in Los Angeles—but nothing too serious. It was only on the second night, August 12, that things began to spin out of control; by the morning of August 13, Califano had come to suspect that the California state government might soon be asking for federal troops. To his shock, he could not get the president to return his calls—something that was never to recur in his years as Johnson's assistant. Under pressure, Califano made his first important solo decision as the president's domestic chief: he told General Creighton Abrams, vice chief of staff of the Army, that the general had "White House approval" to move forward with providing the requested support for transporting National Guard units from northern to southern California via U.S. Air Force planes. Califano was anxious not to reveal that Johnson had failed to return his calls. He decided to call another of Johnson's aides, Jack Valenti, who was at the Johnson Ranch; Valenti, informed by Califano of his action, wrote a note that, upon receipt, led the president to call Califano at 9:09 PM Eastern Standard Time on August 14, stating that he wanted no federal military presence and inquiring who had authorized the army to proceed. Califano explained that, upon the recommendations of Secretary of Defense Robert McNamara and Attorney General Nicholas Katzenbach, who themselves were responding to the requests of California authorities (the governor of California being the commander of the state's National Guard), he himself had made the call. Johnson accepted this without comment. Now recovered from his temporary blackout, so to speak, Johnson instructed Califano to call the most prominent black leaders— Martin Luther King, Jr., of course, and also Whitney Young, head of the National Urban League; Roy Wilkins, executive director of the NAACP; and A. Philip Randolph, head of the then-important Brotherhood of Sleeping Car Porters union, and ask them publicly to condemn violence, explaining his fears that violence in the streets would make it that much more difficult to get desired Great Society legislation, designed to address urban problem, through Congress. A few days later, Johnson instructed Califano to "assemble a package of federal programs to deal with the underlying causes of the riots in Watts" (Califano 1991, 63). Having already been working with the task forces, Califano was able to follow through on this request; he was also asked by Johnson before the month was out to work on reorganizing civil rights efforts that, due to the large number of new laws that had at least apparently spread civil rights enforcement responsibility among a myriad of federal agencies, needed clarification and coordination. Califano had survived this major crisis with the president's confidence in him higher than ever, thus sealing his place at the heart of the White House operation.

As one of the people closest to Johnson, Joseph Califano functioned as a significant conduit of information both ways. Civil rights was clearly an issue that Johnson, who had grown up in a state with legal segregation, was exceptionally passionate about. At the very outset of Califano's service, he was instructed by the president to consult with Attorney General Nicholas Katzenbach so as to bring about a reorganization and consolidation of efforts in that all-important area. A few weeks later, the president communicated to Califano his desire that Vice President Hubert Humphrey be removed from any position of real influence regarding civil rights, apparently on the grounds that Humphrey was not tough enough to handle the variety of opposition sure to arise to any meaningful attempts at enforcement and further progress—thus, LBJ, at a private Saturday lunch, instructed Califano to "put together a plan and get the civil rights programs out from under the Vice President" (Califano 1991, 66). As mentioned, Johnson instructed Califano to remove Humphrey's name from the task force list; furthermore, he ordered his domestic advisor to call Humphrey and tell him to keep quiet regarding any proposals for urban policies, complaining that he didn't "need the Vice President to try to commit him to some crazy, Goddamned expensive idea that Congress will never approve anyway" (114). Johnson preferred to try selling big ideas himself. As mentioned earlier, when a politically inexperienced commissioner of education, Francis Keppel, announced on October 1, 1965, that on account of evidence of racial discrimination, the school system of the city of Chicago would have its federal funds cut off, Johnson, after meeting with the livid mayor of Chicago, Richard Daley, had Califano put together a meeting of a handful of top officials to set Keppel straight as to the exactitudes of the law, as well as the political realities; soon, Keppel was transferred to a less politically sensitive position. Califano was also given the task of communicating directly with Mayor Daley the results of the meeting. From the reverse perspective, outside interests quickly realized that Califano had the ear of the president; for instance, in late December, AFL-CIO President George Meany had a message delivered to Califano warning that the Great Society programs should not be gutted on account of the increased expenses of the Vietnam War buildup.

The 1966 midterm congressional elections showed the historically normal swing away from the president's party, somewhat more pronounced due to the landslide of 1964 and also to the more highly charged atmosphere stemming from the spread of urban disorder. Democrats retained large majorities in each house, however, and a number of the new Republicans elected to the Senate were about as liberal, and thus favorably inclined toward the Great Society, as were the Democrats. It was also still the case that Democratic ranks included many members, mostly but not exclusively southerners, who were growing in their skepticism of more controversial Great Society initiatives. The political situation, then, was on balance more challenging. Johnson and Califano met at the LBJ ranch on December 22, 1966, to ponder new proposals, many taken from the task forces of that year, the content of the upcoming State of the Union address, and the political arithmetic of the new Congress. "As we went over more than [a] hundred ideas that afternoon," Califano recalled in his memoir, "I kept thinking; There will never be enough for this man; he adopts programs the way a child eats rich chocolate-chip cookies" (Califano 1991, 180).

Johnson's troubles accelerated as Vietnam became a more divisive and distracting issue, and with the spread of the long, hot summers of the mid- and late 1960s. Television dramatically brought footage of the seemingly endless riots into millions of homes far removed from the sites of disorder. Califano continued to serve as a sounding board for Johnson and by now felt free to speak his mind, for instance, advising the president that a proposed proclamation of a national day of prayer for July 30, in the wake of serious disturbances in Newark and Detroit, would likely be mocked. Califano also warned, prophetically and unsuccessfully, against the creation of a national commission on the sources of the spreading civil disorders. As is the usual case with such groups, LBJ intended to stack the commission with people favorable to his mindset; after investigation, they would be expected to conclude that the best thing for the nation to do would be to increase funding to Great Society programs. Califano feared the creation of a "political Frankenstein's monster" and that Johnson would not like what it would come up with (probably politically unreal proposals for vastly increased federal government spending). Johnson eventually went ahead with the commission anyway.

With the national pot boiling more than ever, Califano spent the spring and summer of 1967 again on the road in search of new ideas, visiting eight academic centers and meeting with some 115 experts. He found they shared one common theme: questioning of the president's Vietnam policy. With the shifting of political discourse away from friendliness toward Great Society programs and in the direction of criticism of them, Johnson, personally committed but politically realistic and astute, had to consider his response. Members of his own cabinet were advocating significant reductions in Great Society appropriations requests. But Joseph Califano wrote the president on December 4, 1967, urging that backtracking be resisted. Johnson, he advocated, should give a little on the issue of raising taxes (to finance war spending) and not fear the cutting of "obsolete programs" such as "school milk for suburban children," but in the larger sense he should "go forward on a fairly substantial scale with new programs in the area of housing and jobs particularly," holding Great Society spending "at least" to current levels, levels that Califano considered actually rather modest, far below the often grandiose rhetoric the president employed publicly. Regarding the single most powerful figure in the House of Representatives concerning these issues, Ways and Means Chairman Wilbur Mills of Arkansas, Califano recommended that Johnson "tackle Mills head on" since Mills "wants either (or both) (1) to force . . . you to your knees, or (2) to dismantle great hunks of the Great Society." (Califano would continue to advocate standing up to Mills, publicly and privately, as the battle of the proposed tax surcharge and its proposed coupling with Great Society spending reductions proceeded in 1968.) More than ever, due to the unsettled times, presidential leadership would be required. Johnson did not reply to the memorandum, but Califano "watched him test the suggestions at several economic and budget meetings" (Califano 1991, 253). Califano and Johnson spent all day on December 27, 1967, at the LBJ Ranch talking over new proposals for the upcoming State of the Union address.

The address showed that Califano's attempt to steady a wavering Johnson had succeeded. The Great Society was defended, and further extensions of it were proposed, although Johnson delivered the speech in a subdued tone, admitting that complex phenomena such as poverty and pollution could not be changed in a day. In the context of the Vietnam War's Tet Offensive and its aftermath, Johnson continued to submit proposal after proposal to Congress: "The President could not hurl programs at Congress and the public fast enough. He was irritable and impatient when I did not have a draft special message in his night reading to go to Congress the next day," leading to slipups (failure to notify appropriate congressional committee members of what was coming, and poor management of the press) that did not happen in previous times (Califano 1991, 259). This period included a special message from the president, "Health in America," the issue that Califano would focus on the most during the rest of his career in government service in the post-Johnson years, especially as secretary of health, education, and welfare under President Carter, and beyond.

Califano continued to handle the latest issue or crisis that arrived in the day's mail. On February 27, 1968, he was given an advance copy of the final report of the Kerner Commission, the name often used for the National Advisory Committee on Civil Disorders in reference to its weak (if loyal to LBJ) head, Illinois Democratic Governor Otto Kerner, but actually dominated by the very liberal Republican mayor of New York City, John Lindsey, whose thirst for federal money for his troubled city knew absolutely no bounds whatsoever. Califano was sure that Johnson would "erupt" with its harsh condemnations of white racism, indignant demands for "federal spending several orders of magnitude beyond what he had proposed," and relative minimizing of LBJ's accomplishments. Even the commission's most quoted sentence, "Our nation is moving toward two societies, one black one white— separate and unequal," was patently absurd to anyone familiar with the nation's past, which had obviously been far more separate and unequal than was the troubled present (Califano 1991, 260). Johnson's response to the report's eventual release in March was classic: a vague statement that the report would be circulated among appropriate authorities for study, a sure sign that it was going to be deep-sixed, even though Johnson was of course sympathetic to the commission's goals and even its attitude—had there been no Congress of the United States to deal with.

Sometime early in 1968 Califano began to consider his next career move, and came to the conclusion that he would not serve beyond the current administration, regardless of who the next president was. But he remained as committed as ever to Johnson, as trusted, and as effective, even in the face of externalities that augured poorly for the Great Society. A practicing Catholic, Califano observed that Johnson's attendance at mass increased in his last two years of office, from fourteen times in 1967 to nearly every other week in 1968, making Califano wonder if Johnson might consider following his daughter Luci into the Church (he did not ever take this step, remaining a Protestant). "Over time," Califano recalled, "the President talked more often about seeking guidance from the Almighty and praying. I had a sense that he found comfort in his relationship with God, particularly during his final year in office" (Califano 1991, 334). In accepting Califano's resignation, Johnson summed up the role of his chief domestic advisor during the busy and exciting years of the mid-1960s: "You were the captain I wanted and you steered the course well."

Joseph Califano remained an active presence in American life decades after his Great Society years. He wrote several well-researched memoirs of his government service, and returned to Washington to serve as President Carter's secretary of health, education, and welfare from 1977 to 1979, where his interests in health issues blossomed. In 1992 he founded the National Center on Addiction and Substance Abuse at Columbia University in New York City, serving for years as its president and chairman. His 2004 memoir, *Inside*, well summarized his Great Society years and after.

SARGENT SHRIVER
(1915–)

Sargent Shriver was not a Kennedy, but he did marry one, thereby joining and also becoming identified with one of the United States' greatest political clans of modern times. Though in terms of image the Kennedys seemed able to keep, at least for most of the twentieth century, one foot in their politically useful Irish Catholic, immigrant, upwardly striving success story ancestral past, the founding and succeeding generations of Kennedy public servants were even more seen as (and felt themselves to be) the personification of a kind of noblesse oblige gentry—American-style, of course: socially conscious people using their privileged position to advance the conditions and standing of their less fortunate fellow citizens. In a phrase, they turned themselves into American Roman Catholic aristocrats of the best sort. Sargent Shriver was more the real thing, a descendant of an ancient (by American standards) Roman Catholic family from Maryland, the English colony founded by Catholic convert Lord Baltimore originally to serve as a haven for Catholics. Maryland produced Founding Father Charles Carroll, the only Catholic to sign the Declaration of Independence, and the city of Baltimore became the mother church of American Catholicism, its first apostolic see, home of the first American to be named a cardinal, and producer of the Baltimore Catechism that instructed millions of American Catholics in the faith through the middle of the twentieth century.

A wide-ranging career in public service aided by his close family connections brought the already accomplished and well-regarded Sargent Shriver to Washington during the administration of his brother-in-law John F. Kennedy, where he served as the founding director of one of the greatest examples of early-1960s idealism and noblesse oblige on the part of the world's richest county, as well as creative Cold Warrior–ing: the new Peace Corps organization. Like Herbert Hoover, organizer par excellence of food relief efforts during and after World War I, had been to an earlier generation,

Shriver became identified with noble intentions actualized into practical humanitarianism in his creation and administration of the very well-received Peace Corps effort to capture the spirit of President Kennedy's 1961 inaugural address challenge, "Ask what you can do for your country." Given this pristine image, his administrative experience, and of course the fact that via his wife Eunice he was a Kennedy, Sargent Shriver seemed an ingenious choice on the part of President Johnson to become the man assigned to make the brand-new Office of Economic Opportunity, the Great Society's most radical and certainly its most controversial institution, into something that would marshall the forces needed to win the War on Poverty declared by the president in his 1964 State of the Union message. Though the task was beyond anyone's capability, Shriver struggled mightily to translate the ideas and catchphrases, most famously the opaque, endlessly debated "maximum feasible participation," into concrete, measurable progress. Despite finding enemies all around, Shriver, driven on by an eternal optimism grounded in a deeply sincere, lifelong religious faith and practice (he was a lifelong daily communicant) that sought, in the words of Mother Eleanor O'Byrne, to "do the truth in charity," and lacking any ego problem whatsoever, he battled disgruntled local governments, impatient radical activists, and skeptical media, and responded innovatively to new challenges (most lastingly in his Great Society program offering taxpayer-funded legal services to poor Americans, which became institutionalized), even while functioning as the man in the middle between two political enemies, Lyndon Johnson and U.S. Senator Robert F. Kennedy of New York. Sargent Shriver, against long odds and despite many trials, achieved many things as a Great Society warrior against poverty, but even a near-saintly figure such as he could not satisfy all of the continually rising expectations of the turbulent late 1960s.

Some of Sargent Shriver's forebears came to colonial America in the early 1700s, and his Founding Father ancestor David moved south of the Mason-Dixon Line from Pennsylvania into Maryland in the 1760s and established a mill, which still stood during Sargent Shriver's childhood. In 1820 one of David Shriver's grandsons married a Roman Catholic woman who raised their children as Catholics; one of these was Herbert, Sargent Shriver's grandfather, who served in the Maryland legislature as a Democrat; the Shrivers had been among the founders of the Maryland Democratic party. On November 9, 1915, Robert Sargent Shriver was born at home in Westminster, Maryland; both his parents were Shrivers who were each other's second cousins. Sargent Shriver was baptized by James Cardinal Gibbons, archbishop of Baltimore and former sometime roommate of his grandfather Herbert, and as a child assisted him at mass in the Shriver family chapel at Union Mills as altar boy. One of his earliest political memories was listening to radio coverage of the drawn-out 1924 Democratic National Convention, which went to the 103rd ballot before producing a nominee. The family moved to Baltimore in 1923 when his father took a job in banking; there,

Shriver continued his recently begun formal education in parochial schools. In 1929, his father moved the family to New York where he was a founding partner of a new investment bank, not a good move in the year of the great stock market crash. While financial problems plagued his parents, the family was hardly destitute, but in 1930 it was as a scholarship student that Shriver was enrolled in the Canterbury School of New Milford, Connecticut, a rare Roman Catholic top-flight New England preparatory boarding school. John F. Kennedy, one year younger than Shriver, was also a student there but transferred after only a year. Shriver's high school years were happy, and after graduating in 1934, he got his first exposure to the world beyond the United States, spending the summer in Germany under the auspices of a program called the Experiment in International Living, which promoted contact among people of different nations.

He matriculated at Yale University, then overwhelmingly populated by students of his social class and prep school background, in New Haven, Connecticut, in the fall of 1934; he again succeeded academically and socially, most significantly at the highly regarded *Yale Daily News*, of which he became chairman as a sophomore. After Shriver's graduation in 1938 with a bachelor's degree in English, a family friend offered to pay for law school, so he returned to New Haven that fall. A year later World War II began with the German invasion of Poland, and the issue of the day became whether or not the United States should become involved. Shriver joined the America First Committee, an isolationist group, but also signed up for the U.S. Naval Reserve. He was commissioned an ensign in September 1941, shortly after having taken the bar exam. He saw action in the south Pacific theater of World War II, eventually being awarded a Purple Heart and serving on a submarine. With the war over, Shriver returned to New York and began doing routine work for a law firm, which he quickly found tedious; Yale connections helped him get a job at *Newsweek* magazine in early 1946, at which point he also first met Eunice Kennedy, whom he was eventually to marry years later. Through her, he became connected to Joseph Kennedy, her father, who asked him his opinion (which was negative) on a manuscript he had prepared about his son, Joseph Kennedy, Jr., who during military service had died in a plane crash in 1944. Shriver's frankness did not at all offend Kennedy, and a week later the Kennedy family patriarch offered him a job with Joseph P. Kennedy Enterprises. Late in 1946, Kennedy asked Shriver to go to Chicago to supervise his newly purchased Merchandise Mart, an enormous facility that had been built by Marshall Field & Co. in 1930 but had never been profitable, and Shriver accepted. Chicago, which he had never even visited before, was to become his home and the Merchandise Mart his principal occupation for some twelve years.

In 1947, though, Shriver found himself in Washington, at Joseph Kennedy's request; Eunice Kennedy, twenty-five years of age, had accepted a government job in the U.S. Department of Justice as head of a newly organized Committee on Juvenile Delinquency (she had been working in Harlem), and her father asked Shriver to go assist his ambitious daughter for a while in her new effort. So, for the first time, Sargent Shriver was devoting his attention to a contemporary social problem, with a woman to whom he was attracted. Both were soon frustrated at how slowly things proceeded within the federal bureaucracy, and so they resigned in June 1948, forming a private committee to continue addressing the juvenile delinquency problem, and organizing numerous conferences to foster discussion and exchange on the topic. Ideas that would later characterize Shriver's Great Society initiatives were evident: thinking big, antibureaucracy, and the coordination of public and private efforts adding up to "joint community action" (Stossel 2004, 102). Shriver returned to pick up work at the Merchandise Mart in the summer of 1948; Eunice Kennedy moved to the same building in which Shriver lived in 1950. After they both worked on the successful 1952 Massachusetts senatorial campaign of Eunice's brother John, early in 1953, they decided to marry; the wedding took place at St. Patrick's Cathedral, New York City, on May 23, 1953, Francis Cardinal Spellman officiating.

As a successful and well-connected Chicago businessman, Sargent Shriver was naturally often asked to participate in civic life, and did so to an extraordinary degree. In 1952 he accepted the chairmanship of the school committee of the city's prointegration Catholic Interracial Council, and then became its president in 1955. In 1954 his attempt to gain Eunice Kennedy Shriver a seat on the Chicago School Board had inadvertently led to his name, rather than hers, being chosen; he served for six years, during which time he gained favorable reviews for his hard work and openness to experimentation and innovation. Integrating city schools, given Chicagoans' often intense neighborhood identification, which of course could coexist with and overlap racial fears, proved very difficult. Shriver's continuing interest in civil rights led to his participation as a board member of the new National Catholic Conference for Interracial Justice, a group that would be one of the ten official cosponsors of the 1963 civil rights March on Washington.

In 1959, the political ambitions of the Kennedys led Sargent Shriver to give up his civil leadership posts in order to go to work for the presidential campaign of his brother-in-law, John F. Kennedy. Among other tasks, he was put in charge of creating a civil rights division for the campaign. In 1956, Dwight Eisenhower had attracted about 40 percent of the black vote, the highest for a Republican since before the New Deal. On the other hand, the Solid South was still a huge part of the Democratic party's electoral coalition, and a backlash to the *Brown* decision of 1954 outlawing state-sponsored school segregation had reinforced the historical white supremacist tendencies of many (and, in some states, nearly all) southern Democratic political leaders. Shriver helped organize voter registration efforts for the now very substantial black population outside of the South, and it was he who first communicated the idea to John F. Kennedy that he call Martin Luther

King, Jr., who had been jailed in Georgia on minor charges, as an expression of sympathy. This act played very well in the national media and was especially helpful in gaining the support of some black southern ministers, most famously Martin L. King, Sr., who had objected to Kennedy's Roman Catholicism. Given his business experience, Shriver was a natural to work on the Business for Kennedy section of the campaign, too. Kennedy narrowly won the election.

Because his brother-in-law had favorably impressed him during the campaign, as well as due to his wide-ranging connections and contacts, John F. Kennedy asked Sargent Shriver to play a major role in staffing the new administration—his first experience with the high levels of the federal government. He performed well but was not interested in a position for himself, intending to return home to Illinois, in part due to his interest in running for office there. JFK believed, however, that his sister Eunice would want to be in Washington during his administration. President Kennedy therefore called Shriver on January 21, 1961, the second day of his administration, requesting his brother-in-law to head a task force on the Peace Corps, an idea that he had almost casually mentioned as a candidate but that, given its favorable reception, he had decided to make into something, although exactly what he did not know. Shriver agreed, using his many connections and his personal, informal style to do the job; he once described his modus operandi as trying "to get bright, informative, creative people and then pick their brains" (quoted in Stossel 2004, 197). As the work proceeded, Shriver's strong streak of practical idealism was energized. He agreed with those who felt that the Peace Corps needed to think big and bold, not be a minor experiment somewhere in the bowels of the federal establishment. Meetings, wherein Shriver encouraged and moderated freewheeling discussion and debate, continued through February 1961; this continued to be Shriver's way of doing things in the Great Society years, too. On the 24th, he submitted to the president his recommendation that a Peace Corps with institutional autonomy be established at once. Shriver's report was in line with the thinking that he and Eunice Kennedy had expressed in the late 1940s on juvenile delinquency and that he would again push during the Great Society years with "community action": the Peace Corps needed to be "a cooperative venture of the whole American people—not the program of some alphabetical agency in Washington" (205). Shriver found he had to sell the proposal to Kennedy's advisors, and successfully did so; on March 1st, the Peace Corps was created by executive order. By now, it proved not to be difficult for President Kennedy to talk his brother-in-law into assuming the new organization's directorship. With Shriver's energy and dedication, the Peace Corps grew rapidly.

Naturally, there were some problems, the first major one being the opposition on the part of sectors of the federal government's foreign policy establishment to the Peace Corps's independence. Shriver, through contacts, was able to get Vice President Lyndon Johnson to intercede, successfully, with the president, thereby raising his esteem for the Texan. Shriver spent much of the summer of 1961 lobbying members of Congress, many of whom were skeptical or worse, to gain support for the Peace Corps, making many new contacts and new favorable impressions; on September 22, the Peace Corps Act was signed by the president. Shriver's relations with Congress continued to be good—he actually underspent his budgets and returned surpluses (Stossel 2004, 274).

Jacqueline Kennedy asked Sargent Shriver to be in charge of President Kennedy's funeral after his assassination on November 22, 1963, and so the many details of that difficult task fell to her fellow Kennedy in-law. And right away, the new president sought Shriver's advice about such issues of detail as how soon he should take possession of the Oval Office in the White House. Shriver also worked to assure the Peace Corps community that Johnson was in fact a great friend of theirs. Then and in the next few weeks, Johnson made it clear to Shriver that he needed him and hoped to make great use of his talents, and also fostered press speculation as to exactly what position Shriver might fill.

Sargent Shriver was out of the country on an extended trip in the Middle East and points beyond when President Johnson, in his State of the Union address of January 8, 1964, issued his famous declaration of the War on Poverty. The Kennedy administration's modest groundwork in this area had taken place far from the bright lights of Washington press conferences. Shriver's name had been suggested to the president as a potential salesman for the program on Capitol Hill (Stossel 2004, 342). Shriver learned in late January, in Hawaii, his final stop before his return to the mainland, what Johnson had in store for him. Two very large briefing books were handed to him, filled with information on the coming War on Poverty. Shriver was also told that Johnson had tapped him as the man to run the antipoverty program. A car was waiting for him at the airport in Washington on January 31, and he was soon face-to-face with the president and subject to the Johnson treatment, appealing to Shriver's idealism and stressing the great need for a sort of Peace Corps effort within the United States to address the difficulties of what author Michael Harrington had called the "other America." LBJ gave Shriver more material to take home, and then the next day blind-sided him with word that he was that very afternoon going to announce Shriver's appointment at a press conference. Shriver objected that he was no poverty expert; what would he say to the press, and what about the Peace Corps? Johnson gave assurances across the board but was insistent that Shriver become his "Mr. Poverty, at home and abroad, if you want it to be. . . . I want you to get rid of poverty. . . . You'll have an international Peace Corps—one abroad and one at home" (348). Eunice Shriver's positive comments on the position helped settle Shriver down.

What, exactly, was Johnson asking Shriver to do? There had been an *ann-*

ouncement of a War on Poverty, but there was no battle plan, no content to speak of, and certainly nothing concrete—similar to the situation involving the expression "Peace Corps" in January 1961. Johnson's secret Oval Office tape-recording system recorded his charge to Shriver later that evening: "Now you've got to see how in the hell you're going to administer this thing. Then, you're going to have to have to get that bill and that message together . . . you'll have more influence in the administration than any man in it. You'll have a billion dollars to pass out. . . . The sky's the limit. You just make this thing work, period. I don't give a damn about the details . . . this is number one on the domestic front. Next to peace in the world, this is the most important" (quoted in Stossel 2004, 352).

If anyone could fulfill this seemingly impossible task, Shriver, with years of civic-mindedness, contacts, governmental experience in new programming, and family and spiritual resources, was surely as good a candidate to fill the bill as any. The day after the announcement, Shriver had already been able to assemble not only presidential economic advisor Walter Heller and others who had been involved in the formulation of the State of the Union address's "war declaration," but also several potential task force members, including Frank Makiewicz, whom Shriver knew through Peace Corps connections and who himself knew Michael Harrington. At this meeting Shriver learned of the "community action" concept that had been developed beforehand, which seemed familiar enough; as he recalled later, "Community action—which the people in Community Action thought was so revolutionary—was something we had been running in the Peace Corps for four years before it ever got into the War on Poverty. So I thought Community Action was absolutely sort of normal" (quoted in Stossel 2004, 357). It even could be said to fit the states'-rights, local-control kind of tradition that had a time-honored place in American history.

Familiarity, however, did not mean belief in political viability or sufficiency. Poverty often (but far from always) resulted from lack of employment, just as it had during the Great Depression, a period of mass unemployment. Now that "pockets" of poverty were being newly brought to light, any antipoverty program worthy of the name would have to have a solid jobs and training component, something he had considered back in Chicago in the 1950s when, as school board president, he had become familiar with the depressingly large number of deficient-in-skills, and hence unemployable, "products" of the Chicago school system. Ideas were needed. They began to be generated in meetings held at Shriver's Rockville, Maryland, mansion, starting two days later, on February 4, and continuing day and night for a couple of weeks. Dozens of people participated in an atmosphere filled with expectation and hopefulness, though tempered by years of political and social experience. Available poverty *knowledge* turned out to be surprisingly slight. Shriver reached out to people, coordinated the conversations, and kept them moving, knowing that Johnson demanded a real proposal very soon. Shriver had recruited Adam Yarmolinsky, known to be hard-nosed and skeptical, from the U.S. Department of Defense right from the start.

While fostering open debate, Shriver, who was now, thanks to his Peace Corps experience, versed in the ways of Washington, was willing to be insistent on the necessity of thinking and acting big, for instance advising one participant to "add another zero" to his proposal (from $30 million to $300 million) (Stossel 2004, 364). "Community action" proved to be an ambiguous term. Given the extraordinarily negative view of existing state and local welfare departments that prevailed, a key to the appeal of community action was its potential to act outside of the existing welfare order and not be "captured" by it. As to *who* exactly constituted a given "community," and *how* decisions were to be made regarding "action," the phrase that was come up with was "maximum feasible participation," reasonably ambiguous and later to be infamous.

The outcome of the meetings Shriver put together and directed was spectacularly successful: in less than a month, a bill providing for the domestic version of the Peace Corps called Volunteers in Service to America (VISTA), the creation of local Community Action organizations (whose functions were not sharply defined), the Job Corps (mostly training), the Neighborhood Youth Corps (low-skill, temporary, government-funded jobs for the hard-core, near-unemployable youth), and more were put into the proposed Economic Opportunity Act, which also created the new, freestanding government agency, the Office of Economic Opportunity (OEO). As to exactly what the OEO would have control over, the bureaucratic turf wars produced this outcome: the OEO retained a general coordinating authority over all of the programs in the law but actual operating authority over VISTA, the Job Corps, and Community Action. That would prove to be more than enough for starters, though other important and long-lasting Great Society programs would soon emerge out of Shriver's bailiwick.

The Economic Opportunity Act would exist on paper; what would it be in the real world? March 1964 saw more task force work orchestrated by Shriver. He sought to reach out to business leaders, initially through Vernon Alden, a Harvard Business School graduate who served as president of Ohio University in Athens, Ohio, with many corporate contacts. Unlike some poverty warriors, Shriver held no animus toward business; he responded enthusiastically to a suggestion that corporations be encouraged to submit bids to run Job Corps centers, helped make that happen, and was not surprised when the business-run centers tended to fare better than those run by others such as universities. Openness to experimentation was especially important given that, in reality, no one seemed to *know* how to deal with hard-core unemployed young people for whom traditional schooling had not worked. Johnson saw political trouble in allowing the private administration of taxpayer money, but submitted to Shriver's optimism as well as his argument that a willingness to experience the shock of the new was central to the War on Poverty spirit (Stossel 2004, 375–76).

Five months of politically serious lobbying by Shriver and others ensued, in which "Mr. Poverty" stressed that the aim was the fostering of opportunity, the "hand up" rather than "handout" (Patterson 1996, 535). There was much to overcome: possible partisan Republican opposition, especially in the more conservative House of Representatives; and potential opposition on the part of many white southern Democrats, who still constituted virtually the entire southern congressional delegation, who, reeling from the 1964 Civil Rights Act's debate and passage in July, might see the Economic Opportunity Act as a close cousin, especially given that its benefits would disproportionately go to black people (given that they were disproportionately poor). What if "community action" meant money to independent community groups who just happened to be black-controlled? The biggest surprise in the campaign to enact the Economic Opportunity Act was the successful recruitment of Representative Phil Landrum of Georgia, a southern Democrat and member of the House Education and Labor Committee, as a cosponsor. Along with White House aide Lawrence O'Brien, Shriver was able to talk Landrum into the pivotal role of introducing the bill to the House. Shriver himself testified in the committee hearings phase and helped line up an impressive array of witnesses, including many officeholders hopeful of receiving large amounts of money from Washington to deal with their local situations. On May 26, the bill was favorably reported out of committee on a party-line vote (19–11). By that time, President Johnson's Great Society commencement address in Ann Arbor had been delivered, further defining the idealistic context in which the bill would be considered. The Senate Labor and Public Welfare Committee was a much easier hurdle to cross; after brief hearings, the bill was favorably reported out of this committee on July 7 and approved on a roll call vote on July 23, 61–34. When it came to House passage, Shriver's years of fostering good, respectful relationships with House leaders and members, including those philosophically disinclined to support increased federal power, helped get the bill through with only minor amendments. In a deal that indicated Shriver's understanding of and willingness to play the sometimes dirty game of politics for a perceived greater good, he agreed, reluctantly and after fighting long and hard, to "purge" from the antipoverty program one of the chief participants in the task forces whose work had resulted in the bill's creation, Adam Yarmolinsky, which, in one of the periodic fits of irrationality that sometimes break out on Capitol Hill, had become the price that had to be paid because Yarmolinsky had, erroneously and perhaps due to his "foreign-sounding" name and New York background, been labeled a radical (he returned to working at the Pentagon). The Economic Opportunity Act was signed by President Johnson on August 20, 1964.

Now came the *really* hard part: implementation. Amazingly, Shriver re-

mained head of the Peace Corps, which certainly continued to absorb a noticeable amount of his time and remained his very own baby. Yarmolinsky's
sharp questioning of proposals was to be missed at the new Office of Economic Opportunity, and no one of his stature ever appeared to function as
in-house critic. October 19, 1964, was Shriver's first day as director of the
OEO—only a few weeks before LBJ's landslide election win, which also
brought in a more liberal, activist, and Democratic Congress. Meetings of
program leaders took place on Monday, Wednesday, and Friday mornings to
discuss progress in setting up their particular areas and what they planned
to do next. All present were invited by Shriver to critique these reports in an
effort to set them on the best, most thought-through paths. As described by
historian Alice O'Connor, these meetings "became the ultimate test of
toughness for the predominantly male OEO leadership, where individual
presentations would be subjected to 'the roughest tests of imaginativeness,
feasibility, efficiency, praticality, and political salability that his closest associates could devise.' For Shriver, sharpest of all in the cross-examination, the
meetings were also essential tools for planning, generating new ideas, and
making major policy decisions" (O'Connor 2001, 168). Before the end of
November, Shriver could announce that 119 grants had been awarded to projects in thirty-three states. The pace picked up with two more rounds of an-
nouncements by mid-January 1965, involving $100 million and close to 400
programs (Stossel 2004, 396). *Announcing* the *awarding* of money for a
project was still not making the project work. Rapidly in 1965, the news
media began reporting trouble in some of the Job Corps centers and rural-
based camps, which were somewhat modeled on the New Deal–era Civilian
Conservation Corps camps (and sometimes actually used the same sites).
Getting the camps off the ground rapidly, Shriver was sure, was necessary to
create momentum, as had been the case with the Peace Corps, and, it was
hoped, garner initial favorably publicity. Shriver's "guesstimates" before
Congress in the hearings of the previous summer proved so wildly optimistic
that he presided over "Operation 10,000," a stepped-up recruiting effort.
Shriver himself recruited many youth culture celebrities to pitch the Job
Corps to its intended audience. The number 10,000 was, with difficulty, just
barely achieved by the last day of June. It was a case of too much, too fast,
with too little quality control and way, way too little planning and attention
to nuts-and-bolts issues and details. The media reported these shortcomings,
which were all too real and were resulting in a rapid and large drop-away
from the new programs. As the summer progressed, there were also incidents of violence and even rioting at some centers; bad news tended to drown
out good, which was far more subtle and longer term anyway.

   A large part of the problem lay in unrealistic expectations across the
board, especially remembering that "poverty" had been far off the national
agenda since World War II had begun. Shortly after Johnson had declared
war on poverty in January 1964, a Gallup poll revealed that 83 percent of

the public did not believe such a war could be won (Margolis 2000, 134). The doubters and skeptics responded to the negative reports, and the image was set for many. Meanwhile, Shriver terminated the contracts of the most poorly run job centers—most of them run by universities—and made more contracts with businesses such as General Electric, International Business Machines (IBM), and Westinghouse (Matusow 1984, 237). Job Corps participation tripled to some 30,000 by the summer of 1966, and incidents declined radically; serious incidents virtually disappeared (Stossel 2004, 401). However, the high cost per Job Corpsman proved distressing to members of Congress (Matusow 1984, 238).

The Job Corps was, of course, not all there was to Shriver's OEO. Community Action had to be transformed from concept to actuality. The appeal of federal funds to local governments has always been obvious enough: "free" money to allot toward various local needs, never in short supply, without arousing the ire of local taxpayers. Originally, most applications for funding new Community Actions agencies (CAAs, usually written as CAPs, meaning Community Action programs) came from groups reflecting local power structures, usually including duly elected officials, especially mayors. Given that Shriver was anxious to get as many CAAs up and running as possible, most applications, following meetings between the supplicants and Shriver in Washington, were provisionally approved (no formal, bureaucratic guidelines yet existing) with a proviso that the "participation" of those to be served—the poor—be increased as the programs unfolded. But even before 1964 was over, Shriver was beginning to receive many letters of protest from mainstream groups like the National Association for the Advancement of Colored People (NAACP), complaining that "participation" by the affected populations had been sorely lacking. The protests gathered steam as 1965 rolled around and application numbers rose. In some places, alternative CAAs, that is, not involving the local government or political establishment, were filed. The OEO, seeking consensus, would invite competing groups from a given city to Washington, and achieved some success over time. But time could be of the essence, due to roused expectations, and consensus building not only meant delays but also was, of course, not always successful, with losers often finding ways to fight back and gain publicity. Mayors began writing President Johnson to complain. Mayor Richard Daley of Chicago (father of the present mayor) made no effort at all to include *any* "participation" outside of his well-organized and infamous political patronage machine, and called President Johnson personally to "inform" him of how the OEO seemed to want him to fund "subversives" who might challenge his Cook County Democratic party organization, pivotal to hopes for Democratic electoral success in politically closely divided Illinois. Shriver, of course, knew Daley and Chicago; the OEO regional official who had initiated the complaint against Mayor Daley's CAA was fired and replaced by a black machine loyalist, and Shriver rejected complaints over the outcome, even declaring Chicago's CAA the model of the country (Cohen and Taylor 2000, 343–44). The climax came in May 1965 at the annual meeting of the then–highly publicized U.S. Conference of Mayors, when two California Democrats, Los Angeles Mayor Samuel Yorty and San Francisco Mayor John Shelley, proposed a resolution criticizing the OEO for its "maximum feasible participation" requirement, which they presented as a threat to democratically elected local government. Yorty, whom Shriver had been pressuring, attacked "Mr. Poverty" by name: "Mayors all over the United States are being harassed by agitation promoted by Sargent Shriver's speeches urging those he calls 'poor' to insist upon control of local poverty programs" (quoted in Stossel 2004, 405). Johnson sent Vice President Hubert Humphrey to assure the mayors that their concerns would be addressed. Shriver, though he had been surprised by the intensity of the conflict, was no political naïf by any means, and made early-course adjustments, including far more attention to CAA grant applications at the Washington level, including a personal review by himself in each case. What happened in Syracuse, New York, in late 1965 demonstrated the political realities: a Community Action grant to the Syracuse Community Development Association, after bitter complaints by the elected government of the City of Syracuse that reached LBJ's own desk, was subsumed under a new CAA, the Syracuse Crusade for Opportunity, made up principally of the city government and the traditional welfare agencies. Angry activists got a meeting with Shriver in December 1965, but not an overturning of the decision (Matusow 1984, 252). Saul Alinsky, a Chicago-based radical of long standing who became a nationally known radical theorist in the 1960s and had served as a consultant to the now-dethroned Syracuse Community Development Association, sounded like a born-again right-winger in denouncing the War on Poverty as "the greatest boondoggle and feeding trough that's come along for the welfare industry for years" (Stossel 2004, 408).

The OEO had an Office of Plans, Progress, and Evaluations that went about its business as best it could, but the trend was clear; for instance, it dutifully reported to Shriver that an Atlanta CAA called Economic Opportunity, Atlanta, headed up by a white foundation leader and insider Democrat, Boisfeuillet Jones, had no meaningful "participation" from the poor and precious little genuine "community organizing" going on; however, Shriver, basing on his estimation of political reality, overruled the recommended cutting off of funds (Matusow 1984, 255–56). And on December 6, 1965, Shriver was back in Chicago to speak at a War on Poverty conference organized by Mayor Richard Daley, defending the "establishment" even as outside protesters denounced the War on Poverty as a "fraud" (Cohen and Taylor 2000, 345).

Shriver, with his faith, optimistic nature, and insider's perspective, was far from discouraged about the OEO's prospects. It was experiencing birth pangs and needed feeding to continue developing and growing up. He proposed to Johnson that the OEO's budget be steadily increased over the next few years, with more emphasis on job creation and social service provision (Matusow 1984, 251). He was seriously interested in the idea known as the negative income tax, which meant a guaranteed income, but continued to insist to the president that the War on Poverty's emphasis remained "altering society so poor people are able to raise *themselves* above the poverty level through their *own* efforts" (quoted in Davies 1996, 102). Johnson was skeptical overall, but, still attracted to the vision, promised that once Vietnam was "over," funding would go up significantly for the OEO. Johnson, a lifetime professional politician, was responsive to continuing criticism of the OEO and especially "maximum feasible participation." A brief flap ensued between Shriver and Charles Schultze, Budget Bureau director for the White House, who opposed maximum feasible participation, while Shriver publicly defended it. Johnson was worried about the 1966 midterm congressional elections, as well as Vietnam, and was increasingly willing to believe that the maximum feasible participation concept had originated from partisans of Robert Kennedy, with whom he had long had poor relations and whom he increasingly viewed as a potential political rival for the Democratic presidential nomination of 1968. At times he wondered even about Shriver's loyalty, but in the end kept him on, justly believing in Shriver's continued commitment and loyalty to him as well as to the Great Society's War on Poverty.

Despite these troubles, Shriver the Great Society innovator remained open to and potentially enthusiastic about other ideas. He came up with a real winner at the same time the above controversies were swirling: Head Start, the federally funded, compensatory pre-elementary childhood enrichment program, similar to kindergarten, that became a long-term Great Society survivor. (In 1965, publicly funded kindergartens were still unusual in the United States.) Eunice Kennedy Shriver brought to his attention early-1960s studies suggesting the salutary possibilities of "early intervention" into an underprivileged child's life. His wife woke up memories of his Chicago School Board service, where he had learned of the large numbers of arriving first graders who were woefully unprepared for school. Politically, Shriver believed, the idea would be widely popular. So in early 1965 he convened thirteen people to come up with a proposal, which took the form of a seven-page memorandum presented to Shriver on February 19, 1966. A couple of days later, the name "Head Start" came out of an extended, idea-sharing meeting presided over by Shriver. Head Start was to be the first "national emphasis" CAA, coming out of Washington though administered by local CAAs. Shriver's bias remained to "think big," and so he and his colleagues came up with a proposal for an eight-week program for the coming summer of 1965 involving 100,000 children. Not only would the program prove its worth, but additionally, it would gain favorable publicity for the War on Poverty as a whole. An experienced publicity man dating back from his days at the Merchandise Mart, Shriver decided to enlist the first lady, Lady Bird Johnson, who enthusiastically agreed to host a White House tea on February 12, 1965, primarily attended by distinguished women. The plan succeeded in gaining widespread coverage, including on the "society" pages of newspapers, and a favorable response (Stossel 2004, 423). In response to Shriver's mass mailing of invitations, hundred of applications came to the OEO; staffing greatly increased, supplemented by willing volunteers for such a noble-sounding initiative. In response to another Shriver appeal, over 200 universities offered to organize training sessions in June to prepare people to work in the Head Start summer programs. Shriver had originally conceived of 100,000 children as "thinking big"; the actual number proved to be 500,000, and what had been conceptualized as a summer program almost immediately was transformed into a year-round effort. Despite the inevitable problems in some places, and despite a scholarly debate that soon ensued and has long continued as to whether or not Head Start had much *lasting* effect, the Great Society had hit a home run. Head Start became a part of the United States. Spending grew and the programs developed along lines similar to preschools.

Sargent Shriver's other big idea, which became the second National Emphasis program, also proved to be a permanent one: Legal Services for the Poor. The idea had first come to Shriver's attention in April 1964, during the planning stages for the Economic Opportunity Act, after reading an article in the *Yale Law Journal* proposing that legal services be one offering of neighborhood centers (Stossel 2004, 433). A long-standing, though limited, tradition of legal aid societies constituted the existing world that Shriver sought to improve; as it seemed unlikely that such groups would promote their own demise, Shriver looked to the American Bar Association, believing that if this professional association, along with local bar associations, could be brought around to the concept of legal services for the poor, that would virtually in and of itself do the trick. On February 7, 1965, the ABA endorsed the concept; Shriver had successfully stressed the ordinary legal services (and the fees to be gained, paid for by taxpayers) that would constitute the overwhelming traffic of "poverty lawyers," omitting some of the more radical uses to which Legal Services for the Poor might be—and were—put in future years, such as suing city governments. Legal Services really began to get off the ground in 1966. In 1967, Shriver made it policy that Legal Services was to seek "law reform," thus giving a clear green light to a "test case" strategy seeking the judicial establishment of defined rights for the poor. As time went by, criticism of this use of Legal Services rose—especially since its lawyers won most of their cases against the Establishment—but Shriver remained wedded to it. Another initiative launched at the same time, Comprehensive Health Servces Programs, led to the creation of several dozen federally funded Neighborhood Health Services centers.

With the deployment of hundreds of thousands of troops to Vietnam after the commencement of ground combat operations by U.S. forces in 1965, and with the rising "backlash" in the country, largely in response to televised scenes of urban rioting, money became harder to come by for the Great Society, including Sargent Shriver's OEO. Furthermore, as Shriver went to Capitol Hill in the spring of 1966 to testify on behalf of budget requests for the coming fiscal year, he encountered continued criticism, even from some liberal Democrats. The Democrat-controlled Education and Labor Committee of the House favorably reported out the moderately increased OEO budget the Johnson administration had requested, but with an amendment restricting the Community Action program (Stossel 2004, 456). In April, Shriver was to deliver the keynote address for the new Citizens' Crusade against Poverty, an initiative of Walter Reuther and his United Automobile Workers union. His speech, however, which reflected as usual his positive, optimistic, and hopeful view, was rudely interrupted in a planned way in its middle by angry members of the audience, to such a degree that he stopped and walked off the platform; the meeting collapsed (Matusow 1984, 254). Back on Capitol Hill, a Republican member successfully proposed an amendment to the OEO budget authorization bill defining "participation" by the poor as one-third of a CAA board's membership, chosen by vote among "the poor" themselves. The final bill was also well below what Shriver and his OEO leaders had viewed as the irreducible minimum for the OEO to continue to gain any momentum at all.

In November 1966, the midterm congressional elections swung against the Democrats, especially in the House of Representatives, though they retained control; additionally, a closer look at the returns revealed the election of a number of new Republican senators who were by no means entirely hostile to the spirit of the Great Society. At a press conference later in November, Sargent Shriver, far from acting like his usual optimistic self, stated, in moderately guarded yet, for Washington, reasonably frank terms, what would become the conventional wisdom of many in the ensuing decades: the War on Poverty was well on its way to being lost because it was not only being underfunded (with the exception of the wildly popular Head Start), it was being *grossly* underfunded: "In summary, congressional action has curtailed the War on Poverty in 1,000 communities of America for fiscal 1967. And hundreds of additional communities, especially in rural America, will be unable to join the battle" (quoted in Stossel 2004, 460). When, shortly thereafter, Shriver learned of further huge increases in spending for the Vietnam War, he tendered his resignation, delivered to Johnson at the LBJ Ranch on December 19, 1966. After a meeting with the president, Shriver rescinded his resignation, convinced that, despite the many setbacks and the encircling gloom, there was still life in the Great Society's War on Poverty yet.

1967 proved him right. President Johnson, though with no particular visible enthusiasm or effectiveness, had called for increased OEO funding in his January State of the Union address. Encouraged by White House aide Joseph

Califano, Shriver and his OEO colleagues committed themselves to lobbying the new, presumably more skeptical Congress on behalf of their War on Poverty initiatives and programs. As had been the case in previous crusades, Shriver spent an inordinate number of hours on Capitol Hill in the summer of 1967 as Congress held hearings on the OEO's efforts to date. Large numbers of witnesses testified favorably as to Community Action programs of various sorts. But another "long, hot summer" of urban unrest and rioting led to charges, for instance by Mayor Hugh Addonizio of Newark, that some CAAs had whipped up discontent to the point of virtually encouraging rioting. Shriver in response ordered a review to see if there were any basis to such charges, and issued a policy statement to OEO regional directors that money was to be immediately cut off from any CAA that either appeared to encourage or tolerated civil disorder. Testifying before a House Committee on July 31, 1967, however, Shriver reminded the representatives of the root causes of the disturbances: "After the riots began, voices of reason and order swiftly announced: 'We will not tolerate violence. We will not permit lawlessness.' And they are right. But there are voices that say, 'We cannot, as a nation, tolerate the conditions that produce violence and lawlessness.' And they are right, too" (quoted in Stossel 2004, 473). He also reported that his investigation had shown, and he produced testimonies from many local officials in corroboration, that CAAs had played calming, constructive roles in the cities that had suffered from civil disturbances. In another example of his efforts, Shriver wrote Republican Congressman George Bush of Texas that the OEO was "not an anti-riot agency," but rather was "directed at long-range solutions to the basic causes of poverty" (quoted in Davies 1996, 196).

But some members of the House of Representatives, most significantly the respected veteran Oregon Democrat Edith Green, remained unhappy with CAAs and any sense or hint that rioting would "pay off" by increasing federal antipoverty funding in a particular area hit by civil disorder. Far from Washington, however, the riots had indeed generated a wave of support from local governments fearing they might be hit next by rioting. Shriver was successful in getting Republican mayors to join the chorus of praise for OEO-funded antipoverty efforts. And though the OEO publicly opposed Congresswoman Green's amendment to its authorization bill for fiscal year 1968 that required state or local government officials to be in control of all CAAs, subject to "broad federal direction," and that a full one-third of the membership of each CAA board be elected public officials, in reality Shriver fully accepted the amendment as politically necessary and actually was helpful in getting the OEO reauthorization through at least a survivable level (Stossel 2004, 477).

All of the efforts paid off: the OEO achieved the increased budget requested by Johnson, authorized for two fiscal years no less, and without any real hampering of its control. Nor were its more popular programs such as Head Start "spun off" to other areas of the federal bureaucracy, thus potentially leaving the OEO behind as an ugly duckling in danger of future execution. It was a political achievement in which Sargent Shriver played a big role. However, the overall lay of the landscape remained daunting; there was every sign that the Great Society's War on Poverty "moment" had passed, and no sign of getting it back on a growth curve. This was underscored when Shriver met with Johnson at the president's Texas ranch early in 1968, before the State of the Union address. The OEO's budget was to be reduced, money being shifted into politically more palatable areas including jobs schemes and riot prevention. Both Johnson and Shriver knew the end was now near. The president offered him the ambassadorship to France, and after receiving advice from Rose Fitzgerald Kennedy, the family matriarch, he decided to accept the position, so informed Johnson in March, and was sworn in on May 7.

Sargent Shriver, after his well-earned two-year tour of duty in Paris, continued his long career of public and political service for the rest of the twentieth century, filling in as the vice presidential candidate for the doomed Democratic party ticket of 1972, unsuccessfully seeking the Democratic presidential nomination in 1976, and, most significantly, helping Eunice Kennedy Shriver found and nurture the phenomenal international Special Olympics movement, receiving many honors along the way, including the nation's highest civilian honor, the Presidential Medal of Freedom (as did Eunice Kennedy Shriver making them the only married couple both so honored). Given that he was diagnosed with Alzheimer's disease, it may be that his last big public appearance was, somewhat incongruously, on September 7, 2003, onstage with his Republican son-in-law Arnold Schwarzenegger, who had just been elected governor of California.

MARTIN LUTHER KING, JR.
(1929–1968)

While Billy Graham has often been called the nation's preacher, Reverend Martin Luther King, Jr., though even more famous than his fellow Baptist for his public speaking skills, could never have well fit such a role, even had he lived beyond 1968. For while Reverend Graham consistently preached a gospel of individual, personal repentance and salvation, a pure-and-simple evangelical Christianity, King personified the social gospel tradition of American Protestantism, stressing a vision of social transformation via applied Christian ethics in his frequent preaching to both church and also to well-placed, highly influential (especially in terms of national media attention) secular audiences. A son of the (first-generation) educated, professional black middle class of Atlanta, King grew up with the slights of the southern segregation situation never far away, despite a relatively sheltered existence in a mostly self-contained black world of high achievement and aspiration. He was therefore dually educated both in the promise of the United States' ideals and also its failures to live up to them fully. After experiencing a classic Baptist calling, he headed for his father's (and grandfather's, and great-grandfather's) profession, the Christian ministry, going north to receive advanced theological training and thereby immersing himself into a broader, and nonsegregated, world. When Providence took him to Montgomery, Alabama, just in time for the celebrated act of civil disobedience on the part of Mrs. Rosa Parks, followed by the organized and sustained boycott by the Montgomery Improvement Association, King, at the very young age of twenty-six, was suddenly, almost miraculously thrown into the spotlight, first locally and then, very rapidly, nationally. In all humility he soon came to see his role as public spokesman for the boycott as divinely ordained, and it put him on a path toward greatness from which there was to be no turning back. By the time the term "Great Society" began to enjoy general circulation, Martin Luther King, Jr., had for some time been by far the most famous and also most highly respected of all black Americans and one of the most influential Americans in the world. At the same time, to be sure, entrenched and powerful forces in the South viewed him as anathema and remained determined to resist him and his movement. But King sought to overcome. In keeping with the developing spirit of the Great Society, King was not at all satisfied with rather modest and often symbolic, if highly significant, gains, and rapidly moved beyond such specific civil rights issues as nondiscrimination in employment and public accommodations toward the more general issue of poverty in the contemporary United States and what could be done about it, specifically and especially by the federal government. He heartily agreed with Lyndon Johnson's 1965 Howard University commencement address that called for equality not as opportunity, but as fact and result. Martin Luther King, Jr., embodied the respectability of the aspiring black middle class, especially in contrast to the rising tide of youthful black militancy as seen in the black power movement. King's influence with the sometimes vaguely well-meaning Establishment, both reformist liberal and more cautiously moderate, thus rose ever higher, even, ironically, as he became decidedly more radical in his publicly asserted views as to what ailed modern American society and what was needed to deal with these ailments. Far from satisfied with mere "respectability," King continued to ponder the question of the status of black Americans in the wider society, and so he responded enthusiastically to President Johnson's call for a Great Society by broadening his critique of U.S. society, a critique only reinforced by his temporary sojourn up north in Chicago, where he met angry protests and violence. This sadly educational experience for him as to the varieties of intergroup dynamics among the United States' diverse people sent a clear message: while King's moral authority seemed close to unquestioned among many powerful elements of society, this was far from the case when it came to the general population across the board, and not just Klansmen, either. The moral message of King's Deep South–based civil rights effort, extended and broadened into the Great Society crusade, proved to be far less transferable to the very different situation of the urban North. And the open criticism by King of the Johnson administration's policies in Vietnam harmed his relationship with the White House, even as the Great Society seemed to be tottering and as King's own date with tragedy drew ever nearer. He had a dream, and he had been to the mountaintop, but, as he himself so prophetically intoned on the eve of his assassination, he did not live to enter the Promised Land.

Martin Luther King, Jr., entered this world on January 15, 1929, in Atlanta. Two years later his father assumed the pastorate of the Ebenezer Baptist Church, taking the reins from his father-in-law. Family, church, and school were the solid pillars of his childhood and beyond. At the age of five he entered public school and thrived there. Two years at a private high school affiliated with Atlanta University, whose constituent schools included his father's alma mater, Morehouse College, were followed by his completion in 1944 at age fifteen of his precollege training at Booker T. Washington High School, the first public high school for blacks in the State of Georgia. Having already won several oratorical contests, then very popular, he continued to study and practice public speaking in college. Attracted by Atlanta University's great tradition of sociology, the public-minded King gravitated toward that subject and deliberately chose manual labor summer jobs so as to deepen his awareness of social problems and realities. He also participated for the first time in a substantial interracial organization, Atlanta's Intercollegiate Council, where he saw at least glimmers of the potential of white allies in the cause of the betterment of the race.

At Morehouse, King encountered models of an intellectually grounded, modern Christianity, especially in the person of the institution's remarkable president, Benjamin Mays, a minister who also had earned a Ph.D. from the University of Chicago, and George D. Kelsey, chairman of the Department of Religion. King had never taken to emotional, call-and-shout expressions of faith, but from Mays and others he saw that intellectually respectable religion was more than just conceivable; it actually existed. In 1947, his senior year, King determined, without any Damascus-type experience, to enter the ministry; as he later recalled, he was moved by "a desire to serve God and humanity, and the feeling that my talent and my commitment could best be expressed through the ministry" (Warren 2001, 29). Early efforts at public preaching at his father's church went well, and so before the year was out King had been ordained to the Baptist ministry (which did not necessarily require formal theological training or certification) and named King, Sr.'s assistant.

Following his graduation in June 1948, King enrolled as a scholarship student at Crozer Theological Seminary in Chester, Pennsylvania. While taking required courses designed to prepare him professionally for the ministry, King also read widely on his own in the classic of the Western tradition and in more modern works by such authors as Gandhi, Reinhold Niebuhr, and Walter Rauschenbusch, a founder of the American social gospel tradition. In the integrated setting of Crozer, King shone, being named the best student as well as the valedictorian of the class of 1951. Having so excelled academically, King's next stop was Boston University's Ph.D. program in theology, where his intellectuality continued to deepen; while a student there, he met and married Coretta Scott, and was awarded the doctorate in June 1955. Out of a number of alternatives, King deliberately chose to return to his native South and assume, at the age of twenty-five, the pastorate of Montgomery, Alabama's Dexter Avenue Baptist Church (less than a football field away from the Alabama State Capitol, site of the 1861 launching of the Confederacy), where he was to remain for five years.

Of course this proved providential when, on December 1, 1955, Rosa Parks's act of civil disobedience in refusing to give up her paid-for seat to a white man and move to the back of the bus, as required by law, led to her arrest. The Montgomery Improvement Association was founded, the soon-to-be famous bus boycott began to be organized, and King, who had immediately made a reputation for his preaching, was chosen as its president and spokesman. At Dexter he organized a Social and Political Action Committee as a vehicle for applying Christian principles cooperatively as well as individually, and he was active in the Montgomery chapter of the National Association for the Advancement of Colored People. At some unspecified point in 1956, King, as he later recalled, "experienced the presence of the Divine as I had never experienced Him before" and emerged permanently fortified in his sense of doing God's will (King 1958, 114–15). In the wake of the successful conclusion of the bus boycott, King found himself heavily in demand as a speaker, traveled extensively, and made his first appearance on the cover of the influential newsweekly *Time* in 1957, the year he became the first president of the newly formed association of black southern pastors, the Southern Christian Leadership Conference. That same year he made his first significant appearance in the nation's capital at the Prayer Pilgrimage to the Lincoln Memorial on May 17th, which proved to be a sort of dress rehearsal for the dramatic 1963 march to the same locale. In 1957 he called for federal action to ensure voting rights and promised a revolution through balloting (two federal laws of 1957 and 1960, though modest in actual effect, were at least the first civil rights acts passed by Congress since the Reconstruction). His 1958 account of the Montgomery boycott saga, which had concluded successfully with the destruction of the bus segregation system, *Stride toward Freedom*, reflected King's education and wider interests by including a fundamental sociological analysis of what lay behind the white power system: the two separate and highly unequal societies coexisting in Montgomery, the blacks and the dominant whites. Late in 1959, he announced his decision to leave Montgomery and return to his native Atlanta, where as associate pastor to his father at Ebenezer, he would find more time for the ever-increasing list of out-of-parish activities he believed God intended for him. So, as the 1960s began, Martin Luther King, Jr., had been transformed from a youthful minister in a small southern city in the Heart of Dixie to a man in the South's leading city who was without question the most influential leader of black America, well-known for his efforts on behalf of a political agenda of civil equality.

The civil rights movement had slowly been acquiring some real momentum over the course of the 1950s, but with the notable exception of the 1954 *Brown* decision, the action was coming at the local, not state or federal, level, and was overwhelmingly activist rather than legislative. This situation continued in the early 1960s despite the replacement of the more cautious Dwight D. Eisenhower (with whom King had had an audience) with the narrowly elected "new generation" John F. Kennedy, who owed considerable political debt to the old-line southern segregationist Democrats, still a hefty element of the Democratic party structure, especially on

Capitol Hill. Despite closer relations with Kennedy, King's activism in the days of the JFK administration remained local, and his power base the SCLC, whose budget and activities increased enormously during these years. Indeed, King's insistence on forcing the issue of state-imposed segregation and the denial of legally guaranteed voting rights in his native Southland, as dramatically seen in the 1963 demonstrations in Birmingham, ultimately pressured the Kennedy administration to come out openly in favor of more federal civil rights legislation. It would, however, take the ascendancy of Lyndon Johnson—the man most responsible for the two civil rights acts of the late Eisenhower era—to bring these ideas to fruition as part of the Great Society program.

But a few weeks before the Dallas assassination, Martin Luther King, Jr.'s apogee was reached with his unforgettable, televised address from the Lincoln Memorial whose central litany, "I Have a Dream," was to become a part of the national vocabulary. He had tried out the expression in earlier speeches in Detroit and Chicago, but the March on Washington gave him a national audience. A. Philip Randolph, long the most successful black labor union leader in the country, had first threatened a mass march on the national capital to protest racial discrimination during World War II; in the early 1960s, he was again promoting the idea as one whose time had come. Tellingly, the march sought to broaden the agenda of the civil rights movement from its understandable stress on destroying segregation, most visibly (though far from entirely) a southern question, to matters of "economic justice" arising from the gross disparity between blacks and whites in income and wealth. Birmingham, of course, had proven to be an enormous and highly significant struggle, one of whose outcomes was King's "Letter from Birmingham Jail," a product of great frustration with the glacial pace of change and the extreme caution of well-meaning, so-called moderates. This example of the print medium was a private communication that would ultimately become a classic, broadly circulated through many printings, with its simple theme of "we can't wait" and its revelation of the bankruptcy of "moderation" at this late date. But that would come later; in 1963, it remained unknown to the public in an increasingly television-oriented age. Even among the northern activists most interested in the potential of a grand March on Washington, Birmingham had been a major "distraction" from serious planning. Among the many lessons reinforced by Birmingham was the power of the relatively new but increasingly dominant mass medium of television—the dramatic pictures of racial oppression remain ingrained in the memories of millions even a full generation later, and at the time dramatically affected public opinion, making the civil rights movement clearly on the side of the angels. And, more than ever, Martin Luther King, Jr., was seen by tens of millions as the personification of that movement.

With Birmingham "settled," at least for now, King, sensing momentum, became increasingly interested in the proposed Washington march, seeing it among other things as a way to force both executive and legislative action. By early June, King was taking the initiative toward making the march a reality in August. President Kennedy's June 11 televised speech proposing civil rights legislation, given in the wake of the integration of the University of Alabama, excited King and made the "pilgrimage" even more appealing. By the end of June, the August 28 march was official and publicly announced, though still viewed somewhat warily by the Kennedy administration and even by Roy Wilkins, head of the NAACP, and Walter Reuther of the United Automobile Workers, which would wind up providing significant numbers of participants, organization assistance, and, of course, money. King, a leading proponent, played a major role in carrying the day in the private discussions among the United States' black leaders and remained at the heart of the planning that continued during the summer. Fears subsided, and by mid-July President Kennedy had spoken favorably about the coming event. King was one of the eventual ten names officially listed as march chairmen. As the date approached, King took pains to stress that the march was not simply about civil rights narrowly defined, but economic justice, implying large-scale government activism, as well.

King was one of many speakers at the Lincoln Memorial that day. The setting, the national memorial to the Great Emancipator, and the several hundred thousand people present provided a dramatic backdrop for King's oratory. Heavily supported by labor unions (its twin themes being "jobs and freedom") and liberal religious organizations, skeptically received in its planning stages by President Kennedy and other high-ranking administration members, including Vice President Lyndon Johnson, all of whom feared disorder and potential backlash, the march succeeded in every respect as a moment of high American idealism. All the speeches were supposed to be available to the media the day before the event, but King's had yet to be written when he arrived in Washington on August 27, the eve of the march. Its themes, of course, had been addressed by King innumerable times, and so without any trouble he wrote out his "Dream" speech in the earliest hours of the historic date of August 28, 1963.

From the gathering point at the Washington Monument, the assembled marched toward the Lincoln Memorial in the late morning, organizers thrilled at the impressive turnout being captured by network television cameras. Though such marches were to become almost routine in future years, up to this time nothing like it had ever been seen in Washington. King, the climactic speaker, appearing at a point where all three television networks were presenting live coverage, and he delivered a short sermon, less than ten minutes long, firmly situated in the traditions of black American preaching and of American political ideals and the language and imagery of the Holy Bible. The uninitiated witnessed the "call-and-shout" tradition of the black church as the crowd responded frequently to King's heartfelt lines. Black America's full inclusion in the American dream was the message's essence, presented as the moral fulfillment of the unfinished business of the first Reconstruction af-ter the Civil War, and also as the natural extension of the United States' noble ideals. As the preacher continued, he extemporized with familiar biblical al-lusions and a national hymn, "My County 'Tis of Thee," with its concluding line, "Let freedom ring." Moved by the crowd's response, King left his text, employing a phrase he had often used in his many speeches that was to be-come the defining one of the address: "I still have a dream. It is a dream deeply rooted in the American dream. I have a dream that one day this nation will rise up and live out the true meaning of its creed—we hold these truths to be self-evident, that all men are created equal. . . . I have a dream that one day every valley shall be exalted, every hill and mountain shall be made low, the rough places will be made plain and the crooked places will be made straight and the glory of the Lord shall be revealed and all flesh shall see it to-gether" (quoted in Garrow 1986, 283–84).

The conclusion presented a beatific vision from "the old Negro spiritual, 'Free at last! Free at last! Thank God Almighty, we are free at last!' " (quoted in Garrow 1986, 248). The civil rights movement conceptualized and de-fined as a "freedom movement" would resonate strongly with American rhetoric and tradition, both politically and religiously. If the dream were to be achieved, then the white majority would have to be moved out of its com-placency. In this, King succeeded. Like millions of others, President Kennedy, who received King and others immediately after the speech, was suitably impressed and strengthened in his commitment to the cause gener-ally and to his civil rights bill specifically. For King himself, the crowds, the attention, and the reception were fortifying, the message being that the movement had perhaps even more power than it had imagined and was closer to success than it might have dared dreamed. More than ever, he un-derstood the role that God had insisted he play, and despite personal reser-vations and feelings of unworthiness, he knew he had to play it.

The March on Washington inspired hope that Congress might be moved by national pressure. Local pressure via organized campaigns in southern cities continued, and proved no easier than in the past. King spent much of his time in the months following the march trying to continue the pace of change in Birmingham, but with disappointing results; the intransigence of many of Birmingham's white leaders, combined with the caution of some of Birming-ham's black leaders, proved disheartening. So did, of course, the murder of John F. Kennedy on November 22. What would the new administration bring when it came to civil rights?

King was invited to the White House by the new President Lyndon John-son on December 3, and the meeting went well, King coming out believing in Johnson's sincerity of commitment to the cause. Regular meetings in the White House followed as the Great Society began to unfold. Johnson's supreme understanding of the actualities of the legislative process would be pivotal, of course, in the realization of the legislative dreams of the March on Washington. King's role, defined in a bigger sense than ever by his "I Have a Dream" speech, would be that of public preacher, moral teacher, the conscience of a nation. For the short remainder of his life, King's schedule of public appearances remained enormous and exhausting. Such public honors as an invitation to preach at St. Paul's Cathedral in London, being named "Man of the Year" by *Time*, and, on a grander scale, being the youngest-ever recipient of the 1964 Nobel Peace Prize, a private audience in Rome with Pope Paul VI, and a large-scale biracial dinner in his hometown of Atlanta celebrating his Nobel Prize, a social event utterly unprecedented in that city's history and a profound signal that the Atlanta white power structure was indeed reading the signs of the times, ratified and shone light upon his stature.

But to some extent he was also an insider; inevitably, he was one of the handful of black leaders Johnson asked to a private White House meeting on January 17, 1964, for an advance briefly on the "declaration" of the War on Poverty slated for the State of the Union address to Congress. King privately and publicly applauded the initiative, as his ideas regarding civil rights were far broader than mere issues of access, most definitely including federal efforts to promote individual economic advancement. The simple issue of access to better paying jobs had formed a major part of the movement's agenda, and continued to in the mid-1960s, occupying plenty of King's time, which was spent away from Washington and primarily in his native Deep South. But King was more than ever a truly national figure, and as the civil rights movement spread to the North, King could not avoid involvement. The issues were different—legally sanctioned segregation, however broadly defined, was relatively unusual and infinitely more subtle—yet the subservient position of blacks as a group compared to whites was similar. For instance, the mayor of New York City, Robert Wagner, asked King to come help restore calm after a police incident in July had produced rioting. King used the occasion to state more than once that the violence had root causes in need of addressing: "The major problem remains one of economics . . . the need for millions of dollars now for full employment and for the elimination of slums" (quoted in Garrow 1986, 344). The answer was a plethora of government-funded programs—an answer in tune with the developing notions of Johnson's Great Society concept enunciated at the Ann Arbor commencement only a few weeks before.

The dispute over the seating of the Mississippi delegation at the August Democratic National Convention in Atlantic City, a complex power struggle that proved to be the last stand of the old-line, all-white, segregationist Mississippi Democratic Party, embittered many in the civil rights movement against Johnson and also, for some, against King, who was accused of at least passivity in refusing to fight Johnson's insistence on a compromise with the old-line white Mississippi Democratic establishment. Now something of an insider, King was aware to a far greater degree than many more idealistic and younger activists of the realities of the political power game, and also of the tremendous potential for advancing his goals through the person of Lyndon Johnson, however flawed he might seem to outsiders. By the time of the controversy, the Republican Party had already nominated Arizona U.S. Senator Barry Goldwater, whose libertarian values had led him to vote against the landmark 1964 Civil Rights Act outlawing racial (and various other forms of) discrimination in public accommodations and in the workplace, as well as the very idea of large-scale federal antipoverty programs of the sort that King, along with Johnson, were envisioning. Goldwater was anathema to King in every way, and Johnson far more than just an acceptable alternative. King understood the critics—his 1964 book bore the title *Why We Can't Wait*—but did not second-guess his decision, fundamentally agreeing with the analysis of northern civil rights activist Bayar Rustin that the movement was in transition "from protest to politics." King had been an honored guest at the July 2nd signing ceremony for the Civil Rights Act, a dream long deferred, and one whose realization was close to miraculous. There were plenty of reasons for high hopes, especially after the 1964 Johnson landslide over Goldwater produced the most liberal, activist federal Congress and federal government since the fabled New Deal era of the 1930s.

Elections such as 1964's, whose ideological tone revealed, as Barry Goldwater put it, that voters deciding between the two major parties had "a choice, not an echo," reminded everyone that voting could actually matter. Goldwater's "extremism" allowed Johnson to position himself, and many Democratic congressional candidates, rhetorically in the center, and the civil rights question as it had been playing out (especially on television) very much granted the moral high ground to liberalism and its philosophy of a beneficent federal government leading the nation toward the higher paths of true Americanism, so eloquently defined by King's Lincoln Memorial address of August 1963. With a public accommodations/employment law on the books, and a high-stakes election just behind him, King saw as the next immediate issue the right to vote in many (though not all) areas of the South. After that, he stated on the day following the 1964 election, attention should be turned to the "northern" (i.e., outside the South) black urban underclass—one of the targets of the Great Society's already-proclaimed War on Poverty that, via the election landslide and the makeup of the new Congress, stood on the brink of major advances (Garrow 1986, 358). Upon his return to the United States following his Nobel Peace Prize address in Stockholm, King again indicated his interest in the "economic justice" component of Johnson's poverty war whereby the United States might come to resemble Scandinavia, which lacked slums and suffered from no unemployment—benefits brought about by extremely powerful national governments. Following his New York visit, King and his wife and parents were flown to Washington for a welcome home meeting with President Johnson, who spoke privately to the new Nobel laureate about how his vision for a federally led war on poverty would transform the lives of black Americans. In response, King observed that the basic civil right of voting remained in crying need of federal attention in the South; Johnson expressed pessimism that a bill could make it through Congress in 1965 (367–68).

Voting rights were, legally speaking, about as open-and-shut an issue as the civil rights movement faced. The Reconstruction-era Fifteenth Amendment not only forbade discrimination on account of race, but also contained a second article empowering Congress to enforce this standard via legislation. No one could question the appropriateness of federal action, as seen in the enactment in the late Eisenhower years of the first two civil rights acts, both of which involved (convoluted) federal action to ensure voting rights. On the other hand, election procedures, including registration, were fundamentally a state, not federal, responsibility (as they always had been) that was exercised locally. As had been shown in the 1890s, determined, evasive efforts (grandfather clauses, poll taxes, literacy tests) could be used by those opposing equal-opportunity voting—and were, and continued to be into the 1960s. The new idea for 1965 was to empower federal officials to register voters in areas where a simple headcount revealed an enormous discrepancy between the adult citizen population and number of registered voters. Again, King's role would be to organize direct action on the ground, gaining attention for the issue, enlightening people as to the real situation as opposed to mere on-paper "rights," and forcing the issue. The exercise of the right of peaceful assembly and redress of grievances would seem to be as all-American as was the right to vote itself—but, in reality, these "rights" were just as questionably valid in some places as was the "right" to vote. King's efforts were soon to make Selma a locale known in American history and the most influential moment in the story of the enactment of the Voting Rights Act of 1965, one of those laws that truly marked a watershed and produced, in a strikingly short order, a born-again, biracial political South that was to endure.

That biracial political order certainly did not exist in Alabama in 1965; the State Legislature was all white, and voter registration laws included a literacy test that could easily be, and had long been, manipulated in its usage for purposes of massive black disfranchisement. On January 2nd of that year, Martin Luther King, Jr., spoke at the Brown Chapel African Methodist Episcopal Church in Selma, announcing the voter registration drive, the "Alabama Project." On Monday, January 18, King was at the head of a group of 400 marchers who trod from Brown Chapel to the Dallas County Courthouse and attempted to register to vote, with many of the national media present. Hours passed, with not one applicant even shown the inside of the building, let alone allowed to attempt to register to vote. On the second day, dozens of arrests and a relatively minor incident of police brutality began to provide the Selma effort with some much-desired national publicity. Arrests increased markedly on the third day, a trend that continued and was accompanied by a series of mostly relatively minor but nonetheless always quite real instances of the authorities employing physical force, all of which were documented and extensively publicized by the press corps present in Selma; again, civil rights activists joked that the South's law enforcement personnel were, as per usual, unwittingly functioning as the movement's greatest allies. Mediators from the federal government's new Community Relations Service concluded after much effort that there simply were *no* whites to be found in Selma who even remotely saw the historic moment for what it was: a challenge to one of the pillars of institutionalized white supremacy that was not going to be denied, an idea, like the Civil Rights Act of 1964, whose time had come. Rather, an air of mindboggling unreality continued to pervade Selma's whites, including "moderates," who seemed to imagine that, having acquiesced to the integration of public accommodations, that was enough, and no change in the political structure would be necessary.

In early February, after careful consideration, King deliberately sought arrest by participating in a large-scale march that officials said violated Selma's parade ordinance. From his jail cell—only a few weeks after the awarding of the Nobel Prize—King communicated with other leaders regarding strategy, including seeking the involvement of President Johnson, who responded with a clear public statement of support for the Selma cause and a hint of coming increased federal involvement. A few days later, after King's release, a brief meeting at the White House with the president was arranged, after which King praised the president's commitment to securing the right to vote by any means necessary, including new federal legislation. The events in Selma were demonstrating for what seemed to King and other knowledgeable observers for about the millionth time that federal intervention was absolutely necessary for change to come even in so basic an area as the right to vote. As he would publicly sum up the aim on March 1, "We are going to bring a voting bill into being in the streets of Selma" (Garrow 1986, 394).

At this point, seeking further momentum, King and his collaborators began laying the groundwork for the proposed march to Montgomery, with King mentioning this to a reporter, and took the Selma tactics to other Alabama counties, Perry and Wilcox. On March 5 King was back in Washington for an extended meeting with President Johnson that lasted more than an hour, who updated him on the progress of new proposed legislation to ensure voting rights and informed him that Senate Republican Leader Everett Dirksen had promised support on his side of the aisle. King then returned to Alabama in preparation for the scheduled commencement of the attempted march toward Montgomery the following Sunday, March 7. While Governor George Wallace originally favored permitting the march to proceed, believing it would collapse long before reaching Montgomery, thereby embarrassing the marchers (who did not believe the march would be allowed to proceed very far and hence would not be physically prepared actually to complete it), he changed his mind when warned that there was substantial likelihood that the marchers would be attacked along the way, thus further harming whatever was left of Alabama's national image, and also the cause of maintaining white supremacy. King for his part had become more concerned than ever about the unending reports of death threats. He remained unsure of the wisdom of proceeding until the last moment when, pressured, he gave his approval for the march to begin.

And so came the fateful confrontation of March 7, 1965, on the Edmund Pettus Bridge over the Alabama River between the marchers and the state troopers whom Selma officials feared would create yet another embarrassing incident. Their worst fears were realized. About a minute after the declaration of unlawful assembly and its accompanying two-minute warning, the all-white Alabama state troopers advanced, very hard, on the unmoved, utterly unthreatening, would-be marchers. Tear gas followed, as did mounted police. Cheering white spectators provided background noise. All was recorded by the national media, and the unknowing, witless white supremacists continued their collective public self-immolation while exhibiting their ever-diminishing grip on reality. George Wallace, less clueless than many, privately cursed out bumbling officials responsible for the debacle for the white supremacy cause. That evening, national television relayed what had happened, producing the inevitable and obvious response. At the cost of several dozen people's physical abuse (no one died), the civil rights movement made another significant leap toward success. King had made the right call; he and his crusade had been helped by the law enforcement officials and by the national media. Alabama's "Bloody Sunday" had entered history.

The following Tuesday night, President Johnson issued a statement announcing that his administration was writing a bill to ensure voting rights and that a message to Congress was imminent upon the bill's completion. The following Saturday, Johnson, in his first press conference since the Pettus Bridge incident, fully aligned himself with the marchers, and then called King Sunday night to invite him to be present the next evening, Monday, when he would address Congress and propose his promised voting rights act (King did not go, as his presence was required in Selma at a memorial service for a Boston minister and civil rights marcher who had been killed in Alabama a few days before). King's march, then, provided the immediate backdrop for the proposal of what turned out to be one of the most highly significant pieces of 1960s civil rights legislation. In that speech of March 15, after comparing the Selma marchers to the colonial patriots of Lexington and Concord, Johnson employed the civil rights anthem's title: "We shall overcome." King is reported to have cried—something he was never known to do—at this point (Garrow 1986, 408).

Oppressive actions by state and local officials led federal judge Frank M. Johnson, Jr., to approve on March 5 King's proposed march from Selma to Montgomery along Highway 80. At the request of Governor Wallace, who claimed the state could not afford to pay for the needed security, Johnson federalized 1,800 members of the Alabama National Guard to do the job, supplemented by various federal officials. The dramatic march by some 3,000 began on Sunday, March 21, with King, who had been informed of serious assassination threats against him and advised by the U.S. attorney general not to march (Fairclough 1987, 242), in the lead—this time across the Pettus Bridge and beyond, in another stride toward freedom. Observers noted King's obvious exhaustion as the miles and blisters accumulated. Many northerners came down south to join the marchers for at least a part of their trek. On Thursday, King and thousands of others reached the Alabama state capital, scene of his first national fame nearly a decade before. In a famous speech at the state capitol building, King established a call and response with the thousands assembled: "How long? Not long."

It was clear that a strong voting rights act would indeed pass Congress soon, which would in the event be signed by President Johnson on August 6, 1965. There was every reason for King to believe that this law, with federal supervision and enforcement, would make the long-evaded 15th Amendment right to vote at last a reality—and so, rapidly, it did. With this landmark added to the 1964 Civil Rights Act, as it would be soon, the desire to maintain momentum produced the question: what next? King wasted no time after completing the march to Montgomery, heading for Baltimore on March 31 for a Southern Christian Leadership Conference (SCLC) board meeting at which he asked his colleagues to consider expanding the organization into northern cities—a second, more national stage for their southern-oriented civil rights movement focusing on the roots of poverty and its attendant social pathologies. The SCLC duly declared itself in favor of Great Society–like items such as a higher minimum wage, universal federally guaranteed health insurance, and government-funded jobs programs. In a speech at Baltimore's Cornerstone Baptist Church, King publicly stated that his civil rights efforts were going national and heading north, as had so many southern blacks over the course of the twentieth-century great migration.

For King, it proved to be generally alien territory. His own forays into the north, in rather cloistered academic groves, had made him well aware of the national nature of racial discrimination, specifically involving housing. It would take King's own martyrdom in 1968 to get an antidiscrimination bill through Congress, thus giving the death blow (at least legally) to the time-honored and nationally revered concept, "a man's home is his castle," a slogan behind which racial discrimination could, and did, take place. One admitted visitors as one pleased, and rented or sold as one pleased, including restrictively, if so desired. The problems of poverty, now on the national agenda via the Great Society in a new way, were of course as daunting to King as to anyone else, and its connections to racism obvious enough. In July 1965, King began to determine that Chicago should be the place to go to see what he could see about SCLC prospects outside the Southland. After visiting various northern cities, King made his way to the nation's capital in August to report to Johnson on his impressions of the current state of black America in the northern urban areas—negative and ominous—and to witness the signing of the Voting Rights Act—a great triumph.

The Watts riots later that month interrupted King's planned Puerto Rican vacation and took him to Los Angeles, where his already developing sense of the challenge of the nonsouthern meaning of civil rights, with its economic dimension paramount, was underscored. Chicago activists were asking him to bring the movement, and his personal prestige, to their side. King was receptive to this new challenge, which while involving overtly discriminating situations also entailed the subtleties arising from urban complexity, such as "ethnic neighborhoods." With the War on Poverty presumably on the brink of great expansion and advances, the timing seemed right. On September 1, 1965, King and SCLC leader Andrew Young announced the coming of a Chicago initiative. The political establishment of the nation's then-second city, from Mayor Richard Daley on down, were underwhelmed to say the least. Busier than ever, and drawn in many different directions for many different purposes and instances related to the greater goal to which he was devoting his life, King did not make it to Chicago to begin his campaign until early January 1966.

He found the various contradictions that made up the city that was said to work: an extant and disgruntled civil rights movement; a powerful political machine that was white dominated yet to a degree integrated and that the local business community fundamentally accepted; and an overwhelmingly de facto segregated city of "ethnic" neighborhoods with their strong community pride and exclusionary character. King and his aides were unable clearly to define exactly what the movement they were bringing to Chicago might actually accomplish, or even do, to somewhat skeptical reporters a few days after his arrival. More regularly, King began to discuss and even speak vaguely about a need for the redistribution of wealth (which he continued to do with continuing vagueness). An apartment in the Lanwdale ghetto area was rented and renovated, and on January 26th, King moved in. He was in and out of town regularly but intended to be there Wednesdays through Fridays. A March 12 "festival" successfully raised funds, but Mayor Daley kept his distance, his coolness obvious to all. Increasingly, King was making public comments critical of Johnson administration policies in Vietnam, distinctly cooling his relations with many of the administration's leaders. That mysterious but real phenomenon known as "momentum" seemed to be breaking down. The chant of "black power" began to be heard, bothering King, though he well understood where it came from and refused to be pressed into publicly denouncing it, as he feared its potential harm to a dream of integration via either increased black separatism or white "backlash."

Chicago was not quite King's Waterloo, as he inevitably soldiered on in the couple of years remaining to him before his 1968 murder, but it did provide one of the most enduring pictures of the so-called white backlash against civil rights that took form in the swing against the Great Society recorded in the 1966 midterm elections. In late July, King announced that there would be a march to the office of a realtor known to be an active practitioner of racial discrimination (illegal in Chicago since 1963). Fear of the spread of ghettos and the damage to property values, especially important to people whose greatest asset was the equity in their homes, was cresting in Chicago and elsewhere, aided and abetted by the increasing number of riots, one of which had hit the West Side of Chicago in mid-July. White protesters, "greeting" demonstrators with insults and hurled objects, greatly outnumbered the protesters from the Chicago Freedom Movement. King, commonly enough, was out of town during the first march, but naturally felt obliged to appear at a follow-up, which took place on Friday, August 5th, against another realtor's office. Despite a police escort, King was struck in the head by a rock and partially knocked down. While blood was not drawn, of course he was stunned physically, mentally, and emotionally. The picture was given prominence all over the next day's papers. He told reporters that he had never expected "anything so hostile and so hateful as I've seen here today"—which was saying a great deal (Garrow 1986, 500). Marches continued, a vague agreement of sorts was reached that ended them, and Mayor Daley was overwhelmingly reelected mayor in 1967.

King rhetorically asked the question in 1967, "Where do we go from here?" For himself, the answer was in the direction of more radical stances, such as calling for a guaranteed annual income, a concept that Johnson found absurd. King had gone full-fledged into the antiwar movement, which also separated him from Johnson, who was increasingly consumed by Vietnam. The rioting and violence, along with the black power militancy, solidified King's image to most as the respectable civil rights leader, though to some of the more impatient young, that was not a great image to have. Ironically and tragically, it took King's assassination on April 4, 1968, in Memphis, where he had gone to support a strike by black garbage collectors, to again make King a shaper of the Great Society program. The Open Housing Act of 1968, outlawing various forms of discrimination in real estate transactions, was signed into law a mere week after King's death, hurried up as a memorial to him—the first of many that would be constructed on his behalf.

CHALLENGING
THE GREAT SOCIETY

BARRY GOLDWATER
(1909–1998)

When Barry Goldwater died on May 29, 1998, tributes were issued from around the nation and also across the political spectrum. Secretary of the Interior Bruce Babbitt, a fellow Arizonan, longtime political opponent, and also friend, commented in a memorial gathering held on June 3rd at Arizona State University that wherever he went across the world, when people found out that he hailed from Arizona, they immediately identified that western state with two larger than life characters: Geronimo and Barry Goldwater. The longtime U.S. senator and 1964 Republican presidential nominee came to personify the rising influence of the western United States in American politics, but more concretely, as things eventually turned out, also the rise of a modern conservative political movement that became highly competitive in national elections and that was importantly underwritten by as well as reflective of a renewed and influential conservative *intellectual* movement. Yet in 1964, of course, Barry Goldwater was crushed, in both the popular and electoral vote, by Lyndon Johnson, the prime mover of the Great Society; furthermore, Goldwater was blamed for having dragged down the entire GOP ticket, producing the top-heavy Democratic majorities in both houses of Congress that would prove critical for the enactment of a plethora of LBJ's Great Society proposals.

The 1964 presidential race is most remembered for the blunders of the amateurish Goldwater campaign along with the shift, if at least temporarily, of what seemed like almost the entire political center into the camp of the Democratic party. Indeed, it would hardly be an exaggeration, ironically, to "credit" Goldwater with having thereby played, however unintentionally, a critically significant role not only in the birth of the Great Society as a living, breathing entity, but also in the wide-ranging scope of its creation. Not only had Goldwater simply lost, and lost big, the 1964 presidential contest— but more than a few Great Society proponents and partisans (but not, significantly, the politically astute Lyndon Johnson) also took Goldwater's political humiliation as indicative of the birth of a new social-democratic ethos, more in line with Europe's than with the postwar United States', as well as a repudiation of what they saw as an attempt to restore the allegedly halcyon days of Herbert Hoover or even of William McKinley. "Forward, into the nineteenth century," said the Goldwaterites, according to some of their critics. In the short run, of course, these critics were right, and so the Great Society came to be, taking on an enormous form, no less. But to the surprise of many, the apparently vanquished populist-style conservatism that Barry Goldwater did much first to create and then bring to the highest level of American politics lived on to see another day, again not only in politics but also in the realm of ideas, as seen in the soon-to-develop critiques of the fledging Great Society programs that were struggling to be born. With his outsider, rebellious, libertarian, don't-tread-on-me instincts paramount, along with his basic, fundamental attitude of traditionalism where the United States and its traditions were concerned, Barry Goldwater in the 1960s both embodied a losing point of view seemingly out of touch with its times as well as the shape of things to come. Not particularly intellectual himself, as he was the first to admit, he nonetheless articulated reservations about the vision of a Great Society that were developed by intellectually minded activists who themselves primarily worked out of the long-standing American antistatist tradition. In the short run, then, and in significant ways, Goldwater actually proved to be radically *ahead* of his time, for in the long run he played a major role in preparing the ground not only for the 1966 gubernatorial victory of Ronald Reagan in California, but also for Reagan's 1980 presidential success. A sign held up at a Republican gathering in the 1980s paid tribute to Goldwater's historic role, reading, "Barry: Your Truth Is Marching On."

The Great Society view of the world hardly enjoyed any natural connection with the movers and shakers of mid-twentieth-century Arizona, the world into which Barry Morris Goldwater was born on January 1, 1909—at home, three years before the achievement of statehood, and about a month before the death of Geronimo. Goldwater's grandfather, Mike, made an archetypal immigrant's journey in the mid-nineteenth century, from Polish Russia to London to California in 1852. In 1860, Mike became the first Goldwater to enter Arizona Territory, a classic Jewish peddler whose wife and children were based in Los Angeles, where in 1866 Baron, Barry's father, was born. In December 1872, Mike Goldwater and his brother Joe opened what was their second Arizona store, this one in Phoenix, where Mike's son Morris (Barry's uncle) worked as manager. When it failed in 1875, the Goldwaters opened a new store ("Goldwaters") farther north, in Prescott, which quickly thrived. The family became active community leaders, developers, donors, and politicians, Morris being elected Prescott's mayor in 1879 and continuing for ten terms that stretched over nearly a half century; his father Mike also served a term as mayor. Morris, a leader of Arizona's Democratic party, was a crucial actor in the statehood movement, which came to fruition in 1912.

It was Mike's youngest son, Baron, who pushed his brothers to open a new Goldwaters in the fast-growing community of Phoenix. Its opening in 1896 soon led to Baron's following the family tradition by becoming a founding father and community leader for numerous Phoenix institutions. In 1907, Baron married a transplanted midwesterner, Josephine Williams. The lack of a Jewish religious community along with the Jewish matrilineal tradition meant that Barry would be raised an Episcopalian like his mother.

Barry Goldwater thus grew up in one of the founding families of Arizona, a constituency of doers, builders, and pioneers. Like his relatives, he was community minded in a serious way without at all even being tempted to become a professional, full-time politician. He was a man of many hobbies and interests, ranging from western history to Indians to aviation to photography (his first *Arizona Highways* photograph appeared in a 1939 issue). Like millions of Americans, including Lyndon Johnson, the New Deal era proved a formative experience for his political views; in his 1979 memoir, *With No Apologies*, he stated, "I think the foundations of my political philosophy were rooted in my resentment against the New Deal" (Goldwater 1979, 44). The Depression failed to dim his admiration for Herbert Hoover and his philosophy of individualism, free cooperation, and localism; when Goldwater began his career as a syndicated newspaper columnist in 1960, the aide responsible for the column contacted Herbert Hoover's office, writing to Hoover's aide that Goldwater basically shared Hoover's philosophy (Goldberg 1995, 142). Unlike Hoover, however, Barry Goldwater never had to pull himself up by any bootstraps; financial security was a given in his upbringing. Neither book learning nor the family store particularly appealed to his restless mind. In the late 1940s Goldwater became involved in a Phoenix reform effort aimed at introducing the city manager form of government to the city, a classic "bring business principles to government" concept. In 1949, he won his first elective office, to the Phoenix city council, and soon became vice mayor.

The challenge of being a Republican in a state that historically had been overwhelmingly dominated by Democrats appealed to Goldwater. In 1951 he traveled around the state warning against creeping socialism. His underdog 1952 campaign for the Senate was a historic breakthrough for Arizona Republicans. He insisted that he did not oppose government activism and programs per se, rattling off such examples as federal bank deposit insurance, the Securities and Exchange Commission that regulated the stock market, the Federal Housing Agency, and Social Security, none of which he seemed to view as threatening individual liberty (Goldberg 1995, 93). A September 1952 campaign comment regarding a local concern well illustrated, however, his general orientation toward the federal government: "If you want to see the end results of a welfare state look at our Indians" (102).

To know Barry Goldwater was to like him, and Republican senators in Washington did; in 1955, he was already being made chairman of the Republican Senate Campaign Committee, a big step in developing his national image, connections, and reputation, especially when one remembers what a small, almost remote state Arizona still was in the 1950s. He appeared regularly on national television news shows and greatly increased his travels around the United States, especially in his three tours of duty as GOP Senate campaign chief (1955/1956, 1959/1960, and 1961/1962). The United States that he saw in his travels was one in accordance with his individualistic philosophy. In 1958, he stood out (along with Nelson Rockefeller, elected to his first term as governor of New York) in the worst Republican electoral debacle since 1936 in being solidly reelected senator over Arizona political legend and former senator Ernest McFarland.

A rising political star, Goldwater naturally caught the attention of politically minded people, especially conservative Republicans who longed for a champion and who theorized that the poor results of 1958 stemmed from a failure to articulate clearly enough the distinct worldview they held, which they believed was held by a majority of Americans as well. On May 15, 1959, he met with a small group of people to discuss how they might promote conservative ideas around the country; out of this meeting was to emerge the unique "Draft Goldwater" movement. By July of that year, "Americans for Goldwater" chapters existed in thirty-one states plus the District of Columbia (which Goldwater referred to as the land of Oz); among the activists was L. Brent Bozell of Maryland (Goldberg 1995, 143). In 1955, William F. Buckely, Jr., had successfully launched a conservative political magazine, *National Review*, which became a forum for conservative intellectuals as well as practical activists. Buckley's brother-in-law, L. Brent Bozell, a *National Review* founding senior editor (Goldwater was a faithful reader of *NR*) became the ghostwriter for Goldwater's phenomenally successful 1960 123-page tract, *The Conscience of a Conservative*, which became a bible of the Draft Goldwater movement of the early 1960s. Published in late 1960 about as far away as one could imagine from the eastern publishing houses by the Victor Publishing Company of Sheperdsville, Kentucky, the book sold some 3.5 million copies and is sometimes said to be the twentieth century's most-read political book (Edwards 1995, 110). Many years later, long after the Great Society's day had passed, Goldwater would author another book, tellingly and optimistically entitled *The Conscience of a Majority*.

Goldwater spent the first two months of 1960 speaking in thirteen states for Republicans as he was again serving as Senate campaign chairman; in May alone he visited eleven states; by year's end he had made some 800 speeches along with numerous radio, television, and college campus appearances. Additionally, a newspaper column bearing his name was nationally syndicated from the *Los Angeles Times* (a newspaper philosophically unrecognizable from its later liberal incarnation) three times a week. Meanwhile, with an eye toward the longer range, the Draft Goldwater movement had created by the summer 400 "Americans for Goldwater" clubs and "Youth for Goldwater for Vice President" chapters on sixty-four college campus in thirty-two states (Goldberg 1995, 143–44). Richard Nixon's meeting with Nelson Rockefeller three days before the start of the GOP convention on July 22, 1960, known as the Treaty of Fifth Avenue, was seen by Goldwater and Goldwaterites as a Nixon "sellout" to Rockefeller's more eastern-establishment, liberal Republicanism and angered Barry enough to get him to allow the placement of his name in the nomination for president, if only briefly. Once the convention had assembled, Goldwater took the microphone to announce the "withdrawal" of his nonexistent candidacy, called for unity against the "blueprint for socialism presented by the Democrats," and then closed with what was taken by his faithful to be a prophetic utterance: "Let's grow up conservatives. Let's if we want to take this party back—and I think we can some day—let's get to work" (145).

The Conscience of a Conservative (1960) is representative of the political worldview of the "Taft Republicans," descendants of "Hoover Republicans," those for whom the New Deal remained a living example of what *not* to do with the national government. At the outset of his manifesto, Goldwater made explicit an orientation as far removed from that of the soon-to-be-dawning Great Society as one could imagine: "I have little interest in streamlining government or in making it more efficient, for I mean to reduce its size. I do not undertake to promote welfare, for I propose to extend freedom. My aim is not to pass laws, but to repeal them" (Goldwater 1960, 23). Ideas had consequences, and Goldwater continued to call the political drift he had first noticed in the New Deal era by what he considered to be its true name: socialism. In a 1958 speech broadcast statewide from Prescott, Goldwater had warned, "If you do not wake up, socialism will be a reality in the United States within another election" (Goldberg 1995, 127). The traditional American philosophy of limited government, Goldwater argued, was as relevant as ever, being no more out of date than the Ten Commandments. Federal programs such as public housing or "urban renewal" not only should not be expanded, but they should also be eliminated, lest they encourage "Socialism-through-Welfarism." Some 80 percent of Goldwater delegates at the 1964 Republican convention reported that they had read the book (202).

An alternative version of this manifesto appeared in Goldwater's Senate floor speech of January 11, 1961, "A Statement of Proposed Republican Principles, Programs and Objectives." Written by Michael Bernstein, minority counsel for the Senate Labor Committee, it offered an alternative to the impending "New Frontier" mentality of the incoming Kennedy administration. Goldwater had first met John F. Kennedy in the 1940s in Arizona and, as did most, found him personally appealing if suspiciously lacking in strong

political principles; in contrast, the Arizonan strongly disliked the incoming
vice president, Lyndon Johnson, whom he had of course come to know during the latter's years as Democratic Senate leader in the 1950s and whom he
regarded as "the epitome of the unprincipled politician" (Edwards 1995,
197). In his Senate speech, as in his book, Goldwater warned of the drift in
American society away from valuing freedom and individualism and the
continuing threat of interest group politics, a New Deal legacy. Government
downsizing, not expansion, was needed, most especially at the remote federal level. Kennedy's slogan of the 1960 campaign was unimpressive to
Goldwater, amounting to "socialism of some order or another. Khrushchev
recently promised free housing, free medical care, and free transportation.
And here we are with the New Frontier promising pretty much the same
thing" (Goldberg 1995, 151). Unsurprisingly, Goldwater went on to deride
a long-standing liberal proposal, federal aid to primary and secondary education, which would become a cornerstone of LBJ's Great Society, with its
implicit threat to local control.

When Americans of the late 1950s and early 1960s spoke about the federal government and education in the same breath, most likely the issue was
that of school integration, itself one of several increasingly visible manifestations of the growing civil rights movement. No one who got to seriously
know about Barry Goldwater ever accused him of personally being a bigot;
he took pride in his Jewish background even while acknowledging that his
name alone might turn some voters against him. Goldwater's store had employed black people long before other department stores did, and Goldwater
had financially contributed to the National Association for the Advancement
of Colored People chapters in Phoenix and Tucson as well as the Phoenix
Urban League, voted to desegregate a restaurant at the Phoenix airport, and
insisted on taking his black legislative assistant, Kathrine Maxwell, with him
to the Senate cafeteria in 1953 (Edwards 1995, 231). He voted for the Civil
Rights Acts of 1957 and 1960, which involved highly technical and ultimately unsuccessful efforts to ensure black voting rights in the South (Goldberg 1995, 121). In this matter, the Fifteenth Amendment explicitly stated
that Congress had the right to enact appropriate legislation to secure the
right to vote. Similarly, Goldwater saw the appropriateness of federally mandated integration orders involving interstate transportation, given the federal
responsibility for interstate commerce. Things were different, however,
when it came to the question of public school segregation. It was the *Brown*
decision of 1954 that marked the beginning of Goldwater's "problem" with
civil rights.

The essence of the problem was Goldwater's deeply held philosophical belief in states' rights. He denied the logic of the *Brown* decision and thus
thought it wrongly decided from a legal and constitutional view; schools
were and always had been local institutions and history universally demonstrated that segregation had always been viewed as legally possible, though

not required; Goldwater remained a strict constructionist, for any other position would lead inexorably to judicial tyranny. Goldwater did not favor school segregation and said so on many occasions. He consistently opposed laws that *mandated* segregation, but that did not mean that states did not have the legal right to enact such laws, as many long had. He was openly critical of President Eisenhower's deployment of troops to Little Rock, Arkansas, in 1957 to enforce a federal court order to desegregate Central High School. In *The Conscience of a Conservative* he continued to deny federal authority in local public schools—though he dropped this position a few years later, before the 1964 campaign, explicitly affirming the Eisenhower position that the law as defined by the U.S. Supreme Court was, in fact, the law, and would have to be enforced. In 1962, during the integration crisis at the University of Mississippi, Goldwater opined that the segregationist position of the Mississippi governor was immoral but also, in Goldwater's eyes, constitutional, despite what the Supreme Court had ruled (Goldberg 1995, 154). But by the fall of 1963, with a presidential candidacy looming, Goldwater stated that it was proper, if required, to deploy federal troops to the South to enforce court-ordered desegregation (175).

A few weeks later, on January 4th, 1964, Barry Goldwater declared his candidacy for the Republican nomination for president. In his announcement, Goldwater expressed openly his by-now well-known philosophical approach to politics: he believed in limited government and "individual responsibility against regimentation." Expressing fears of Americans becoming "just cogs in a vast government machine," he promised for 1964 voters what was to become a familiar catchphrase: "a choice, not an echo" (Goldberg 1995, 181). Four days later, in his State of the Union address, President Lyndon Johnson declared "unconditional" war on poverty. Goldwater's response to this "declaration" came in the form of his first important speech, on January 16th, before the Economic Club of New York. In this setting, the Arizona senator, far from his home environment, delivered a stinging attack on "the Santa Claus of the free lunch, the government hand-out, the Santa Claus of something-for-nothing and something-for-everyone" (184). Regarding poverty itself, Goldwater had the temerity to point out that, despite loose talk of lack of skills and inadequate education, "The fact is that most people who have no skill, have no education for the same reason—low intelligence or low ambition" (184).

The biggest debate in terms of issues in the country in that year was centered on Capitol Hill and the 1964 Civil Rights Act. Inevitably and, for this issue, quite accurately, "states' rights" and "local control" conflated with the often euphemistic attempts to defend institutionalized southern white supremacy. Most of the defenders of the old order were the southern Democrats; as Johnson himself pointed out in an October campaign appearance in Louisiana, the 1964 civil rights bill garnered the votes of two-thirds of Senate Democrats and *three-fourths of Senate Republicans* (Margolis 2000, 247).

In the precable era, television network coverage of the eighty-three-day debate was intense and inevitably, unavoidably favorably inclined toward the civil rights cause. Goldwater opposed the cloture bill that ended the filibuster mounted by southern Democrats, a procedural vote deemed so important by television news that regular programming was interrupted to report it. On June 18, 1964, the day the Senate voted, Barry Goldwater took to the floor to speak on the issues involved in civil rights as he understood them. Virtually at the outset, he made his personal, moral position clear: "I am unalterably opposed to discrimination or segregation on the basis of race, color, or creed, or on any other basis; not only my words, but more importantly my actions through the years have repeatedly demonstrated the sincerity of my feeling in this regard" (Lokos 1967, 88). While the issue was "fundamentally a matter of the heart," it was true that laws could help— "laws carefully considered and weighed in an atmosphere of dispassion . . . and in the light of fundamental constitutional principles" (89). Regarding the central public accommodations and employment sections, Goldwater concluded, "I find no constitutional basis for the exercise of Federal regulatory authority in either of these areas" (90–91). (In the litigation that followed the Civil Rights Act's passage, the federal government defended the public accommodations section on the grounds that the federal government was regulating interstate commerce via the law. As far as states and localities went, Goldwater not only believed that they had the constitutional right to enact laws mandating nondiscrimination in public accommodations, but he also publicly endorsed such a bill being considered in Phoenix in June; see Lokos, 123.)

Goldwater moved then from constitutional philosophy to practical implementation, and expressed concerns, warning that enforcement of the Civil Rights Act would require "the creation of a Federal police force of mammoth proportions" along with "the development of an 'informer' psychology in great areas of our national life—neighbors spying on neighbors, workers spying on workers, business spying on businessmen" (Lokos 1967, 91–92). As his remarks neared their end, Goldwater stressed, "I repeat again: I am unalterably opposed to discrimination of any sort"—but, "I am unalterably opposed to the destruction of our great system of government and the loss of our God-given liberties" (92). In the most important Senate votes of that year, Goldwater was one of twenty-seven nay votes.

Barry Goldwater had finished a distant third in the March 10th New Hampshire Republican primary, but as the campaign moved south and west, he sped toward his hard-fought, grassroots-oriented California victory over New York Governor Nelson Rockefeller's enormous spending advantage, thus clinching the nomination at the July convention held at San Francisco. On Saturday, July 11, Goldwater's "brains trust" gathered to discuss Goldwater's all-important acceptance speech. Goldwater wound up asking Harry Jaffa, a political scientist at The Ohio State University, to play the leading role in the construction of the speech, and played a significant role in the final outcome. Angry at what he considered to be scurrilous attacks from liberal, northeastern Republicans, Goldwater decided to use the moment to signal that his call four years prior to conservatives to grow up and take over the Republican party had borne fruit. Significantly, the group composing the speech included only one practicing politician—Goldwater himself (Edwards 1995, 268–69).

On July 12th, Goldwater appeared before southern delegates at the GOP convention, saying that segregation was "wrong morally, and in some instances, constitutionally." He further promised that the Civil Rights Act would be enforced under his administration, and promised to use the bully pulpit of the White House to combat discrimination (Lokos 1967, 125). Three days later came his famous acceptance speech. Introduced by Richard Nixon on July 16, Goldwater began his speech, which thematically stressed overall the positive value of freedom per se, as in freedom from oppressive government not only abroad, as in the Cold War fight, but also at home, as in the Great Society that was being born. In 1964, it was still the case that the three television networks provided complete coverage of the political conventions. Hence the acceptance speech, probably *the* principal highlight of often dreary proceedings, provided a tremendous opportunity for a candidate, especially a challenger from the minority party. Goldwater and his speechwriters of course took it seriously, living in a world where such a moment afforded a far greater chance to communicate with the mass electorate than was to be the case in the later cable-television age.

The speech naturally covered many different political issues, such as the whiffs of scandal associated with Lyndon Johnson's image as a wheeler-dealer, and, inevitably most prominently, the Cold War; Goldwater stated ominously that the United States was losing in Vietnam, despite Johnson's unwillingness to talk about it, and the speech overall was pervaded by a tone of anxiety about impending doom, unless the people revive themselves. When it came to the domestic policy realm, Goldwater, rather than enumerating specific programmatic points, offered instead a sharply articulated *philosophy* of what America should be that differed radically from the Great Society's view. "The Good Lord," he began, "raised up this mighty Republic to be a home for the brave and to flourish as the land of the free—*not* to stagnate in the swampland of collectivism" (Lokos 1967, 184). When he warned that the "tide has been running against freedom," he was not simply referring to the Soviets: "Our people have followed false prophets" (184). The "single resolve" of his campaign, and of the Republican party of 1964, was "*Freedom!*" This core value underlay the United States' position in the divided, Cold War world—but it was also fundamental to grasp that "we *must renew* freedom's vision in our own hearts and in our own homes" (184). Besides its international errors, the present administration was held responsible for disturbing internal trends: "We have lost the brisk pace of diversity and the genius of individual creativity. We are plodding at a pace set by centralized planning, red tape, rules without responsibility, and regimentation without recourse" (185). The growth of federal power had led to the rise of "bureaucratic make-work" rather than "useful jobs" for far too many. The rising concern about public disorder, especially in the big cities, was noted with alarm.

What lay behind these discouraging and forbidding trends? Morally challenged political leaders? Out-of-date policies? Goldwater drew a thick line in the sand: "We Republicans see all this as more, *much* more than the result of mere political differences, or mere political mistakes. We see this as the result of a fundamentally and absolutely wrong view of man, his nature, and his destiny" (Lokos 1967, 186). In short, the entire philosophical worldview of the political opposition was being drawn into the spotlight and was found threatening to basic American values.

The Great Society vision was being constructed by those "who seek to live your lives for you, to take your liberties in return for relieving you of your responsibilities. . . . Those who seek absolute power, even though they seek it to do what they regard as good, are simply demanding the right to enforce *their* version of Heaven on earth" (Lokos 1967, 186). The source of the error was "false notions of equality," certainly a word very much in the air in the mid-1960s with the powerful focus of national attention on the civil rights struggle. Wrongly understood, "equality" could lead "first to conformity and then to despotism." Freedom, not equality wrongly understood, was Goldwater's god. Freedom was not easily attained or kept: "I know that some men may walk away from it, that some men resist challenge—accepting the false security of governmental paternalism" (186, 190). The Cold War was far from won, and Goldwater, always a firm proponent of military spending and a forceful foreign policy, pledged to continue the struggle until victory. Freedom was America's hard-won birthright, and it would be not only defended but also held up to others as a beacon. This was why domestic affairs mattered to much: "Our example to the world must, like charity, begin at home" (190).

The United States, to be sure, had to be a society of involved, caring citizens, "never abandoning the needy or forsaking the helpless." Goldwater, with his lifetime of civic activism of all sorts, did not really worry about that possibility. What needed to be stressed, rather, was "the liberation of the energy and the talent of the individual—otherwise our vision is blind at the outset" (Lokos 1967, 191). His Republican vision was of "a nation of men and women, of families proud of their roles, jealous of their responsibilities, unlimited in their aspirations—a nation where all who *can*, *will* be self-reliant" (191). Key to this was the "sanctity of private property," which Goldwater had seen threatened by the Civil Rights Act against which he had voted. In opposition to LBJ's expansive Great Society vision, Goldwater offered an alternative: "We do not seek to live anyone's life for him—we seek only to secure his rights, guarantee him opportunity to strive, with government performing only those needed and Constitutionally-sanctioned tasks which cannot otherwise be performed." Yes, there was a place for government—but "we Republicans define government's role, where needed, at *many* levels, preferably the one *closest* to the people involved." In practice this meant, "Our towns and our cities, then our counties and states, then our regional compacts—and *only then* the national government! *That* is the ladder of liberty built by decentralized power" (192).

Goldwater's speech was destined to immediately and lastingly become known for the first half of the following dramatic statement with which its argument concluded: "*Extremism in the defense of liberty is no vice. Moderation in the pursuit of justice is no virtue*" (Lokos 1967, 193). Nothing in the campaign that followed could overcome the dominant interpretation that prevailed: Goldwater and his ideas were "extremist." From Goldwater's point of view, however, as the speech in its entirely made clear, the stakes in the 1964 election were indeed high, and the need to offer a "choice, not an echo," as was often said that year, was great and inevitable.

The GOP platform committee, dominated by Goldwaterites, similarly portrayed the federal government as a source of potential abuse of power and something to be concerned about, a far cry indeed from the Great Society view of it. Promises were made of reduced federal spending and lower federal taxes, and criticism was leveled at federal regulations, bureaucracy, and the overall centralizing trend that seemed inexorably on the rise in American politics. While the platform did promise "full implementation and faithful execution of the Civil Rights Act of 1964," it also expressed opposition to what it termed "inverse discrimination" and also to the abandonment of the neighborhood school concept so as to foster desegregation as an end in itself (Goldberg 1995, 203). While talking points for long-range future political discourse of the late twentieth century and beyond may easily be discerned in this Republican platform, it proved to be radically out of sync with the dominant spirit of 1964.

Would there be a serious debate in the 1964 presidential election campaign over the philosophical foundations of the War on Poverty, and the soon-to-be-announced Great Society programs? It was not to be. Barry Goldwater certainly broke all the rules in his presidential run. He criticized the War on Poverty in a speech delivered in Appalachia; he questioned what would be born in 1965 as Medicare at a Florida retirement home (Lokos 1967, 14). Political liberals prophetically sensed a golden opportunity to take the center of the electorate and had little trouble arousing fears of the destruction of such New Deal icons as Social Security, let alone any Great Society extensions of the welfare state. The image of Goldwater as trigger-happy was famously underscored with a much-discussed television commercial aired on September 7th featuring a girl picking off the petals of a daisy as a voice in the background counted down from ten to zero, followed by an atomic explosion, with a message following that suggested the world itself might be blown up should Goldwater assume the presidency; a similar message was delivered on September 13 featuring a girl and an ice cream cone. (In an echo of this scenario, President Jimmy Carter in 1980 claimed that his little daughter Amy had expressed fears to him of a nuclear holocaust should Ronald Reagan be elected; in the much-changed atmosphere of that year, however, Carter was roundly ridiculed.)

On Election Day, the association of Goldwater's "states' rights" beliefs with white supremacy was fundamentally confirmed: besides his own Arizona homeland, Goldwater won only five Deep South states, most of which had *never* in the twentieth century voted for a Republican presidential candidate. Vermont voted for a Democratic presidential candidate for the first time in the twentieth century. For 1964, Goldwater was indeed too "extreme." The War on Poverty and the Great Society were just being born, and the center of the American electorate was more than willing to give them a try, in the spirit of LBJ's campaign speech to the United Steelworkers convention at Atlantic City, wherein he promised, "We will extend the helping hand of a just nation to the poor and the helpless and the oppressed. We will do all these things because we love people instead of hate them, because we have faith in America, not fear of the future" (Goldberg 1995, 227). Goldwaterism, then, here was rhetorically represented as unhelpful, unjust, oppressive, hateful, faithless, fearful, and backward-looking, and this representation was dominant in the narrow national media of the day. True, some "backlash" against the civil rights movement was observable, in large part a reaction against televised pictures of rioting (which would greatly increase as the 1960s wore on), but Martin Luther King, Jr., Lyndon Johnson, and even many mainstream conservative Republicans such as House GOP Whip Gerald Ford and Senate Minority Leader Everett Dirksen sided with the landmark Civil Rights Act of 1964 as an idea whose time had come. As the syndicated newspaper columnist Tom Wicker observed, most came to believe—quite correctly—that Goldwater "would act, in some way, outside the vital center, against the national consensus" (quoted in Lokos 1967, 25).

In years to come, in fact quite soon, the Goldwater critique of many War on Poverty and Great Society programs would become mainstream, boilerplate, and even dominant in American political discourse. At the same time, however, as Johnson had hoped, much of the paradigm shift proved permanent, and the national government greatly increased its role in such areas as health care and education, as seen in the early twenty-first century, when an all-Republican-controlled national government understood to be "conservative" enacted a prescription drug benefit/entitlement as part of Medicare with a colossal price tag and enacted national standards subject to testing for precollege educational institutions receiving federal funds (which meant all public schools). Goldwater's philosophically libertarian, nonracist states' rights–based opposition to federal guarantees of equal treatment in public accommodations and employment, however, would not rise to fight another day, despite controversies over such things as the acceptability of various forms of affirmative action lasting into the twenty-first century.

Goldwater's term as Arizona's U.S. senator ended, giving him more time than ever to attend to the speaking circuit; he remained very much in demand, continued his newspaper column, and did not disappear from television news programs. After the August 1965 riot in the Los Angeles neighborhood known as Watts, Goldwater almost sounded like a Great Society man; rioters, he said, were "fed up with not being able to get job, with not being able to live as well as other people live," and he suggested job training and economic investment in urban areas (Goldberg 1995, 246). But his heart remained to the right. Goldwater tied rising inflation to "excessive" federal spending; criticized the rhetoric of civil rights leaders, including Martin Luther King, Jr., for falsely and unrealistically raising expectations; and cheered the 1966 midterm swing to the GOP as a repudiation of Johnson personally as well as of his Great Society—"a backlash against dishonesty in government, runaway inflation, welfare state socialism and a no-win policy in Vietnam" (247). Goldwater was largely preaching to the choir at this point; the GOP pickup in 1966, though large, was predictable and included many liberal Republicans as well as moderate and conservative ones. Goldwater would return to the U.S. Senate and serve for many more years, fundamentally sticking to his largely libertarian conservative guns and living long enough to see both himself and the movement he did so much to start outlast much, though far from all, of LBJ's Great Society. He continued to favor big government in the military sphere, continued to worry about tax cuts leading to deficits through the vogue of President Reagan's 1980s supply-side economics, and on social questions became increasingly libertarian on the whole. Barry Goldwater remained a rugged individualist.

WILLIAM F. BUCKLEY, JR.
(1925–)

In the early twenty-first century, a Web page of links to conservative sites included, naturally enough, the online edition of *National Review*, the influential magazine of opinion started by William F. Buckley, Jr., in 1955 and continually edited by him through the late twentieth century; its annotation to the *NR* link, in an allusion to historically minded insiders, stated that the publication was "still standing athwart history." Left out was what had come next, in the original setting: standing athwart history, "yelling, Stop, at a time when no one is inclined to do so, or to have much patience with those who so urge it" (*National Review*, "Publisher's Statement," November 19, 1955). This cri de coeur's tone is that of radical alarm while also suggesting political impotence, awareness of unpopularity, and lack of influence, suggesting being a virtual voice crying in a wilderness, and time rapidly running out before some dreaded apocalypse. This famous statement may be taken as authentically representing the feelings not only of Buckley but also of his collaborators in the always shaky venture of a new magazine, right in the midst of the Eisenhower age, a time when, somewhat similarly, impatient liberals with memories of the then-not-so-distant New Deal era for their frustrated part bitterly complained from the other shore about the politics of "dead center," that the bland were leading the bland. The liberals' mood would begin to improve with the dawning of the Kennedy era, brief as it proved to be, and then positively boomed in 1964 with the declaration of the War on Poverty and the pronouncement of the Great Society by President Lyndon Johnson. 1964 also brought encouragement to William F. Buckley, Jr., and his band of conservative intellectuals, writers, and activists with the Goldwater campaign. But the crushing defeat of their paladin did a great deal to create such mammoth Democratic majorities in Congress that the Great Society steamroller, if only for a single congressional term, soon flattened everything in its wake as it sought to construct a new political and social order.

This, however, did nothing to stop the usually cheerful, energetic, and peripatetic William F. Buckley. In the pages of his magazine, which itself immensely benefited from the Goldwater campaign; in his failed campaign for the mayoralty of New York City, which he used to promote his own notions of the correct understanding of problems as well as solutions to the modern urban scene; and in the creation of his long-running television interview program, *Firing Line*, nationally broadcast on what was still known as "educational television," Buckley did what he could to spread his ideology and enlighten his fellow citizens according to his conservative lights. The enfant terrible of the early 1950s, who had scandalized the northeastern liberal establishment with his attacks on the alleged secular, leftist bias of his alma mater in *God and Man at Yale* (1951), defended Joseph McCarthy in *McCarthy and His Enemies* (1954), and at least amused 1950s students with his frequent appearances on the then-popular college lecture circuit, assumed a new, more mature role as the most significant impresario of a conservative intellectual movement that would grow exponentially in the latter third of the twentieth century. Buckley, who from day one sought to distinguish his brand of conservatism from right-wing extremism, had significant difficulty dealing with the civil rights issues, as the moral high ground was easily occupied by the liberal left while his principled states'-rights terrain was crowded with white supremacists who were morally unsavory as well as politically objectionable. He had an easier time poking holes in and encouraging impatience with the problematical Great Society attempts at resolving social problems, and the turbulent maelstrom of the late 1960s made his conservative critique more appealing to millions. Through it all, Buckley's sense of style helped create the persona of the leader of the new, modern conservative movement as an intriguing (not moss-backed), intellectually challenging (not reactionary), respectable, nonthreatening figure within the acceptable mainstream of American politics. William F. Buckley, Jr., became conservatism with a witty, half-cocked, smiling face, destined for a long career that ran well past the Great Society's brief, shining moment.

William Francis Buckley, Jr., born November 24, 1925 (he insisted on changing his middle name to "Frank," after his father, at age five), was an "immaculately conceived" cradle conservative, with a particularly rebellious, ideosyncratic streak, and the credit would have to go to his extremely strong-willed father most of all—Will Sr., a Texas-born Irish immigrants' son whose mother had instilled in him a very strong Roman Catholic faith and identity that he was able successfully to pass on to his children. Fluent in Spanish and a graduate of the University of Texas in law, Will Sr. moved to Mexico where he made and then lost a small fortune (via confiscation) in the oil business. Expelled from that turbulent country in 1921, he was back in the United States where he successfully rebuilt his finances to a level that allowed William Jr., sixth of ten children born to the founding patriarch and Aloise Steiner Buckley of New Orleans, to have a most unusual and highly privileged childhood at an isolated family compound in Sharon, Connecticut, located in the rural, northwestern part of the state. The Buckley children were educated at home and were tutored in Spanish and French from the age of five. In 1926 they lived in Venezuela; from 1929 through 1933, the family lived in Paris where Will Sr. was working, thereafter returning to Connecticut. The patriarch worked in New York during the week, but when he was home on weekends he used the family dinner table for educational purposes, forcefully expounding his own hard-earned philosophy of free enterprise, antirevolutionism, isolationism, and a rock-solid Catholic faith while continually challenging his children to report what they had learned that week and to discuss and debate the issues of the day. None rebelled against the father; quite the opposite. And of all the children, Bill Jr. came most to resemble his namesake personality-wise; he was argumentative, increasingly the center of attention at the dinner-table discussions, a great reader who loved discovering and using words, uninterested in team sports while excelling at sailing and horseback riding, musically talented on the keyboard, quick-witted, and sarcastic, and from an early age he exhibited a religiosity that matured into a deep and life-sustaining faith. All these characteristics he would carry with him all his days. He spent the fall of 1938 at St. John's Beaumont, a Catholic school in England, the next spring touring Italy, and then returned to Sharon; in 1940, he entered a small, nearby Protestant prep school, Millbrook, where, given his preparation to date, he excelled academically, musically, and in debate, graduating in 1943. Health delayed his entry into the Army until 1944; he passed the war uneventfully in extended training in the southern United States, greatly improving his social skills, which had been notably lacking to date.

Upon entering Yale College in September 1946, William F. Buckley, Jr., nearly twenty-one years of age, possessed a rare cosmopolitanism that had an intriguing Americanizing finish to it via his military service. His first campus activity became debating, where he exhibited a style of sarcastic humor and competitiveness that stood out even in that realm, and then the campus newspaper, the *Yale Daily News*, of which he became chairman after his sophomore year. In this post he attacked liberal professors, denounced communism with an unusual vehemence, and created controversy and interest on all sides. Graduating in 1950 and marrying Patricia Taylor in Vancouver shortly thereafter, Buckley taught Spanish and composed his first book, *God and Man at Yale* (published in the fall of 1951), an attack on the liberal establishment that he claimed dominated Yale and that taught, sometimes subtly, sometimes not, its students that sophisticated people were morally relativistic and that good-hearted people were socialistic, hiding behind the shibboleth of "academic freedom." The liberal Establishment reacted predictably, including with substantial doses of overt anti-Catholicism as well as charges of extremism and authoritarianism, and there were criticisms from more conservative quarters, too, but the book sold and established

Buckley's reputation beyond New Haven and Sharon. Buckley was not exactly a conservative as that term was then understood; rather, he sought to shake things up and to change them, seeing himself as a paladin struggling against an embedded, irritatingly smug establishment. As the book sold and the controversy raged, Buckley did a nine-month tour of duty with the Central Intelligence Agency in Mexico, after which he and Pat moved to New York.

Having experienced the thrills of journalism in college, Buckley decided to accept a position as an associate editor at *The American Mercury*, an established magazine that he rapidly discovered to be fiscally in crisis. An editorial dispute brought his tenure to a quick end in a matter of weeks. Buckley and his brother-in-law, Brent Bozell, a close friend and collaborator from college days, decided to write a lengthy magazine article about the controversy surrounding Senator Joseph McCarthy; this developed into the book, *McCarthy and His Enemies*, which, while offering some criticisms of the Wisconsin senator's sloppiness, even recklessness, nonetheless firmly came down on the side of a continuing crusade to expose un-American "security risks" both inside and outside of government. Published in March 1954, the book's timing proved excellent—a matter of weeks before the so-called Army-McCarthy hearings. Buckley made many appearances, live and via the media, some in prominent venues, others not, ridiculing the alleged reign of terror and pointing out the unending lionization by the Establishment of all critics of McCarthy as heroic, brave, and selfless. For its part, such Establishment organs as *Time* and *Newsweek* deigned not to recognize the book's existence. As John Judis, Buckley's 1980s biographer, summed up, "If *God and Man at Yale* had given Buckley the reputation of an enfant terrible among the eastern intelligentsia, *McCarthy and His Enemies* made him a pariah" (Judis 1988, 111).

William F. Buckley's most lasting contribution to the United States' great debates, of course, is *National Review*. Since leaving the CIA, he had off and on expressed interest in buying a periodical or starting one, but his decision to write the book on McCarthy turned out to be his project of these years. In collaboration with Willi Schlamm, a Jewish refugee from Hitler's Europe who had become an associate of *Time* publisher Henry Luce, a prospectus seeking support went out in 1954 to prospective financial supporters, and Buckley began touring to raise money (his father donated $100,000). The prospectus expressed great dissatisfaction with the alleged moderate conservatism of the Eisenhower administration: "Middle-of-the-Road, *qua* Middle of the Road, is politically, intellectually, and morally repugnant"; referring to the British socialist tradition, the prospectus spoke of the dangers of "an identifiable team of Fabian operators . . . bent on controlling both our major parties—under the sanction of such fatuous and unreasoned slogans as 'national unity,' 'middle-of-the-road,' 'progressivism,' and 'bipartisanship'" (Judis 1988, 133). The acceptance of New Deal–ish welfare statism by "modern conservatism" of the Eisenhower sort was unacceptable and to be fought.

National Review's debut issue, in November 1955, showed that, among respectable elements, only the isolationist Old Right was excluded from the effort to create a new forum for conservative thought; disreputable elements smacking of such crudities as anti-Semitism were excluded as well, though the states'-rights position of the white supremacist South in criticizing the pro-integration U.S. Supreme Court *Brown* decision was supported, usually out of a principled fear of a stronger central government. As a magazine of opinion, it of course would never have a circulation of millions (it did not take long for the weekly, due to financial problems, to become a fortnightly), or anything close to it; its targeted audience were "opinion-makers," either conservative or at least those willing to entertain the possibility of a supportable conservative viewpoint on a given issue, and political activists of a right-wing bent. Bad ideas, emanating from an elite, explained much of what was wrong with the world; conscious of occupying a position that was very much a minority one within the educated, intellectual world, Buckley in 1956 commented, in what would become one of his most famous turns of phrase, that he would "sooner be governed by the first two thousand people in the Boston telephone directory than by the two thousand members of the faculty of Harvard University" (Judis 1988, 217). No fan of the sentimental fetish of the "common man," Buckley distrusted the plans and schemes of the descendants of New Deal–era "Brains Trusters" even more. Much of the magazine was taken up with foreign affairs, as the communist threat was seen as the clearest and most present danger. While Buckley spent the lion's share of his time tending to his infant magazine, he continued to make numerous public appearances, both live and via media, and was strongly in demand due to his entertaining and witty persona. His philosophy combined strong anticommunism with an ambition, as he told a television interviewer in 1957, aimed "at overturning the revised view of society pretty well brought in by FDR" (162). In 1959, a collection of his writings revealing his continuing indebtedness to his father's dislike for the New Deal approach to things, *Up from Liberalism*, was published. In 1960, *National Review* celebrated its fifth anniversary at the Plaza Hotel in New York, John F. Kennedy was narrowly elected president over Eisenhower's vice president, Richard Nixon (Buckley, disliking the politics of both, was neutral and wrote *NR*'s presidential vote editorial accordingly), and the 1960s began in earnest with William F. Buckley a rather eccentric, none too influential in actuality, yet real feature of the nation's intellectual and political landscape.

The 1960s overall would prove to be American liberalism's heyday, and to some extent its Waterloo, but it has been increasingly realized that a new American Right was also developing and growing in those years, if not successfully in a narrowly political sense, especially at a national level, where the Great Society and liberalism dominated the landscape during the mid-1960s. At a weekend meeting of several dozen youthful conservative activists held at the old Buckley family estate in Sharon in the fall of 1960, a new student organization, Young Americans for Freedom, was born. The host was the personification of what the attendees aspired to become.

In 1961, several activists associated with *National Review*, in a protest of the domination of the New York State Republican Party by Governor Nelson Rockefeller's penchant for governmental activism and also by his money, established the Conservative Party, whose greatest achievement would come in 1970 with the election of James Buckley, Bill's brother, as a U.S. senator from New York. After some tactical uncertainty, Buckley and his magazine definitively distanced themselves from the then-growing and, to some liberals as well as conservatives like Buckley, potentially threatening right-wing John Birch Society, despite its overlap with activists promoting a presidential candidacy of Arizona U.S. Senator Barry Goldwater, whom Buckley very much liked and supported. In the not-so-very-long run, the John Birch Society, though it survived, faded from the central political scene, while William F. Buckley's star continued to shine and, despite the mid-1960s' liberal hour, rise. In late 1961, he was contracted to write a syndicated newspaper column, first called "A Conservative Voice" and eventually "On the Right," which survived into the twenty-first century and which vastly increased awareness of him. He began to be profiled by such mass-circulation magazines as *Esquire*, *Playboy*, and *Mademoiselle*. A failed attempt to construct a philosophically minded book solidified in Buckley's own mind the appropriateness of his role as a polemicist and editor. Both in his own writing and his continuing fostering of the growing conservative movement's "home," *National Review*, Buckley was right at the center of political conservatism, both in its practical and intellectual terms.

By 1964, *National Review*'s circulation reached 90,000, a very respectable number for a political review and nearly twice the number in 1961 when Barry Goldwater had allowed his name to be signed to a successful subscription-increase letter (Judis 1988, 221). Buckley's brother-in-law Brent Bozell had served as the ghostwriter for Goldwater's successful political tract, *The Conscience of a Conservative*, and both *NR* and Buckley the columnist treated Barry Goldwater as conservatism's popular face insofar as national politics was concerned. The Draft Goldwater for President movement came substantially out of efforts organized by central figures involved in *National Review*, though not Buckley himself. But once the actual Goldwater campaign organization began to take shape, it became clear that Buckley would not be invited into the inner circle of Goldwaterites, some of whom perceived Buckley and the *NR* set to be a little too far to the right, others of whom simply did not want rivals to their own positions of influence. The debacle that was to be the Goldwater campaign unfolded without any direct involvement by William F. Buckley, Jr.

In fact, Buckley almost from the start was, unlike the other top brass at *National Review*, a doubter regarding the viability of Goldwater's candidacy; increasingly in contact with circles in New York City, where he was now spending most of his time (save for his regular and lengthy skiing vacations to Switzerland), he was less and less confined to a conservative ghetto, and thus more in contact with people who regarded a Goldwater candidacy as barely above the level of a joke, not to mention political analysts with experience in the real world of national-level American politics. Lyndon Johnson had declared the War on Poverty in January 1964, the same month in which Goldwater declared himself a candidate; what might the effect of a weak, poorly run Goldwater campaign be on the longer range prospects for American conservatism? In the spring, at Ann Arbor, Johnson's University of Michigan commencement address announced the coming of the idealistic-sounding Great Society. Buckely in his June newspaper columns wrote openly of the likelihood of Johnson's winning in November. The Civil Rights Act of 1964 made it through Congress in the summer, in fact with the support of any number of conservative members of Congress such as Senator Everett Dirksen and Congressman Gerald Ford (though not with Goldwater's), a high point for the liberal view of the civil rights question. In his usual speech to the annual meeting of Young Americans for Freedom, held in New York City in September, Buckley spoke openly to an intensely attentive audience of young conservative activists of Goldwater's impending defeat, of the need to take the longer view, and of the necessity of thinking about what conservatism would do next after Election Day 1964. Here and elsewhere, Buckley demonstrated his connectedness to the realities of American politics. Goldwater's nomination had indeed been a triumph for conservatism within the Republican party; but American conservatism had miles to go before it was to make it to the mountaintop. Overall, 1964 was to be Lyndon Johnson's and liberalism's year, not Barry Goldwater's, conservatism's, or Buckley's. But, Buckley added, conservatism, and he himself, would live to fight another day.

Not only was Goldwater routed, but so was the Republican party, whose only positives were to be found in the somewhat (yet far from entirely) welcome "conversion" of some southern white supremacist Democrats to Goldwater Republicanism, the first step in a movement of the highest long-term significance. *NR* was the logical place for public discussion of the "Where do we go from here?" sort, and it so functioned, as it was to do for the rest of the 1960s and mostly until the 1980s, as conservatism's town hall. Conservatism, surprisingly to some, rebounded well from the Goldwater debacle. Buckley himself soon made a surprising decision: to be a candidate for mayor of New York City in 1965, using the campaign to bring attention to conservative approaches to government, approaches far removed from the developing mentality of the Great Society. Much of Buckley's concerns, expressed on his own and in the issues of *National Review*, involved international questions, and as the 1960s Vietnam issue loomed larger, that would continue to be the case. But in his mayoral campaign, Buckley exclusively addressed the kinds of domestic questions that the Great Society debate was all about. He was particularly interested in publicly debating Republican Congressman John Lindsey, an epitome of liberal Republicanism and an embodiment of the fact that Great Society thinking was not confined to the Democratic Party of Lyndon Johnson; Lindsey, in fact, was *more* liberal than most Democrats in Congress. Buckley hoped for a "campaign of ideas," whose serious purpose was largely educational and that, if the truth be told, was not to be taken too seriously at all—he admitted in his first press conference that he did not believe he had any chance of winning; appropriately enough, he entitled his book about the entire adventure *The Unmaking of a Mayor* (1966).

His maiden campaign press conference, held on June 24th, addressed various issues of rising concern in New York City and in the nation. The "urban crisis" of the 1960s was beginning to be sensed all across the political spectrum, and the Great Society view of how to deal with it, thanks to the top-heavy Democratic majorities in Congress that had resulted from the Johnson landslide, were moving through Capitol Hill committee-hearings rooms and corridors on their way to congressional floors, the White House, and then actualization via new bureaucracies in Washington and then beyond the banks of the Potomac. John Lindsey's approach to the Great Society—do more of it, and faster, and locally, too—was well within the mainstream of New York City's post-Depression political center and in the tradition of the last Republican mayor of New York, New Deal supporter Fiorello LaGuardia. William F. Buckley, Jr., represented something quite new and different—a dissenting alternative. New York's fiscal deficit, for instance, was not blamed on insufficient federal aid, but rather on Mayor Robert Wagner's courting of voting blocs' favor, such as labor unions, who should be dealt with more firmly. Regarding welfare costs, Buckley called for a one-year residency requirement for those seeking aid, in the hopes of discouraging migrants from other states who were allegedly attracted by New York's higher dole. The most important issue, Buckley said, was crime, the solution to which was not improved or increased government-funded social programs, along the lines of the Great Society, but rather more police and greater sympathy and support for the police (Judis 1988, 239–40).

Clearly this was something different for New York City in the 1960s. Local press coverage proved to be decent, even helpful. The campaign itself proved to be an educational experience for Buckley and for the conservative movement of which he was a representative. At the outset, while never believing he could win, Buckley and his circle did imagine the possibility of denying Lindsey the mayor's office by taking away Republican votes. However, they were also aware, as the people who had established the New York State Conservative Party, that the Republican Party of New York State was Governor Nelson Rockefeller's party; both Rockefeller (who endorsed Lindsey) and Lindsey had declined to support Goldwater even after his nomination; furthermore, those Republicans who basically wanted to win more than make a statement would eventually be proven correct in believing that Lindsey was electable. Instead, the audience within the city for Buckley's arguments and even his act, to some degree, were the "outer-borough," white, Catholic "ethnics" of Irish, Italian, and Polish extraction from Queens, Brooklyn, and Staten Island, most of them registered Democrats. These were not exactly people Buckley had often come into contact with; on the other hand, it did not take him too long to see the connection, nor was he all that surprised to learn that they could form an audience for his conservative political message. Those whom the national news media would later term "Reagan Democrats" in the 1980s would be described in the 1960s as the bringers of "white backlash" to the civil rights and Great Society idealism.

William F. Buckley, Jr., talked about welfare in his mayoralty campaign of 1965 in a way unknown in New York City's modern political history. His heresy to the "mainstream" of New York politics was profound, and total; predictably, his gospel largely fell on deaf ears. But not entirely. The conservative candidate scoffed at the Great Society idea that increased spending on government-run programs would be of any substantial help in alleviating the problems of urban minority residents. To a black audience he expressed agreement that American blacks historically had labored under unique disadvantages, but added that "socializing" the country was nonetheless not called for; rather, following the basic argument he derived from the 1963 study of New York City's various groups by Nathan Glazer and Daniel Patrick Moynihan, *Beyond the Melting Pot*, he stated, "The *principal* problems that are faced by Negroes today, and that were faced to a lesser extent by other groups, are *not* solved by government. They are solved by the leadership of their own people. Will *you* kindly tell *me* what the government has proposed to do, for instance, about the problem of illegitimacy? . . . The mayor of New York has got to be modest in his pretensions. He must not approach the Negro people and say, 'I will transform your life' " (Buckley 1966, 166).

A three-week newspaper strike meant that the mayoral campaign moved to television, where Buckley performed strikingly well and gained far more attention than heretofore. Significantly noticed far beyond the precincts of the five boroughs in an era when New York was imagined to be central to American politics, Buckley, the television version, began to sow seeds in the heads of some that he should move into the electronic medium. Buckley began to take the whole campaign somewhat more seriously, not in the sense that he imagined he would be elected, but rather that conservative ideas might gain substantially wider currency through his efforts. As the election approached he was increasingly attacked, by such organs of the liberal establishment as the editorial pages of the *New York Times*, as pandering racism; he reacted sometimes with ridicule, sometimes with anger to such talk. His final tally, nearly 350,000 votes, some 13.4 percent of the total, was easily the highest yet in the brief history of the youthful New York Conservative Party, overwhelmingly from ethnic outer-borough neighborhoods, hardly at all from the traditional home of city Republicanism, the wealthy Upper East Side (Judis 1988, 255–56).

William F. Buckely, Jr., may have lost the mayoral election, but he came out of it a far better known man to the nation as a whole. More newspapers picked up his column (he had continued writing it during his campaign as well as continuing his *National Review* work), and in early 1965 began serious discussion that the following year produced the television program *Firing Line*, which featured Buckley and a guest in a discussion-debate. His entertaining account of his campaign, *The Unmaking of a Mayor*, published in 1966, substantially broadened his audience beyond the narrower confines of right-wing conservative political activists. He continued to appear quite frequently at college campuses and elsewhere on the public lecture circuit in the late 1960s and consistently drew substantial crowds. (His 1971 book, *Cruising Speed*, and a 1983 book, *Overdrive*, both of which originally appeared in *The New Yorker*, give a sense of his tremendously demanding schedule and catholic interests.) He appeared on mass-circulation magazine covers such as *Time* and on television programs, and was profiled in mass-circulation publications. The greatest mass medium of them all, television, proved, as it had during the mayoral campaign, a perfect setting for the Buckley persona.

Firing Line debuted on an independent New York City television station on April 30, 1966. It did especially well for a serious public-affairs program, was enjoyed by people across the political spectrum, and was nationally syndicated on the emerging network of educational television stations beginning to be known as "public" stations. Its audience was not, of course, in the league of commercial programming, but when it came to the realm of the politically active, it was major league. Eventually, transcripts of his program could be purchased. Buckley often had liberals on the program, but he used the show to advance his critique of the Johnson administration's policies, both foreign and domestic. The Great Society, of course, had no appeal whatsoever for him, and he once stated that the Great Society deserved to be ignored; unfortunately, the question had to be asked, "But will the Great Society ignore us?" On a *Firing Line* program with Alabama Democratic Governor George Wallace as the guest, Buckley differentiated *his* brand of conservatism's from Wallace's based on an antipathy for the Great Society approach to public issues that dated to his father's disdain for the New Deal; speaking of spending programs for the poor and elderly, Buckley opined, "This is a free-enterprise country and . . . we have a tradition here of private philanthropy, of philanthropy conducted by private people and under programs that haven't required mobilization of the machinery of the state at the federal or state or local level. . . . [T]he whole tradition of your kind of Democrat is one of enormous enthusiasm for federal handouts" (Judis 1988, 285). In 1968, Buckley was a firm Nixon man, not a Wallace economic populist at all. As a devoted anticommunist, he continued to support the Vietnam War while heaping scorn on antiwar protesters and the liberal Establishment who had lost its nerve. In his 1970 introduction to a collection of primary sources from America's conservative tradition, subtitled *Did You Ever See a Dream Walking?* Buckley, in keeping with his philosophical underpinnings and oft-repeated debating rhetoric of a quarter-century, made resistance to and defiance of statism a fundamental stance from which to see and analyze the world: "It is essentially the modernist view that only the state can negotiate the shoals that lie ahead of twentieth-century man. We are accordingly urged to believe in the state as the primary agent of individual concerns, a belief that is embedded in the analysis and rhetoric of socialism. Yet we are resisting, in America, the beatification of the state, most particularly in the past few years, when American conservatives have been joined by prominent liberals in expressing skepticism for the capacities of the state" (Buckley 1970, xxvii).

Just beyond the Great Society era, in the early 1970s, Buckley would make contact with a group of New York editors, writers, and intellectuals of a social scientific bent associated with *Commentary*, a midcirculation magazine established in the late 1940s by the American Jewish Committee, and *The Public Interest*, a much smaller circulation quarterly already known for publishing articles critical of the Great Society in form, if not (in the early years, anyway) in intent. Such figures as Irving Kristol, Daniel Patrick Moynihan, Norman Podhoretz, Midge Decter, and Nathan Glazer, who collectively would come to be labeled "neoconservatives," began to partner with Buckley and *National Review* in a way that even in 1965 would have been unthinkable, their actual bylines even appearing in the magazine in the early 1970s (and well beyond). A new intellectual-political alignment was in formation that would have long-term consequences of high significance, and William F. Buckley, Jr., was in the thick of it. His brand of conservatism—urbane, educated, refined, east coast, neither country club nor Chamber of Commerce—was far more hospitable. From Buckley's point of view, the neoconservatives he welcomed added a social science–based intellectual depth previously lacking in most conservative political discourse. While there were various factors in this story, including many connected with foreign policy questions, disillusionment with the Great Society as it had turned out was paramount in this significant new intellectual departure.

Buckley's biographer, John Judis, appropriately termed the founding editor of the *National Review* the "patron saint" of the conservatives. As longtime journalist and frequent presidential candidate Patrick Buchanan wrote in his 1988 autobiography, *Right from the Beginning*, "It is difficult to exaggerate the debt conservatives of my generation owe *National Review* and Bill Buckley. Before I read *NR*, there was virtually nothing I read that supported or reinforced what I was coming to believe. We young conservatives were truly wandering around in a political wilderness, wondering if there was anyone of intelligence and wit, any men of words, who thought and felt and believed as we did" (221). In the 1960s, Buchanan recalled, Buckley's magazine "was a *vade mecum* for young conservatives; it was our Iskra, 'the Spark' of the revolution; it maintained our morale and spirit, kept us in communion with our leaders, our philosophy, our cause. We waited for *National Review* in those years; and then we quoted it back at our critics and tormentors" (247). Later generations of intellectually minded conservative activists faced no such shortage of venues in which to find and express and work out their values and ideas. It was in recognition of William F. Buckley's impact in creating this alternative "counter-Establishment" to the old, liberal establishment that Yale University, against whom its youthful prodigy had railed in 1951's *God and Man at Yale*, chose to honor its prodigal son with an honorary degree on the occasion of his fiftieth reunion.

TOM HAYDEN
(1939–)

Like all significant social and political movements, the Great Society emerged and developed in a context; the civil rights movement, more than any other single social phenomenon of the times, drove a reform spirit and a questioning of the degree to which the United States as a whole had really achieved the "American dream." A demographic source of the ferment of the 1960s was the coming of age of a new generation, originally led by elder brothers and sisters whose memories stretched back to include at least some of a world war they had experienced as children. In the late 1950s, a "New Left" began to emerge to fit new times. Tom Hayden of Michigan, a state in which (in Hayden's coming of age) modern, socially and politically active labor unions were especially influential, found himself ideally situated to play a major role in the articulation of the vision of the progressive wing of a politically engaged rising generation. First as a college student and then an aspiring activist-intellectual, Hayden, like another Midwesterner, Bob Dylan of Minnesota, became a "spokesman for his generation," most memorably in the well-known early-1960s New Left manifesto, "The Port Huron Statement." In a sign of the genuine interest on the part of Establishment figures in shaping a new federal assault on poverty, Hayden surprisingly found himself brought to the White House and consulted with regarding the formation of early War on Poverty strategies.

Not content merely to write or discuss, Hayden then took to the front lines of the struggle to bring what came to be known as "maximum feasible participation" on the part of the poor themselves to fruition, hoping that the poor could, with organization, become a new and powerful element in American cities that the power structures who governed them would not be able to ignore. As any soldier would report, the action in the field would prove to be a far greater challenge than the classroom training. Well-known due to his authorship of the Port Huron Statement, which was seen in the

1960s as a true portent of what followed, Hayden had much to say during the 1960s' turbulence and troubles. Not really part of the power elite, but with good connections and access, Hayden was always seeking to advance public policies in the direction of empowering the traditionally powerless. Hayden's formation in these struggles proved to be a lifelong one, eventually leading to his joining the Establishment and becoming, in his own way, a practicing member of it. He had hoped for something more radical, but remained throughout his long and politically engaged life a committed activist of the 1960s vintage sort.

Thomas Emmett Hayden, named for St. Thomas Aquinas, was born in Michigan on December 11, 1939, to an assimilated, established Roman Catholic family whose forebears had come to the United States from Ireland; his grandfather had held many governmental offices and had helped establish a law school in Milwaukee where he had also taught. From his parents he learned lasting values: "education, enterprise, fairness," and no particularism of either the ethnic or religious sort. The family lived in a two-story house in Royal Oak, a suburb twelve miles north of Detroit; politically, his father was an "Eisenhower Republican" and his mother a "Stevenson Democrat." They divorced when Hayden was a child, and he continued to live in Royal Oak with his mother, while his father remained strongly involved in his life; the boy frequently visited him in Detroit and went on summer vacations with him in Canada, and they took many fishing trips together, including, among other sites, one in Port Huron, Michigan. His first eight years of formal education were spent in the parochial school of his parish church, the Shrine of the Little Flower (dedicated to the nineteenth-century French saint, St. Thérèse), under the pastoral care of Father Charles Coughlin, the famed "radio priest" of the New Deal era who had accepted his silencing by order of the Archbishop of Detroit in the early 1940s, an era characterized by greater ecclesiastical order than would be the case in decades to come. By the second grade, Hayden's intelligence was being noted at school, and at George A. Dondero High School he became editor of the school newspaper. As a high schooler, he developed a sense, shared with a few friends, of dissatisfaction and unease with what seemed to be the prevailing set of values: "those of the comfortable middle class." Perhaps being the child of divorce in an age when that was fairly unusual gave Hayden his feeling of difference.

In September 1957, Tom Hayden matriculated at the University of Michigan at Ann Arbor, an institution with a distinctive and changing profile that would be the setting for a number of historic occurrences associated with the 1960s. Here the idea for the Peace Corps would first be articulated; Students for a Democratic Society, the most significant leftist student organization of the 1960s, would virtually begin here; the first "teach-in" over the Vietnam controversy would be held; and, of course, in Michigan Stadium, President Lyndon Johnson would deliver the 1964 commencement address in which he would outline his vision for a "Great Society." Similar to the University of

Wisconsin–Madison, and unlike most of the other large midwestern Big Ten universities, Michigan attracted noticeable numbers of students from back east, who sometimes brought with them a different perspective from that of the typical student, who, like Hayden himself, would be a graduate of a Michigan public high school. Reflecting the school's base, large numbers of students who matriculated—in his memoir, Hayden said it was 40 percent— never earned their degrees, reflecting the impersonal nature of the enormous university. Michigan, like other ambitious institutions, was increasingly becoming known as a research university, something more and more appreciated in what Harvard University President Nathan Pusey called "the age of the scholar." Problem solving, with federal financial underwriting, was increasingly the hallmark of institutions like Michigan.

It did not take Hayden long to gravitate toward the university's student newspaper, the *Michigan Daily*, which became his principal interest and activity (though he did compile solid grades in his courses). He steadily gained increasing recognition for his work on the paper, but continued to exhibit nonconformist attitudes; as he recalled, "My drive for success was tempered by a disquiet about the world around me. I rejected, for example, the campus honorary societies that automatically incorporated rising *Daily* editors along with fraternity and student government leaders in their exclusive ranks" (Hayden 1988, 29). As a rising figure at the large-circulation school paper, Hayden was in a position to participate in the editorial decisions as to what stories to focus on. For example, he chose to put on page 1 a photograph of a march in Washington, D.C., in 1958 in support of desegregation that attracted thousands of students. A year later, he became acquainted with a New Yorker attending Michigan, Al Haber, who was the son of a college professor and New Deal–era vintage Democrat. Haber was one of a small number of students, including a couple of people with ties to the United Automobile Workers union, a significant force in the State of Michigan, and another New Yorker, who began seeking the revitalization of a near-moribund, old-line social-democratic organization, the Student League for Industrial Democracy (founded in 1905), the "youth arm" of the similarly aged and weakened League for Industrial Democracy. Hayden was interested and connected with Haber and company, but continued to focus on the newspaper as well as other interests, such as a group promoting the creation of a "peace corps," an idea derived from the establishment in 1958 of the British Voluntary Service Overseas organization and picked up by presidential candidate John F. Kennedy in 1960, who endorsed the idea in a speech at Ann Arbor that Tom Hayden, who was seated next to the candidate, found "dramatic and thrilling" (Miller 1987, 55). Hayden was clearly one caught up in the "search for a national purpose" that followed in the wake of Sputnik, which supposedly revealed United States with a disjointed value focus and a misappropriated, misdirected wealth, and, like millions, he would respond to JFK's slogan to "get this country moving again."

In the spring of 1960, Hayden's dream came true: he was now editor of the *Michigan Daily*. At the same time, Haber's idea for an on-campus conference on the increasingly visible civil rights issue was successfully realized, thanks in large part to a grant to Haber of $10,000 from the UAW union, which was thanks to the connection of Sharon Jeffrey, another Michigan student, a fellow activist, and the daughter of influential UAW leader Mildred Jeffrey, an associate of the Reuther brothers who dominated the organization's leadership. What Martin Luther King, Jr., would call the "beloved community," at least in secular form, was on Hayden's mind that spring, as he used his forum in the newspaper to argue for the university's calling of another conference on a matter of local concern: the future of the campus community, which could only be developed via greatly increased participation and a "democratization of decision-making," which could work against trends of "alienation" (Miller 1987, 54). The civil rights conference suggested not only Haber's talents but also the real potential of his ideas, including the creation of a new, far more vibrant student organization out of the near ruins of the Student League for Industrial Democracy, which would soon become the very famous and influential Students for a Democratic Society, or SDS (officially born in 1960).

Hayden continued to expand his connections in the summer of 1960. He hitchhiked to California, his eventual adult home, to check out the activism he had heard about at the San Francisco Bay Area's University of California campus at Berkeley; student activists took him to a farm in Delano, California, where he learned about the treatment of Mexican farm workers, giving him material for articles in the *Michigan Daily* on the "new student movement." Then he went south to Los Angeles for the Democratic National Convention. Though warned by Michigan friends that Kennedy was a "phony liberal," he found himself moved by the Massachusetts senator's speech at the Los Angeles Memorial Coliseum. He met the inspiring political activist Michael Harrington, and also Martin Luther King, Jr., who along with Hayden was manning a picket line outside the convention, seeking a strong civil rights plank on the party platform; Hayden recalled in his memoir being told by the civil rights leader, "Ultimately, you have to take a stand with your life" (Hayden 1988, 35). Later in August, before leaving California, he spoke at a conference on student political activism near Monterey on the need for the small, enlightened minority who saw through society's pretensions to take the existential leap of faith and, in evangelical fashion, seek courageously to work to effect the possibilities of making a new and better world (Miller 1987, 48).

Hayden's final stop in his far-flung summer was Minneapolis for the second national conference of the then-influential National Student Association, which primarily brought together young leaders from college student government associations and campus newspapers. Along with Hayden, Al Haber was also there, spreading the word about his vision of the new Students for a Democratic Society. Hayden here met and was impressed by some student civil rights activists from the South, most importantly Sandra Cason, a graduate student in philosophy from the University of Texas, Austin, whom Hayden would marry. As he recalled in his memoir, meeting representatives of the new Student Nonviolent Coordinating Committee proved to be "key to my own transformation." In them he saw much of himself and what he hoped to become: "young, politically innocent, driven by moral values, impatient with their elders, finding authentic purpose" (Hayden 1988, 36).

In his senior year at Michigan, 1960–61, Tom Hayden continued to develop himself in the same groove. Through his editorials in the *Michigan Daily*, he effectively sought to use his position of opinion-molding influence to help create the "new generation" he continually wrote about. In his final editorial for the campus paper, May 30, 1961, he wrote, "My deepest fear about the university is that we are adrift intellectually and humanly" (Hayden 1988, 47). Now that he was graduating, he had to choose among various options, including an excellent job offer from the *Detroit News* in its Washington, D.C., bureau; however, he "did not want to report on the world; I wanted to change it. But how?" (48). The yearlong effort by Haber and his allies to attract him to SDS culminated in victory, thereby providing Hayden his answer. He and Sandra Cason had decided to get married, and she wanted to continue her civil rights efforts in the South. After a summer together in New York, home base for SDS and its parent League for Industrial Democracy yet not too far from the Philadelphia national office of the National Student Association, to which Hayden was still attracted, Hayden chose SDS. He and Cason were married in an Austin wedding ceremony, and they moved in September to Atlanta, where Hayden became the field secretary for SDS's new office there; Cason could continue developing her work for SNCC in the South's unofficial capital city. Hayden could continue his journalistic efforts, thereby promoting awareness of the South's realities to youthful "northern" audiences who, with their consciousness levels now raised, would be attracted to SDS.

Hayden now got around in the South and developed a feel for its deeply entrenched system of white supremacy as well as its significant levels of poverty, especially compared to the rest of the United States he had known and experienced. He was jailed in McComb, Mississippi, and Albany, Georgia, and was debriefed in Washington by Federal Bureau of Investigation agents and an assistant attorney general for civil rights, who (unsuccessfully, of course) sought Hayden's aid in convincing some of the Mississippi activists to withdraw due to well-founded safety concerns. The lack of progress by the campaign for civil rights effort in Albany, Georgia, sowed various seeds of doubt concerning the political Establishment in Hayden and his fellow young idealists: "We had not lost our vision or moral fervor, but we began to suspect that our parent society had" (Hayden 1988, 72).

Hayden continued to write for publication, seeking to spread his moral and political vision. The winter 1961 issue of *The Activist*, a small-circulation

"New Left" magazine read by fellow left-wing political activists, reproduced an Associated Press photograph of Hayden being subjected to physical abuse in McComb, Mississippi; it also ran his article, "A Letter to the New (Young) Left." Here he discussed the Cold War's freezing of human possibilities for peace and also such domestic problems as "the failures of the welfare state to deal with the hard facts of poverty in America" and "the persistence of a racism that mocks our principles and corrupts everyday life" (Cohen and Hale 1967, 2–3). He warned of the dangers of liberals' acceptance of excessive political and moral "realism" when it came to considering social problems and the not-always-so-hidden conservative implications of this alleged realism (3). Action was needed: "We must move ahead concertedly with our goal—the changing of society. . . . This means writers and theoreticians as well as organizers and picketers" (8). Hayden knew of the many doubts that the dissatisfied shared regarding the odds and the outlook of such activism— he frankly stated that he shared them—but called on his readers, the actual and potential leaders of a movement for social change, to reject the immobilizing tendencies of a so-called mature attitude. "We doubt our ability to effect change, we doubt our ability to understand enough. . . . I do not recommend that we banish doubt . . . but I would suggest that it is possible and necessary to begin to think and act—provisionally yet strongly—in the midst of our doubts" (9).

Tom Hayden returned to his alma mater in December 1961, where he met with some forty people who sought to help in establishing a new national student movement. Here he decided to write a "manifesto of hope" to become an "agenda for a generation." Looking back, Hayden admitted, "I still don't know where this messianic sense, this belief in being right, this confidence that we could speak for a generation came from. But the time was ripe, vibrating with potential" (Hayden 1988, 74). Back in Atlanta, he spent time studying the writings of Columbia University sociologist C. Wright Mills, one of the greatest intellectual influences on the slowly growing, soon-to-burst-forth New Left, most significantly back in Big Ten country at the University of Wisconsin–Madison; his 1961 article for *The Activist* had taken its title from Mills's own 1960 essay in the British *New Left Review*, "Letter to the New Left." Hayden was especially impressed with Mills's most popular formulation, which formed the title of his most influential book, *The Power Elite*, published in 1956 and a bible for the New Left (two years later, Hayden would write "Radical Nomad," an M.A. thesis at Michigan, on Mills); however, he felt that Mills provided little guidance for what to do about the situation he so brilliantly and pointedly diagnosed. He returned to Michigan's campus in March 1962 to speak at the Michigan Union, his words becoming an SDS pamphlet, "Student Social Action," which was "literally a first draft of the manifesto I was preparing for Haber and the upcoming SDS convention" (82). Borrowing a phrase from one of his college teachers, Hayden favored the promotion of "participatory democracy." He spoke at many colleges on behalf of student activism and the new organization to promote it, SDS.

During this time, planning proceeded for SDS's convention in Port Huron, Michigan, some ninety miles north of Detroit, at a camp/conference center owned by the United Automobile Workers union, who proved willing to rent it at an affordable rate. Hayden holed himself up in Manhattan to complete his manifesto, which would serve first as the talking points of the gathering, and then, as revised, as its product and call to the rising generation of activists. He completed his forty-nine-page draft on June 1, less than two weeks before the scheduled June 12 commencement of the Port Huron SDS conference, which began with fifty-nine registered participants representing eight of the eleven SDS campus groups, some "elders" sympathetic to the effort and influential in the formation of its organizers, and various reform-oriented student organizations (Miller 1987, 106–7). The participants had had Hayden's words in their possession for only about a week before the Tuesday on which the conference began.

On Friday, June 15, formal, open-session discussion of what would become "The Port Huron Statement" began, continuing into the night and achieving completion on Saturday (some wording was later amended). The final, sixty-three-page document contained many critical statements regarding U.S. government Cold War policies; was naturally friendly to the idea of increased federal government activism, whose necessity when it came to civil rights was utterly obvious to all present; included the call for "participatory democracy," a vague, undefined term apparently not debated at Port Huron; and overall hoped to inspire citizen activism from the new generation, so "that decision-making of basic, social consequence be carried on by public groups" (Hayden 1988, 97). The hope was for "*participation*—not new representatives, but new constituencies acting in the historical process" (97–98). Twenty thousand copies were printed (there were ultimately four official printings and some 60,000 printed), and excerpts were frequently quoted and anthologized as the 1960s unfolded.

Only years later would SDS develop an image as a threatening, subversive, extremist organization. At the time of its conception, by contrast, this new, youthful, idealistic political grouping existed within the mainstream, on its left edge of course, but no more demonic than its counterpoint on the right, Young Americans for Freedom, also founded in 1960 and actually *far less* connected to the politically dominant forces of the time than was SDS. For instance, right after the Port Huron convention, Hayden and Al Haber drove to Washington to meet with presidential assistant and on-leave Harvard University history professor Arthur Schlesinger, Jr., a quintessential insider of the highest order, who promised to inform President Kennedy of its goings-on. YAF in 1962 could only dream of such access; no presidential assistants, let alone presidents, expressed any interest in *its* manifesto, the Sharon Statement of 1960.

Tom Hayden, therefore, had reason to believe at least that the Kennedy administration was "teachable," and had firsthand knowledge that it contained elements at least interested in the new SDS. For the rest of the years allotted to JFK, however, SDS, Hayden recalled, "remained mostly an intense subculture of discussion" (Hayden 1988, 105). In keeping with the vision of "participation," Hayden and SDS, two days after the August 1963 march on Washington for Jobs and Freedom, which was highlighted by Martin Luther King, Jr.'s "I Have a Dream" speech, launched a new initiative that became known as the Economic Research and Action Project (ERAP). In September in Bloomington, Indiana, home of Indiana University, an SDS leadership conference established ERAP as a northern parallel to plans in the works among civil rights activists for a Deep South voter registration drive the following year that would gain fame as the Freedom Summer. ERAP would attempt to organize the poor to put pressure on American political and economic institutions; "ERAP," Hayden recalled in his memoir, "was a product of intense thinking about the intertwined issues of race and poverty and how to bring them to center stage in a nation consumed by the Cold War" (125). The old connection with the United Automobile Workers union via Mildred Jeffrey obtained $5,000 in seed money to help establish ERAP's national office in Ann Arbor. ERAP would occupy much of Hayden's attentions during the rest of the 1960s.

SDS's ERAP began starting up in advance of President Johnson's January 1964 State of the Union address in which he declared War on Poverty, which was naturally welcomed as a sign that "our movements were again setting the agenda—as we had in civil rights—and the government was responding, giving us legitimacy and a sense of effectiveness"(Hayden 1988, 125). Given the president's statement, ERAP's role would be to experiment and to prod the establishment, free of the constraints of coalition politics, a kind of updated, Progressive-era settlement house with a decidedly more political slant. No matter what the War on Poverty turned out to be, Hayden and company "knew that the ultimate official effort would be a token in comparison with the real needs" (125). Hayden continued to involve himself in other matters, such as the nuclear arms question and the then-fashionable discussion of the imagined impending crisis said to be resulting from the spread of automation, and he was also trying to finish his master's thesis on C. Wright Mills at the University of Michigan. In 1964, he moved to Newark, New Jersey, which would serve as his base for the next three years.

The spring of 1964 saw not only continued discussion but also the birth of various ERAP efforts, mostly in northern cities. Hayden coauthored an ERAP paper, "Toward an Interracial Movement of the Poor?" with Carl Wittman, a graduate of Swarthmore College who had started an ERAP chapter in nearby Chester, Pennsylvania; it was Wittman who suggested that Hayden go to Newark, a city he had never visited. Newark, close to New York City and by far New Jersey's largest city, was home to some

400,000 people. It appeared to be under the control of liberal Democrats, yet despite its black majority, there was only one black member of the city council, whose principal interest seemed (to Hayden) to be patronage; Hayden found Newark to be run in the fashion of Richard Daley's Chicago. Social statistics such as infant mortality and crime rates indicated Newark's many challenges and needs. Into this setting in the Clinton Hill neighborhood, to live modestly and to work, went twenty-four-year-old Tom Hayden and a dozen other ERAP organizers—all but one white, middle class or higher, and graduates of prestigious academic institutions. It was tremendously challenging and proved educational, as Hayden recalled: "None of my reading or class work prepared me to know the ghetto, or know concrete economic realities, or know the real operation of political machines. And here I was to organize, as if I knew something that those living here didn't know" (Hayden 1988, 123).

Central to ERAP's vision was involving the neighborhood residents themselves, helping them "overcome their fears and self-doubts and go on eventually to become their own community organizers and leaders" (Hayden 1988, 118). The typical day began with a staff meeting at 9:30 AM, neighborhood visits for the rest of the morning in teams of two, seeking information regarding problems, and trying to drum up interest in participating in creating a community activist group. The work, unsurprisingly, proved far from easy, with about a 10 percent positive response rate; an individualistic mentality prevailed of "blaming individual weakness as the cause of social ill." In the battle for hearts and minds, at meetings staff would first encourage residents to talk and then encourage them to transfer blame from individuals to institutions. Still, after a few weeks some fifteen block groups could be counted involving at least tentatively some 250 people. A new organization, the Newark Community Union Project, was born.

The Great Society's "official," federally directed and funded War on Poverty began to take shape in 1964–65. Hayden was far from a true believer in the Johnson administration; present at the 1964 Atlantic City Democratic National Convention, Hayden, like many other youthful idealists, had been especially upset by the Mississippi delegation dispute that had ended in a rather standard political compromise that ill suited the new, morally inspired politics; Hayden recalled the experience as "a turning point in political history and a thoroughly embittering experience for the movement. . . . What was needed from the liberals was not an expedient compromise formula, as if they were dealing with mere self-interest, but a *moral* and *emotional* recognition of the essential rightness" of the noncompromisers (Hayden 1988, 118, 120). However, these feelings did not mean that he withdrew from opportunities tendered by an Establishment with which he was ill at ease. Nor did this Establishment ignore him. Hayden was invited to Washington by Frank Mankiewicz, head of the Peace Corps, to consider the possibility of developing common projects. He offered to have

NCUP train volunteers in the new domestic version of the Peace Corps, Volunteers in Service to America, but despite some extended discussion over the course of several meetings, the offer was never accepted.

Hayden was based in Newark but continued to get around and make his voice heard. He attended the February 1965 National Poor People's Conference in Cleveland and published excerpts from a diary he was keeping that fall in the influential intellectual quarterly *Partisan Review*. Here he attempted to articulate what was *new* about ERAP and why this new approach was necessary: "Most political reform movements seek to make change *for* people instead of *through* people . . . the 'solutions' are imposed administratively on people, life-patterns are disrupted willy-nilly, and new problems are created" (Hayden 1988, 139). The programs fail because "they do not make the promotion of democracy their key value" (139).

Hayden was similarly critical in his article for the initial 1966 issue of *Dissent*, another intellectual journal out of the Old Left but one that labeled itself "socialist," which was revised and expanded for inclusion in a sour 1967 collection of essays whose subtitle suggested its collective theme, *The Great Society Reader: The Failure of American Liberalism*. Things were getting *worse*, he insisted, his tiredness and frustration with the actualities of his Newark experiences palpable, with the federal government's new initiatives barely making a dent on the increasingly dark situation: "The trend is *toward*, not away from, increased racial segregation and division, greater unemployment for Negroes than whites, worse educational facilities in the slums, less job security for whites, fewer doctors for nearly everyone; in essence, the richest society in all history places increasing pressures on its 'have nots' despite all talk of the 'welfare state' and 'Great Society.'" LBJ's initiatives were grossly underfunded, misdirected to a corrupted establishment, and "should evoke little optimism. The amount of money allotted is a pittance, and most of it is going to local politicians, school boards, welfare agencies, housing authorities, professional personnel and even the police." Hayden's rejection and even dismissal of such institutions showed his longing for a radical reconstruction of social relations, for which he was toiling with such limited results in a barren vineyard. The community involvement known as maximum feasible participation was being "frustrated by the poverty planners' allegiance to existing local power centers" (Gutterman and Mermelstein 1967, 479).

Hayden and others in the Newark Community Union Project tried to implement local community participation. The local leader of the Office of Economic Opportunity was genuinely open to the idea, and so the NCUP helped get Newark divided into seven districts for purposes of the antipoverty initiative, each to have an area board. Again, it proved challenging actually to get local people involved—but not impossible; NCUP "studied the rules of the area boards until we understood them better than anyone. We organized the members of NCUP block clubs to attend their local area board meetings as they would a political convention" (Hayden 1988, 146). Small but real successes ensued, including memberships in boards, the successful founding of community service centers that provided such needs as legal aid, and relationships with urban planners and economists, all in the face of an at-best uneasy local political establishment. Hayden's focus on and up-front experience with the black, urban underclass underlay his critical perspective of the War on Poverty fight as it actually was turning out on the ground: "The official politics promoted opportunities for a new stratum of middle-class blacks, political brokers, middle managers, and professionals increasingly removed from the vast and permanent underclass of people outside the scope of the antipoverty program." The very real "ghetto" social pathologies that Daniel Patrick Moynihan had been attacked for pointing out in his report could not be ignored by Hayden and his colleagues, nor were they; "We tried . . . building self-esteem and power" even while insisting on "drastic external improvements in jobs, education, and housing." Techniques included "everything . . . petitions, demonstrations, electoral politics, rules skirmishes within the War on Poverty." But the outcome was strongly disappointing: "All our efforts failed to turn the antipoverty program around" (149).

Besides *living* his beliefs, Tom Hayden continued to write about them. The riots in Newark of July 1967 brought a greater awareness of the city's problems to a wide readership via Hayden's accounts, first in the *New York Review of Books* and later, in expanded form, in his book, *Rebellion in Newark: Official Violence and Ghetto Response* (Hayden 1967), which appeared in an inexpensive paperback edition. (Among other things, Hayden provided a drawing of a Molotov cocktail, on a napkin, to a writer from the *New York Review*, which wound up in unforgettable cartoon form, drawn by David Levine, on that periodical's cover a month after the riot.) Hayden's preface indicated his radical concerns: to inform readers as to the root causes of the riots—continuing racial inequality and the woefully inadequate efforts to deal with it—and the open question as to whether or not the United States was really capable of dealing with it.

Newark "elites," Hayden explained, had been proposing "pouring money into job training and social service programs through the existing agencies of government," wanted to rebuild and shore up the city's middle class, and favored "downtown" development projects like a convention arena, highways, and a medical school designed to "urban renew"—that is, destroy—a "blighted" neighborhood. Activists, however, including Hayden himself, sought "power, rather than money" (Hayden 1967, 6). The riot had long been expected to come, sooner or later, by informed local residents; as James Baldwin had put it, the "fire" was coming next time, and next time was now here. When it did, the city government attempted conciliatory measures and concessions, but it was too late; having "been indifferent to the community's demand for justice," the people were "now going to be indifferent to the authorities' demand for law and order" (26). Widespread stealing from stores, especially those white-owned, involving "respectable" blacks as well as the underclass, Hayden reported with equanimity: "People voted with their feet to expropriate property to which they felt entitled. . . . A common claim was: this was owed me" (30). As it turned out, the theft "proved more effective against gouging merchants than organized protests ever had been" (30). Hayden dutifully reported the concern of New Jersey authorities at the "carnival atmosphere," but responded that the "community" saw the happenings as "more like the celebration of a new beginning. People felt as though for a minute they were creating a community of their own" (32).

The New Jersey state government, declaring an "obvious open rebellion" and "criminal insurrection" to exist, sent in state troopers and National Guard units to supplement the Newark police, thus ending the rioting with military force and occupation that resulted in the over two dozen deaths and numerous injuries. Hayden stressed the nearly all-white makeup of the outside forces and discussed at length their abuses of authority in putting down the riot, while acknowledging the apparent popularity of their mission among the public outside of Newark. Hayden believed that the mutual negative stereotypes of black urbanites and white suburbanites for each other wound up being strongly reinforced by the riot's suppression. How big might the fire be next time? New Jersey Governor Richard Hughes met with Hayden during the riot and, upon the activist's advice, withdrew the National Guard (Matusow 1984, 363).

The conclusion to Hayden's *Rebellion in Newark* was entitled, "From Riot to Revolution?" Here he excoriated American society for the "fact that no national program exists to deal with the social and economic questions black people are raising" (Hayden 1967, 63). What about the Great Society? The context had changed. The 1967 riot occurred the year after the 1966 midterm elections, termed by the dominant news media a "backlash" against the riotous images that middle America was seeing on its television screens and resulting in a partisan swing to the Republicans (though more than a few of them, especially in the Senate, were not necessarily against increased federal social programs). The Vietnam War was escalating, thereby "crowding out" increased federal social spending. Hayden noted the "exhaustive hearings" on these issues of the past few years but asserted that there was "no apparent commitment from national power centers to do something constructive" (63). He quoted with obvious disapproval President Johnson's televised speech of July 28th condemning the rioters and insisting that government officials were obliged in such circumstances to focus their attentions on ending the disorders, not on their alleged roots or causes. Hayden predicted that Congress, when it got around to it, was "likely to lament the failure of past civil rights, welfare, and anti-poverty programs, rather than focus on the need for new ones" (64). As for the traditional, tired cry of self-help and the fatuous parallels to poor immigrants groups that had sup-

posedly pulled themselves up by their own bootstraps, Hayden was unequiv-
ocal: "Self-help does not build housing, hospitals, and schools" (64).

As his analysis closed, Hayden, who had worked in Newark for some three
years, pulled back from romantic revolutionary rhetoric: "This is not a time
for radical illusions about 'revolution'" (Hayden 1967, 68). He knew too
much about the stagnation and even conservatism in the ghetto. But he still
judged the riot to be "people making history," people who were "barred from
using the sophisticated instruments of the established order for their own
ends. . . . Rocks and bottles are only a beginning, but they cause more attention than all the reports in Washington" (69).

The Great Society, then, according to Hayden, had utterly failed, at least in
the North. He and others had created a poor people's movement in Newark,
but it led to "no permanent redistribution of power to the poor" (Hayden
1988, 165). Hayden left Newark, becoming involved in the massive protest
movement against U.S. involvement in Vietnam, and traveling to North Vietnam in 1968. He participated in the "student rebellion" at Columbia University in New York City in the spring of 1968, in an effort to "bring the war
home" that succeeded in shutting down the university, whose officials decided to bring in police who successfully "cleared the buildings" while engaging in a police riot. Hayden moved on to Chicago to participate in the
antiwar demonstrations there, earning some fame as one of the "Chicago 7"
indicted and convicted for inciting a riot (he was one of the planners of the
protest), a conviction later overturned. His bitterness over Vietnam even led
him to speak out against assisting Vietnamese refugees after the communists
won the war. From 1971 forward, he lived in Los Angeles, writing many
books and articles, lecturing frequently, and serving as an elected Democratic
officeholder in both chambers of the California Legislature beginning in
1982, until his career was ended due to the success of the term limits movement, but he remained extremely politically active, with the star power of being a living link to the 1960s, a special time. He concluded his 1988 memoir
on a wistful note: "I miss the sixties and always will" (507).

STOKELY CARMICHAEL
(1941–1998)

"Black power!" These two words, uttered in 1966 before a cheering, chanting crowd in Mississippi by civil rights activist Stokely Carmichael of the Student Nonviolent Coordinating Committee and picked up by the news media, proved to be his signature expression. As for himself, he preferred the title of his posthumously published memoir, *Ready for Revolution* (2003), a phrase with which he liked to end his many public speeches and writings. The need for black power in early-1960s, white supremacist Mississippi, the most militantly segregationist society of the Deep South, seems obvious enough, especially when such realities are recalled as the fact that at the time, less than 10 percent of the state's black population, who constituted more than one-third of the whole people living there, were even registered to vote. Black power, nonetheless, rapidly made Carmichael the public face (along with Malcolm X, assassinated the previous year but still a strong presence) of a new stock figure of the 1960s social struggles—the "black militant." He preferred the term "organizer," and his years of struggle more than justify his self-selection. Once affixed, the "militant" label stuck, and fittingly enough, throughout the remainder of Carmichael's life, which took a serious pan-African turn in the late 1960s when he made a permanent move to the mother continent. Guinea became his home, and he adopted the African name, Kwame Ture, by which he would be known until his death in 1998. In the 1960s, Carmichael, a total outsider to the Great Society's efforts, Washington-based and otherwise, remained an unstinting critic of the national government's feebleness and inaction when it came to civil rights questions, dating back before Lyndon Johnson's presidency to be sure but also continuing. What limited chance there ever was that Carmichael might develop any concrete connection with Johnson's Great Society was forever destroyed by the Mississippi delegation credentials fight at the 1964 Democratic National Convention, held at Atlantic City, and its aftermath.

Carmichael had become too radicalized to appreciate the Great Society; as he recalled, referring to the years 1961–65, "Mississippi was my real education. . . . I learned a lot in Mississippi. . . . I probably *unlearned* twice as much. . . . [B]y the time I would leave Mississipi, I would be clear on what my life's work was to be. I had discovered what I was—an organizer—and that the movement was my fate" (Carmichael 2003, 277, 278). Carmichael's roles in the Great Society era were twofold: first and foremost, grassroots organizing, promoting with some real success at social change from the bottom up (a sometime Great Society goal); and second, by embodying and articulating a radical alternative, seen by increasing numbers of Americans living through the long, hot summers of the late 1960s as potentially violent, to the civil rights Establishment, and especially, despite the actual relationship between them, its most prominent figure, as a radical alternative to the apostle of nonviolence and friend of Stokely Carmichael, Martin Luther King, Jr. Carmichael—grassroots political organizer, leader, and, by the late 1960s, frequently seen and heard public figure—significantly helped pressure American society to face the disturbing realities of institutionalized white supremacy, thereby playing an important role in laying the groundwork for some of the Great Society's institutional achievements, namely the landmark civil rights bills of the 1960s. Stokely Carmichael, first of several created "media figures" of the type known as black militants, may also be said to have played a large role in the spread of fear, backlash, and misunderstanding that helped bring the Great Society moment to its rather sudden end—a point at which he reinvented himself, transforming Stokely Carmichael, African American, into Kwame Ture, African.

Stokely Carmichael was born at the home his father had built in Port of Spain, Trinidad, a colony of the British Empire, on June 29, 1941, to a family with varied Caribbean identities, including American, as his mother, May Charles Carmichael, had been born in the U.S. Canal Zone. His unusual first name, given to him by the Anglican priest who baptized him, was that of one of the priest's former teachers. His mother determined to move to the United States, leaving behind her husband and three children in October 1944. A year and a half later, Adolphus Carmichael joined her in New York, the children remaining to be raised by relatives; the death of Grandmother Cecilia Carmichael in 1952 meant that Stokely and his two sisters landed at La Guardia Airport, New York City, the following June, joining their parents in an area of the South Bronx dominated by immigrants from either the Caribbean or the southeastern United States. The following January, the family moved farther north in the Bronx, close to the Bronx Zoo, becoming the only black family in their new neighborhood, where they quickly gained acceptance; in his memoir, Carmichael could "remember no instances of overt racism from the neighborhood kids" (Carmichael 2003, 62). His hardworking father and stay-at-home mother provided a strong home and encouraged their son's early propensity to read voraciously and widely. The

Carmichaels became the first black family to join nearby Westchester Methodist Church, where again they were welcomed and became active members (their son rose to the rank of Life Scout, second only to Eagle, in the church troop). Given this background, Stokely Carmichael's academic success in the public schools was predictable; in 1956, he began the ninth grade at the prestigious, highly competitive Bronx School of Science, New York City's best-known selective public school.

Carmichael's time at Bronx Science included playing on the soccer team and studying Latin for four years. The school also brought him into contact with a far wider range as well as a greater number of intellectually precocious teenagers—including numerous "Red Diaper" types, that is, sons and daughters whose parents' political backgrounds were of the far left, including communist. Carmichael participated in various left-wing student activities, both discussion and street demonstrations, without actually enrolling in any particular group; his political education in the vocabulary on the modern European radical tradition proceeded even as he approached graduation. His political education was also furthered in Harlem, where he regularly went to get his hair cut, both in the proverbial freewheeling barbershop conversations and also on 125th Street, where he would observe "stepladder speakers" seeking to inform the community on such black nationalist issues as the rising tide of independence among the Caribbean and African colonial peoples, and also regularly visit the African Bookstore.

Of course the high school–age Stokely Carmichael was aware of Martin Luther King, Jr., who had become nationally prominent in 1956 with the eventually successful and favorably publicized Montgomery, Alabama, bus boycott. In 1960, Carmichael's senior year at Bronx Science, the first nationally publicized "sit-in" occurred at the Woolworth's lunch counter in Greensboro, North Carolina; Woolworth's and other national store chains became the subject of pickets in which Carmichael and other Bronx Science students participated.

But it was a trip to Washington, D.C., that previous fall that cemented Carmichael's eventual decision to attend college in the nation's capital. Joining a demonstration in opposition to the House Committee on Un-American Activities, Carmichael was attracted to a large group of protesters who were black. They turned out to be students from Howard University, organized as the Nonviolent Action Group (NAG), soon to be an affiliate of the Student Nonviolent Coordinating Committee (SNCC, pronounced "snick"), which would be organized the following spring under the guidance of Ella Jo Baker. Nearly at once, Stokely Carmichael determined to go to Howard.

Howard, Carmichael recalled, was "a veritable tissue of contradiction, embodying the best and the absolute worst values of the African-American tradition" (Carmichael 2003, 113). Historically black, uniquely supported by and hence tied to the U.S. Congress, preprofessional, inclusive of an enormous "college life" social scene, and founded during the post–Civil War

Reconstruction era, the Howard University of 1960 also contained many memorable faculty (such as Rayford Logan, E. Franklin Frazier, and especially Sterling Brown, whom Carmichael got to know) committed to the uplift of the race, some tradition of student activism, and, significantly, a large number of Caribbean and African students, who furthered Carmichael's internationalist and black nationalist perspectives. It was also at Howard that Stokely Carmichael encountered large numbers of black Southerners.

The Nonviolent Action Group, which had attracted Carmichael to Howard in the first place, soon became his activist home. This small group of a few dozen people sought to act both on campus and beyond, and as Carmichael recalled, "History was kind to us. We had come along at an extraordinary historical moment that presented black youth with an unprecedented opportunity to engage society militantly. . . . What bound us together was a great interest in and respect for our people and a passionate identification with the African struggle everywhere, whether in Mississippi, Mozambique, or Montserrat" (Carmichael 2003, 144).

On campus, NAG members became influential in the student government and the *Hilltop*, the student newspaper (with Michael Thelwell, a Jamaican who later edited Carmichael's memoir, becoming editor-in-chief). These official organs were used both to obtain funds to support students in their political activities as well as to raise consciousness of the burgeoning civil rights movement and other issues, for instance, organizing a speaker series known as Project Awareness, notably between Bayard Rustin and Malcolm X. But early on, Stokely Carmichael sought to go where the action is: to fight on the front lines. That meant the still-unfamiliar South. NAG members educated themselves in the tradition of nonviolent confrontation, led especially by the longtime black political activist Bayard Rustin's writings; Rustin had gone to Montgomery at the start of the bus boycott to educate the youthful Martin Luther King, Jr., on the same topic. In the spring of 1961, as it happened, the Congress of Racial Equality, a traditional civil rights organization that had been founded in Chicago, was organizing its pro-integration Freedom Rides, which changed Carmichael's life "as they did the direction and character of the student movement. This was when I decided, definitely, to be seriously involved in this struggle. From now on, serious commitment"—a seriousness and a commitment that would never wane (Carmichael 2003, 165).

The Congress of Racial Equality (CORE) Freedom Riders were testing to see if the now federally mandated integration of interstate bus travel, applying both to seating and to bus stations, was effectual throughout the South; of course everyone knew that it was not, but what would happen in a given place if the issue were, peacefully of course, forced? One member of NAG, Hank Thomas, joined the riders, who departed from Washington on May 4, 1961, seen off by Carmichael and others. Television coverage brought national awareness to the attacks suffered by the riders in Anniston and Birmingham,

Alabama, but with Thomas's participation especially, Carmichael and other NAG members felt personally involved. They were underwhelmed at the federal government's relative invisibility and especially offended by the statement of Attorney General Robert Kennedy to the effect that "extremists on both sides" were responsible for the incident (Carmichael 2003, 185). CORE's leader, James Farmer, was pressured to "suspend" the rides—but SNCC, beginning with the Nashville affiliate, decided to catch the falling flag. Carmichael arranged to complete his examinations early and then moved to join the struggle firsthand. He took a plane to New Orleans and prepared to take a train—ensuring that all involved facilities were integrated—to Mississippi. An unruly mob had gotten through in order to board the train, and upon arrival in Jackson, Carmichael was arrested for sitting in the white waiting room at the station. SNCC's strategy for the summer was "jail, no bail": continue to fill up the jails by refusing to post bail. The success of this tactic in Carmichael's case meant that he was soon transferred to Parchman Penitentiary in the northwestern corner of the state known as the Delta region. Parchman's bad conditions were the subjects of folk songs that Carmichael had heard at clubs in Greenwich Village, New York. The prison lived up to its squalid reputation, and Carmichael spent his twentieth birthday in jail. CORE, without asking SNCC's opinion, decided soon after publicly to call an end to the Freedom Rides of 1961, and also for legal reasons to bond all Freedom Riders out of prison. Upon returning to New York, Carmichael appeared at a press conference and periodically over the summer made speeches, often at fundraisers before wealthy people, as a veteran Freedom Rider.

In August 1961, Carmichael went back South, to Nashville, for a four-week-long "political seminar" at Fisk University, put on by the Nashville SNCC and designed to further develop the movement, its leaders, and its strategy as to where to go next. The meeting included representatives, who sought to direct the movement toward voter registration, with which the Washington insiders proposed to assist (eventually, the Voter Education Project would play a significant role in this process). Historically grounded via his college history course with Rayford Logan at Howard, Carmichael was aware of the Reconstruction struggle over black suffrage. Hours of discussion, in which Carmichael participated heavily, led to a tactical decision to move away from the public accommodations sit-ins and toward the ensuring of the right to vote for black people in the South. This, of course, far from precluded continuing "action projects"—while in Nashville, for instance, Carmichael and others organized a picket line at a store where black people shopped but were not employed. To whites who offered the pickets insults and abuse, Carmichael—literate, verbal, and self-confident with his first-rate education—enjoyed responding in kind rather than suffer in quiet, dignified silence (Halberstam 1998, 525).

Under strong family pressure, Stokely Carmichael returned for his sophomore year of college, 1961–62; the death of his father on January 21, 1962, and his mother's insistence cemented his commitment to finishing college. Carmichael changed his major from premed to philosophy and continued to be a full-time student during the academic years that followed. There was plenty to do politically on campus, of course, as well as nearby. In March 1963 it was discovered that a segregated labor force was constructing a new building on campus. A meeting arranged with the black chairman of the President's Committee on Equal Employment Opportunity—the man was a protégé of Vice President Lyndon B. Johnson, who had been given responsibility for this effort by President Kennedy—resulted in a proverbial runaround, which then led the Howard student government to announce a demonstration at the building site if no satisfactory answer were received to the so-far-unanswered letters sent by the student organization. Soon thereafter, a public statement was issued by the Labor Department threatening action against the involved contractors and unions. A victory rally was held on campus—but, as Carmichael noted in his memoirs, "a splendid victory . . . on the inside. I believe the electricians may have taken on three Negro apprentices that year" (Carmichael 2003, 276). He and other NAG members were also involved that year in continuing desegregation efforts in Cambridge, Maryland, during which disturbances Carmichael was struck with tear gas.

In June 1962, the school year having ended, Carmichael went to join the famous activist with the providential name, Bob Moses, in the Delta town of Greenwood, Mississippi, which had a vast, dirt-poor black population; he would continue to work there through 1965. The people, however, were not poor in spirit, and Carmichael was so impressed by them that he concluded, "The most important thing Mississippi first taught me was to really love my blackness . . . *really* to love it" (Carmichael 2003, 282). SNCC's aim was on the same wavelength as that of the Community Action Program organizers of the soon-to-be-born-and-named Great Society: "Our way is to live in the community, find, train, or develop representative leadership within strong, accountable local organizations or coalitions that did not exist before, and that are capable of carrying on the struggle after we leave. When we succeed in this, we will work ourselves out of a job. Which is our goal" (302). Voter registration was of special interest in the Delta because it was part of the "black belt" (black referring to the soil) of the South in which black people constituted a clear majority of the population. In the pre–Voting Rights Act (1965) world, it proved to be slow going. And it was far, far away from Washington.

Stokely Carmichael, a frontline soldier in the crusade for social change, remained generally unimpressed with the Kennedy administration's approach to civil rights, though he was surprised to find himself impressed with the president's televised speech in 1963 calling for a civil rights bill. As an organizer gaining more and more experience, and as a child of the television age, he understood the significance of the August 1963 March on

Washington highlighted by the famous Martin Luther King, Jr., "I Have a Dream" speech. But as a leader of SNCC, he knew the inside story of the heavy-handed pressure brought to bear on John Lewis, SNCC's leader, to tone down his prepared remarks at the Lincoln Memorial that preceded King's.

It took the Freedom Summer of 1964 to bring true national attention to the ongoing struggle in Mississippi. By that time, of course, a new president, Lyndon Johnson, had succeeded the slain John F. Kennedy, and early in that year he had first declared war on poverty and then called for the construction of a Great Society. The mind of activist Stokely Carmichael, however, was elsewhere—in Mississippi. Though he originally was skeptical as to the value of the Freedom Summer concept, whereby hundreds of young activists would follow the pioneers of SNCC, taking up residence in the veritable belly of the segregationist beast, and seek to bring voting rights to the literally disenfranchised, Carmichael soon understood the historic impact of the drama that unfolded, given the tremendous media coverage. Since Bob Moses, whom Carmichael knew, respected, and trusted, was promoting the idea, Carmichael went for it; furthermore, he knew firsthand how painfully slow progress had been (only a few hundred blacks had been able to register to vote), given the tremendous resistance by the powerful forces of institutionalized white supremacy, and hence the need for some new departure. There had been a successful "freedom election" involving tens of thousands during the November 1963 statewide elections, wherein the excluded had been organized via a SNCC-led campaign to cast mock ballots, thereby demonstrating the desire for the real thing—actual voting rights—while also developing a stronger statewide organization for future purposes. Some student activists had assisted in this effort, and Carmichael came to believe that their presence not only attracted some national media attention but also diminished the incidences of intimidation and violence leveled against the freedom movement. And so, in the spring of 1964, Carmichael and other members of SNCC, which by now had a greater number of organized chapters in predominately white universities, began serious planning for the Freedom Summer. As the Mississippi white governmental Establishment and white-controlled media loudly warned of the coming "invasion" and their determination to resist it by any means necessary, Carmichael noted that, despite efforts by SNCC activists in Washington, no one from the Johnson administration had any words of encouragement to offer regarding either the cause itself or the safety of the activists. Not only was it an election year, but in 1964 the southern delegation in Congress remained overwhelmingly Democratic and also in possession of enormous influence on Capitol Hill due to their accumulated seniority in regard to years of service, on which rank in congressional committees, as well as committee chairmanships, was almost entirely based. Additionally, Lyndon Johnson was shepherding the landmark 1964 Civil Rights Act through Congress while also seeking to launch the Great Society antipoverty programs, for which he hoped, with reason, to gain some southern Democratic support (toward this end, Congressman Phil Landrum of Georgia was successfully drafted to serve as a cosponsor of the basic enabling act of the War on Poverty). The world of Capitol Hill intrigue was an alien environment to Carmichael. He was heading for Mississippi again.

Shortly after the spring 1964 semester at Howard ended, Carmichael went to Oxford, Ohio, to participate in training exercises for the Freedom Summer volunteers. Here John Doar, from President Johnson's Department of Justice, addressed the volunteers, and in response to questioning stated that the federal government would *not* be able to protect them in Mississippi—a statement, however realistic, that was seized upon by the Mississippi media. Before the training sessions had ended, three civil rights activists, two white Northerners (Andrew Goodman and Mickey Schwerner) and one black Southerner (James Chaney), were reported missing, having last been seen in Philadelphia, Mississippi. All had been murdered. Despite the despondent mood in Ohio, few volunteers went home; instead, they went to Mississippi; Carmichael returned to Greenwood for an amazing ten weeks.

Strokely Carmichael's responsibilities were varied. His most enjoyable turned out to be the "freedom schools," in which not only academic basics but also black pride and black nationalist ideas were fostered. He entertained Martin Luther King, Jr., who visited, heavily escorted by FBI agents. Politically, he sought to build on the 1963 mock election by helping Bob Moses, whose idea it was, create the Mississippi Freedom Democratic Party. This group, which would prove to be SNCC's greatest success, was created in order to force the issue of black exclusion from the all-dominant, all-powerful, all-white "regular" Democratic Party, which held not only every statewide office, including the entire congressional delegation, but also *every single seat* in *both* houses of the State Legislature. Sixty-six delegates, most of them black, were chosen in Jackson at a state MFDP convention to go to the Democratic National Convention at Atlantic City, New Jersey, where they would challenge the credentials of the "regular," all-white delegation. In 1964, all three television networks carried "gavel-to-gavel" coverage of the two majors parties' conventions; as Johnson's convention was a "coronation," with the president facing no opposition to his nomination, the news media would be looking for stories. The Mississippi story at Atlantic City proved to be a dramatic one indeed, and its outcome further embittered Carmichael as well as others from the national Democratic party establishment.

Carmichael, of course, knew that Johnson had played a major role in Congress's enacting the Civil Rights Act, and was also aware that Republican presidential nominee Barry Goldwater, on libertarian grounds, had voted against it. Political insider, civil rights sympathizer, and United Automobile Workers chief counsel Joseph Rauh helped immensely both by agreeing to

represent the MFDP at the convention credentials committee and also by lobbying fellow Democratic party liberals on behalf of the challenge. At the
hearings, Mrs. Fannie Lou Hamer, whom Carmichael knew well, stole the
show with her dramatic testimony regarding her violent abuse at the hands of
white supremacists and the lengths to which the white Mississippi political
establishment had gone to exclude her, and others like her, even from voting.
She literally embodied the freedom struggle in all its righteousness to a degree
that was nothing short of heroic.

But as she began to testify, a dirty political trick was played by the Johnson administration. In 1964, if the president called a news conference, television covered it. Johnson himself made sure that Mrs. Hamer's testimony
was not seen live; however, the story proved compelling enough just the
same, and her testimony was broadcast in its entirety later that night as part
of the "gavel-to-gavel" convention coverage. The essential justice of the
MFDP's position was self-evident.

But this was becoming high-level, national politics. Representative Edith
Green of Oregon, a party regular and the most influential woman in the
House of Representatives, proposed the seating of both delegations on the
condition that each delegate pledge fealty to the national Democratic ticket,
whereupon each would receive a half-vote. The MFDP, whose aim was inclusion, found this acceptable. Now, however, Carmichael and his fellow activists experienced the famous Johnson treatment secondhand, as hard-line
political pressure of all sorts was successfully brought to bear on people who
up to that point had been allies of the credentials challenge effort. The Freedom Democrats were only to have two "at-large" seats, while the "regulars," who collectively constituted most of the principal state officeholders
and duly elected political leaders, took their seats as per usual; the rest of the
Freedom delegates were to be "honored guests." The administration even
"announced" who the two MFDP delegates were to be. It was also made
clear that all future delegations to Democratic conventions had to be chosen
in a nonracial basis.

The compromise was rejected by both Mississippi delegations. Pressure
was brought to bear on the MFDP even by civil rights pioneer Minnesota
U.S. Senator Hubert Humphrey, whose potential selection as LBJ's running
mate helped bring some liberals in line, including Bayard Rustin and Martin
Luther King, Jr. In the end, the MFDP went home, but realized that they had
gained enormous publicity for the conditions of their daily lives.

The credentials challenge inspired SNCC to attempt the same gambit in
early January 1965, when the most liberal Congress since the early New
Deal years convened. Similar to the party convention, an early order of
business was the presentation of credentials by the duly elected members,
thus providing an opportunity for challenges to their elections, a matter
nearly always routine and perfunctory of course. Were the Mississippi
members of Congress—all white Democrats—legitimately elected if it could

be demonstrated that the Fifteenth Amendment guaranteeing the right to vote without respect to race or color was not only flouted, but *institutionally* flouted, even by said congressional members? Now more than ever, feigned ignorance of the political situation in Mississippi could not be taken seriously. Carmichael was part of 250 black Mississippians who traveled to Washington to lend support to the challenge to three congressmen, which garnered, on a forced roll-call vote, an astonishing 149 votes in favor of the challenge, which meant the seating of the white Mississippi delegation was merely provisional during the nine months Congress spent investigating the challenge, the idea of which had received no support from the national civil rights organizations or from the Establishment liberals supposedly now dominating the national government. There *had* been political support from across the country via various grassroots organizations, many of them religious, including the Friends of SNCC. The continuing investigation formed a backdrop to the debate over the Voting Rights Act of 1965, a pillar of Great Society legislation.

SNCC, along with others, sensed momentum in its favor. It had more money than before. It also faced the question of "What now, what next, at the grassroots?" What about efforts in the rest of the South, which had been pushed to the background with all the focus on Mississippi? How could the organization cope with its growth? Should the freewheeling SNCC, run by seemingly endless discussion followed by consensus, now, in changed circumstances, seek to become more "organized"? With actual voting rights on the immediate horizon, what should black Southerners do with them—affiliate with a national party, or organize their own, as Carmichael tended to think? No easy answers were forthcoming. Stokely Carmichael graduated from Howard University in the spring of 1965 and went to work full time for SNCC, but now in Alabama, in the small community of Selma, still focused on organizing around the voting rights issue. Violent repression, including the deaths of two local black men, brought in Martin Luther King, Jr., and others from his Southern Christian Leadership Conference. This then led to the call for a march from Selma to Montgomery, the state capital, and the violent scene, perpetrated by (all-white) Alabama state troopers on the Edmund Pettus Bridge (named for a Confederate general) crossing the Alabama River, which rapidly got out of control and whose repression was filmed and shown over and over on national television. As Carmichael well summarized, "As usual, racism [was] its own worst enemy. . . . The gratuitous brutality and unconcealed racism in that footage, flashing across the nation and around the world, succeeded in embarrassing even [Alabama Governor] George Corley Wallace, let alone the administration in Washington. Even Southern segregationist congressmen found it necessary to appear in the media distancing themselves . . . from 'this deplorable behavior'" (Carmichael 2003, 449).

King now came to Selma to lead a second attempt at crossing the bridge, temporarily restrained by a federal court order that had successfully been attained by Alabama state authorities, only to turn back halfway across the bridge, which left a sour taste in Carmichael's mouth as well as that of many others. Soon, however, attention was turned from the disappointment and confusion of King's decision to the latest murder of a northern white activist, this time Reverend James Reeb. When President Johnson went out of his way to express concern and support for the Reeb family, including the use of government-owned planes, Carmichael was singularly unimpressed; as he wrote decades later, "The march had been called . . . in response to a local African man's murder. Where was LBJ's and the nation's response then?" (Carmichael 2003, 452).

Carmichael had reservations about the march—what, exactly, was it for?—and about SCLC's media-oriented tactics, which he termed "hit-and-run," more generally; what was needed, he always believed, was grassroots organization that would last, long after the cameras and outside marchers had departed. However, he was fully aware of the unique stature of Martin Luther King, Jr., and therefore argued within SNCC that if King had decided on a march, a march there would be. Locally, Carmichael won SNCC members over to his side, but a press release from the Atlanta headquarters stating that the organization would not officially participate in the march was indicative both of the lack of clear consensus as to the advisability of the march as well as the discombobulated state of SNCC itself.

Stokely Carmichael proposed to use the march to foster voter registration, especially in Lowndes County, on the other side of the Pettus Bridge from Selma's Dallas County, whose social structure (the vast majority of the rural population was landless) and political situation (literally, virtually *no* blacks were registered to vote, in a county where they constituted a large majority of the population) were reminiscent of the Mississippi Delta. As the soon-to-be-famous march to Montgomery proceeded down Highway 80, Carmichael and his fellow SNCC activists followed along, talking to local people who turned out to see the marchers, making contacts, and promising to return for organizational, long-range purposes. Carmichael correctly believed that the right to vote really was coming very soon; the Voting Rights Act became law in August 1965, and shortly thereafter Lowndes County was given a federal registrar to supervise voter enrollment. Then what? Whatever answers came to whatever questions were posed, organization would be needed. In the event, Carmichael succeeded in helping to organize an independent party, the Lowndes County Freedom Organization, which would come to be known as the Black Panthers and later gain much greater fame via its California namesake. He had no desire to join the southern Democrats, the vast majority of whom he continued to view as "Dixiecrats."

Personally, the answer to the question "What next?" that Stokely Carmichael desired to give was to move North—in his particular case, he hoped, back to Washington, a city he knew that at the time, given its peculiar status under the U.S. Constitution, did not even have an elected local government, let alone one effectively dealing with the needs of its majority black population, in Carmichael's eyes. The tremendous civil disturbance in the area of Los Angeles known as Watts, which had followed closely on the heels of the Voting Rights Act's signing, underscored the notion that civil rights was not just a Deep South problem.

But there were many "What nexts?" to consider—such as "What next in Alabama?" On January 23, 1966, Alabama staffs of SNCC and SCLC met to discuss political strategy, the basic choice being either a separate, local party, or affiliation with the national Democratic party, which was in firm control of the federal government and building the Great Society. Carmichael forcefully argued the nationalist line against coalition politics (Fairclough 1987, 312). His orientation was local and grassroots in an Alabama still under the political control of southern Democrat Governor George Wallace, the man who had "stood in the schoolhouse door" in a futile attempt to prevent the integration of the University of Alabama and who had unforgettably cried in his inaugural address as governor for segregation to last forever. The divide between the two visions of where black Americans should go next, itself a variation on a very traditional theme, could not be worked out in January 1966.

A meeting of SNCC leaders took place in May 1966 near Nashville to elect the group's officers, as well to continue the discussion of the "What next?" question. A very long, late meeting resulted in Stokely Carmichael being voted in the new chairman of SNCC. He would serve in that capacity for the next year, setting a more militant tone and a more nationalist agenda that critics, both far and near, insisted was separatist; Carmichael himself, upon becoming chairman, publicly stated, "We see integration as an insidious subterfuge for white supremacy in this country" (Hayward 2001, 134). He was uninterested in, and even contemptuous toward, a White House Conference on Civil Rights called for June 1–2 by Johnson to consider life in the new, post–Voting Rights Act era, viewing it as "a totally cosmetic, public relations . . . ploy to co-opt the new black vote for the Democrats," and was disgruntled when now-former SNCC Chairman John Lewis chose to attend (Carmichael 2003, 479).

Being SNCC chairman meant he would be based in Atlanta, the organization's headquarters and also the home of Martin Luther King, Jr. The two men were together much more often, and Carmichael remained as impressed as ever by the movement's most prominent leader. SNCC's independence was crucial for Carmichael, who had no interest in joining the "acceptable-to-the-establishment-and-administration" (Carmichael 2003, 492) crowd, or in becoming a subsidiary of either the Great Society or the Democratic party, which would continue to be dominated by segregationists in the South for a few more years. By 1966, the Johnson administration's Vietnam policy was becoming more of a public issue. With his radical foundation dating back to his days at the Bronx School of Science, Carmichael naturally led SNCC into a public antiwar, antidraft declaration in his first few weeks as chairman. Coverage of his first press conference in Atlanta proved disheartening, as he noted the media's eagerness to report, or perhaps create, a "split" between King and "young black militants." The shooting on June 6, 1966, of James Meredith, one of the greatest symbols of integration as the first black person to attend and graduate from the University of Mississippi (his 1962 matriculation, under federal court order, had set off a serious riot), on the second day of his one-man "March against Fear" created a new demand among the civil rights movement for another organized march. Initially skeptical, Carmichael rapidly swung around to the possibility of using a new march as a politically useful organizing tool, as had happened during the final Selma-to-Montgomery march the previous year.

Carmichael represented SNCC at a Memphis "summit" to plan the march with several people, including King and two Establishment figures with whom he was increasingly impatient: Roy Wilkins of the National Association for the Advancement of Colored People (NAACP) and Whitney Young of the Urban League. These men were proud to be "insiders," linked to white allies such as labor unions, the national news media, and above all, the Johnson administration. Unlike King, who knew the South in his bones, Wilkins, in Carmichael's estimation, "clearly had no respect for the experience or contributions of mass activism. . . . In his mind, whatever the movement had accomplished—the legislation—was entirely because of the insider contacts and skillful influence of the NAACP. It never occurred to him that they had never been able to get *any* legislation—not as much as an antilynching law—until masses of black people had taken to the streets in nonviolent direct action" (Carmichael 2003, 499). Carmichael was often frustrated during the heated meeting, but persevered; his solid, established relationship with the civil rights movement's great leader paid off when King firmly sided with Carmichael on the two disputed matters: first, providing security for the marchers via a Louisiana group with whom Carmichael had dealt before, and second, insisting that the march be set up to function as a recruiting and organizing tool for the local community in the long term, rather than as a staged spectacle and nothing more. According to one eyewitness, Carmichael claimed that President Johnson was a bigot, and Carmichael was confrontational, and not the least bit deferential, with his civil rights movement elders, Wilkins and Young, who eventually walked out (Fairclough 1987, 314–15).

The march to Jackson did take place, with no loss of life though of course with the usual "low-level" intimidation such as King being gratuitously knocked over by a law enforcement official, and unfriendly crowds at particular points. At Greenwood, a large gathering of black Mississippians turned out, many to welcome Stokely Carmichael back. Here the young activist, having just been released yet again from jail in yet another instance of official harassment, on June 16, 1966, gave what proved to be his most famous speech. To him, it was the usual: register, vote, and gain and exercise power—black power—"nothing new, we'd been talking about nothing else in the Delta for years. The only difference was that this time the national media were there" (Carmichael 2003, 507). As reported by the *Washington Post*, Carmichael, after noting that he had just been through his twenty-seventh arrest, added, "I ain't gonna be arrested no more. . . . [T]he only way we're gonna get justice is when we have a black sheriff. . . . Every court house in Mississippi should be burnt down tomorrow so we can get rid of the dirt" (quoted in Fairclough 1987, 316).

The next evening, June 17th, in a variation on the familiar call-and-response tradition of southern-style worship, the crowd picked up the chant "black power" as a response to the cry "What do you want?" A voter registration drive in Greenwood added many new voters to the rolls, the encamped marchers were attacked with tear gas by harassing authorities, and the march moved on toward Jackson, where it would eventually conclude on June 26th. King had requested federal protection for the march but had been rebuffed; a new request was now rejected by Johnson's attorney general, Nicholas Katzenbach, who claimed that the marchers had been trespassing (Fairclough 1987, 318).

But Stokely Carmichael soon learned that the news media, many of whose members lacked any substantive understanding of life in the black belt South, were playing up the "black power" slogan as the totem of a supposedly newly militant strand in a now-fracturing civil rights movement. Carmichael, now more than ever a battle-hardened movement veteran, was not the apologetic type, and so announced that he and other SNCC leaders would no longer speak to white reporters (Halberstam 1998, 528); though he failed to keep the promise, the words reinforced his image as a "black separatist." Given the reception of the phrase, King, committed as ever to integration, sought in his many remarks as the march proceeded to avoid any hint of black separatism while calling over and over for more power *for* black people. King met with Carmichael and tried to convince him that the slogan did more harm than good (Fairclough 1998, 318). But King also declined to offer any full-scale repudiation of black power, then or later, despite much pressure, though he publicly allowed that the expression had apparently been misunderstood and was "unfortunate." It turned out that way.

With the march to Jackson successfully completed, Carmichael, twenty-five years old, spent the year of his SNCC chairmanship moving around the nation, making numerous appearances in churches, on campuses, with the press, and on television. A late-summer 1966 Harlem church appearance by Carmichael was memorably profiled in the January 1967 issue of *Esquire* magazine (then at the height of its influence with its well-received New Journalist accounts of the 1960s United States) by Bernard Weintraub: in a profile, Weintraub wrote, "His style dazzles. He shakes his head as he begins speaking and his body appears to tremble. His voice, at least in the North, is lilting and Jamaican. His hands move effortlessly. His tone—and the audience loves it—is cool and very hip. No Martin Luther King We Shall Overcome oratory. No preacher harangue. No screaming" (Weintraub [1967] 1971, 670). The next day, in Newark, Carmichael spoke to an older audience about "white power," and a "system in this country that locks black people in, but lets one or two get out every year. And they all say, 'Well, look at that one or two. He's helping his race.' Well, Ralph Bunche hasn't done a damn thing for me" (672). Besides skillfully using humor, Carmichael hit his central point, the one about power: "Brothers and Sisters, we have to view ourselves as a community and not a ghetto and that's the only way to make it. The political control of every ghetto is outside the ghetto. We want political control to be *inside* the ghetto. . . . Black power is the demand to organize around the question of blackness," concluding with his personal mantra, "*Organize!*" (673).

Many people received him very well, but nonetheless, he found that he had been labeled the "militant" with a separatist "black power" ideology. "Suddenly rendered menacing, sinister, and subversive of public order and stability, the two words would, in short order, have me denied entry into France and Britain, declared *persona non grata*, and banned in thirty territories of the former British Empire, including even the country of my birth. They would make me the object of vilification and, on more than one occasion, put my life at risk" (Carmichael 2003, 524). As a SCLC staff member recalled it, "Stokely . . . threw the words out, and before he could explain it the press had taken it and used it as a bludgeon" (quoted in Fairclough 1967, 319). Carmichael found himself attacked by the civil rights Establishment, especially Roy Wilkins of the national NAACP (although Carmichael continued to have fine relations with many grassroots NAACP chapters and members). Martin Luther King, Jr., however, continued to refuse to join the chorus, following his strict rule of never criticizing other civil rights groups. Administration figures were not so reticent; on July 5th, President Johnson criticized the concept, and then on July 6th, Vice President Hubert Humphrey told the NAACP convention that black power was a variation on the theme of racism.

In response to what he regarded as a disinformation campaign, Carmichael, along with activist colleague Michael Thelwell, spent a weekend producing a SNCC position paper, "Toward Black Liberation." Here an obsessive focus on "integration" was frankly questioned. The question for the black minority in the United States *was* power, simply enough. It was said by the civil rights Establishment, including King, whom Carmichael always retained full respect for, that the Johnson administration and its Great Society effort deserved support. "Toward Black Liberation" argued that little had been accomplished, that fundamental realities remained glaring though often, despite all, still unseen: "When unknown racists bomb a church and kill four children, that is an act of individual racism. . . . But when in that same city, Birmingham, Alabama, not five but five hundred Negro babies died each year because of a lack of proper food, shelter, and medical facilities, and thousands more are destroyed and maimed physically, emotionally, and intellectually because of conditions of poverty and deprivation in the ghetto, that is a function of *institutional* racism. But the society either pretends it doesn't know of this situation, or is incapable of doing anything meaningful about it" (quoted in Carmichael 2003, 533). However, the thinking in Carmichael and Thelwell's statement was on the same wavelength as the Great Society's when it came to imagining local community organizations acquiring some power, with maximum participation by local people themselves. Carmichael and Thelwell stressed *independent*, that is, black-led, organization, as a necessary foundation: "When the Negro community is able to control local office and negotiate with other groups, from a position of organized strength, the possibility of meaningful political alliances on specific issues will be increased" (533). Their focus was on the mass black population, not the achievements of a few "tokens" such as Carmichael himself, who had been admitted to and graduated from the most prestigious public high school in New York City.

The above position paper was included in Carmichael's memoir, published in 2003. Another SNCC position paper of the same time, "The Basis of Black Power," however, exhibits a more disquieting tone. A white coming into a meeting of black people, it was argued, would "change the complexion of that meeting. . . . People would immediately start talking about 'brotherhood,' 'love,' etc.; race would not be discussed." Regarding the obvious conclusion to be drawn from this claim, the exclusion of whites from black groups, the paper argued that said exclusion was "because the effects that one is trying to achieve cannot succeed because whites have an intimidating effect." White antiracist activists were thanked for their invaluable assistance in the Mississippi struggle but were advised now, as the struggle entered a new phase given that basic political rights had in fact been won, to go into white communities to combat the problem. SNCC should be "black-staffed, black-controlled, and black-financed," and avoid being used as a "tool of the white liberal establishment" (quoted in Bloom and Breines 1995, 153–56).

But the context in which these analyses were offered was that of the post-Watts era. 1966 would bring the second of what proved to be four consecutive so-called long, hot summers of widespread rioting in American cities; Carmichael himself was arrested during disturbances in Atlanta that September. Did militancy and allegedly rhetorical excesses like black power cause riots? "Toward Black Liberation" saw things much as did the advocates of Great Society Community Action Programs: riots were "not the products of 'black power,' but of the absence of any organization capable of giving the community the power, the black power, to deal with its problems" (quoted in Carmichael 2003, 536). This rational point was hard to argue with. But the image of militancy was rapidly having an effect. SNCC was finding it much harder to obtain money, thus returning to its impoverished past (it got even harder when, in 1967, Carmichael took a pro-Palestinian stance in the wake of the Six-Day War). A perception developed, pushed by the media, that white people were being "run out" of SNCC. Carmichael, the media-designated spokesman for the slogan of the moment, got more speaking invitations and television appearances than ever, and as he got higher fees, he spoke as often as practicable so as to raise money for SNCC. In his memoir, Carmichael summed up his late-1960s public persona and how it was formed: "Whatever was or could be made to sound confrontational or controversial got featured, usually to the exclusion of serious supporting arguments or context. Of course, I take some responsibility in this. While I didn't set out to offend anyone, I certainly wasn't about to bend over backward merely to *avoid* giving offense either. I was going to tell the plain truth" (543). Sometime in the late 1960s, Brian Lamb, who would later found the Cable Satellite Public Affairs Network (C-SPAN), heard Carmichael speak in a church. He recalled it this way: "Well, of a thirty-minute speech, probably, and maybe two minutes was incendiary. The rest of it was thoughtful and intelligent and very well stated" (759). But when it came to the televised report that night, "What made it on was the fire and brimstone" (759). As the Great Society's moment was being burned away, Carmichael's publc image was contributing to its destruction.

Carmichael tried to explain himself on numerous occasions. Writing on "What We Want" in the September 26, 1966, issue of the *New York Review of Books*, for instance, he argued for the need for a new organization that could "speak to the growing militancy of young black people in the urban ghettoes," as the tone of the civil rights movement had been "adapted to an audience of liberal whites" (Carmichael [1966] 1967, 109). The violence he had both witnessed and experienced had stayed with him: "For too many years, black Americans marched and had their heads broken and got shot." Regarding the now-familiar slogan "black power," Carmichael insisted, "For once, black people are going to use the words they want to use—not just the words whites want to hear." Violence, he hoped, would not come, but if it did, "Responsibility for the use of violence by black men, whether in self-defense or initiated by them, lies with the white community." As for integration, it spoke "not at all to the problem of poverty, only to the problem of blackness." In the end, "We can build a community of love only where we have the ability and power to do so; among blacks" (108–20).

Carmichael also decided to write the book *Black Power*, coauthored with Charles Hamilton and published in 1967, in an attempt to define to a wide audience the truism that had somehow become controversial (it remains in print in the early twenty-first century). The book's tone is reformist and non-threatening, though some of its stances are appropriately labeled radical. Integration, for instance, is associated with middle-class aspirations whereby "a few blacks 'make it,' leaving the black community, sapping it of leadership potential and know-how . . . these token Negroes—absorbed" (Carmichael [1967] 1992, 53). Coalitions are deemed obviously necessary in the pluralistic United States, but coalition politics are subjected to a critical and historical eye, having all too often existed "only at the leadership level; dictated by terms set by others; and for objective[s] not calculated to bring major improvement in the lives of the black masses" (60). Organized labor's record of racism is disclosed, and the Mississippi Freedom Democratic Party saga of 1964 is discussed at length and in detail. The Great Society programs are said to have floundered in the face of Deep South white supremacy (45–46). What is needed is institutional control by black communities of their own institutions, such as public schools (166).

At the spring 1967 SNCC meeting in Atlanta, Carmichael announced he was giving up the chairmanship to return to grassroots organizing, his calling. (He was replaced by former Howard classmate H. Rap Brown, who would later become associated with his own catchphrase, "Burn, baby, burn!" of whom Carmichael quipped, "You'll be happy to have me back when you hear from him. He's a bad man" (quoted in Davies 1966, 192). He traveled to London, then to Cuba, China, North Vietnam—and then Africa. He would make Guinea the base of his efforts to build the All-African People's Revolutionary Party for he rest of this life, thus substantially removing himself from American political life, most obviously in its mainstream forms. He and SNCC had dealings with the developing Black Panther movement of California, whose leaders were destined to replace him as the public face of black militancy, and also participated in the 1968 Poor People's Campaign in Washington, planned by Martin Luther King, Jr., and continued by Ralph David Abernathy after King's murder in April, but its stunning failure reinforced Carmichael's notions that he belonged back in Mother Africa, to which he soon returned, after having been "expelled" from SNCC in a factional dispute he believed to have been fomented by U.S. government authorities. Although he took up residence in Ghana, he often returned to the United States, frequently speaking before students and others during black history celebrations. After a generation's worth of toiling in the political wilderness there, Stokely Carmichael succumbed to cancer in his long-term home of Conakry, Guinea, on November 15, 1998.

STROM THURMOND
(1902–2003)

As Strom Thurmond approached the completion of his 100th year in the early twenty-first century, still holding, incredibly, the South Carolina senate seat he had uniquely won as a write-in candidate in 1954, and stood poised to become the first centenarian U.S. senator in history (which he accomplished), he might well have reflected on the axiom of Cardinal Newman that to live is to change, and to live well is to have changed often. As the 1948 presidential standard-bearer of the segregationist States' Rights Party that bolted the Democratic Party, so long the automatic and apparently natural home for the overwhelming majority of southern whites, in protest of the party's historic adoption of a civil rights plank as part of its platform, Thurmond had certainly traveled a long, long way in the near half century that had ensued; in fact, he had become nothing less than a South Carolina, as well as a U.S. Senate, institution. His July 2003 funeral and memorial service in Columbia was said to be the grandest state ceremony in the Palmetto State since the passing in 1850 of John C. Calhoun.

No one who survives in modern elective American politics even half as long as Thurmond did can possibly do so without attending well to his or her constituency, both in the realm of rather mundane, if important, services to citizens seeking assistance of various sorts from their federal government, and also in the broader sense of "bringing home" at least a reasonable share of the plethora of federal dollars increasingly made available over the course of mid- to late-twentieth-century American history. All agree that Thurmond was one of the very best at this classic political game. And Thurmond's longevity is indeed in a class by itself in Senate history; it is hard to imagine that it will ever be matched, or probably even approached, again. But matters such as these do not make one a figure of lasting historical importance.

No one ever imagined Strom Thurmond to have been at any time one of the key insiders, power brokers, or truly dominant figures of the U.S. Senate.

Rather, Thurmond's lasting importance is to be found in his key role in the realignment of American politics that came out of the 1960s, largely in response to the Great Society efforts of President Johnson, most especially, of course, in the pivotal area of civil rights. In 1960, the so-called Solid South, a familiar name describing that lasting and apparently eternal fixture of the country's basic political structure that dated to the defeat of Reconstruction in the 1870s, was continuing to show a few cracks at least at the presidential level (1944 was the last presidential election in American history in which the Solid South, meaning the eleven states of the old Confederacy, all voted for the Democratic presidential candidate). But not in South Carolina, which in casting (by a narrow vote) its electoral votes for John F. Kennedy kept intact its perfect, 100 percent Democratic voting record in twentieth-century presidential elections—for the last time, as things were eventually to turn out. Yet when it came to Congress, even in 1960 the Solid South prevailed *entirely* in the Senate—there were *no* Republican senators from *any* of the former Confederate states—and the Democrats continued to control all but a tiny handful of southern congressional seats, save for a few so-called mountain Republican areas like East Tennessee. It was Strom Thurmond who played the role of harbinger of an emerging Republican majority in the (white) South, when in 1964, just as the Great Society revolutions were getting underway, he joined the party of Lincoln, now the party of Barry Goldwater, foe of the Great Society and opponent (in Goldwater's case, on libertarian rather than white-supremacist grounds) of the Civil Rights Act of 1964.

By the early 1970s, Thurmond had adjusted himself relatively painlessly to the new realities of a significantly biracial electoral constituency that swiftly emerged in South Carolina, as elsewhere in the South, following the enactment of the 1965 Voting Rights Act. Abandoning the trappings of white supremacy, he yet remained philosophically and "constitutionally" a staunchly reliable conservative, a states'-rights man, throughout the rest of his career, just as he had been in his earlier incarnation as a Jeffersonian Democrat of the old, Solid South sort. This fact is highly suggestive; his negative view of at least the grander notions of the War on Poverty and of the overall centralizing, big-government trend of the Great Society was grounded in a tradition that, if historically related to, was nevertheless genuinely distinct from and ultimately *detachable* from that of the doomed, old-style southern white supremacy. If a supposed national conservative majority were ever effectively to challenge for real, lasting political power at the federal level, southern conservatives would somehow have to get over their instinctive aversion to the word "Republican." Thurmond's first national fame had been gained in the failed 1948 third-party "Dixiecrat" effort, which shortly proved to be merely another of the many illustrations in American political history of the futility of trying to crack the extraordinarily entrenched two-party setup. No, however hard it might be to abandon the party label of one's forebears, conservative southern Democrats would have to become conservative southern Republicans.

It was metaphorically said that black Americans in the 1930s turned the Lincoln portraits adorning their parlor walls backwards as they cast their first Democratic presidential votes for Franklin D. Roosevelt. Similarly, descendants of Confederate veterans would have to make the partisan switch (newcomers to the South from other regions of the country, an increasingly important and numerous constituency in the post-1960s South, often brought their Republican identity with them and faced no such historically grounded dilemma). Strom Thurmond played a significant role, in 1964 and beyond, in effecting this historic change, which was to lay the ultimate foundation for the political lineup of the late twentieth century and beyond. In 1996, at the age of ninety-three, Thurmond, in announcing his candidacy for a seventh term as senator, declared his continuing "mission to right the 40-year wrongs of liberalism" (quoted in Frederickson 2001, 1). He continued the fight until his death on June 26, 2003, at the age of 100.

James Strom Thurmond was born at home to a comfortable family on December 5, 1902, near the courthouse square of Edgefield, South Carolina, an "upcountry" community on the Savannah River in the western part of the state, the seat of Edgefield County, whose political tradition was strong enough to have produced a number of contentious figures: William Travis of Alamo fame; Preston Brooks, the caner of Massachusetts U.S. Senator Charles Sumner; and perhaps most famously, at least within the state, Ben Tillman, memorialized in statuary form on the state capitol grounds in Columbia. Tillman, whom Thurmond met as a small boy, was the Palmetto State's version of the extreme white supremacist populism prominent across much of the South during the late nineteenth and early twentieth centuries. The Civil War was certainly a vivid, living memory in Thurmond's early days—he had a grandfather who had served in the Confederate army—and so was Reconstruction, during which time Edgefield had a black majority population and Tillman had been a central participant in the vigilante activities that had brought about "redemption"—the restoration of Democratic party control and of institutionalized white supremacy. His father, J. William Thurmond, was a practicing attorney, a landowner whose large holdings were farmed by sharecroppers, a sometime state legislator, and a community leader with political ties to Tillman, whom he had once served as his campaign manager and who eventually named him a U.S. attorney for South Carolina. Many prominent officeholders visited the Thurmond home, discussing political matters as Strom watched and listened.

White supremacy pervaded the young Thurmond's world; segregation did not always extend by any means to interpersonal, private relations, but it was prominent in public life, and in all settings, the races had clearly distinct "places," there being no doubt which was on top and which was on the bottom—despite the fact that, at the time of Thurmond's birth, blacks constituted the majority of South Carolinians (but not, with the rise of the Great Migration northward, from the 1920 census forward). By the time Thurmond was growing up, the "race issue" had apparently been settled—which didn't stop numerous office seekers from "using" it in their campaign speeches, decade after decade. By the time he was a teenager, Strom Thurmond had determined that he would seek political office. Completing the ten grades of the local public high school in 1918 at the age of sixteen, Thurmond matriculated at nearby Clemson College, South Carolina's land-grant institution for whites, where he was an extremely active, energetic participant in many extracurricular activities of all sorts, especially athletics, while earning a degree in agriculture, Clemson's "default major," in 1923. He immediately was hired to teach farming in a nearby public school. Soon he was teaching Sunday School, coaching sports at the school, and writing articles for the local paper on farming.

Five years of this went by before he made his first run for political office, Edgefield County school superintendent, in 1928; he easily won. While fulfilling the duties of this office, he studied law privately under his father's supervision and was admitted to the state bar in 1930. He was elected to the South Carolina State Senate in 1932, easily defeating Ben Tillman's son, combining calls for improved education (via a lengthened school year, at least for whites) with opposition to higher taxes on the general public (special fees were preferred to raise revenues). In the 1935 session, several of his bills to improve education were enacted, indicating that he was beginning to make a mark and also bolstering his growing reputation. Back in Edgefield, he represented both whites and blacks in his legal practice and effectively lobbied for state and federal dollars for local institutions, both white and black, though certainly not equally so. This legal work led him toward a contested candidacy for a state judgeship, to which the legislature, in an upset, elected him in 1938. His service on the bench continued until he left in 1942 for military service.

His wartime exploits, such as his participation with the 82nd Airborne Division in D-Day, 1944, kept his name before the Palmetto State public. In October 1945, he again donned his judicial robes, but he resigned in May 1946 so as to prepare a run for the state governorship, stressing the postwar possibilities for progress; none of the candidates for the Democratic nomination that was tantamount to election spent any time on the race question. Thurmond was easily elected. In his inaugural address, he gave education the spotlight, including the education of blacks, pointing out what was obviously to anyone remotely informed: the state needed to provide its black citizens improved educational facilities, the lack of which was chiefly behind the high illiteracy and low overall educational standing of South Carolina compared to other states. A few weeks into his term, Governor Thurmond acted forcefully and historically in condemning the kidnapping and subsequent lynching of a black man being held in upcountry Pickens County's jail for the crime of murder; beyond words, Thurmond ordered state authorities to apprehend the lynchers, resulting in the arrest and historic trial of thirty-one men and gaining him the applause of South Carolina blacks and even out-of-state liberals (Cohodas 1993, 99–100). (None, however, was convicted.)

1947 saw two law cases arise out of South Carolina challenging the continuing practice of the "white primary" among the monopolistic Democrats, in defiance of a prior U.S. Supreme Court ruling (*Smith v. Allwright*, 1944), and one challenging the segregated dual-school system on the grounds that in practice it was not remotely "equal" although it was surely "separate" (eventually "bundled" into what became 1954's *Brown* decision). 1947 was also the year of Jackie Robinson's riveting saga of baseball integration with the Brooklyn Dodgers and the release of *To Secure These Rights*, the pro-integration, profederal action report of the presidential commission on civil rights released on October 29. Thurmond kept quiet about the racially charged events of the year; his personal highlight was the ending of his bachelor status with his marriage to Jean Crouch, the day before which he stood on his head for a photographer whose snapshot then appeared in the subsequent issue of *Life* magazine; the predictions that this photograph would appear in his obituary were fulfilled in the summer of 2003.

It was 1948 when Strom Thurmond became a national figure with his presidential run. The so-called race issue proved impossible to ignore—President Harry Truman made sure of that with a landmark, first-of-its-kind speech devoted to civil rights delivered to a rare joint session of Congress on February 2nd. His legislative proposals were in retrospect amazingly moderate, including neither school integration nor the basic antidiscrimination requirements of the 1964 Civil Rights Act regarding public accommodations and employment practices; however, the white supremacists were on target in seeing these proposals as inevitably constituting an opening wedge toward gaining the enactment of the other two-thirds of the 1948 commission proposals. The entire South Carolina Democratic party establishment denounced Truman; this included Governor Thurmond.

As it happened, the Southern Governors' Conference was set to meet in the Florida Panhandle town of Wakulla Springs, near Tallahassee; its meeting was dominated by discussion among the governors, all Democrats, of Truman's "heresy." Thurmond, living up to his moderate image, successfully suggested a forty-day-long, Lenten-like period of consultation with the president and quiet meditation as to what to do next. His public statements mixed calls for restraint with denunciations of the proposals as "un-American" and unacceptable to the white South. South Carolina Democrats cancelled their traditional fundraising event, the Jefferson-Jackson Day. In a meeting with the Democratic party chairman held at Washington on February 23, Thurmond dominated as the leader of the southern governors and made it clear that he opposed any compromises; the Democratic national leaders responded in kind.

Back in South Carolina, Thurmond also took the lead in the state Democratic party's public declaration of opposition to Truman's receiving the 1948 presidential nomination. Thurmond went back to Washington for the March 13 collective call by several southern governors for southern Democrats to oppose all civil rights candidates and for state party organizations to delay the selection of nominees for presidential electors until after the national party convention. On May 10, Thurmond, in Jackson, Mississippi, for a states'-rights convention dominated by Deep South partisans and political leaders, solidified his position as the increasingly obvious leader for a states'-rights crusade, declaiming, "The fight is on, and we will not lay our armor down until the present leadership of the Democratic Party is repudiated and the South is again recognized as a political entity of these United States." Even in this militantly white supremacist setting, Thurmond called for economic development to advance both races in the South; he quickly defended segregation as essential to the "racial integrity and purity" of both races, and stressed opposition to potential federal interference in employers' right to hire whomever they wished—"Every man's private business would almost be made a public one" (Frederickson 2001, 105–6; Cohodas 2003, 146). (Late in 2003, after Thurmond's death, a press conference was given in Columbia, South Carolina, by Mrs. Essie Mae Washington-Williams, a black woman who revealed that she was Strom Thurmond's oldest child; her mother, Carrie Butler, had been a maid who worked for the Thurmond family. She spoke well of Thurmond and his involvement during her life, and it was revealed that the Thurmond family acknowledged her story's veracity.) A wait-and-see resolution was enacted, but plans moved ahead for a potential third-party presidential effort.

The Democratic National Convention of July 1948, held in Philadelphia, featured considerable drama and melodrama. Strom Thurmond was present, but in this setting was but one of many southern leaders who as a group opposed civil rights but were hugely uncertain as to how best to go about it. Residual loyalty to the Democratic party remained a powerful force, though increasingly, and openly, challenged. On July 14, the Democrats adopted a pro–civil rights plank by a relatively close vote, setting off melodramatic speeches announcing the withdrawal from the convention by half of the Alabama delegation, followed by all of the Mississippians. South Carolina was not among them. Thurmond in fact gave a seconding speech for the nomination of Georgia U.S. Senator Richard Russell, who finally became the candidate southern delegates voted for, even as President Truman was overwhelmingly nominated.

Birmingham, known as the Pittsburgh of the South due to its steel industry, was the site of an already-planned gathering of States' Rights Democrats, as they soon labeled themselves, and thousands gathered there only a couple of days after the Philadelphia meeting (originally a few hundred people had been expected). Organizers, exhibiting some awareness of public relations and the potential national audience, put only U.S. flags and decorations in the auditorium, but many attending purchased Confederate battle flags for their personal use; for these stars-and-bars wavers, the "Southernness" of the cause of states' rights was obvious. Few first-line southern leaders participated; Thurmond was one of these few. Speakers immediately made clear anew the racial basis of the convention attendees' fears. During an afternoon strategy meeting, he agreed to accept the convention's presidential nomination, which came that night.

From then until November 2, Strom Thurmond campaigned tirelessly around the South and occasionally beyond it, making explicit that the white South was standing up against outside attempts to promote integration, at times observing that de facto racial segregation overwhelmingly prevailed outside of Dixie. Rarely did he speak about, or get asked about, anything else. His protest candidacy carried four Deep South states: South Carolina, Louisiana, Alabama, and Mississippi, in each of which Thurmond was the official, "regular" Democratic party candidate, thanks to Dixiecrat control of the state parties. This was a relatively disappointing if ultimately unsurprising showing given the lack of funding, lack of professional political expertise involved, and, of course, the narrow and often unpopular focus of the message. Especially disappointing was President Truman's victory. Notably, Thurmond nominally remained a Democrat as he returned full time to his duties as governor, and, significantly, he declined to participate in efforts to make the states'-rights movement a permanent feature of the southern political landscape. Despite the presidential outcome, as Thurmond well understood, Southerners remained a pivotally important element in the Democrats' newly regained congressional majority. Truman's civil rights proposals got absolutely nowhere, and their failure, largely due to southern domination of the involved Senate committees, allowed southern politicians like Thurmond to remain Democrats; in fact, remaining Democrats, it could now be argued, was the best practical way to stop civil rights legislation. Nothing in the 1950s challenged this situation, and thus the Dixiecrat revolt of 1948 produced in the short to moderate run no political realignment after all.

Governor Thurmond resumed his state duties and much of his voice as an advocate of South Carolina's progress. Outsiders then and later might have been surprised to see the governor address the needs of "our colored citizens" in the educational realm, whose "productive potential" was "perhaps our largest undeveloped economic resource as a State" (Cohodas 1993, 197). Former teacher Thurmond called for improved education, "the means whereby we can most quickly equip our colored citizens to make their maximum contribution to the State's total economy, to the great advantage of both races" (197). Thurmond addressed the black schoolteachers' association in early 1949 and lent his presence to a dinner to raise funds for a new black hospital in Sumter. To this all-black audience, Thurmond spoke of increased opportunities for black people; condemned "outside agitators"; called "race fear" a terrible thing that gave "rise to race prejudice and race hatred," which brought in their wake "violence and death"; and promised decisive action against any mob violence. Race relations would continue to improve as South Carolina economically progressed (197–99). All of this was, in Thurmond's mind, perfectly compatible with the continuation of state-sponsored segregation; as he said in a speech during his first senate campaign, "I have done more for the Negroes of this state than any other governor of the state has. . . . I am not prejudiced when I speak against the breakdown of segregation" (211).

In 1950, Strom Thurmond, whose term as governor was expiring, experienced something unique in his lengthy life: a failed political campaign, against incumbent U.S. Senator Olin Johnston in the Democratic primary; despite Thurmond's efforts, it proved impossible to succeed in branding the equally segregationist Johnston "soft on segregation." Ironically, Johnston narrowly prevailed apparently because the estimated 40,000 black votes cast strongly swung against Thurmond (Frederickson 2001, 215). For the first time since Reconstruction, significant numbers of black South Carolinians, due to court orders and persistence in fighting the many subsequent attempts by government officials at evasion, had exercised the franchise. One of the few clear differences to emerge in the campaign came over the possibility of federal aid to education, which would become a centerpiece of the Great Society program—Thurmond correctly feared that aid would come conditionally and that federal money was inherently and rapidly addicting, and, in spite of his quite genuine interest in improving the substandard South Carolina educational setup, opposed it (Cohodas 1993, 209). Following his loss to Johnston, Thurmond went back upcountry, practicing law out of Aiken (close to his hometown of Edgefield) and remaining out of politics until releasing a public statement on November 2, 1952, that he would be voting for Dwight Eisenhower for president (Frederickson 2001, 230). This would prove in the long run to be a straw in the wind, though in the short run it had no effect—Eisenhower lost South Carolina by a substantial margin to Democrat Adlai Stevenson.

"Black Monday"—May 17, 1954—remains one of the most significant dates in American history. The U.S. Supreme Court, in the famous *Brown* decision, unanimously ruled that de jure (state-supported) segregation in schools (and, implicitly, elsewhere) was unconstitutional, in violation of the fourteenth Amendment's Equal Protection Clause. While far from a total shock to the informed leaders of the southern white supremacist cause, to the mass, voting public, it was. The ground was well prepared for white supremacist efforts of various sorts, both elite and grassroots, producing an era known as "massive resistance." Still in his private citizen phase, Thurmond made no comment on the ruling. In September, he received a gift from the political gods when South Carolina U.S. Senator Burnet Mayback died of a heart attack. The state party nominated Edgar Brown, who had retained significant ties to the national Democratic organization, rather than hold a special primary. Thurmond quickly made himself the personification of the resulting widespread unhappiness over the hand-picked Brown, and, with his unparalleled name recognition, successfully waged the only winning write-in senatorial campaign in American history, receiving close to two-thirds of the vote in a contest where, despite the recent *Brown* ruling, race hardly came up. This put him in the senate seat he was to hold until retirement at the dawn of the twenty-first century. Early in the campaign he promised that he would be a Democrat for Senate organizational purposes, thus retaining influence for the state.

Now Strom Thurmond, who took office on December 24, 1954, upon the resignation of an interim senator appointed after Maybank's death, had a national stage destined to last—but he remained a Southerner, a regional leader of a specific cause to most, both friends and enemies: not the abstraction "states' rights," but rather the maintenance of segregation as a southern "way of life," "heritage," "custom," or "tradition." As the Democrats had a perilous two-seat majority in the Senate, the Democratic leadership accepted Thurmond despite his record of bolting, and he was quickly busy in the routines of the work, including the gaining of favors for South Carolina. On May 31, 1955, the U.S. Supreme Court issued its somewhat ambiguous follow-up to the *Brown* decision, usually referred to as *Brown II*, which recognized the difficulties in implementing the prior decision but called for a "prompt and reasonable start toward full compliance." Thurmond publicly reiterated his opposition to the decision, lent his support to the new White Citizens' Councils movement spreading across the South, and in 1956 took the lead in putting together a "Declaration of Constitutional Principles," immediately known as the Southern Manifesto, publicly announced on March 12th and signed by all but three southern members of Congress, which denounced the Supreme Court's departure from well-established precedent, made coherent historically based arguments, commended peaceful resistance to it, and sought to stress the bigger issue of "judicial encroachment" and fundamental "constitutional principles." On the floor of the Senate and later on television, Thurmond spoke at length about the determination of whites to maintain segregation, and he continued to speak on the matter from time to time.

In 1957, the Eisenhower administration, which had cautiously dealt with the civil rights question to that point, regularly offering some rhetorical support and less often anything terribly concrete, decided to push a bill labeled "Civil Rights" involving the clearest, least controversial issue possible—the right to vote. Black voter registration in the South had dramatically increased in the past decade, but all knew that the right to vote was far from solidly secure across Dixie. Eisenhower also proposed the creation of a Civil Rights Commission. The Senate's tradition of "unlimited debate," known popularly as filibustering, provided Thurmond an opportunity to gain lasting fame along the lines of his standing-on-his-head photo from the 1940s: the longest (by about two hours) speech in Senate history—twenty-four hours, eighteen minutes, from 8:54 PM on August 28 through 9:12 PM, August 29 (Cohodas 1993, 294). The bill passed anyway, Thurmond's arguments being as ineffective as those of all filibusters, but Thurmond's opposition to integration remained popular among southern whites.

He continued to warn all who would listen about the implications of civil rights. His constituent newsletter of January 25, 1960, for instance, noted that the now-operating Civil Rights Commission had recommended the creation of federal registrars to assume control of voter registration in parts of the South with low enrollment—what would turn out to be the key practical element to the Voting Rights Act of 1965, a centerpiece of Johnson's Great Society civil rights program. On April 1, 1960, as another civil rights act designed to increase black voting in the South made its way through Congress, Thurmond spoke at length with familiar arguments and then had the remarks printed and distributed to the media. His legislative assistant J. Fred Buzhardt, Jr., the son of a former legal colleague who had come to work with him in 1956 and would be instrumental in Thurmond's historic conversion to the Republican party, did most of the research and writing for it (Cohodas 1993, 310). Thurmond issued a press release after the Democratic Party Platform of 1960 was voted on with the usual heartfelt condemnations: it was "directed not at Americans and citizens as such, but at innumerable special interest groups, blocs and minorities"; it was "a blueprint for a welfare state and an end to individual liberty and dignity in the United States of America"; and it sounded "the final death-knell of the Democratic Party known to our forebears and completes the transition to a party dedicated to socialism, welfare statism, conformity and centralization of power" (312–13).

Thurmond, himself reelected overwhelmingly in November 1960, never endorsed the Democratic presidential ticket or even said he would vote for it, given the platform on which its candidates ran (South Carolina, true to deeply historically embedded form, voted for Democrat John F. Kennedy, who campaigned from the State Capitol steps in Columbia and told the crowd that the only thing the Republican party had ever done for South Carolina was send General Sherman, anyway).

Thurmond's rhetoric was beginning to associate the drift of the Democrats with socialism and welfarism, terms with negative connotations when used by the senator. Were it not for the continuing and nearly unbelievable absolute employment of the label "Democrat" in South Carolina state politics (the legislature continued to have *zero* Republican members), there would seem to be no reason for Thurmond to remain a Democrat. However modest and incomplete they appeared in retrospect, however, the Republican administration's civil rights steps of the second Eisenhower administration—two civil rights bills and the use of federal troops to enforce court-ordered integration in Little Rock, Arkansas, in 1957—meant that Thurmond had no particular reason to become a Republican; Richard Nixon in 1960 seemed no less committed to the mainstream civil rights agenda than did John F. Kennedy. It was the Goldwater movement's success that would change the situation.

Thurmond continued, as the Kennedy administration unfolded and as dramatic points in the civil rights struggle transpired in the early 1960s, to make public arguments of a "constitutional" nature, arguing for local and states' rights as more reflective of the beliefs and values of communities; of course he considered legally enforced segregation to be a defensible, moral value that a particular community might possess and express in its laws, and he enjoyed pointing out the extensive de facto segregation that prevailed, as everyone knew, outside of the South. He always condemned violence, correctly pointing out that it injured the prosegregation side, and always blamed the violence ultimately on the "outside agitators," who were associated, he repeatedly claimed, with communism. He was the most visible and outspoken South Carolina officeholder to oppose the integration of Clemson, his alma mater, by court order of course, in 1963. In the spring of that year, Thurmond charged the Kennedy administration with placing "greater stress on equality than personal liberty. . . . [T]he cry of the equalitarians is not the American creed, but rather it is the creed of Marxism and the come-on of communism" (Cohodas 1993, 337–38). Thurmond had plenty of company from a host of southern elected officeholders, editorial writers, and political leaders, together constituting the overwhelming majority of the southern leadership class.

In his first speech to Congress after November 22, 1963, President Lyndon Johnson called for the enactment of the martyred President Kennedy's civil rights bill as a fitting memorial. To no informed person's surprise, Strom Thurmond immediately found himself in opposition to all that the new administration stood for, but most importantly, civil rights legislation. Thurmond participated in debates, for instance with Minnesota U.S. Senator Hubert Humphrey (whose relationship, of sorts, had begun with Thurmond at the 1948 Democratic National Convention) on television in March, but his positions were familiar to all and influenced virtually no one. The Senate filibuster against the 1964 Civil Rights Act was broken on June 10th, and the Senate passed the bill on June 19th, 73–27 (with the nays coming from six Republicans, including Barry Goldwater, and twenty-one southern Democrats). Thurmond remained completely unbowed and continued his rhetorical assault on the whole civil rights matter as if nothing had happened and as if nothing were about to happen in response to the laws.

The historic nomination by the Republican party at San Francisco of Arizona U.S. Senator Barry Goldwater at least potentially put many southern Democratic officeholders in an interesting position. Thurmond had missed his first Democratic convention in decades, and given its nominations of Johnson and Hubert Humphrey (whom Thurmond regarded as a socialist), along with its Great Society platform, it was probably just as well. What kind of future did Thurmond have in a Great Society Democratic party? He had not yet accumulated enough seniority to gain any committee chairmanship. Like almost everyone else who knew Goldwater, Thurmond liked him, and while he could never agree with Goldwater's often-repeated statements that segregation was immoral or even with Goldwater's long-standing opposition to laws mandating segregation laws, the South Carolinian did indeed share Goldwater's constitutional belief in the states'-rights philosophy, his dread of the growth of power in Washington, and his aversion to the Great Society vision for the United States' future. Two of Thurmond's longtime and most trusted advisors, J. Fred Buzhardt and Harry Dent, observing the success of the Goldwater movement, had been suggesting for some time that Thurmond join the Republican party. Many South Carolinians whose advice Thurmond sought still found the very notion unimaginable; it was still very, very lonely to be a Republican in South Carolina, not to mention the utter lack of any politically powerful offices or organizations under the GOP banner. A few straws in the wind were available to be grasped at by those who saw a Republican future in the Old South, yet in 1964 it was as elusive a dream as that of a genuinely integrated southern world.

The pivotal moment came in a visit Thurmond paid to Senator Goldwater, who encouraged not only Thurmond's promised public endorsement but also his party switch; Goldwater, too, had pioneered the growth of a conservative Republican party in a state that had historically been predominantly Democratic. Most South Carolina people to whom he mentioned the possibility continued right up until his announcement to tell him he was crazy; like social integration to some, it was literally unthinkable. Thurmond did it anyway. The story was first reported on the evening of September 15th.

On September 16, 1964, Thurmond, speaking on statewide television, told South Carolinians of his decision. He condemned the modern Democratic party as a captive of various special interests, first among them minority groups, threatening individual rights in the same way that the libertarian-leaning Goldwater liked to say—"individuals will be destined to lives of regulation, control, coercion, intimidation and subservience to a power elite who shall rule from Washington" (Cohodas 1993, 359). He would, he insisted, always remain an independent mind, putting South Carolina's interests first, yet he recognized the realities of working within the two-party system. Now, however, he was switching to the "Goldwater Republican Party," with "freedom and constitutional government at stake" (359–60). Thurmond followed up the announcement by vigorously campaigning for Goldwater in the South and, to a lesser extent, out west. Despite Goldwater's landslide loss to Johnson and the tremendous swing to the Democrats in the congressional elections, South Carolina voters listened to

Thurmond and easily chose Goldwater, their first Republican choice for president since the disputed election of 1876. Seven new Republican House members were elected from areas in the Deep South that had not done such a thing since Reconstruction. Thurmond remained the sole Republican statewide officeholder in South Carolina, however, and the Democrats still held the overwhelming majority of House seats from the South. Realignment would take a very long time, and, with the continuing rise in the importance of the black vote in the South, would never come close to eviscerating the southern Democratic party.

The South Carolina returns made clear that Thurmond was not in fact going to lose his seat over his new Republican label. Within the Senate, the diminished GOP accepted him with little difficulty, so he was not a man without a party; while the Republican Senate of the mid-1960s included any number of liberals as well as moderates, conservatives, even Goldwater conservatives, were a part of the landscape. Thurmond therefore continued to oppose Great Society proposals such as the Voting Rights Act of 1965. His arguments were "constitutional"—he stated publicly many times that denying the right to vote on grounds of color was "unconstitutional, discriminatory and wrong" (Cohodas 1993, 374), but he expressed only disdain for "sociological" arguments that, for instance, argued against literacy tests on the grounds that, even if fairly administered, they would wind up disproportionately disenfranchising poorer and blacker populations. Economic development and better funded (by local and state taxes) public schools, not sociologically based government programs, termed "socialism" by the senator, was Thurmond's "war on poverty." Philosophically consistent, Thurmond opposed President Johnson's 1966 proposal to outlaw various forms of discrimination in housing transactions.

Thurmond's many public statements and speeches criticizing judicial activism had their origin in the *Brown* decision, but other actions of the U.S. Supreme Court under Chief Justice Earl Warren also disturbed him, notably the 1962 case prohibiting state-sponsored prayer in school; the ruling remained unpopular with large numbers of people. The Warren Court upheld the Civil Rights Act of 1964 and became increasingly impatient with the not-so-deliberate speed with which integration was proceeding, even upholding "school busing" schemes that further fueled criticism. In 1968, Republican presidential candidate Richard Nixon, whom Thurmond supported, made a campaign issue out of appointing "strict constructionists" to the federal judiciary, especially the Supreme Court.

During the Great Society's heyday, Strom Thurmond was a marginal figure on Capitol Hill. The Republicans were far from where the action was, and his brand, Goldwater Republicanism, was seen by most as having been thoroughly discredited by the 1964 election results. Furthermore, and in spite of what a close look at Thurmond's exact political discourse consisted of, liberal and centrist people always thought of 1948, the ludicrous 1957 filibuster, and fellow-traveling with clear white supremacists when Strom Thurmond came to mind. His extremely thick, Deep South accent reinforced his image as a man of a past struggling to die. His arguments, many of which would be deployed in decades to come by a later generation of conservatives, were tainted in the 1960s by their undeniable association with an increasingly unpopular and thoroughly anachronistic tradition of white supremacy. Thurmond personally lived long enough to have more than a few last laughs on his many critics. In 1968, he was a key figure in resisting a regional, old-line Dixiecrat-type George Wallace presidential candidacy, declining to follow the Alabama Democratic state governor (which itself was following Thurmond's historic 1948 example) in an insurgent campaign but instead becoming a key player in Richard Nixon's successful presidential "Southern strategy," which included the Deep South in its calculations. By then, other issues were coming to the surface, and the Great Society was overwhelmingly on the defensive. In 1970, Thurmond became the first member of the South Carolina congressional delegation to hire a black aide, Thomas Moss. Strom Thurmond's career went on and on and on, long after the Great Society debate had seemingly run its course even in the academic sense. His reputation for obtaining federal money, to some, belied his states'-rights views, though he never saw it that way. He was able to fulfill his odd dream of being the only 100-year-old senator in American history in the last weeks of his final term, dying a few months afterward.

EDWARD BANFIELD
(1916–1999)

In the early twenty-first century, it seems harder than ever for a single book, especially a genuinely intellectually serious one, to occupy, even briefly, a central space in the "national discussion," now carried out by a seemingly ever-expanding number of outlets of varying media by a larger than ever multitude of voices. It was the achievement of Edward Banfield, a professor of government at Harvard University, to produce in 1970 the single most influential, and devastating, critique in toto of the Great Society, *The Unheavenly City*; selling well enough to go through an amazing twenty-two printings, it was unrepentantly reissued after the ensuing storm of discussion in significantly revised form in 1974 as *The Unheavenly City Revisited*. With a historical approach framing a commanding grounding in the data-rich social science methodology so favored by intellectual enthusiasts of the Great Society project, a readable style reflecting Banfield's earlier experience in journalism, and the prestige of the author's intellectual home base in the government department of the United States' oldest and wealthiest university, *The Unheavenly City* proved to be a true landmark: a thundering, howling reproach to the entire conceptual schema of Lyndon Johnson's envisioned utopia. Unsurprisingly (in the original preface, Banfield predicted that his book would "probably strike many readers as the work of an ill-tempered and mean-spirited fellow"), its author was described in the many articles and symposia brought forth by *The Unheavenly City* as diabolical, a heretic, and, inevitably as he knew it would, a racist. Nonetheless, the book was read, talked about, and frequently employed then and for years to come in university classrooms. He was a logical choice for the new Nixon administration to head the Presidential Task Force on Model Cities. Banfield was soon being frequently associated with a group of prestigious, well-placed intellectuals who began to become known as the neoconservatives, but his intellectual grounding in the University of Chicago's famed free-market economic tradition, as well as his many publications on urban problems and related issues of various sorts, made it obvious to any student of his work that there was little that was "neo" about his fundamentally conservative critique of latter-day liberal reform efforts. As his conservatism was intellectual as opposed to political, though, it made a bigger impact and proved to be a lasting one even after his book-of-the-moment was replaced by others.

Born on November 19, 1916, in Bloomfield, Connecticut, Edward Christie Banfield, after growing up partially in Hartford and much of the time on a farm in a rural, upstate area, attended the state's land-grant institution, Connecticut State College at Storrs, later renamed the University of Connecticut, in anticipation of studying one of its specialties, animal husbandry. Journalism attracted his interests, as he wrote for and eventually edited the campus newspaper while majoring in English; after his graduation in 1938 he worked for a weekly paper in Rockville, Connecticut, selling advertising and doing some writing. In his extended forays into journalism, he resembled Daniel Bell and Nathan Glazer, two other students of modern-day social problems who also eventually found homes in the groves of academe and who would also be among those accused of having become "neoconservatives" in the 1970s. He greatly differed from Bell, Glazer, and other neoconservative names found among the famous coterie of social thinkers known as the "New York intellectuals," however, in his original grounding in rural issues, reflecting his nonurban background and education at what was in his day still an agriculturally oriented college. Banfield worked in journalistic capacities for the U.S. Forest Service, the New Hampshire Farm Bureau Federation, and the U.S. Farm Security Administration (FSA) in public relations, first in Upper Darby, Pennsylvania, just west of Philadelphia, then Indianapolis, and finally Washington, D.C. Increasingly disillusioned, he left the FSA in 1947. In response to a request by an economist at the University of California, Paul S. Taylor, whom Banfield knew, he used soon-to-be discarded FSA files to prepare a study of a failed cooperative farm project begun under the auspices of the Federal Resettlement Administration and later shut down. Banfield in his study expressed the difficulties faced by reformers: the limited impact of reason on the complex and ever-changing nature of social reality, and especially the great distance between the social planners' assumptions and that hard-to-pin-down reality. Impressed, Taylor sent Banfield's work to a prominent ex–New Deal "Brain Truster" then at the University of Chicago, Rexford G. Tugwell, a former head of the New Deal's Resettlement Administration, who contacted Banfield and brought him to the Midwest to study and teach the planning process in a new program Tugwell was establishing. Banfield began graduate study in political science, working and studying with, among others, the conservative sociologist Edward Shils, with whom he did some collaborate work; and Frank Knight, founder of the "Chicago School" of market-oriented economics, whom he deemed especially influential on his intellectual formation. (Years later, he would get to know future Nobel Prize–winning economist Milton Friedman, who with his wife Rose owned a farm near the Banfields' own in Vermont.) Via sociology professor Herbert Blumer, he read the often cynical writings of William Graham Sumner, a late-nineteenth-century Yale University professor whose criticisms of the pretensions of social reformers warned of unintended consequences; he also continued his study of agricultural economics with Theodore W. Schultz. Banfield's intellectual development was gradual—he continued to work with Tugwell, collaborating with him on papers that continued to argue for injections of more rationality into a much-needed planning process, and he published works in the *Journal of Farm Economics* that concretely analyzed the irrationality and ineffectiveness of FSA programs even while continuing to genuflect ritualistically at the continuing, alleged benefits of a planned government farm program (Wilson 2003, 69, 70–71). "Planning" continued to be a mantra invoked in these and other of Banfield's early published analyses, though the term was employed in vague and unconvincing ways, almost as a ritually invoked statement of faith. Banfield completed the Ph.D., based on his original FSA report that had gotten him "discovered" and subsequently drawn him to Chicago, and published it under the title *Government Project*. He found that while the cooperative farm in question, at Casa Grande, Arizona, had been reasonably well designed and honestly administered, and that rationally the income of the poor farmers resettled there had in fact risen, in the end, failure resulted due to a lack of cooperation, associated with a lack of solid leadership, among the farmers involved. Banfield continued to write and teach at Chicago before moving to Harvard University in 1959, joining his old collaborator Martin Meyerson, who had strongly recommended his appointment.

In the mid-1950s Banfield began writing on urban problems in collaboration with Martin Meyerson, a city planner whom he had gotten to know as a graduate student at Chicago. Meyerson was a future president of the University of Pennsylvania who would recruit Banfield to Philadelphia in 1972, shortly after the storm over *The Unheavenly City* broke (he would return to Harvard in 1976 and complete his academic career there). In 1955, Banfield and Meyerson's first book, *Policy, Planning, and the Public Interest*, was published by The Free Press of Glencoe; it analyzed via the housing issue the local political life of Chicago in a way implicitly skeptical of good-government "reformers" and more favorably inclined to established political organizations with a proven track record of getting things done. A "machine" leader, for instance, was sympathetically quoted: "What I look for in a prospective [precinct] captain is a young person—man or woman—who is interested in getting some material return out of his political activity. I much prefer this type to the type that is enthused about the party cause or all hot on a particular issue. Enthusiasm for causes is short-lived, but the necessity of making a living is permanent" (Banfield and Meyerson 1995, 70–71). Banfield and Meyerson discussed the planning difficulties and controversies surrounding the new Chicago housing projects—attractive to city politicians due to the federal largesse involved, soon to expand significantly, and, due to strongly expressed public feeling expressed by many whites, sited in racially segregated areas—as prone to the production of new social difficulties of all sorts, most with strong racial components.

Banfield, with the collaboration of his wife, Laura Fasano Banfield, whom he had met at the University of Connecticut and married shortly after his graduation, returned to his rural concerns in his controversial 1958 book concerning southern Italy, *The Moral Basis of a Backward Society*, produced after some nine months' residence with his wife's Italian family in a hilltop village, "Montegrano" (actually Chiramonte). The "Southern Question" had loomed large in Italy since the *risorgimento* unification movement of the nineteenth century, and in certain ways paralleled the United States' own history of regionally uneven economic development, whether referring to the South versus the North or rural versus urban. Why did the South of Italy continue to lag behind its North in terms of economic, social, and political development, and in spite of numerous government-sponsored programs over the course of many decades? Banfield stressed the *cultural values* of the region as a neglected explanatory factor. The book was translated into Italian and widely available in Italy for years to come, but received limited attention in the United States on the whole until much later. The central value of the village people was labeled by the Banfields "amoral familism," summarized as follows: "Maximize the material, short-run advantage of the nuclear family; assume that all others will do likewise"—a rational survival strategy given prevailing conditions (Banfield 1958, 85). A lack of civic identity, founded on a profound, deeply rooted lack of civic trust, was at the root of continuing backwardness and poverty. If possible at all, given this entrenched inheritance, the needed political change that would underlie any hope for common economic advancement could likely come only slowly and in small increments; grandiose schemes of the future would founder, as had misguided efforts in the past, on the lack of social capital in the community. These ideas would return and be applied in the American context in Banfield's writings on the "urban crisis," reaching full flower in *The Unheavenly City*, but they were formed and substantially worked out, and in a very different setting from that of the contemporary urban United States, long before that notorious book appeared.

In response to an invitation accompanied by funding, Banfield returned to the subject of Chicago politics, the product of which appeared in 1961 as *Political Influence*. He attempted a micro study of six decisions made in local Chicago politics, focusing on the classic "who/whom" question (who gets what from whom). Banfield found that decisions were made via the guidance of the local political organization, Mayor Richard Daley's famous Cook County Democratic Central Committee, and involved various interest groups who for a time duked it out before being led to the bargaining table by elected officials sensitive to the variety of interests involved, which wound up producing results that those involved could at least live with. While in the abstract this might seem like a humble achievement, Banfield presented it as a success and also as a realistic reflection of the Chicago that actually existed, not an imagined, pure, Utopian "White City" such as the phantasmagoria at the popular turn-of-the-century World's Fair. The much-criticized political "machine" of Chicago Democrats, then, came out looking reasonably good, and certainly better than the "expert" planners and reform-obsessed critics who knew far less than they thought they knew and far, far less than the ears-to-the-ground local elected officials. Banfield took his manuscript to Mayor Daley, whose only substantive plea was that profanity attributed to him be removed; Banfield complied.

Relocated in the Boston area, Banfield began collaborating with new Harvard University colleague James Q. Wilson, whom he had met in 1956 when Wilson, a Californian, had been a graduate student at Chicago. Building on his study of Chicago, Banfield, with Wilson, now produced the more general study, *City Politics*, published in 1963. The book built upon studies of some thirty cities published by the Joint Center for Urban Studies, a collaborative venture of Harvard and the Massachusetts Institute of Technology founded in 1959, the director of which was none other than Martin Meyerson. The book's introduction writes matter-of-factly about its underlying view that city government is "a political process," in contrast to the "usual approach to the subject" that said government is more a product of "administration" than "politics," with "administration" implying professional, rationally based, disinterested control. In the United States, people, as individuals and as organized interests, *directly participated* in the decision-making process, which was understood to be far too important to be left to mere so-called experts. And due to this reality of heavy political activity, there also needed to be greater attention paid to more *informal* means whereby opinions were promoted, issues threshed out, and actual decisions made, ultimately by elected officials more than by civil service administrators. Urban problems involving such matters as crime, racism, and poverty in the United States were fundamentally *political* rather than *administrative* problems: "It is not for lack of information that the problems remain unsolved. Nor is it because organizational arrangements are defective. Rather it is because people have differing opinions and interests, and therefore opposing ideas about what should be done" (Banfield and Wilson 1963, 1–2).

Significantly to the critique of the Great Society that would later come from Banfield, the introduction to *City Politics* expressly *denied* that increased knowledge of how city politics actually functioned would necessarily produce a greater likelihood of "solutions" to the problems of the modern urban United States; as previously explained, the lack of solutions reflected the uneasy coexistence of people of widely differing opinions, sometimes even with regard to what "urban problems" actually consisted of, and sometimes, as in the case of crime rates, with regard to even basic elements of proposed or anticipated "solutions." The introduction *did*, however, offer two rather unheroic outcomes of increased knowledge, though neither was likely to be welcomed by most of those who concerned themselves with what was getting to be known as the "urban crisis." First, Banfield and Wilson opined that a new city planner or other highly educated and credentialed type would benefit from reading *City Politics* because he or she could "learn . . . to be more aware of the limitations upon him and more tolerant of them. This may help him to make plans that are more likely to be carried into effect" (Banfield and Wilson 1963, 3). Secondly, *City Politics* just might "reduce the amount of well-meant but often harmful interference by citizens in the workings of political institutions" (3). Such people, usually called reformers, might close the book chastened and "more willing . . . to allow politicians to do their work without obstruction" (3–4). Obviously enough, the above was hardly the spirit of very many of the men and women of good hope who threw themselves into the creation of the Great Society. A gigantic exception to the above, however, was Daniel Patrick Moynihan, whom James Q. Wilson met in 1962. Wilson succeeded Martin Meyerson both as Banfield's collaborator and as director of the Harvard-MIT Joint Center for Urban Studies, and in 1966, following the controversy over the so-called Moynihan Report, deliberately resigned his directorship while lobbying to have Moynihan replace him, which he did.

In the fall of 1965, a new quarterly, *The Public Interest*, made its debut. This influential small-circulation periodical, which continued publication into the twenty-first century, was coedited by two of the New York Intellectuals, Irving Kristol and Daniel Bell, who, like Banfield, shared significant journalistic and "real-world" backgrounds. Banfield recommended to his junior colleague Wilson that he get in touch with the new magazine's editors and seek to publish there, and so a connection was soon born; Wilson's first contribution appeared in the second issue (in the winter of 1966). As for Banfield, his maiden contribution did not come out until the sixteenth issue (dated summer 1969) and reflected an analysis of the Great Society on which he had been working for the past few years. "Welfare: A Crisis without 'Solutions'" (Banfield 1969) was in effect a precis of *The Unheavenly City*, whose first edition would come out a year later, in 1970. It also paralleled a fall 1968 article in *Daedalus*, the Journal of the American Academy of Arts and Sciences, provocatively entitled "Why Government Cannot Solve the Urban Problem."

The analysis of the recent Great Society era was harsh, even blunt. City welfare departments, under the spell of the new dispensation, had of late "become much more liberal," the most significant general outcome being "that the federal government, through the various Great Society programs, has taught people to regard welfare as something that is theirs by right and has put the local welfare departments under pressure to give them all that they are legally entitled to" (Banfield 1969, 92). In Baltimore, for instance, the local Office of Economic Opportunity–financed antipoverty agency had "made people aware of the availability of AFDC and stimulated them to apply for it" (92). And why was this supposed to be undesirable? Banfield minced no words. First, he charged, the welfare system "causes the breakup of a great many families." Second, the system "enables a great many people who should work to escape work," a group from which he hastened to exclude mothers with dependent children, most of whom *should not* be working, given their other responsibilities (95). Third, the system created powerful disincentives against moving in search of better opportunities elsewhere, thereby tending to trap people in areas comparatively lacking in many opportunities to get out of the system. Finally, Banfield charged that the system strongly encouraged "wholesale lying and cheating." Where he came out was radical: "I conclude that *no* welfare system can be satisfactory"(99).

A magazine article is bound by severe space limitations and thus can only hint at the underpinnings of a given analysis, especially a radically challenging one. *The Unheavenly City* was the culmination of years of reading, writing, and reflection on the contemporary urban United States' changing situation, written in a style designed to appeal to the educated reader rather than the technical specialist. The ensuing reaction was, despite enormous hostility, a social scientist's dream: the book *mattered* to people. Symposia and review articles considering Banfield's arguments appeared in such varied locales as the *Social Science Quarterly, UCLA Law Review, Fortune,* the *Atlantic,* and the *New York Review of Books.* It became a widely used text in college and university courses for years to come. Banfield offered his overall response in 1974 as *The Unheavenly City Revisited,* justifying himself in his preface by noting that the cities' situation had changed (politically, with the end of the Great Society and its replacement by the Nixon administration, the change was monumental and, as things turned out, lasting) and more data were available, but most significantly of all, he sought to respond to suggestions and criticisms engendered by the phenomenon that was *The Unheavenly City.* Especially, Banfield wrote, he had tried to clarify points that had been misunderstood, in hopes of reducing, at least, the "amount of outcry over views erroneously attributed to me"—though he hastened to add, "although experience tells me that I should not expect too much in this respect" (Banfield 1974, ix). However, the book's argumentative stance remained: "I cannot find a way to make the book much less controversial" ( ). The bottom line, though, came out as follows: "My 'revisit' has . . . not changed the book in any essentials. . . . [T]hose who did not like it before will not like it now" (ix).

The Unheavenly City's title, of course, is ultimately derivative of the vision traditionally attributed to St. John the Evangelist as recorded in the Book of Revelation, the apocalyptic final book of the Bible, at whose conclusion, following the Final Judgment, a "new heaven and a new earth" come about, including the "heavenly city" named the New Jerusalem. In this beautiful, well-lit (via the Almighty's personal luminescence), perfectly ordered city, whose streets really are paved with gold and through which flows a pure, clear, unpolluted river of life, God and man live together in perfect harmony for ever and ever, Amen. Specifically, Banfield (in both editions) chose as his book's epigraph a 1710 quote from colonial Puritan leader Cotton Mather, who wrote in his *Theopolis Americana: An Essay on the Golden Street of the Holy City* of colonial America as a "Holy City" wherein might be built "an Heavenly CITY. . . . A CITY to be inhabited by an Innumerable Company of Angels, and by the Spirits of Just Men" (quoted in Banfield 1974, 1). Banfield, of course, believed in no such city in this fallen world, siding rather with Founding Father James Madison's observation in *The Federalist* that if men were angels, there would be no need of government. Hence, his "city" was *un*heavenly, existing in the "real world" of here and now.

Yet he began his first, introductory chapter with good news: "The plain fact is that the overwhelming majority of city dwellers live more comfortably and conveniently than ever before. They have more and better housing, more and better schools, more and better transportation, and so on" (Banfield 1974, 1–2). Next, he asserted that all signs pointed to further improvement. Finally, while admitting that poverty and racial discrimination continued to exist, he flatly stated that there was "less of both than ever before" (3). Banfield then posed what was perhaps *the* central question of his study: what, exactly, *was* the so-called urban crisis that so much ink had been spilled over in recent years, and around which so many Great Society programs had been shaped?

Taken literally, claims that the United States had developed into an "urban" nation had to include the rapid growth of suburbs, areas destined to constitute the home base of the absolute majority of the American population by the close of the twentieth century—but, of course, talk about an urban crisis did not include such districts. Rather, the "serious problems directly affect only a rather small minority of the whole urban population" (Banfield 1974, 10)—and what people usually had in mind when speaking of the urban crisis were "poverty areas," some very large, "psychologically—and in some degree physically—cut off from the rest of the city," which Banfield agreed constituted "a potential hazard not only to present peace and order but—what is more important—to the well-being of the society over the long run" (12). Where had these enclaves come from?

Banfield's historical sketch matched that of many analysts. The federal highway programs had encouraged suburbanization, overall contributing to segregation and increasing the difficulty of city residents finding suitable employment. Even more damaging had been those federal programs, dating back to the New Deal, falling under the rubric "housing and renewal," which had also encouraged suburbanization and, most explicitly and directly via mortgage appraisal instructions, segregation. Federally sponsored construction projects within city limits had produced the widespread physical displacement of poorer people from their homes and the destruction of their neighborhoods. Partisans of the Great Society effort would have found these points most amenable.

But Banfield began his book asserting that things were getting better. Did he include the core city areas in this positive view? Yes. He cited various statistics and social indices, for instance school attendance, to back this up, and later offered an extended analysis to the effect that so-called flight to the suburbs, usually motivated primarily by a desire for a free-standing house and more room, benefited city residents by opening up a significantly higher quality of housing stock than that which had been previously available to the poor. The "crisis talk" resulted not from the actual realities, but rather from the social reality that "the improvements in performance, great as they have been, have not kept pace with rising expectations. In other words, although things have been getting better absolutely, they have been getting worse *relative to what we think they should be*" (Banfield 1974, 22).

In *The Unheavenly City Revisited*'s third chapter, Banfield directly addressed a conceptual category that in the nation's public political discourse had often been avoided or even denied, though it had been subject to significant scholarly inquiry: class. After carefully defining exactly what he did and did not mean, and describing various classes, Banfield proceeded to get into analyzing the "lower class," the one associated with the "urban crisis." The slum was more than a location; it was "a way of life with its own subculture . . . norms and values . . . reflected in poor sanitation and health practices, deviant behavior, and often a real lack of interest in formal education" (Banfield 1974, 71). By no means were all slum neighborhood residents lower class people as Banfield here defined—many were better understood to be working-class people, and, due to the history of residential segregation, a significant number of middle-class people also lived in so-called slums. It was fundamental to any policy considerations, either by public or private parties, that these class realities be understood.

The rise of the middle class in American society, and the ever-greater numbers inhabiting the *upper* middle class, produced a continuing elevation of standards for society as a whole; this reality was the underpinning for the erroneous belief that urban problems were getting worse, when by objective measures urban life had substantially improved, even radically so. Banfield now played the game of pop psychologist in his analysis, postulating that the "ascendancy of the middle and upper middle classes has increased feelings of guilt at 'social failures' . . . in the upper-middle class view it is always society that is to blame. Society . . . could solve all problems if it only tried hard enough; that a problem continues to exist is therefore proof positive of its guilt"(Banfield 1974, 75–76). Banfield's entire scholarly career had made manifest that this was hardly a belief he shared.

Banfield next turned his attentions to the central domestic marker of the 1960s national discussion on social problems: race, a phenomenon at the core of "urban problems" given that the "most conspicuous fact of life in the city is racial division" (Banfield 1974, 77). As a foil and a point of departure, Banfield briefly quoted black psychologist Kenneth Clark, whose 1965 book *Dark Ghetto* was presented as the "mainstream" view of the regnant establishment: "The dark ghettoes are social, political, educational, and—above all—economic colonies. Their inhabitants are subject peoples, victims of the greed, cruelty, insensitivity, guilt, and fear of their masters" (77). Of course, Banfield then stated that the "view to be developed here is altogether different from this one" (77). It had been observed as a commonplace on many occasions in Banfield's book that racism still existed—who could possibly deny anything so obvious?—but he immediately added, here, quoting the then–barely known black economist Thomas Sowell, that discrimination had been faced by many groups in the past and that, today, the early 1970s, discrimination itself (distinguished from the *historical legacy of* discrimination) was *not* the main obstacle retarding urban black people's social advancement. Rather, it was that, like Puerto Ricans and Mexicans, a poor urban black person was "the most recent unskilled, and hence relatively low-income, migrant to reach the city from a backward rural area" (78). Furthermore, Banfield again injected class into his analysis. Much of what is seen as racial prejudice was "really *class* prejudice. . . . Similarly, much of what appears (especially to whites) as 'Negro' behavior is really lower-class behavior. The lower class is relatively large among Negroes" (87).

Banfield noted the rise, in far from optimum circumstances, of the black middle class in the 1950s and 1960s and declared its continuation "as inexorable as that of all other groups." Already higher-end black neighborhoods and suburbs were developing, meaning that "the time has come when many Negroes who find the slum intolerable can leave it without at the same time having to leave the society of other Negroes" (Banfield 1974, 96)—for, Banfield suggested, quoting Malcolm X, genuinely voluntary self-segregation by group was common enough and predictable, though not universal.

However, this inexorable trend would have consequences: "As more and more Negroes withdraw into middle- and upper-class communities, the concentration of the lower class in the slum will necessarily increase" (Banfield 1974, 96). Banfield predicted that this would be seen by the "mainstream" "not as a consequence of the improved position of Negroes generally, but rather as further evidence of callousness and neglect by the 'white power structure'" (96). After quoting a Watts resident complaining about "absentee leadership, absentee ministers, absentee merchants," and observing that the speaker apparently "thought that this was a problem that someone—presumably the government—should do something about," *and* agreeing that the increased isolation of the lower class *was* problematical, Banfield delivered in no uncertain terms where he came out with respect to this particular situation: "It is hard to see what can be done about it. The upper classes will continue to want to separate themselves physically from the lower, and in a free country they probably cannot be prevented from doing so" (96–97)—notwithstanding the desires of reformers, Great Society warriors, or guilt-ridden social commentators. Banfield closed his chapter with more pop psychology with regard to the "higher . . . psychic cost of being Negro" given the continuing misunderstanding, and sometimes knowing misstatement by people who knew better, of contemporary positive trends in black America; the "overemphasis on prejudice encourages the Negro to define all his troubles in racial terms" (99).

Banfield's next couple of chapters in *The Unheavenly City Revisited* considered the problem of urban unemployment, an item that the Great Society efforts principally hoped to address via the Job Corps program. With his University of Chicago training, unsurprisingly, Banfield described the baleful effects of minimum wage laws, which the Great Society's supporters viewed as axiomatic and ever in need of increases, on job creation. Banfield quoted Paul Samuelson, the most widely read (through his highly used introductory textbook in college courses, then and long after) economist and well-known as a thoroughly mainstream liberal Keynesian, "What good does it do to a black youth to know that an employer must pay him $1.60 an hour—or $2.00—if that amount is what keeps him from getting a job?" (quoted in Banfield 1974, 108). Most, though not all, evidence suggested that the minimum wage reduced the likelihood of "the least capable (the inexperienced, the unskilled, and so on) . . . because *the price of their services makes it unprofitable to employ them*" (107). But that was not all: "Those with few skills and below-average education are often not productive enough to permit the employer to pay them the minimum wage *while also providing on-the-job training and opportunity for advancement* that they desperately need" (109).

Unions, civil service tests measuring alleged "merit," and state licensing exacerbated the difficulties. Besides economic theory, there was the social perception that a minimum-wage law was damaging to one's standing in one's circle or community; Banfield noted two examples of federal employment schemes of the late 1960s in Detroit that had been unable to find enough takers. Then there was the competition from the illicit, underground economy such as drug sales, and then simply from the various amusements and distractions from a rat race, "grind," working lifestyle available in the modern, action-packed city. Finally, the labor market in urban areas was also changing in the direction of more service jobs as opposed to blue-collar, physical-labor situations. This, too, posed problems for some hardcore unemployables: "No one cares if a factory worker speaks crudely, scratches himself in the wrong, places, or is physically unattractive. . . . In many service jobs, on the other hand, it is essential that the service worker 'make a good impression' on the middle-class people he serves" (Banfield 1974, 117).

Could minimum wage laws and licensing requirements be repealed or amended? Banfield regarded such a notion as "hopelessly Utopian. . . . (Bayard Rustin, the Negro leader, said that he would gladly trade the whole war on poverty for an increase to $2.00 in the minimum wage)" (Banfield 1974, 119). As to the "familiar suggestion" of training programs, the key was not the skills, but the inculcation of "certain qualities—reliability, motivation to learn, and adaptability to the demands of the work situation" (120). Federal efforts as seen to date in the Manpower Development Training program had documented the theoretically obvious difficulty. Tax exemptions and subsidies for business to get them to remain in, or even relocate to, depressed areas? Only if they were very large, which was highly unlikely given cities' needs for revenues, and anyway, this would be to go against a huge trend; more likely, "The city must adjust to becoming a center for services and exchanges rather than for the production of goods" (120). Could the unemployed urbanites be induced to move where the jobs are? They were not likely to want to do so, and as a group would be unlikely to be welcomed with open arms elsewhere were they to be coming via a government-sponsored or -encouraged relocation plan. The one idea Banfield thought had a genuine shot was the improvement of public transportation so as to make suburban jobs more easily accessible to inner-city residents.

What about the Great Society's Community Action Programs? Banfield saw this as the latest in a string of conceptualizations for how to help the poor, from the "friendly visitors" of the nineteenth century to the "settlement houses" of the Progressive era to the profession of social workers and their associates in the mid-twentieth century. Organizers of the 1960s tried mobilizing existing neighborhood leaders, seeking to form and train new ones on ways to fight city hall via mass action and media manipulation, all the time assisting them in overcoming their feelings of inadequacy and hopelessness. Banfield cited research suggesting a limited response to the organizing efforts, with one odd exception: youth gangs. But these individuals, Banfield stated, "did not suffer from feelings of powerlessness and were not representative of the class for which mobilization was to provide therapy—and what they did, in Chicago and New York, for example—was to terrorize and destroy" (Banfield 1974, 147).

The reader of *The Unheavenly City* by this point has long since figured out Banfield's view of the world, and thus is not surprised to read, as the author moves on to discuss education, a mantra of American reformers long before the Great Society era, that "the possibilities of improving the city by reforming its schools are sharply limited" (Banfield 1974, 149). Regarding the more grandiose expectations that people had, Banfield had nothing but cold water to throw on them: "If we want to equalize the educational attainment of children from different economic backgrounds, we will probably have to change not only their test scores and financial resources, but also their attitudes and values" (159). Banfield cited an early study of a million-dollar compensatory school effort in Newark, as well as the famous 1965 Coleman Report, *Equality of Educational Opportunity*, to highlight the extremely limited success of such efforts to date. Data suggested that what happened to a child at a very early age, even prekindergarten, was critical, but so far, Head Start had not produced lasting gains (168, 248–49). Banfield suggested lowering the school-leaving age to fourteen so as to free up more resources for those still enrolled, as well as to provide opportunities for learning outside the school walls for those who clearly enough were not benefiting from continued time confined therein.

After discussing various other matters, including crime, Banfield ended his book with a final chapter, "What Can Be Done?" He insisted on feasibility as a top criterion for evaluation of any idea; anything else was "a Commencement Day Oration." The other fundamental issue was lack of knowledge, which needed to be faced squarely: "The plain fact is . . . that no one knows how to change the culture of any part of the population" (Banfield 1974, 263). Banfield was peeved at some of the things he found himself reading: "What can an educational psychologist, Jerome Bruner, mean by writing that the plight of the poor in our society probably cannot be changed without first changing 'the society that permits such poverty to exist' and that accordingly his 'first recommendation, as a commonsense psychologist and a concerned man, would be that we should transform radically the structure of our society'?" (263). Banfield listed some thirteen specific recommendations, most employing economic incentives, but freely admitted their adoption was unlikely. An additional problem was the perversity of public opinion, particularly the dominant "political style . . . formed largely in the upper classes and, within those classes, mainly by people of dissenting-Protestant and Jewish traditions," adding up to two simple ideas: "First, DON'T JUST SIT THERE. DO SOMETHING! And second, DO GOOD!" (273–74).

With the recent Great Society episode in mind, Banfield criticized "the feeling of exhilaration when a bold step is taken. . . . Believing that any problem can be solved if only we try hard enough, we do not hesitate to attempt what we do not have the least idea of how to do and what, in some instances, reason and experience both tell us cannot be done" (Banfield 1974, 274). The reference was applicable to the public posturing of politicians overselling a program: "The politician, like the TV news commentator, must always have something to say even when nothing urgently needs to be said" (276); as for the scholarly evaluations, these were more down to earth, and Banfield cited them frequently in his book. The *best* way to help the poor was "to keep profit-seekers competing vigorously for their trade as consumers and for their services as workers"—not a popular thing to say, as this was "not a way of helping that affords members of the upper classes the chance to flex their moral muscles or the community to change its commitment to the values that hold it together" (275). The War on Poverty was "a sort of secular religious revival that affords the altruistic classes opportunities to bear witness to [their own] cultural ideal and, by doing so, to strengthen society's adherence to it" (275). Banfield concluded his chapter with a doleful observation. "If we look toward the future, it is impossible not to be apprehensive. The frightening fact is that large numbers of persons are being rapidly assimilated to the upper classes and are coming to have incomes—time as well as money—that permit them to indulge their taste for 'service' and doing good in political action. . . . Doing good is becoming—has already become—a growth industry, like the other forms of mass entertainment, while righteous indignation and uncompromising allegiance to principle are becoming *the* motives of political commitment" (278).

Interest in Banfield's polemic proved to be extremely high. Much of the reception was decidedly, and not unexpectedly, unfriendly in the extreme, for he was suggesting a deep incoherence at the core of the Great Society vision. Sociologist Richard Sennett, for instance, in *The New York Review of Books* termed the Harvard professor of government "an innocent, blind to the facts of class and race in America today, and taking refuge from the storm of modern events in an old-fashioned small town mythology of class and the individual's place in history" (Sennett 1970). In his 1974 revised edition, Banfield included Sennett's diatribe in his appendix of symposia and articles that had come out of *The Unheavenly City*. Collectively, Banfield seemed under severe attack indeed; the forces about whom he worried at the conclusion of his book were fighting back, seeking both to destroy him and to advance a new birth of Great Society-like programming.

Edward Banfield was too pessimistic. There were many ways for the upper classes to do good, and by no means was "everyone" assimilated into the reforming class whose increase he feared. A critique of the Great Society approach to things, in whose creation Banfield played a huge role, proved to have legs. Conservatism, though far from unchallenged and far from uninfluenced by the Great Society, would have a stronger future in the generation that followed the publication of *The Unheavenly City* than would Great Society–style liberalism. Edward Banfield played a large role in helping create a more intellectual, more sociological conservative critique of contemporary American society, first labeled "neoconservative" in the 1970s (he referred to himself as a Burkean conservative). He completed his academic career and died on September 30, 1999.

BOTH FOR AND AGAINST

WILBUR MILLS
(1909–1992)

Wilbur Mills represented the Second Congressional District of Arkansas from 1938 to 1977 and served as chairman of the pivotal House Ways and Means Committee from 1958 to 1974. In holding this position, he was one of the most influential figures during the Great Society period. After having paid his dues and established his position and reputation in Congress, Mills was a man of well-known values, a man with whom one could do business, and a central player who preferred to keep his own counsel; those who dealt with him knew these things and usually acted accordingly. A believer in the contributory social insurance scheme enshrined in the creation of Social Security, his decision to take on and support Medicare, an idea that had been around for decades, was centrally important to the passage of the legislation creating it in 1965. His continuing fiscal conservatism, however, led him to insist on holding the line on Great Society spending as the financial challenges of the Vietnam War exploded in the late 1960s, and even Lyndon Johnson could not turn him around. Hence Mills was influential both in creating one of the major achievements of the Great Society and also in helping to choke off the potential expansion and development of its central War on Poverty elements.

Mills's initial election to Congress, appropriately, came at the midterm of Franklin D. Roosevelt's second term, 1938, a year that confirmed the downturn in the fortunes of the New Deal that had first been marked during the court-packing controversy of 1937. The strong swing to the Republicans in 1938, however, only meant that the minority party had now returned to a respectable status in terms of congressional membership; the Democrats remained the majority by a comfortable margin. Mills represented a huge, somewhat anomalous element in the Democratic coalition: the old Solid South, from the states of the old Confederacy of Civil War days, usually from one-party areas. As late as 1960, for instance, there was *not a single*

Republican senator from the southern states. Arkansas, Mills's home state, was a classic example of this setup. There was really no Republican party in the state at all, though there was a barebones Republican apparatus that sent delegates to the quadrennial national Republican conventions. No Republican presidential candidate ever came even remotely close to carrying Arkansas; no Republicans held any statewide offices; it was far from a sure thing that there would even be a Republican name on the ballot for the vast majority of offices; it was far from uncommon for the state legislature to have zero Republicans among its membership. In this situation, politicians of any and every ideological/philosophical stripe ran under the label "Democrat."

The New Deal ushered in two generations of political dominance in Congress by Democrats: in the sixty years following FDR's initial election in 1932, Republicans won control of the House of Representatives in only two elections, 1946 and 1952, and in each case immediately lost that control at the next opportunity. This meant that during Mills's congressional career, Democrats were nearly always the majority; during his days (1958 forward) as chairman of the Ways and Means Committee, not only were Democrats always in the majority, but there was also rarely any serious danger of their losing this majority. But it is important to comprehend that the *nominal* majority of "Democrats" did *not* mean that a "New Deal" mentality prevailed in the Congress as a whole during most of these decades of Democratic control.

The expression "bipartisan conservative coalition" came to be employed to describe those who set Congress's dominant philosophical orientation from the 1938 election returns forward up until the 1964 election, the Johnson landslide. The New Deal moment had allowed the creation of a federal welfare state, among other things, but that moment had passed; the negative reaction to the court-packing plan and to the wave of sit-down strikes served to discredit the New Deal in the minds of many, including more conservative Democrats, especially from the South, where unions were to remain quite weak throughout the twentieth century. New initiatives designed significantly to expand the entitlements of the federal welfare state—in other words, to get back on the New Deal track—remained deeply desired dreams of many politically active and influential people, but in the event they were not able to succeed in the face of the bipartisan conservative coalition. Incremental increases and expansions in the coverage of those entitlements already created, as in the case of Social Security, did continue to be enacted by Congress, but on paths already worn. FDR, of course, became overwhelmingly preoccupied with the international crisis, which ultimately led to, as he put it, Dr. New Deal turning into Dr. Win the War. While on occasion he rhetorically expressed support for the extension of the welfare state's provisions, circumstances did not lend themselves to such a focus. After suddenly becoming president in 1945, Harry Truman did eventually try to push national health insurance during his presidential terms, but came up woefully short given the realities of the bipartisan conservative coalition. This situation continued until the coming of the administration of congressional master Lyndon Johnson and then even more so with the results of the 1964 election.

Wilbur Mills is best understood as a mainstream member of the bipartisan congressional conservative coalition. Given his governmental and social philosophy, had he been born elsewhere, he might well have naturally gravitated to the moderate-conservative wing of the Republican party—but this was not possible in Democratic, Solid South, one-party Arkansas (which has hardly disappeared: into the twenty-first century, it was still the case that Republicans *had not even remotely come close to contending* for control of the Arkansas legislature). He also spent his career in the old congressional setup, which lasted until the 1970s Watergate scandal–inspired reforms, that was characterized by the strongest congressional committee system in history, under committee chairmen whose powers were extremely strong, bordering on autocratic. Career Democrats rose to power as chairmen based on the strictest seniority system, which produced a disproportionately southern look to the chairmen, itself a product of the utter lack of party competition for most of the South. In such a setup, a serious, hard-working congressman like Mills, if he kept at it, could rise to the top.

Mills was born on May 24, 1909, in Kensett, Arkansas, a small town some fifty miles northeast of Little Rock, the first of three children of a successful store owner, who eventually became a local bank president, and a homemaker. At an early age Wilbur was being taught double-entry bookkeeping by his parents, who sent him to a local high school where he graduated valedictorian and then to Hendrix College, a liberal arts school in Conway, Arkansas, considered the finest institution of higher learning in the state. At Hendrix he was again an outstanding student academically, participating in debating and literary activities and graduating as salutatorian in 1930. He entered Harvard Law School that fall, where he felt quite out of place, received mixed grades, and left one semester before graduating, returning home to work in the bank owned by his family. Nonetheless, he was admitted to the Arkansas bar in 1933.

In the following year Mills first stood for election, campaigning as a reformer against corrupt practices in the probate court of his native White County. He continued in this work, learning a great deal about the ins and outs of give-and-take politics with the usual low-level (at least) corruption. Indicative of his personality, upon marrying Clarine Billingsley in 1934, he took only a one-night honeymoon at a Little Rock hotel before returning to work. At age twenty-nine, in 1938, he was elected to Congress from the Second District, a poor, rural, agricultural region. In keeping with his career to date, Mills became known as a workaholic congressman who rarely attended Georgetown parties, read vociferously and studied hard, and was often back in his district making speeches and staying in close touch with his constituents. He made taxation his specialty, winning a place on the House Banking and Currency Committee in 1939. He soon aspired to a place on the highly influential Ways and Means Committee, as did many others, and achieved this goal late in 1942 with the help of House Speaker Sam Rayburn of Texas, who took a liking to Mills and began introducing him to influential people on the Democratic side of the aisle, both veterans and relative newcomers such as fellow Texan Lyndon Johnson. Mills was thoroughly socialized to the insiders' view of Congress: respect the institution, do your homework, go along, wait your turn, seek consensus. He compiled a mainstream voting record, supporting federal largesse in general and only bucking the national Democratic party on the ultrasensitive issue of civil rights and on questions involving labor unions, whose powers were virtually nonexistent in his state (e.g., like all members of the Arkansas delegation, he signed the 1956 Southern Manifesto denouncing the U.S. Supreme Court's antisegregation *Brown* decision). Southern Democrats were expected to meander away from the national party in these respects, so in following this practice, Mills was doing little if any harm to himself.

Rather than civil rights, Mills was interested in the financial realm. As he recalled in a 1980 interview, he spent the 1940s (and beyond) studying and learning: "I undertook to memorize the Internal Revenue Code. . . . I spent an awful lot of time studying it, and Social Security legislation, reciprocal trade legislation, debt legislation, welfare programs, unemployment compensation, all these matters that were within the jurisdiction of the Ways and Means Committee" (Zelizer 2000, 37). The committee system became even stronger in the postwar decade, with a reduction of the number of standing committees and a doubling of the number of staff (40). A rule was passed (the "closed rule") for Ways and Means that usually made it impossible for the full House of Representatives to amend a committee proposal, which could only be voted up or down as reported out. This had the effect of making the real decision making take place within the committee.

Mills was well within the mainstream of his party when it came to his support for the gradual expansion and improvement of Social Security benefits, and a firm believer in the contributory scheme rather than the general revenue scheme of financing, as this created a sense that the individual was "buying" the pseudo-insurance and thus was truly entitled to its reception upon retirement. His impressive and knowledgeable participation in the House debate that ultimately produced the 1950 amendments to the original Social Security law added to his general reputation within the House while demonstrating both his belief in the system and his discomfort with "welfare." Symbolism was important here to Mills and others who were negatively disposed to a "dole" or straight-out welfare-state setup. Cogent objections to this shell game, notably from Representative Carl Curtis of Nebraska via his Subcommittee on Social Security, were brushed aside, sometimes nervously, sometimes angrily, and certainly successfully.

Throughout the 1950s the hard-working Mills continued to add to his reputation as a man of solid expertise on issues with which the Ways and Means Committee dealt, especially taxation. Insiders interested in the various questions he addressed all agreed that Mills knew what he was talking about and was a man with whom one could do business. Mills elicited scholarly contributions on various matters via panels of experts commissioned by his subcommittee of the bipartisan Joint Economic Committee in the mid-1950s. He continued to prefer contributory social insurance programs over direct welfare doles. Upon the death of Tennessee Representative Jere Cooper in 1957, Mills stepped up as the exceedingly well-prepared new chairman of the House Ways and Means Committee.

In a 1962 speech, Mills remarked that "slogans about conservatism or liberalism have very limited value" (Zelizer 2000, 151). He would have continued to identify himself as a fiscal conservative, but he had never particularly opposed government activity interfering with the economy, even at the federal level; in this, his New Deal origin never fully left him. He felt no attraction to Barry Goldwater's radical-sounding conservatism at all (Arkansas voted for Johnson). However, Mills held to the traditional conservative position that government programs should not lead to "dependency." Contributory social insurance he saw as a completely different animal, for it tied "entitlement" to contribution.

With the coming of the Great Society, Wilbur Mills was in full command of his position of influence as Lyndon Johnson planned his effort to construct one of the pillars of the new American welfare state's structure, the long-dreamed-of Medicare program, an entitlement to medical services on behalf of senior citizens. Washington insiders of the mid-1960s rated him one of the half dozen most influential people in the nation's capital. Without Mills's approval, it would not be possible for interested parties to add health care benefits to the Social Security setup. As a fiscal conservative, Mills worried about paying for new entitlements. Social Security was funded by a specific tax, whose proceeds were allegedly deposited into a mythical (yet oft-invoked) "trust fund"—the contributory scheme that Mills believed in. How could health entitlements be funded? How much, exactly, should they be? Where would existing entities—private insurance, doctors as represented in the then-powerful American Medical Association, traditional welfare programs of this class that provided aid for the "medically indigent," et alia—fit into the new structure? Could it be done? If it could, all agreed, Wilbur Mills would have to sign on and take a leading role in making it happen. It also took a change in the political arithmetic, which the 1964 Johnson landslide provided, as well as the commitment of President Johnson himself. All of these pieces came together in 1965, and Medicare was transformed from dream to new reality.

During the Kennedy administration, Mills opposed proposals that circulated in those years to add health insurance to Social Security, fearing unpopular higher taxes that would call Social Security itself into question and also worrying about the potential upward push on health costs (which in reality would eventually turn out to be far greater than the greatest fears of Mills and others). A serious proposal called King-Anderson, named after two members of Congress, was kicking around during these years. It created a contributory system of hospital insurance and a few other benefits, but did not include covering the costs of visits to doctors, due to fears that AMA abhorrence of interference with their financial prerogatives would doom the idea from the outset. Mills's way of opposing King-Anderson was to state publicly that it did not have the votes in Congress, an estimation that was consistent with that of the Kennedy administration, especially Robert Ball, veteran of the Social Security Administration, and point man Wilbur Cohen, another longtime Social Security insider and an associate of Mills's for decades. Cohen was firmly of the opinion, then and later, that Mills was a reality who had to be dealt with; furthermore, Cohen held a high opinion of Mills, viewing him as eminently reasonable as well as politically astute. Cohen and his aides worked on discovering alternatives palatable to Mills and dealing with his concerns. In the summer of 1963, Mills attended a White House meeting and was clearly entertaining serious proposals involving such things as higher taxes or tax deductions for purchases of private health insurance. He accepted two new pro-Medicare members for his Ways and Means Committee, and began to drop hints in public statements of his openness to new approaches for new times.

Lyndon Johnson expressed serious interest in Medicare within a week of his suddenly being thrust into the Oval Office in November 1963. Wilbur Cohen and Robert Ball were given the go-ahead to deal with Mills on the issue. Johnson understood Mills's personal obsession with "actuarial soundness," at least as measured by the Social Security shell game, and his style of playing the game cautiously, his unwillingness to support anything of such historical significance unless his count showed that Congress as a whole would go for it. Part of his reputation depended on leading "winners" through Congress. Mills had decided in September 1963 that Medicare in any of its permutations was dead for the current session, but had already shown his openness to serious discussion and real proposals.

And so, in early 1964, Mills's Ways and Means Committee continued working on the question and was in regular contact with Cohen and Ball, to whom Johnson had delegated authority to represent his interests; it was said that Cohen "lived with" Mills over the course of the next few months. Mills's conception of how to be a leader was well exhibited over the course of the considerations. In the end, as chairman, the signals he sent and the calls he made would likely be decisive; therefore, at the more preliminary stage of the process, in which various ideas and proposals were brought forth, dissected, and kicked around, Mills remained elusive as to his own thoughts, keeping his options open, observing which proposals were able to gather the most support of the varied interests involved. Veteran social security actuary Robert Myers, whom Mills had worked with for decades, provided Ways and Means data and estimates in the spring of 1964, the key questions being, "What exactly would the benefits turn out to be?" and "How, exactly, would they be paid for?" This was the essence of the situation; politicians might on the outside speak grandly or in noneconomic terms about certain notions of social justice or even the Great Society, but within the Ways and Means Committee, the question was, "What will the setup be?"

Lyndon Johnson considered Medicare to be right at the heart of his Great Society vision. He was going to fight it out if it took all summer, or even longer. On May 18, 1964, he had a long telephone conversation with Lawrence O'Brien, his chief congressional liaison officer, about how things were going. The word was encouraging. While Mills, predictably, declared that Johnson would not be able to get everything he wanted, he was at the same time still clearly on board regarding the general proposition: a new and significant entitlement to health care for the old. Johnson had also been concerned that Mills might be upset by stories in the Washington press suggesting that the committee was getting nowhere fast, but O'Brien reported that Mills had dismissed such reports as the usual. Furthermore, real progress was in fact being made: Mills said there would be an actual proposal before another week had passed. Still, Mills was being Mills, refusing to commit to anything in particular, yet, and preferring to continue the pace of very deliberate speed. Johnson was all too familiar with the Mills way, and expressed frustration to O'Brien: "Tell him they're [the press corps] asking me questions and I don't know what the hell he's doing. A Democratic President ought to know what a Democratic chairman is doing" (Zelizer 2000, 225). But even Johnson simply had to deal with Mills the way he was.

Johnson restrained himself for a few weeks, but then made a call to Mills on June 9, 1964, trying to encourage the process toward completion. He flattered Mills, expressed confidence that he was moving in the right direction, offered technical help from the executive branch, and stressed the historical moment: "There is not anything that has happened in my six months or that will happen in my whole term, in my judgment, that will mean more to us as a party or to me and you as individuals in this piece of legislation. . . . It'll be a bill that you and your folks will never forget and I will come in and applaud you." Mills was pleasant, expressed concern about the taxes that would be required, and expressed hope for some Republican support so as to make Medicare bipartisan. Johnson retorted that Republicans always opposed antipoverty programs, but Mills replied, "They are not always against Social Security" (Zelizer 2000, 226). Indeed, there was clearly Republican support for particular elements of the health benefits proposals.

This brief exchange between Mills and Johnson concerning partisan politics is a reminder of the ever-present realities of Washington. 1964 was a big election year, and the coming electoral test, as per usual, tended to make faint hearts fainter. Creating a huge entitlement was a major, major step; any choice meant rejecting alternatives that might include this or that item that had been definitively appealing to a particular constituency. The AMA's long-standing campaign against "socialized medicine" had imprinted that expression in the consciousness of millions—and, whatever it might actually mean, it sounded bad. Hints of this possibility were clearly present even in the spring, when Johnson still considered it realistic to hope for action in the current session, but by late June 1964, Johnson was beginning to fear the handwriting on the wall. Lawrence O'Brien's headcounting supported Mills's belief that Medicare in any form at the present moment would not quite get a favorable vote within the Ways and Means Committee. Should the administration go for King-Anderson, taking the incrementalist line that they could always hope to get more later? But Mills had long publicly opposed King-Anderson; surely he would not feel he could convert to something he had long criticized?

He did not. On June 24, Mills publicly reiterated his opposition to King-Anderson, warning of the uncertainties of its tax implications. In a couple of weeks Ways and Means favorably reported out an increase in Social Security payments, a perennial election year favorite, whose cost seemed to crowd out for the moment the creation of a new entitlement in the health insurance area. Ignorant media commentary was published complaining that Mills had exercised a "one-man veto" on Medicare, which grossly misunderstood what was actually going on. He by no means opposed Medicare at this time, and continued to encourage discussion and negotiation as 1964 progressed.

The Senate included U.S. Senator Clinton Anderson, of King-Anderson fame, and this New Mexico Democrat, with Republican Jacob Javits of New York adding leading bipartisan support, got a version of Medicare added to the Social Security benefits increase law by a vote of 49–44. This was the first time that either house of Congress had ever passed a Medicare bill. But Mills's opposition was crucial in seeing that it did not survive the conference process.

November 3, 1964, saw the greatest political victory for the vision of an activist federal government since the Depression era. The next Congress would be the most Democratic since the 1930s; specifically, three Republican members of the Ways and Means Committee who had opposed Medicare were defeated. As Mills himself had no philosophical opposition to the Medicare concept, he wasted no time in stating to reporters on the day after the election that he "would be receptive to a Medicare proposal" in the new Congress (Zelizer 2000, 231). The new Ways and Means Committee would reflect the increased Democratic majority in the House, giving the Democrats an 18–7 majority as opposed to the 15–10 lineup of the previous Congress. This made it much easier for Mills to make something happen, and he moved to ensure this outcome, asking the Social Security Administration to come up with a new proposal, this one to include a separate "trust fund," which came out in early January. A day later, the Johnson administration unfolded its new, improved version of King-Anderson, which had been prepared with many of Mills's concerns in mind, such as the separate trust fund. It was presented as fitting into the contributory mode of social insurance. That the whole ball game had been changed by the election results was dramatically indicated when the AMA presented its own proposal for means-tested, taxpayer-funded, voluntary health insurance that included doctor visits and prescription drug costs. The big difference was the presumption that all of this was strictly for those who fell below a to-be-determined income level, while those above it were expected, as per usual, to take care of themselves. In other words, this was welfare, not across-the-board entitlement, and certainly not universal contributory insurance. On January 27, 1965, Ways and Means resumed hearings with these revised ideas now on the table.

Several weeks of closed hearings in executive session produced technical discussions regarding the nearly unending possible combinations of taxes and benefits. Various experts disputed projections and the assumptions on which they were based; in the end, all participants grossly, radically underestimated the costs that very shortly presented themselves in the ensuing years. Mills continually expressed his concerns about public support for the entire worldview of contributory social insurance, including Social Security, if taxes got too high, which they might if the cost of the benefits promised somehow got out of control. That was what was behind his talk about actuarial soundness. For these reasons, Mills was most uneasy with talk about the use of general revenues to fund Medicare. In the Social Security world, one's "contributions" (a misnomer since they were not voluntary—yet the term was used by supporters of the program) created not only a pseudo-right to money, but also the *attitude* that benefits paid out had been "earned." He articulated this faith during Ways and Means hearings: "whenever you have a program financed by a specific tax, the willingness of people to pay that tax, that specific tax, limits the benefits of that specific program. . . . If you put a program, then, into the general fund of the Treasury, there is less likelihood that you control the package of benefits initially enacted than there is if you put it in a trust fund. . . . I can't help but reach the conclusion that a specific fund, supported by a payroll tax, is a more conservative method of financing something than to do it out of the general fund of the Treasury" (Zelizer 2000, 236).

This was Wilbur Mills the *fiscal* conservative—not someone philosophically opposed to government intervention, but one who in this setting employed the term "conservative" to financial matters in a way that suggested prudence, care, and careful consideration—all desirable things to produce a "sound" outcome and a scheme in which the bills could be paid. Nebraska Congressman Carl Curtis was still around complaining about the misleading rhetoric and conceptualizations used in the discussion, but, even more than usual given the new political arithmetic, he was more or less ignored—the bottom line was, as everybody recognized (given the increasing numbers of elderly and their increasing longevity), the expansion of available treatments. Medicare in some form was an idea whose time had just about come. Much of this debate exhibited the relatively familiar symbolic distinctions between contributory insurance and welfare, but to Mills, symbols in this realm had real meaning and real significance, providing a brake on spending that was consistent with his fiscal conservatism. Curtis's conservatism included a perfect willingness to consider government health care spending for the poor, that is, means tested, but balked at across-the-board (in effect, mandatory) schemes for all. Curtis had a much tougher sell at any time, and in the atmosphere of the newfound enthusiasm for the Great Society approach to things, he had no chance whatever.

By early March, three reasonably coherent proposals had been produced by the hearings, reflecting a contributory approach (based on the administration idea), a welfare approach (the AMA idea), and a souped-up welfare approach concocted by a veteran Republican member of the committee with whom Mills had worked for years, Wisconsin's John Byrnes, that was more dependent on general revenues but had a higher means test for determining what individuals had to pay in taxes. At this point Mills stepped up and acted decisively, mixing together elements of the three proposals so as to provide for both doctor fees, in an optional insurance program, and hospital insurance, plus what would come to be known as Medicaid—entitlement to federal funding of medical services for the poor. In mid-afternoon on March 2nd, at a meeting of the committee with HEW officials present, Mills surprisingly "declared himself" and asked Wilbur Cohen to come up with something combining these features. Cohen had a busy night.

For many at the time, and certainly in retrospect taking into account how things actually worked out, this was the key moment in the whole saga. Those favoring the Great Society's expansive attitude toward welfare state provisions were ecstatic that a solid, respected, fiscally respectable Mills had put his seal of approval on an expansive Medicare scheme. Broad support had seemingly been guaranteed, as different constituencies had each made their contribution, balanced by Mills, whose timing proved perfect. From March 12 to 19, the Ways and Means Committee held its usual closed hearings, going over the new data provided line by line, surrounded by technical experts. It was critically important to Mills that the Medicare tax be listed separately on people's W-2 tax forms from the Social Security tax, which would thereby be kept politically quarantined and thus "safe" should any problems ever develop regarding Medicare costs. What was eventually known as "Part A," the hospital insurance entitlement, was directly linked to the Social Security tax but had its own "trust fund"; "Part B," the optional medical insurance covering doctors' fees, came from general revenues plus fees charged against the Social Security benefits checks of those who chose to participate; "Part C," Medicaid, came from general revenues. Cost-containment efforts took up the committee's agenda on March 17th and 18th, with much uncertainty, followed by finishing details such as the place of blood banks and the definition of who was a "doctor" as opposed to a mere provider of "hospital services." On March 23, 1965, on a party-line vote of 17–8, the bill was reported out of committee favorably.

Congressman Byrnes's criticism of the "Part A" setup on the floor of the House led Mills to respond on April 7th, claiming that the new system was fiscally prudent and sound, and that Social Security remained sacrosanct: "There is not one single, solitary thing in this bill which would permit or allow for $1 of the money which is set aside to go into the old-age and survivors disability insurance trust funds [i.e., Social Security] to ever get into the hospital insurance trust fund" (Zelizer 2000, 249). Mills's reputation, along with the large Democratic majority, ensured the sanctity of the committee's proposal, now being called the Mills bill. His speech received a bipartisan standing ovation upon his presentation. The House passed the Mills bill on April 8th, 313–115. Naturally the Senate bill was a little different, requiring the usual conference committee sessions, in which Mills was the leading participant, making various compromises (especially in the realm of cost-containment efforts), resisting others (keeping the AMA more agreeable by fighting to exclude various non-M.D.s from the hospital insurance program). The Conference Committee completed its work on July 20th, and Medicare became law.

Wilbur Mills would have to be given tremendous credit for this achievement, one of the Great Society's greatest. The monetary benefits associated with Medicare and Medicaid went a long way toward keeping many of the elderly out of poverty, and so in this sense Mills made a strong contribution to the War on Poverty waged involving seniors. But Mills had far less enthusiasm for much that the Great Society was trying to do about poverty involving those not yet at retirement age. Much of Mills's professional activity as a congressman had dealt with taxation questions—social security was not his only bailiwick. But when it came to welfare per se, especially programs that amounted to what he considered to be more or less handouts, he had no personal investment, in fact no great interest.

One thing Mills *did* have an interest in was the traditional orthodoxy of the desirability of a "balanced budget" for federal expenditures, and, as a fiscal conservative, the fear of ever-growing demands on the taxpayers' money. The coming of the war in Vietnam, the criticisms of the antipoverty efforts, and the increase in the rate of inflation that marked the second half of the 1960s all allowed Mills, having just been the point man in what would have to be acknowledged as the creation of a huge new entitlement, to step in as defender of financial orthodoxy by insisting—that is the word for it—on a holding of the line in the War on Poverty. Presidential assistant Joseph Califano recalled Mills expressing his attitude in a private meeting with Lyndon Johnson late in 1967: "Mr. President, across town from my mother in Arkansas a Negro woman has a baby every year. Every time I go home, my mother complains. That Negro woman's now got eleven children. My proposal [a freeze on welfare payments] will stop this. Let the states pay for more than a small number of children if they want to" (Califano 1991, 245–46). Clearly, Mills had little interest in further payments for more children, should they arrive.

This comment was made in the wake of Mills's activities during the fall regarding "welfare abuse." In the context of Social Security amendments involving the usual federal funding for Aid to Families with Dependent Children of that year, the Ways and Means Committee had gone on record expressing concern about two things: increased costs to taxpayers, and the dependency culture behind these galloping costs. The two "solutions" included in the bill were to freeze federal contributions, on which states significantly depended to pay for the money on which the beneficiaries lived, and to institute a work requirement for "appropriate" beneficiaries (Davies 1996, 180). Mills was out front in the ensuing debate as the bill moved to the Senate side, where liberals severely, vehemently criticized it. By the end of the year, however, a modified version of it had passed Congress. It should be noted that the same bill included very large increases for the recipients of "regular" Social Security checks.

When Johnson proposed on August 3rd an income tax surcharge that was supposed to help pay for the war, and thus allow continued spending on his beloved Great Society programs (as a political necessity, a couple of billion dollars' worth of cuts in proposed spending accompanied the proposal), Mills saw an opportunity to make a strong statement that would wind up renewing congressional control over federal spending in general. Medicaid, it turned out, was way, way above Mills's hopeful, narrow projections, upsetting enough to him that he eventually came to refer to the program as the most expensive mistake of his career. Welfare caseloads shot up in the late 1960s, and so did the spending required of them, increases that were not directly budgeted but that had to be paid for. Mills began speaking out publicly on the dangers of out-of-control federal spending, and as a powerful leader of Congress (his Ways and Means Committee had no direct control over general revenue spending—that was the Appropriations Committee's business—but it did control the proposed surcharge tax), he was of course centrally located in the power structure to do something about it. Fiscal year 1968's deficit as a percentage of GDP was a postwar record, and, following the orthodoxy of the day, Mills associated this with the uptick in inflation.

By late 1967, it was public knowledge that the White House and Chairman Mills were at loggerheads. Mills would not move the tax bill without a promise for expenditure control that was anathema to the Great Society camp. Mills gave public interviews claiming that members of Congress reported their constituents to be uneasy about the huge increases in domestic federal spending and activity, and the figure of $5–6 billion in reductions or proposed expenditures was kicked around. In October, Mills had his committee put off any action on the surcharge. Great Society skeptics were not only greater in number after the swing of the midterm 1966 elections, but they were also emboldened. In explaining the committee action, Mills opined that what was indicated was "the anxiety which many Members of the Congress feel—fortified by the uneasiness they found in their constituencies over the recent Labor Day recess—about the recent sharp rise in federal outlays and the proliferation of federal government activity" (Zelizer 2000, 265).

Mills painted a picture of a federal budget rapidly getting out of control. Not only were cries for new spending, under the Great Society mentality, ever-growing, but there was also the problem of the "built-in" increases implicit in previously agreed-to laws, including such things as cost overruns, pay increases for government employees, and the open-ended entitlements of things like Medicare. The *rate* of increases in government spending, reflecting a Great Society mentality, threatened those with more traditionalist views of things, like Mills. This was thought to "heat up" the economy, encouraging inflation; thus a reduction in government expenditure would "cool down" the macroeconomy. There was no immediately cooling down slated for Vietnam, Mills viewed Social Security as sacrosanct, and many government operations really could not be cut; this left discretionary government spending programs—like the Great Society.

By November 1967, the administration had come to accept the general picture that there would have to be more reductions if a surcharge was to make it through Congress; it suggested $4 billion worth, twice as high as its "opening bid." In November, Mills's committee resumed hearings on the proposed surcharge, with the chairman challenging the economic analysis on which the administration based its proposal. It all depended on the model one preferred, but barely concealed were the broader preferences regarding the Great Society. By the end of the month, the hearings were over, but the committee, under Mills's guidance, postponed any action until after the Christmas holiday. He was glad to see that the Johnson administration had upped the ante when it came to expenditure reduction, but he wanted a few billion more.

The debate continued in 1968, the crucial difference being whether to cut $4 billion out of a federal budget of $184 billion, or $6 billion, as preferred by Wilbur Mills. The administration fought so hard because of the threat it perceived to the War on Poverty, which, it believed, would be gutted under the Mills conceptualization. Mills continually claimed there were not enough votes to pass the surcharge without the significant expenditure reduction, but in fact by far the most significant lack of vote was his own. Mills perhaps fought even harder upon discovering that the Appropriations Committee appeared to share neither Mills's sense of where Congress was nor his economic assumptions; in short, they were not poised to go for the far bigger spending cuts, and hardly seemed worried at all at the trends in federal spending seen since the dawn of the Great Society era. Mills proclaimed himself disgusted by this, and despite great political pressure and much maneuvering, he would not retreat.

Johnson, having stunned the political world on March 31st by announcing he would not be a candidate for reelection, hoped to change the political dynamic on Capitol Hill as well. But Mills's concerns involved something far bigger than short-run politics. His fiscal conservatism was quite real and deep-seated. After the month of April failed to change the situation, Johnson decided to move in Mills's direction. A search was ordered for the least harmful way to come up with a couple of billion dollars more in spending cuts. Warned that his political power on the Hill could be destroyed by this fight, Johnson at the same time tried to keep up the public pressure on Mills—but the pressure left the Arkansas "lifer" in Congress unmoved. Before the first week of May was out, Mills had substantially won. The surcharge was accompanied by most of the spending reductions and controls on future spending that Mills had insisted upon, as seen in the "Revenue and Expenditure Control Act of 1968," and the federal budget actually wound up balanced—for the last time in a generation, as things turned out.

Mills continued to furbish his image as the guardian of the public's money, delivering speeches, granting interviews, and writing on the topic. This became his new crusade in the post–Great Society years and even led him on a brief attempt to gain the Democratic nomination for president in 1972. He presented himself as the expert legislator, the man most responsible for the extension of Social Security, not only in terms of retirement benefits but also in its coverage of the disabled and the fatherless—in short, he claimed much of the modern welfare state for his own. He also ran as a man who would hold the line on taxes, again citing his record. His failed candidacy resembled Johnson's in 1960, in that his Washington "insider" expertise and skills proved impossible to translate to the mass of voters outside the Beltway. His long career of service, during which he had privately dealt with alcoholism, ended in tragic farce in 1974 when he became involved in a Washington scandal involving an "adult" entertainer. He lost his Ways and Means chairmanship in the aftermath, declined to stand for reelection in 1976, worked as a tax consultant, and died in Arkansas on May 2, 1992.

EVERETT DIRKSEN
(1896–1969)

Longtime Illinois U.S. Senator Everett Dirksen personified the midwestern, heartland tradition of the Republican party in its post–New Deal, congressional minority party phase. Heir to the principled conservatism that instinctively disliked the welfare statism whose second coming the Great Society represented, Dirksen found himself the leader of an opposition party that struggled to find a common voice in the wake of the 1964 Goldwater debacle. A prominent member of the senatorial "club" who deeply respected its traditions, personally popular across the ideological and partisan divide, and a sui generis character of immense appeal, Dirksen had a well-established and warm relationship with President Lyndon Johnson that proved especially significant at the most critical point of the civil rights movement's hour of destiny, the 1964 debate over the Civil Rights Act. The historically aware Dirksen, who hailed from the Land of Lincoln, aligned himself and the majority of his party, whose very birth in the 1850s had been connected with the United States' greatest freedom struggle, with what he famously called an idea whose time had come.

Everett Dirksen, born to German immigrant parents on January 4, 1896, in Pekin, Illinois, can fairly be said to have been born into a Republican party family. He was given the middle name "McKinley," after William McKinley, then governor of Ohio and soon to be elected president in the famous Battle of the Standards (the gold standard versus a combined, bimetallic gold/silver standard) later that year; his twin brother was named Thomas Reed Dirksen, after the Republican Speaker of the House of Representatives, and he had an older brother named Benjamin Harrison Dirksen, named for another midwestern, late-nineteenth-century president from the Grand Old Party. These names reflect the reflexive Republican identity of the area forged by the Civil War experience and its long-lasting fallout; in the late 1950s Dirksen commented, "I am Republican, period—no tags, no labels, no qualitative adjectives" (Hulsey 2000, 114). Indeed, Dirksen may have been the last American politician actually to refer to President McKinley, invoking his name in public discussion over the Cuban missile crisis. Raised in modest, respectable circumstances, Dirksen was the only one of the five Dirksen brothers who showed the intellectual bent to finish high school (still unusual in those days), where he developed an interest in dramatics and a skill in forensics that were to remain with him and make him nationally famous. Graduating in 1913 as class salutatorian, he continued on to college for three years at the University of Minnesota, where his need to earn money forced him to work nights, cutting into his study time; the result was mediocre grades in a law-oriented curriculum. With the entry of the United States into World War I in 1917, Dirksen left college (he was never to earn a degree) to join the Army, serving in France and seeing various parts of Europe.

A popular World War I song asked the question, "how could you keep the servicemen down on the farm after they'd seen Paris?" But this did not apply to Dirksen, who returned in Pekin in 1919 and tried various jobs in the local town economy while working in town theater productions (including as an actor) and sometimes filling in as preacher at church. His principal civic activity came via his membership in a new organization formed by veterans of World War I, the American Legion, which he joined in 1922. In 1926 he became the commander of a legion "district" whose boundaries were the same as the sixteenth congressional district (whose representative in the 1840s had been Abraham Lincoln), and Dirksen began regularly speaking to various Legion groups and thus becoming more widely known. 1927 was a landmark year in Dirksen's life: he married Louella Carver, he and his brothers began a successful bakery, and he was elected to his first office as a town councilman in Pekin.

Deeply involved in the community and possessing a solid work ethic and a growing ambition, Dirksen naturally responded to suggestions that he consider higher office. He tried for the congressional seat in 1930 against an entrenched Republican incumbent, and his narrow loss in the party primary established him as a man to watch and whetted his appetite for the next round. In 1932, the Great Depression was hitting bottom and the desire to change helped shift the margin in Dirksen's rematch with the much older congressman as he won the Republican nomination, virtually tantamount to election, as an agent of positive change. Dirksen, who had never been to Washington, thus joined the Congress that would gain fame for its "Hundred Days" of New Deal legislation. Although a member of a hugely outnumbered minority (the House had 318 Democrats and 117 Republicans), Dirksen conceded the obvious that the nation faced an unprecedented peacetime emergency and that new thinking regarding the role and potential of the national government was clearly called for. Like most congressional Republicans at this point, he supported the majority of the early New Deal measures designed to promote economic recovery and provide relief. He added to his lawmaker credentials in 1936 when, after private study, he gained admission to the Illinois bar. As time went on, however, Dirksen exhibited more traditional conservative suspicion of the trend toward big government, opposing the creation of the Tennessee Valley Authority and fearing the drift toward U.S. involvement in the new European war. As his congressional career lengthened, and especially as a partisan Republican, Dirksen naturally and increasingly employed the rhetoric of the fear of centralized presidential power. Inevitably, he became embroiled in the internal bickering of the Republican party, then divided into regional blocs; as a Midwesterner, Dirksen found it easy to feel alienated from the east coast Republican Establishment; in 1944, he briefly promoted himself as a candidate for the party's presidential nomination, condemning the New Deal, the "doctrine of collectivism," and the "march toward centralization" that was being accelerated by the nation's involvement in World War II (Hulsey 2000, 20).

However, despite such campaign oratory, he was by no means an unreconstructed states'-rights believer, accepting such direct postwar federal programs as housing for veterans and also more ideological, theoretical signs of a continued federal economic role as the 1946 Employment Act. Nor did he oppose such Truman administration steps into the dawning Cold War as the Marshall Plan, fearing communism's potential spread abroad more than the trend toward a Leviathan state at home. Especially by the standards of midwestern Republicanism, whose best personification was "Mr. Republican" himself, Senator Robert Taft, son of President William Howard Taft and a figure of one of the United States' greatest state-level political dynasties (Ohio's governor in 2004 was Bob Taft), a strong isolationist, Dirksen was seen as one of the moderate conservatives. Serious trouble with an eye forced him to decide against standing for another term in the 1948 election, and he returned to Pekin for what he hoped would be a short interlude in his officeholding career.

That proved to be the case. Dirksen, whose vision quickly improved, spent much of 1949 making speeches and pondering a campaign for the senate seat held by a longtime friend and fellow Legionnaire, Scott Lucas, now majority leader of the Democrats in the U.S. Senate. He announced his candidacy in September 1949 and had the advantage of holding few responsibilities, allowing him to travel around and about the state, often with his wife Louella, becoming better and better known as he rallied Illinoisans against the "creeping socialism" of President Truman's so-called Fair Deal, an attempt further to extend federal involvement in the nation's economy and society in general in the tradition of the New Deal. Dirksen eventually delivered well over 1,000 speeches during the fourteen months he devoted to his Senate campaign and received outside help from other Republicans including freshman U.S. Senator Joseph McCarthy from Wisconsin. 1950 was a good Republican year, in contrast to 1948, and nothing more was heard of the Fair Deal. Rolling up large majorities outside of the Democratic machine in the city of Chicago,

Dirksen won by the wide margin of 300,000 statewide and interpreted his election as a repudiation of the drift toward big government, by now a familiar theme in his political repertoire that would never go away.

Two questions—alleged communist infiltration of American society, and who ought to get the party presidential nomination in 1952—divided Republicans in the early 1950s, and Dirksen sided completely with the Midwesterners against the "eastern Establishment" types. He favored Ohio Senator Taft over General Dwight Eisenhower in 1952, famously crying, during the convention debate, to the eastern delegates, "We followed you before and you took us down the path to defeat!"(Hulsey 2000, 45). A Republican who worried about whether or not Eisenhower was truly committed to his own heartland view of the world, on matters both domestic and foreign, Dirksen was also a strong and consistent supporter of Senator McCarthy right through the Wisconsinite's end in December 1954, when he was censured by the Senate (Dirksen voted against the motion). The earlier picture of Dirksen as a sort of moderate midwestern member of Congress was thus thoroughly overturned by the mid-1950s. However, at the same time he had not destroyed any bridges within the narrower world of congressional Republicans, serving and working hard in the early 1950s as chairman of the Republican Senatorial Campaign Committee. It took the demise of McCarthy to make Dirksen's relationship with the Eisenhower administration a consistently sound one. The president had to seek out allies in the Senate since he had a terrible relationship with the Republican leader, California's William Knowland, and Dirksen was at least sometimes susceptible to Eisenhower's efforts. Both won second terms in 1956.

In early 1957, Dirksen was elected the party whip (second in command) of the Senate Republicans, and since the party leader announced that he would not seek another senate term in 1958, Dirksen was immediately the heir apparent. In this position, Dirksen became a highly informed inside member of the Senate club. His new position as an official Republican leader in the Senate meant that his tendencies toward Eisenhower's more moderate, so-called modern Republicanism were accentuated. Along these lines, Dirksen played a role in developing debate over civil rights legislation. In a very mild, 1950s fashion, Dirksen had supported some steps, calling for a federal civil rights commission in 1953 and arguing for the acceptance of the 1954 U.S. Supreme Court school integration decision. By 1957, Dirksen was the ranking minority member on the Senate Judiciary Committee, controlled by Democrats, and he worked in tandem with Eisenhower's attorney general, Herbert Brownell, to get a bill focusing on voting rights, unambiguously a federal question under the Fifteenth Amendment, out of committee and into the statute books. The Senate's Democratic leader, Lyndon Johnson of Texas, proposed the potentially crippling "jury trial" amendment, requiring such a device if a voting official (naturally, a white) were charged with violating the voting rights of a citizen (naturally, a black), which Dirksen strongly and publicly opposed—so much so that he forfeited what leverage he might have had when it came to working out its final form. In the end the jury trial amendment was included in the law, and despite their suspicions and disappointment, most civil rights proponents accepted the bill as at least a first step in the direction of the meaningful enforcement of voting rights.

Held in a recessionary environment, the 1958 midterm congressional elections swung strongly against the Republicans, reducing their numbers to mid-1930s proportions and setting off another round of self-questioning on the part of the nation's minority party. Knowland, the previous Senate Republican leader, had retired from Washington as promised, and so the leadership position in fact opened up. Liberal Republican senators came up with Kentucky's John Sherman Cooper, educated in wealthy eastern schools and a first-termer, as their candidate, while a few conservative Republicans were unhappy with what they saw as Dirksen's excessive accommodation with Eisenhower Republicanism. One of Dirksen's greatest strengths was his image as someone who knew the Senate inside out, important given the man on the other side of the aisle, Democratic leader Lyndon Johnson, a genius at legislative procedure and protocol. Everett Dirksen was elected leader of the Republican minority in the Senate on January 7, 1959, by a vote of 20 to 14. He would retain this position until his death in 1969.

Key to the role he would play is the term "minority." In a Senate career that spanned nearly two decades, Everett Dirksen was for only two years (1953–54) ever a member of the majority. For the entire decade in which he was Republican leader, he led a minority whose "minority status" and oppositional position in the Washington political game seemed more striking and near-permanent than ever. Furthermore, Dirksen's troops were divided within themselves ideologically to a far greater degree than was to be the case in the 1980s and 1990s, during which years Senate Republicans would again hold the majority more often than not. Dirksen's Republican Senate, at the time he took office as party leader and continuing throughout his tenure, contained a significant number of identifiable liberals along with the larger number of conservatives. It contained no members from the Deep South whatsoever, and even at the point of his departure in the first year of the Nixon administration, southern membership, though growing in number, was small. This lineup, so different from the Republican majorities seen in the U.S. Senate in the last two decades of the twentieth century, had a significant effect on the role the Republicans played in the crucial votes over the Civil Rights Act of 1964, at which point Dirksen gained his greatest fame and strongest external adulation.

When Everett Dirksen assumed his post as Republican leader, the Democrats in the Senate had been following the formidable Lyndon Johnson of Texas, a senator first elected in 1948, as their majority leader since 1955. In the conduct of Senate business, especially given the existence of a Republican president, Dirksen and Johnson found themselves together on a daily basis, often for considerable blocks of time. They got to know each other very well and had little trouble cooperating in an atmosphere of trust and mutual respect. Johnson for his part was far removed from his later Great Society, big-government liberal positions, while Dirksen, with the McCarthy era receding into the history books and by virtue of his new responsibilities as party leader, was back in his more moderate conservative mode. At the conclusion of the 1959 session, Dirksen's first as party leader, he wrote an appreciative note to his colleague across the party divide: "We have fought—gently, I hope—but always with understanding. We have asserted our various party causes, but always in good grace. We have shared a high mutual pride in the Senate." Johnson replied in a fashion he knew Dirksen would like, but also with obvious sincerity and admiration: "Of the leader with whom I have served, there have been none who can wield the partisan stiletto with quite the gusto and the zest that you do. But even though the stiletto cuts deep, it never stings" (Hulsey 2000, 119–20). The relationship had jelled, and Johnson, like the departing President Eisenhower, regarded Dirksen as a dependable, responsible party leader. They cooperated in getting through the Senate another civil rights bill in 1960, also narrow in scope as had been the 1957 act, but still seen by most as at least a step in the right direction. Dirksen also continued to support some social spending, such as increases in Society Security payments.

John F. Kennedy, elected by a tiny margin in 1960, had a Congress to deal with whose nominal Democratic majorities were large—in the Senate, the lineup the day after the 1960 election stood at sixty-five Democrats to only thirty-five Republicans. When it came to civil rights, however, the still-powerful remnants of the old "Solid South" political system held great sway in the Senate. Not one Republican represented a state of the old Confederacy, though John Tower's election as Texas senator (replacing Lyndon Johnson, who had been allowed under Texas law to stand for reelection even while running for vice president under Kennedy) in 1961 changed that. The seniority system in Congress was strong and increased the influence of the southern Democrats even more, especially in the Senate, where unlimited "debate," a delaying tactic known as filibustering, was a powerful weapon. These realities, along with the fact that Kennedy's electoral college coalition had included a number of Deep South states, made the cautious approach of the administration toward civil rights a near lock. While Dirksen got along fine with Kennedy, having gotten to know him during their years of mutual service in the Senate, he brooked no enthusiasm for any "New Frontiers" predicated upon increased federal spending and control, of which he remarked in 1961, "It may be called the New Frontier, but the Kennedy program is the old New Deal taken out of an old warming oven. It was hot stuff twenty-five years ago but time has passed it by" (Hulsey 2000, 154). Similarly, it might also be added that Dirksen's rhetoric had the ring of the familiar, and he continued to indulge in it with regularity.

Dirksen's political stature grew with the institutionalization of his weekly press conference, along with the House Republican leader, Charles Halleck of Indiana, designed to provide a Republican voice in a Democratic-dominated government. His theatricality made him "newsworthy" to many in the Washington press corps, and he enjoyed the attention that grew with the significant television coverage afforded his appearances. Critics were many, some finding his "performances" cornball, and others, especially more liberal Republicans, fearing a too-conservative image for their party; but Dirksen was becoming better known than ever, and nobody disliked him personally—quite the contrary. He enjoyed an incredibly favorable press, especially from the dozens of regulars in the Washington press corps who attended his weekly "shows" with House Republican leader Halleck and who found him an engaging and entertaining "character."

Beginning in 1963, most especially with the crisis that developed in Birmingham, the Kennedy administration was both forced and also motivated by events to shift its civil rights stance. Criticism of the controversial decision by the civil rights partisans there to use children in their street demonstrations was quickly overshadowed by the decision of public officials to employ fire hoses and police dogs that, as the activists hoped, made for powerful television. There was no longer any place to hide for anyone; the moment to decide had come. Within the Kennedy administration, Vice President Lyndon Johnson advised a reaching out to congressional Republicans, especially in the Senate that, with its filibuster possibility, would be by far the tougher nut to crack of the two chambers on Capitol Hill. Kennedy chose to invite both Democratic and Republican leaders to the White House before delivering his landmark, televised address of June 11, 1963, stressing the moral question at stake and declaring that civil rights legislative proposals would soon follow. Dirksen was included in meetings that followed in which the details of such proposals began to be threshed out. With the passing of the Birmingham crisis, however, momentum stalled, and Washington's attention soon shifted to the proposed nuclear test ban treaty. Dirksen's support for the treaty gained him more favorable press from the media and Washington establishments.

Suddenly, on November 22, 1963, Lyndon Johnson was thrust into the presidency. Once the immediate shock had passed, Johnson rapidly began to assess his priorities and how to achieve them, and civil rights was at the top of the list. The acknowledged master of the U.S. Senate during his years in the late 1950s as its majority leader, Johnson knew more about it and about most of its members than anyone living. And he certainly knew a great deal about Everett Dirksen. Like the Illinoisian, Johnson was conscious of the gap between himself and a still powerful, sometimes parochial "eastern Establishment." Johnson and Dirksen had worked together well in the waning days of the Eisenhower years, and they picked up where they had left off almost immediately. The difference, of course, was that Johnson was now president and could—and did—use the unparalleled authority of that office to press for what he wanted, which was a great deal indeed. Johnson from the start of his presidency constantly kept after Dirksen, including him in a way that he knew would be flattering to the Republican Senate leader. Especially at the height of the Cold War, "bipartisanship" was often held to be a political virtue, and Dirksen had a proven track record of cooperation and reasonableness covering many, if not all, issues and occasions. While he had strong political prejudices and instincts, he could not fairly be counted among those who were true ideologues. It was well known that he was already a part of the growing consensus that the time for some substantial federal action in the area of civil rights had arrived. And finally, and not insignificantly, Dirksen was known to enjoy the dramatic, some might say melodramatic—in fact, he could be quite a ham, which could not be doubted by anyone familiar with his weekly "show" for the Washington press corps.

Johnson was determined to make 1964 the year for hardcore federal civil rights legislation. The House of Representatives proved to be no problem at all, passing a strong bill early in the year that included such controversial sections as the prohibition of discrimination in most public accommodations and in employment and promotion policies in private business. Other sections dealing with such matters as voting and the continued existence of the Civil Rights Commission were noncontroversial as far as Dirksen was concerned, but he could not say the same for the idea of creating a new federal agency, the Equal Employment Opportunity Commission (EEOC), that would have the power both to investigate claims of discrimination and also to file suit on behalf of alleged victims of such discrimination. His fears of centralized power, more instinctive than seriously philosophical, were nonetheless quite real, and he publicly expressed his reservations. However, Dirksen refused to commit, and even in private Washington insiders expressed uncertainly as to where he could come out.

Dirksen seemed to enjoy being the center of attention as the drama played out in the spring and summer of 1964. With many of the southern Democrats known to be committed to filibustering the bill to death, and the necessity for a two-thirds majority vote to invoke cloture, stop the "debate," and allow a straight-up vote on the bill (which was sure then to pass; by Senate tradition, "unlimited" debate was the norm; cloture meant cutting off the extended stalling known as "filibustering" and required a hard-to-obtain two-thirds margin). The votes of the Republican members were deemed critical, and Dirksen would have the greatest impact on swaying many of these votes. Johnson advised his Democratic Senate whip, Minnesota's Hubert Humphrey, to keep after Dirksen: "Ev is a proud man. So don't pull any damned protocol. *You* go see *him*. And don't forget that Dirksen loves to bend at the elbow. I want you to drink with him till he agrees to vote for cloture and deliver me two Republicans from the mountain states" (Hulsey 2000, 189). Humphrey, whose own political career had taken off in 1948 when, as a youthful mayor of Minneapolis, he had gained national attention at Philadelphia's Convention Hall where he successfully orated on behalf of a civil rights plank for the Democratic platform, was a committed believer in the cause and hence more than willing to give it his all when it came to keeping after the Republican Senate leader. Progress was slow, not only because of Dirksen's own concerns about the increased federal power inherent in the bill, but also because he was far from certain that he could in fact deliver the votes—yet. Outside of the halls of Congress the civil rights struggle continued to enjoy center stage, and the generalized yet real pressure on public officials to enact meaningful legislation was impossible to miss.

In April, Dirksen introduced two proposed amendments to the bill reflecting his down-home dislike of federal power. The first would limit the power of the EEOC to initiate suits, and the second would give the states preeminence over the federal government in employment discrimination cases. Dirksen's "states'-rights" beliefs were untainted by white supremacy attitudes, but of course to civil rights activists of the moment, academic-sounding discourses about federal versus state power seemed little short of grotesque. Lobbying intensified, which intensified the pressure on uncommitted senators. This may even have been Dirksen's intention, at least at some level, though he may also have regarded the amendments as trial balloons floated up in order to see where they went.

In a meeting with Hubert Humphrey on April 21, 1964, Dirksen for the first time committed himself to coming up with the necessary number of Republican votes so as to cut off Senate debate, should cloture prove necessary. He still did not know, however, if he could in fact deliver, but he pledged himself to trying as hard as he could. The possibilities of various legislative and parliamentary machinations, techniques, and gimmicks continued to swirl within and outside of Washington at an especially high rate, for the civil rights issue was one that by this point a great many people passionately cared about. There had also developed a powerful sense that a truly historic moment might be at hand. On April 29, Johnson, increasingly worried and becoming more and more impatient, pushed Dirksen as hard as he could. Dirksen remained convinced that the bill could only pass if the concerns addressed in his proposed amendments were somehow dealt with. In May, meetings took place (symbolically, in Dirksen's Senate office), as Humphrey, at Johnson's direction, braved loud criticism from many liberals and civil rights activists from Martin Luther King, Jr., on down who feared the watering-down effects of the amendments. On the other side of the political divide, some conservatives publicly complained about Dirksen's involvement with the administration's bill; in the background, the growing campaign momentum of Arizona Republican U.S. Senator Barry Goldwater, an opponent of the bill, did not make Dirksen's balancing act any easier. Meanwhile the Senate filibuster successfully continued, despite the large Democratic majority. With the Democratic senators hopelessly divided on the civil rights question, and their own southern minority blocking their own administration's top legislative priority, the breaking of the deadlock, if it were to be broken at all, demonstrably depended on what the Republican senators, guided by their leader, did. As a decided minority since 1958, this was a rare moment for the Senate GOP. Dirksen made the most of it in the end.

On May 13, Dirksen, whose Senate office hosted top Johnson administration officials including Humphrey, Senate Majority Leader Mike Mansfield of Montana, and Attorney General Robert F. Kennedy, moved closer to making the 1964 civil rights bill a reality. A week and a half of back and forth climaxed in the working out of an agreed-upon package. One of Dirksen's amendments had proposed enjoining the new EEOC bureaucracy from filing suits on its own. Dirksen argued that this would by no means preclude the Department of Justice from doing so upon the commission's recommendations; the administration determined it could live with that. When it came to the question of the prioritizing of state over federal "fair employment" activities, including enforcement, it was Dirksen's turn to give way to compelling arguments that many of the southern state governments gave every indication of being eager to exploit any device available to sabotage the entire "fair employment" effort, an effort in which they did not believe. Dirksen agreed to give the state fair employment a maximum of sixty days in which to act, after which time an appeal might be made to the national commission. The bar was also raised when it came to the standard required for the filing of a federal antidiscrimination suit to a "pattern and practice" of discrimination. At the conclusion of the pivotal May 13 session, everybody involved was smiling, and Dirksen announced to the press that a good agreement existed.

On May 19, Republican senators caucused to look over print copies of the new agreement produced by their leader in tandem with administration officials. He was hardly surprised to receive some harsh criticisms from the more ideologically driven foes of federal power, such as Iowa's Bourke Hickenlooper. Shortly after the caucus broke up, Dirksen staged a media event in his office that would prove to be the single most dramatic moment of his political career. Exerting leadership that would take most Republicans with him, Dirksen told the assembled press corps that he was still sure that the deal was a good one, and then, speaking slowly, uttered the words for which he would be most remembered: "No army is stronger than an idea whose time has come." When it came to civil rights, he declaimed, "Today the challenge is here! It is inescapable. It is time to deal with it! No one on that floor is going to stop this. It is going to happen" (Hulsey 2000, 196). As President Kennedy had framed the question, so now did Dirksen: civil rights now had to be understood as a fundamentally *moral* issue.

And so it did, though not without substantial lobbying on the part of the skilled and experienced Dirksen. The Dirksen substitute bill, with the support of Vice President Humphrey, was introduced to the Senate on May 26.

Responding to critics, the historically minded Dirksen defined the present question as possessing "a deep moral aspect," which meant that there was "a duty on the part of Republicans to do their full share if they hope to be worthy of the Republican tradition . . . and Abraham Lincoln" (Hulsey 2000, 199). The final bit of political wrangling involved Dirksen agreeing to a vote on three rather technical amendments by Senator Hickenlooper in exchange for the Iowan's promise that, after a vote on his proposals (one of which was adopted) to take place by June 9, the cloture vote would proceed, and he (and his allies) would vote for it.

Hickenlooper kept his word. On June 10, the vote for cloture was taken, the national news media providing live coverage from Capitol Hill, though not from inside the Chamber, which was not then permitted. In recognition of Dirksen's role, Majority Leader Mansfield set it up so that the minority leader got the last speech of the debate before the vote was taken. Invoking his earlier phrase, Dirksen stated, "The time has come for equality of opportunity . . . in government, in education, and in employment. It will not be stayed or denied. It is here. . . . There is no substitute for a basic and righteous idea" (Hulsey 2000, 201). The vote to conclude debate was 71–29; twenty-seven of the thirty-three Republican senators voted yes, a higher percentage than among the Democrats.

Everett Dirksen had long been popular with the press corps, as he was with nearly everyone who knew him; in the wake of his role in the Civil Rights Act, his already-good press image soared to new heights. Dirksen also received great praise from such people as Martin Luther King, Jr., Roy Wilkins, and, of course Lyndon Johnson, who said to him: "You are the hero of the hour now. They have forgotten that anyone else is around. Every time I pick up a paper it is 'Dirksen' in the magazines. The NAACP is flying Dirksen banners and picketing the White House tomorrow" (Hulsey 2000, 202). Some conservatives, notably "the" Republican of 1964, Barry Goldwater, disagreed with Dirksen's position on the question—Goldwater believed the public accommodations and employment sections of the Civil Rights Act to be unconstitutional—but disagreement on this important issue did not preclude Dirksen's endorsing Goldwater for president. Dirksen, in fact, had deliberately delayed the vote on cloture until after the pivotal California Republican primary, in which Goldwater had defeated New York Governor Nelson Rockefeller, so as not to embarrass GOP senators who supported Goldwater for president but nevertheless, unlike the Arizona senator, wanted to vote for cloture (199).

Some liberal commentators expressed disappointment with Dirksen's backing of Goldwater, but it was hardly surprising to those who knew and understood him and the political culture he represented. Much of Goldwater's antistatist rhetoric fit Dirksen very comfortably indeed, and it was obvious enough that, after California, Goldwater was going to be the nominee, meaning that party regulars should fall in line behind him. Dirksen and

Goldwater were friendly and went way back; the Illinoisan had been one of those encouraging Goldwater to seek a Senate seat back in 1951. Neither was associated with the more liberal, eastern brand of Republicanism. In 1952, Dirksen had backed Ohio Senator Robert Taft, paladin of the midwestern conservative Republican tradition, against "eastern Establishment" favorite Eisenhower. Dirksen agreed to give the nominating speech for the Arizona senator at the 1964 convention, and in that speech was even willing to describe the libertarian Goldwater's vote against the Civil Rights Act of 1964 as an example of "moral courage not excelled anywhere in any parliamentary body of which I have any knowledge" (Edwards 1995, 264).

The 1964 landslide put into place the largest Democratic congressional majorities since the 1930s, making possible a tremendous expansion of governmental programs and spending. But Johnson, fully anticipating that someday the political winds would turn, maintained his excellent relationship with Dirksen, though in the short run it could not be said that the Republican party had much influence on Capitol Hill or in the federal government. (Johnson soon valued Dirksen's unwavering support over Vietnam especially.) But again in 1965, civil rights took center stage with the enactment of the all-important Voting Rights Act, which fulfilled its designers' hopes by making, once and for all, the Fifteenth Amendment's guarantee of the right to vote without regard to race a reality as opposed to a goal. Again Johnson instructed his aides to cultivate Dirksen, as the president anticipated another filibuster. Johnson was happy when Dirksen agreed to cosponsor the bill with Majority Leader Mike Manfield. Cloture was voted on May 25, 1965, with twenty-three of the thirty-two Republicans joining the majority of seventy. When it came to much of the rest of the Great Society spending proposals, including landmarks such as federal aid to elementary and secondary education, federally subsidized college scholarships, training schemes, and Medicare, as well as more conventional expenditures, Dirksen voted with the large majorities in support of such new departures. The Republican senators did not offer *collective* resistance to any of these Great Society notions in the Eighty-Ninth Congress, whose time, in the estimation of Dirksen, who could read the election returns, had, like civil rights, also come, though in these cases he played no significant role except the negative one of not attempting to organize any opposition view. Other issues, such as prayer in public schools and court-mandated reapportionment, which were beyond the ken of the Great Society, exercised his attention.

When it came to Johnson's proposal in 1966's State of the Union address to outlaw racial discrimination in housing, however, Dirksen was one of many who argued the bill's unconstitutionality. The notion that a man's home was his castle was not seen by Dirksen and some others as the same thing as either the right to vote or the right to equal treatment in public accommodations. Administration attempts at compromise (making the bill apply only to reasonably large-scale, open-to-the-public housing) were of no avail. Without Dirksen's help, cloture was not invoked; it would take the assassination of Martin Luther King, Jr., in 1968 to move Congress finally to adopt the Fair Housing Act.

The 1966 Republican surge in Congress has often been labeled a "backlash" against the Great Society, and to a degree it certainly was; however, the midterm elections also produced a raft of younger and reasonably liberal Republican senators as well, such as Charles Percy from Dirksen's own Illinois, Mark Hatfield of Oregon, and Edward Brooke of Massachusetts. This was seen in the cloture vote in February 1968 over open housing; Dirksen opposed it, but there was a huge jump in the number of Republican senators voting for cloture—namely, the class of 1966. Dirksen's influence, then, was clearly waning but not yet inconsequential, as the vote had in fact failed. Ever the political realist, Dirksen now shifted in favor and worked to help bring along a few more recalcitrant Republicans, commenting to the press, "One would be a strange creature indeed in this world of mutation if in the face of reality he did not change his mind" (Matusow 1984, 207). But now he was being reactive, and the press attention was going to the younger Republicans. The Senate passed the bill, and the House of Representatives, in the wake of King's assassination, followed suit.

Dirksen's health problems increased as he moved toward the end of his life, diminishing to a degree his influence on Capitol Hill, especially in light of the ambitious group of new Republican senators elected in 1966. Dirksen himself was reelected in 1968, a good year for Republicans in Illinois. As a supporter of the Vietnam War, he maintained good relations with Lyndon Johnson. After renewed medical difficulties he suddenly died on September 9, 1969, and was subsequently honored by bipartisan tributes that all knew to be heartfelt.

RICHARD DALEY
(1902–1976)

One of the biggest stories of the 1960s was the "urban crisis," and this theme formed a central justification for the Great Society efforts of President Lyndon Johnson and the congressional majorities who voted for the many and varied proposals and programs that constituted one of the United States' greatest reform thrusts. Richard J. Daley, then mayor of what was still the United States' "second city," Chicago, was a pillar of the Democratic Party's national coalition, the very epitome of the somewhat quaint-seeming leader of an urban political organization—or, as critics and even some friends termed it, a political "boss." *Boss*, a commercially successful 1971 biography by another Chicago fixture, longtime city columnist Mike Royko, was an almost inevitable title. Daley's importance to Democratic politics within Illinois, then still usually considered a swing state, had been famously, or infamously, made manifest in the extremely narrow electoral success therein of presidential candidate John F. Kennedy in 1960, when for some reason Cook County, Chicago's locale, reported its results at the midnight hour, providing just enough to get Kennedy by and help ensure his election. After many years of service in the city Democratic organization, of which he became chairman two years before his election as the city's chief executive, at age fifty-two Daley was elected mayor in 1955. He died in office in December 1976, shortly after the election of former Georgia Governor Jimmy Carter, a man from a very different branch of the party and the first Democratic president of the twentieth century who found it unnecessary to adopt a programmatic slogan, such as "Great Society," to describe his administration.

As the product and eventual chief of a traditional urban political "machine" of the most venerable sort, Daley was naturally familiar to a considerable degree with the general desire behind the Great Society to help those in need and also to assist those who had not yet made it in American society to become enabled to rise. "Urban renewal" had certainly come to Chicago in the 1950s, and Daley, who presided over Chicago's maturation from a Democratic-dominated to a typical one-party, overwhelmingly Democratic big city of the older northeastern/upper midwestern belt, was certainly in the thick of government-business cooperation in the creation of a "renewed" Chicago core; any version of "hands-off" or limited government was simply an unknown to him and his type. His Chicago, involving business-government partnerships, was America's famed "city that works." And so, additional funding from Washington for the sort of thing that Chicago was, in Daley's fundamental estimation, already doing and had been doing from the start of his mayoralty was welcome enough. What was most assuredly *not* welcome was much, if any, interference on the part of federal authorities with the continued running of a well-tempered, nationally famous political machine, heavy on old-school patronage, which Daley was sure had served the city and its inhabitants very well over the course of his lifetime. And finally, when civil rights, formerly considered by Daley to be an issue involving places like Mississippi and South Carolina, came to Chicago in the mid- and late 1960s, its base the outmigration from the South of hundreds of thousands of blacks, mostly to the South Side, pushed along by the Great Society wave and then cresting into waves of violence, Daley, like so many of the white, "ethnic" Chicagoans he both represented and personified, was angered and appalled.

The Great Society, for a moment, envisioned a radically restructured Chicago. Richard Daley wanted none of that and fought to prevent it from developing. For millions of Americans outside of the Midwest's greatest city, Richard Daley became associated with the police conduct surrounding the tense 1968 Democratic National Convention; often forgotten is that, if opinion polls were to believed, millions of Americans *identified with* Daley's police, with the mayor himself, and with his own memorably expressed outrage, captured on live television in a day when the only three networks that existed all simultaneously carried the convention as it unfolded. A smaller group on the political left at that moment ironically joined sentiments with the traditional conservative Republican heartland base in viewing Richard Daley as the personification of the grotesque, institutionally corrupt, old-style Democratic political machine. Daley, however, survived the doom of the Great Society and the barbs of all his critics, old and new; the demise of his organization would come, but after his death.

Richard Daley was a man of a classic geographical type in American history: the immigrant, ethnic neighborhood, in his case, Bridgeport, south of Chicago's famous Loop, near Comiskey Park, home of the unfashionable (as compared to the much-celebrated Cubs of the North Side) White Sox baseball team, a neighborhood known to all as an "Irish," Roman Catholic one of the 11th Ward, a part of the western "Bungalow Belt." Despite the fact that Daley was a third-generation American, he was "Irish," too, and the fact that his neighborhood was identifiable to all as, with few exceptions, housing an identifiable type was too normal to be remarked upon. Born on May 15, 1902, at home, in a house at 3502 South Lowe in which he would live as a husband and father of seven children and that he would never leave or aspire to leave, Richard Daley was an only child of a respectable, successful sheet-metal worker and unionist and a homemaker who was active both in the women's suffrage movement and in Nativity of Our Lord parish, at whose school Daley was educated. Daley had a good formation; he was a daily communicant throughout his lifetime, and was never accused by anyone of personal corruption. Respectability and order were hallmarks of his upbringing and of his adult life and career. He attended a Roman Catholic "commercial" high school, De La Salle, under the auspices of the Christian Brothers order; in 1955 Daley became the third consecutive mayor from the school, as its neighborhood took the moniker "mother of mayors." At the same time, Daley was an active member of his neighborhood club for young men, the Hamburg Athletic Club, practicing and developing organizational skills and meeting politically active people, especially Alderman Joseph McDonough; in 1924, Daley was elected club president and continued to serve for fifteen years.

Upon finishing high school, Daley, following a norm for the local neighborhood population, went to work at one of the local stockyard's commission houses, doing some physical labor along with substantial office work. He began his political activities as an assistant to Alderman McDonough, who named him a precinct captain in the Cook County Democratic Organization in 1919, already a dominant force in the city, and also took him to work in his city council office, where he met more people and learned by doing how local government and politics operated in Chicago. (Cook County is dominated by the city of Chicago but also includes many suburban areas that became increasingly important as the suburbanization trend accelerated over the course of the twentieth century.) Here, Daley's "regularity" was reinforced, as that was how the system operated. Precinct captain work entailed being out and about in the neighborhood, assisting people with any and all problems imaginable, from employment to city services issues. In 1923, he began studying law part time in the evenings after work at DePaul University, eventually earning a degree in 1933. Three years earlier, Alderman McDonough had been elected Cook County treasurer, and Daley, who accompanied him to his new position as his deputy, wound up doing nearly all of the actual work, thereby steadily adding to his expertise and mastery of the details of city budgeting and the connections among patronage appointments (both governmental and in private industry, said to number at its peak some 40,000 positions; see Cohen and Taylor 2000, 157), "friendly" (contributing) bank officers, and city financial decisions (practices also known to city Republicans, then still a presence but on the brink of steep decline). His work was impressive, such that after McDonough's death in 1934, Daley retained the deputy treasurer position, though he lacked enough political influence to be named to the vacant position himself.

1936 proved to be a pivotal year for Richard Daley. He married Eleanor Guilfoyle, began the practice of law, and, due to a timely (for Daley) death, was elected to the Illinois State Legislature representing his Bridgeport neighborhood. In Springfield he rapidly established an excellent reputation as a competent, informed legislator who utterly stayed out of trouble, was a man to ask about budgetary matters, and supported such causes as shifting the tax burden from sales to income and corporate levies and funding school lunches. At the same time, another timely death opened up the position of deputy Cook County controller, and Daley was a logical appointee. His timing continued to be excellent with yet *another* timely death, which allowed him to win an open state senate seat in 1938. Three years later he was named minority leader of the Illinois State Senate. Nevertheless, his heart, and family, remained in his Chicago neighborhood. The Chicago Democratic organization, facing one of its periodic fights with negative publicity regarding the institutionalized corruption that served as its foundation, tapped the well-regarded, known-to-be-honest Daley as its candidate for Cook County sheriff in 1946, but in that terrible year for Democrats, Daley, along with many other Democrats, even in Chicagoland, lost. He was still assistant controller, though, and in 1947 attained the position of 11th Ward precinct captain. 1948 was a better year for Democrats, with President Truman's surprise victory the head of a Democratic surge, and Governor-elect Adlai Stevenson named Daley director of revenue for Illinois and allowed the father of seven to work out of Chicago in state offices across the street from City Hall.

Daley continued to be preposterously lucky in terms of political deaths, for the position of Cook County Clerk opened up in early 1950 due to the officeholder's sudden death; Daley succeeded in getting himself named to this patronage-laden position. As usual, he diligently worked to bring about concrete improvements in the delivery of the services—such as marriage licenses, which were handled by this office—and was rewarded by the voters with election to the position in his own right that fall, in the wake of another bad year for Illinois Democrats who were being subjected to another wave of investigation for scandal. Daley hoped to become chairman of the Democratic Cook County Central Committee, but had to settle for the post of first vice chairman. Finally, on July 21, 1953, Richard Daley reached the top, at age fifty-one, being elected Democratic leader of Cook County.

Reelected county clerk in 1954, Daley soon maneuvered to gain the official endorsement of the Democratic Organization over the reelection-seeking incumbent, Martin Kennelly, who had gained many enemies with his sometime interest in modest political reforms. Daley's campaign was based entirely on the mobilization of the party organization and the celebration of its many virtues. All the incumbent had was television, then in its infancy as a political force. Daley won the Democratic nomination over Kennelly and a third candidate by a margin of 100,000 out of 750,000 votes cast. A strong Republican candidate made a good run, but Daley was elected Chicago's mayor, receiving about 55 percent of the vote, and was inaugurated to what would turn out to be a lifetime job on April 22, 1955.

By this time Richard Daley knew as much about the government of the City of Chicago as anyone. He intended to use his hard-earned power, and began by arranging for the City Council to be removed from any serious influence in budgeting matters, which proved easy to do given its overwhelming machine Democratic makeup. Civil service reform was reversed by putting a clear opponent of the concept in charge of the city Civil Service Commission. Daley strongly believed in the patronage system, reflective of an old, Jacksonian, democratic ethos that believed one man to be about as good as another for nearly all nonspecialist positions. For Daley, this was a given, requiring no thought at all, despite the system's attendant waste, which Daley the master of budgeting was completely aware of. His main interest, rather, was the revitalization of the city itself; as he presciently told a magazine in an interview shortly after his inauguration, he sought to "bring people back from the suburbs to our city" (Cohen and Taylor 2000, 165). The new mayor sought cooperation with the state government, dominated by Republicans, and traveled downstate to Springfield, the state capital, to seek its assistance in promoting an infrastructure redevelopment of the city in such areas as improved airport facilities, highways, and convention facilities; he also sought higher taxes to finance these and other expanded governmental projects, such as hiring more policemen. City cleanliness was a Daley obsession throughout his decades of service as mayor.

"Urban renewal," which had begun in the late 1940s with the federal Housing Act of 1949, also received Daley's enthusiastic and influential support, bolstering his ties with a downtown business establishment that had not supported his candidacy. The essence of urban renewal was the eradication of "blighted" neighborhoods, to be replaced with institutional anchors such as exposition centers or university campuses designed to draw in at least middle- and, it was hoped, upper-middle-class traffic. Downtown redevelopment united Mayor Daley and the business community. In 1957 he established Chicago's Department of City Planning, which grew tremendously in the next decade while establishing a commendable professional reputation. Another big issue was public housing, and, in a classic New Deal tradition, Chicago's mayor wanted to maximize the federal assistance available, providing union jobs at high-end "prevailing wages" to people who were largely loyal supporters of the Democratic organization. What the mayor was *not* interested in doing was promoting racial integration in said projects. For one thing, Daley knew that his fundamental constituency, the very people from whom he had risen, would not stand for "scattered" public housing projects that they believed would threaten the value of the only substantial investment the vast majority of them would ever achieve, their own "bungalows." Additionally, to Daley, a neighborhood fundamentally defined by its dominant group was a natural thing, not a social problem.

In 1957, Daley was in Washington, lobbying for more federal money; back home, he successfully campaigned for a $113 million bond issue for more local government spending. The mayor announced a large-scale scheme for downtown's redevelopment, formed in close consultation with the business community's organization, the Central Area Committee, in 1958, and successfully supported an urban renewal plan for Hyde Park, the neighborhood surrounding the University of Chicago; he also lined up behind the university's vehement opposition to any public housing projects in its vicinity. He was back in Washington in 1959, claiming that Chicago "had" to have another $100 million during the 1960s for additional slum clearance. Federal largesse was appealing, and Daley knew how to spend it most effectively.

Reelected mayor in 1959 with 71 percent of the vote, Daley's star was rising, and not just at home. He was elected that July as the president of the U.S. Conference of Mayors, solidifying his national reputation as a leader in solving modern urban problems; several national publications gave his efforts in Chicago highly favorable coverage during the years of his second term. (The same year, the new U.S. Civil Rights Commission reported Chicago to be "the most residentially segregated large city in the nation"; see Cohen and Taylor 2000, 347.) He sponsored another $66 million bond for infrastructure improvements, easily approved by the voters, in November, thus continuing his big-spending ways. He worked hard into the early 1960s to bring a full-fledged University of Illinois campus to Chicago, within the city limits rather than in a suburban locale, and with heavy-handed efforts won the day. Of course in 1960 Chicago was at the center of speculation when President Kennedy won Illinois's electoral votes due to an amazingly high turnout and record margin in Chicago, whose precincts just happened to be among the very last to report their results to Springfield. Responding to vehement postelection criticism, Mayor Daley was indignant: "It's a joint effort by Republican conservatives in the north and Dixiecrats in the south to prevent the man elected by the people from becoming President of the United States" (268). (Actually, Kennedy would have still prevailed in the electoral college vote even had he lost Illinois.) In the mayor's rhetorical vocabulary of 1960, "conservatives" and southern Democrats were the enemy of his organization and of good, modern, urban, problem-solving government.

Now that there was again a Democratic administration in Washington, Richard Daley's lust for more federal money for his ever-expanding urban renewal plans was naturally intensified. Seeking more money for public housing, the Chicago mayor testified to a congressional committee that, with enough funding, Chicago's slums could be eliminated in a decade—or less

(Cohen and Taylor 2000, 281). Daley, in complete control of the City Council, continued to raise taxes to finance ever-increasing city spending. But in the spring of 1962, Daley's latest bond proposal referenda—six of them—were, for the first time during his administration, defeated, suggesting that federal revenues would be more important than ever if Daley's vision of a revitalized Chicago were to be realized. The minor tax revolt emboldened Daley's enemies to make more hay out of the never-hard-to-find scandals that were endemic in Chicago's institutionalized corrupt politics, and so his 1963 reelection was considerably more difficult than had been the case in 1959; he won with 56 percent of the vote, sharply down from the 71 percent of four years before—but still plenty enough. Intriguingly, though, Daley had made it through again due to the black vote, receiving over 80 percent of it, while getting only 49 percent of the white vote (301). His opponent's public opposition to "open housing" laws, which would outlaw various forms of discrimination, including racial, in real-estate transactions, was key; Daley had not commented on the contentious question. Civil rights activists had a tough time dealing with the fact that, despite their complaints about Daley's reticence on the open housing question as well as their contention that Chicago's schools were de jure segregated, he so overwhelmingly won the support of black voters. In 1963 a small group of hecklers at a fourth of July civil rights assemblage caused Daley to cut short his speech, and it took more heavy-handed tactics than usual to get the City Council to pass a very modest housing bill that prohibited various practices by real estate brokers as "unfair." Still, Daley prevailed.

After the assassination, new president Lyndon Johnson wasted little time in contacting as important a figure in the Democratic party as Richard Daley, and they forged an effective working relationship despite the radical differences in their backgrounds. The coming of the Great Society was welcomed by Richard Daley, who knew a potential gold mine when he saw one. As usual, the mayor proposed significantly increased spending for 1964 to his rubber-stamp City Council, who rubber-stamped it. But criticism outside the machine was growing about the big-taxing, big-spending administration, as well as about Chicago's school segregation (which resembled that of other older, northern and upper midwestern cities). Hence, federal money would be especially welcome. In March, President Johnson proposed as key to his War on Poverty the Economic Opportunity Act, with its new bureaucracy, the Office of Economic Opportunity, which included the possibility of the participation of nongovernmental organizations in funding opportunities for "community action." Mayor Daley publicly commented, "We think the local officials should have control of this program" (Matusow 1984, 125). Daley was happy to greet President Johnson upon his arrival in Chicago in April 1964, where he spoke of his commitment to the War on Poverty he had announced in his State of the Union address the previous January and to the "Great Society" (he employed the term in Chicago) he was, so to speak, formally announce at the University of Michigan commencement a few weeks later. The Chicago delegation to Congress naturally voted for the Great Society programs with their promised federal dollars for the in-fashion "urban crisis," as signified by the creation of a new cabinet-level office, the Department of Housing and Urban Development.

Regularity and loyalty continued to be strong virtues for Daley. At the August 1964 Democratic National Convention held at Atlantic City, Mayor Daley, most predictably, sided with President Johnson in the emotional, televised melodrama concerning the seating of the Mississippi delegation, getting some of Chicago's black aldermen to lend their names to the national "regulars" under Johnson who opposed seating the telegenic Fannie Lou Hamer, an immediate darling of the media whose heartfelt, convincing testimony concerning the evils of white supremacy became the sensation of the convention, and her allies. The 1964 Democratic landslide promised an expansion of aid from Washington, and so Daley felt enabled to present a 1965 city budget that broke with the recent tradition of calling for huge spending increases. He was seated on the podium for President Johnson's January 20, 1965, inauguration and had a place of honor in the presidential box at the Inaugural Ball. He was someone who expected to do business with the president, and with whom the president could do business, too.

This was demonstrated vividly in the spring of 1965 in a confrontation over alleged de jure segregation in Chicago's public schools. A decades-long campaign for federal aid to precollege educational institutions had at last triumphed with the passage of the Elementary and Secondary Education Act, a pillar of Johnson's Great Society hopes and largely directed toward the poorest achieving school districts. An official complaint was filed on July 4th by a Chicago liberal activist group, the Coordinating Council of Community Organizations, whose members had clashed with Mayor Daley from the group's inception in 1962. The U.S. Commissioner of Education, Francis Keppel, found the submission compelling in places—city government action had indeed deliberately fostered school segregation, in fact quite obviously, though admittedly dating back to an era when this had been not only legal (i.e., pre-*Brown*) but also virtually unquestioned. These practices, involving such things as the drawing of school district lines, had continued into the 1960s, again obviously, and up till the present time. Did the *Brown* decision of 1954 have anything to do with things like this? Keppel and his bureaucrats began mulling over their response, one whose outcome would speak volumes as to the realities of the Great Society as implemented in Richard Daley's Chicago.

In the setting of this slow-developing controversy, Martin Luther King, Jr., came north to Chicago on January 22, 1966, moving into a slum apartment in an attempt to broaden his integration crusade by taking it north and drawing attention to the deprived conditions to be found in many black northern ghettoes. The Midwest, and particularly its unofficial capital city, were terra incognita in the main to King. "White ethnics" were not a part of the southern landscape wherein he had toiled for most of his days. King did not know Daley but of course knew of the country's most famous mayor, a builder and urban renewal figure of the first order. If one could get Richard Daley on one's side when it came to Chicago, things could get done—perhaps even school and residential integration? The answer, of course, was no, not at all—what some called "segregation," Daley thought of as a parish and neighborhood. Daley the practicing Roman Catholic was also culturally nonattuned to King's Protestant prophetic moralism. The only way up in American society, as Daley knew from personal and family experience, was working through the political and economic system. Black people in Chicago were a part of his Cook Country Democratic Organization, which was as it should be. Controversies were to be worked out in private so as to keep a common front and keep the community together. Street protests were anathema, giving unwarranted attention to troublemakers, publicity hounds, showmen, and self-appointed pseudo-leaders; those in authority should defuse them, ignore them, and wait for them to fade away, as they inevitably did. Protests by local Chicago activists into Daley's Bridgeport neighborhood were countered by the mayor's use of 11th Ward Organization people to ensure that confrontation was avoided, thus denying the marchers the publicity that hoped for. This was largely though not entirely successful; after a minor disturbance in August, Mayor Daley, quite accurately, spoke negatively of the marchers, stating, "I don't think it helps their cause to be marching in residential areas. I think they are surely trying to create tension" (Cohen and Taylor 2000, 341–42). To the marchers, of course, this was the "creative tension" that King had written of in his famed "Letter from Birmingham Jail," among other places.

To Daley, King, the outsider, really had no business in Chicago. Nevertheless, with his view of political leadership as negotiation and community maintenance, with years of experience regarding the control of public images, Mayor Daley made sure that he had only nice things to say in his public statements upon King's visit to Chicago and its suburbs, and associated himself with the Great Society's generic goals: "We must root out poverty, rid the community of slums, eliminate discrimination and segregation wherever they may exist, and improve the quality of our education" (Cohen and Taylor 2000, 340). To Daley, these items did not call for, let alone necessitate, a radical reconstruction of Chicago's political system, which of course would threaten his lifework. Far from it.

Great Society money was fine with Daley, especially aid for housing projects, now receiving criticism but still defended by the much older Daley—but not federal control over local political structures. The trouble came over the new idea of "participation" on the part of the poor, to the "maximum feasible" extent, in the new programs. This was deliberately designed by radical thinkers who disdained as quaint the traditional patronage-based urban political organizations, who were believed to be unsympathetic to the genuine problems of the disenfranchised, especially if they happened to be black. Should the efforts to "empower" the poor via the new Community Action Programs (CAPs) of the Office of Economic Opportunity, headed by Sargent Shriver, a Kennedy in-law and longtime Chicagoan, actually amount to anything at all, they would establish a kind of alternative, parallel universe to the political machine's mechanisms. Indeed, that was just the point of its idealistic architects who, along with the increasingly active and noisy black Chicago civil rights activists, disdained in the extreme not only Daley himself, whom they saw as the epitome of the white ethnics whose ill-concealed racism—not, as in the South, a product of an ideology of white supremacy but rather of a strong sense of their own particularism, turf, or neighborhood/parish, along with a fear of the loss of the value of what was for most the only substantial investment they possessed, their homes (an assessment with a genuine basis)—they were determined to expose and challenge, but also, even more so, the black "leaders" in the Democratic organization who were, in their eyes, sickeningly subservient to Mayor Daley, souls who had sold out the race for a mess of patronage pottage. Daley, a mature, deeply experienced political leader, saw it all right from the start and had no intention of permitting such a thing to develop in his city, in his political organization, in his Chicago. And, as an experienced insider with a relationship with LBJ, he was sure that he would still be able to get the federal money anyway.

Daley was used to critics decrying election returns as tainted. But despite his awareness of the existence of corruption of various sorts, he believed in them just the same. In early 1966, responding to criticisms of the Chicago CAP's composition and modus operandi, he testified before the House Committee on Education and Labor in opposition to the "maximum feasible participation" concept, maintaining that projects "must be administered by the duly constituted elected officials of the areas" (Cohen and Taylor 2000, 318). While the phrase, destined to become famous, especially among critics of the War on Poverty, was embedded in the law creating Community Action Programs, how participation was to be defined remained unspecified. Daley, who knew whereof he spoke, continued to articulate that local elected officials and their appointees were not only perfectly capable of administering federal antipoverty funds, but they were also, given that public funds were involved, the appropriate persons for this task. Appropriately enough, he had named himself chairman of the new Chicago Committee on Urban Opportunity, whose director was a black Daley loyalist and whose ninety-member board was almost entirely composed of reliable, friendly faces, including the five black aldermen who were faithful members of the Democratic organization.

From the top down, Daley's men appointed the controlling majority of local, "grassroots" representatives to positions on the newly constituted CAP boards, with the help of local Democratic ward committees. No projects with radical-sounding intentions or unreliable sponsors would be funded by Chicago's CAP. Non-Daley groups such as the Woodlawn Organization complained to sympathetic reporters and sometimes directly to the Office of Economic Opportunity in Washington. Results of such protests reflected power realities, beginning at the top. OEO Director Sargent Shriver was an old Chicagoan well-experienced in coexisting with Daley; while he might make trouble for some cities who were ignoring or minimizing the spirit of maximum feasible participation, he did nothing of the kind when it came to Daley's Chicago. Similarly, President Lyndon Johnson had no intention of crossing swords with Richard Daley. When it came to the battle for desegregation, Johnson was extremely occupied with his attempted destruction of the old white supremacy system of the South that he knew so well and that he correctly believed was tottering and would therefore collapse if given a prolonged series of firm pushes. He also knew very well as a sometime victor in close elections that the Chicago Democratic Organization was pivotal to national Democratic politics. Daley, of course, fully understood all of this as well. As a high-ranking official in OEO recalled, "We had problems with Daley on *everything*, and he always went to the White House, and always won" (Cohen and Taylor 2000, 344).

Street demonstrations and theater left Richard Daley ice cold. Self-created societies and self-appointed spokesmen could not remotely compare with duly elected officials, products of established democratic processes that had certainly worked beautifully for Daley and for people like him. Like many politicians, the mayor complained bitterly about the news media giving publicity to people he regarded as nobodies and troublemakers. As for the OEO functionary who, in early 1965, actually sent notification to the Chicago CAP that its funding might be cut off due to a lack of maximum feasible participation on the part of the poor, that person was rapidly replaced by a black Daley machine loyalist. Critics such as those from the Woodlawn Organization got a hearing and platform later that year before a House of Representatives subcommittee, there denouncing the machine and complaining that no War on Poverty existed in Chicago and that its leader, Mayor Daley, held a plantation boss mentality (Cohen and Taylor 2000, 343). Congressional sympathizers tried to make trouble for Daley and his machine.

Such slings and arrows impressed Daley not at all. Chosen chairman of a newly constituted War on Poverty Committee at the summer 1965 assembly of the U.S. Conference of Mayors, he worked with other big-city mayors to organize resistance to federal CAP domination. In no way did he oppose the federal money or wish to end the funding of the War on Poverty in its many manifestations. The issue was control. It came up again in the fall of 1965, when, in response to complaints by local, nonorganization groups, and after investigators from the federal Department of Health, Education and Welfare had visited Chicago, a preliminary finding was issued by U.S. Commissioner of Education Francis Keppel that Chicago's schools were indeed de jure segregated, in violation of the *Brown* ruling and of the 1964 Civil Rights Act, thus jeopardizing the flow of federal money. Daley had no trouble getting the entire elected Illinois Democratic establishment to raise the hue and cry.

Keppel's letter came on October 1st; two days later, Mayor Daley was in New York, and was so insistent that Johnson meet with him that the president wound up being a few minutes late to his scheduled visit with Pope Paul VI. Johnson got right on it the next day, harshly speaking with Keppel and HEW Secretary John Gardner, then dispatching trusted friend and HEW Undersecretary Wilbur Cohen, Daley's fellow Midwesterner and, like the Chicago mayor, the epitome of an Establishment figure whose life story had reinforced in him the belief that doing things properly and regularly could indeed improve the world. A face-saving gesture was announced with a few extremely modest changes, and Cohen announced that funding would not be cut off. Activists and regulars in Chicago's politics utterly agreed as to which camp had won—and so rapidly, and with such relative ease. Back in Washington, very shortly Keppel was promoted away from dealing with such matters and replaced with a more politically astute, reliable sort. From thence forward, the Johnson administration set new procedural regulations requiring a far higher standard of proof of racial discrimination and also that efforts be made to work things out with local officials before any cutoffs of funding were threatened. Daley thus shaped policy far beyond Chicago.

By the time Martin Luther King, Jr., brought his civil rights crusade to Chicago early in 1966, then, Daley was experienced in successfully handling this new form of insurgency, civil rights, against his orderly machine. Again, Daley sought to steal King's thunder by predicting that Chicago's slums, which he termed "bad housing," would be gone in only a couple of years, or even less, if only enough money was provided to the city government by Springfield and, especially, Great Society Washington; he also promoted yet another bond issue. He took care to speak kindly of King in public and ducked all confrontation. As mayor, he was able to unleash a string of actions in the spring that bolstered his image as a fighter against slums. After a March meeting with Daley, King stated publicly, "I'm not leading any campaign against Mayor Daley. I'm leading a campaign against slums" (Cohen and Taylor 2000, 372). By the summer, however, King was becoming increasingly convinced that Daley was "just trying to stay ahead of us just enough to take the steam out of the movement" (383).

King cleanly broke with Daley on July 10, 1966, at a gathering of several tens of thousands, well below organizers' hopes, held at Soldier Field. He called for an open housing campaign and for a voter registration drive, implying that Chicago's blacks would determine who served the next term as mayor, and then led a march to City Hall, taping a list of fourteen demands to the door. The following day, King and Daley got together for a previously scheduled meeting that lasted for three hours. Here the mayor enumerated his many programmatic efforts to combat poverty among Chicago blacks and others, and continued to comport himself with great self-control, avoiding all confrontation and rejecting per se nothing that King demanded. In the press conference that followed, Daley reiterated that the city would continue to seek the alleviation of slum living, adding, in response to a reporter's question, that no violation of law associated with street demonstrations would be tolerated. Relatively minor civil disturbances broke out later that week (in the context of heat in the 90s), which Daley was able to keep under control, though only with the assistance of the Illinois National Guard. This led the mayor to criticize "some" elements in King's Chicago Campaign, though not the reverend himself. King, angered, wound up waiting at City Hall for Daley to return (after failing to get an appointment with him scheduled), and here Daley was again under masterful self-control. When open-housing marchers in white neighborhoods produced highly publicized, highly negative reactions from residents, Daley spoke generally of the need to preserve law and order, condemning no one. Sensing correctly that King was on the verge of having had more than enough of the strange midwestern city, which King accused of harboring hatred more severe than that he had come to know in Mississippi, the mayor sent his black City Council political associates to convince King to leave town, offering minor face-saving gestures of a noncontroversial nature.

King and his southern associates continued to find it hard to believe that Mayor Daley *really did* have significant black allies in Chicago, more than a few of whom did little to conceal their aversion to King, seeing him and even characterizing him as—shades of the Deep South—an outside agitator. Daley enlisted such influential figures as the cardinal archbishop and high union officials to pressure King's movement to cease marches and confrontation and instead to deal with the established power structure. A so-called summit on fair housing mostly revealed Daley's political skills at containment (though out of its deliberations did come a new group, the Metropolitan Chicago Leadership Council for Open Housing, which in years to come did actively promote the concept, aided tremendously, of course, by the 1968 federal law). On August 16, 1966, the mayor sought a court order halting fair housing marches in Chicago neighborhoods, an action supported by the Chicago City Council, 45–1, including all seven black aldermen (Cohen and Taylor 2000, 415).

Mayor Daley certainly continued to be an enthusiastic supporter of "mainstream" Great Society elements; speaking about the impending 1966 Illinois senatorial election between incumbent Democratic Senator Paul Douglas and Republican challenger Charles Percy, Daley wrote for the *Chicago Tribune*, "It is the Democratic Party that has given the people Medicare and expanded social security; federal aid to schools, including expanded opportunities for attending college; the minimum wage and increases in minimum wage; and measures to rebuild cities that provide decent housing, end air and water pollution, and improve transportation" (Cohen and Taylor 2000, 425). He continued to succeed, as long as the Great Society remained in place, in gaining millions and millions of federal dollars for city projects of all sorts. Richard Daley never became anything remotely close to a political conservative of any sort. Like Lyndon Johnson, Daley saw the Great Society as fundamentally an extension of the New Deal. It was not an engine for social revolution in his city of Chicago, which he continued to dominate despite all criticism—in 1967, for instance, despite the bitterness of the civil rights controversy, he won 83.8 percent of the black vote in Chicago (437). If the Great Society meant more federal government efforts to improve society, especially creating patronage-type jobs, and more money to do it with, Daley was a cheerleader for it and a beneficiary of it. On May 9, 1967, Lyndon Johnson and other leading Democrats named Chicago's mayor "Democrat of the Year."

Of the many memorable images that came out of the fabled year 1968, the Democratic National Convention, awarded to Chicago both as a demonstration of Mayor Daley's influence and as a reward for his continued public support of President Johnson, including over the Vietnam War, one of the most vivid is that of the mayor himself. He had originally hoped the convention to be a shining hour for his city, not only drawing attention to (so that committees from all sorts of organizations would consider it as a locale for their future convention sites) but also showing off "Daley's Chicago," the city that worked under its competent mayor. With the assassinations of King and Robert F. Kennedy having already shocked the nation in the last few months, security concerns were naturally high. Daley had refused any permits for protesters and deployed an enormous police force, supplemented by the Illinois National Guard. On the evening of August 28, word spread inside the convention hall, the Ampitheatre, of the police brutality being perpetrated against protesters who had come in moderately large numbers to Chicago to protest the convention of the party in charge of the government that had given the country Vietnam, all televised. U.S. Senator Abraham Ribicoff of Connecticut, in a speech nominating South Dakota U.S. Senator George McGovern, decried the "Gestapo tactics" of the Chicago Police Department. The Illinois delegation happened to be seated close to the podium, and cameras caught their pure rage, led by Mayor Daley, shouting what looked like obscenities that could not be heard but could be lip-read at the senator, who replied, "How hard it is to accept the truth." Richard Nixon narrowly carried Illinois in the 1968 vote.

The longest serving mayor in Chicago history, Richard Daley, was reelected in 1971 with 70 percent of the vote. In 1972, he and his Chicago delegation to the Democratic Convention were denied their seats as a result of their having failed to comply with the reform selection process voted in as a result of dissatisfaction with the 1968 process; Nixon again carried Illinois. Jimmy

Carter, on the other hand, paid proper respects to Daley, who helped him obtain the 1976 nomination, though the Republicans for the third time in a row carried Illinois. Richard Daley died in office very suddenly of a heart attack on December 19, 1976. In 1989, his son, Richard Michael Daley, was elected to the first of five consecutive four-year terms as Chicago mayor.

EDITH GREEN
(1910–1987)

In the late 1960s, Edith Green was sometimes called the most powerful woman politician in the United States. That a good case can be made for this statement, and also that outside of Oregon, at least, her name is unlikely to be recognized today save by aging Washington insiders or researchers on the Title IX sports controversy, may be taken as a sign of the dearth of genuinely influential female officeholders in the days of the Great Society. Another of Green's nicknames in the 1960s was "Mrs. Education." This issue, traditionally of special interest to females, had indeed long been of interest to her, going back to her days as a schoolteacher in the 1930s and her early political career in Oregon as a lobbyist for increased state funding for schools. As a member of Congress, Green favored federal aid to precollege-level education, one of the landmark achievements of the Great Society effort as enshrined in the 1965 Elementary and Secondary Education Act. Green had achieved the considerable power she wielded the old-fashioned, Capitol Hill way: consistent hard work, responsible personal behavior, and, most importantly of all, the piling up of years and years of seniority, during which she built up a well-deserved reputation for expertise in her chosen field, education, while remaining in touch with her constituents back home in Oregon, to which she returned in 1975 upon completing her two decades as a member of the U.S. House of Representatives. A Democrat, Green spent her entire congressional career as a member of the party in control of both houses of Congress. Hence, she was well placed, as the Great Society era dawned and began to take shape, to play a role in both its creation and development. It should have been a happy story, and it was by no means altogether an unhappy one. But where Edith Green came out would have surprised, even shocked, most who knew of her early career, thought perhaps not quite so much those who knew her better.

One of the oddities of the U.S. Congress is the tradition of politeness in public proceedings, so unlike so many other representative assembles around the world. Members thank and yield, most of the time, to "distinguished gentlemen" in floor and committee debates. Colleagues of Edith Green liked to joke that she was a not-so-gentle "gentlelady." From the Johnson administration point of view, she became at a critical point a troublemaker, first via her various amendments to Great Society proposals, collectively known as Green Amendments, then later as a harsher critic of the bigger trends that the Great Society represented for both the nation and also the Democratic party, to which she had devoted a great deal of her life. Federal *aid* to education she favored; centralized *control* over local education, and the mentality she saw lying behind this philosophy, she opposed vigorously, and these stances led her in the end to turn her back on the political party to which she had devoted her career in public service.

Edith Green's election to Congress in 1954 from the Third Congressional District of Oregon (greater Portland) was a logical next step in a career characterized by civic involvement and achievement, focused primarily on the field of public education, for most of her then-forty-four years of life. Born on January 17, 1910, in South Dakota, Edith Starret was the daughter of two teachers and the third of five children. At age six she was taken with her family to Oregon, and they moved in 1926 to Salem, the state capital. She became an active high school debate team member, winning various contests, and was chosen that year as the "Outstanding Girl of Oregon." This honor took her to Philadelphia, where the nation's sesquicentennial was being observed, and then down to Washington, D.C., for her first trip away from home and her visit to the seat of the federal government, where she met President Calvin Coolidge. In 1927 she graduated as valedictorian of her high school class, the first girl at her school to achieve this distinction. After a couple of terms elsewhere, she entered the Oregon College of Education in Monmouth in the fall of 1929; as was then common, she obtained a teaching certificate after completing two years of college and began working as a sixth grade teacher in Salem in 1930, at the age of twenty. She continued working toward a bachelor's degree via the University of Oregon in summers; this was awarded in 1939. In 1933, she married Arthur Green; after their first son, James, was born in 1934 she returned to the classroom for the fall term.

Edith Green's entry into public political life came in 1938, when she entered a speaking contest jointly sponsored by Portland's Congresswoman Nan Wood Honeyman, who had been elected in 1936 and was the first Oregon congresswoman ever, and the Women's Division of the Democratic Party's Central committee on the topic of "The New Deal in the History of the Northwest." This led to her being asked to do some radio spots for Oregon's governor, a Democrat, who was seeking reelection. By now teaching junior high school, she saw her life change with the entry of the United States into World War II. She gave birth to her second son, Richard, in February

1942, and then accompanied her husband to Portland due to his assignment there by the U.S. Navy. Given her effectiveness as a speaker, she tried her hand at a new career, part time, during the war, in radio, at KALE in Portland, and became interested enough in the medium to spend the summer of 1944 studying radio in Palo Alto, California, at Stanford University. Back in Portland, she was given her own radio show that involved playing music and also doing some talking directed toward housewives coping with wartime rationing and shortages; however, with the end of the war, she returned to the classroom for another three years.

Edith Green at this point began to get involved with the Oregon Parent-Teachers' Association, responding to talk about organizing a campaign to seek increased state funding for education (the State Basic School support bill), and soon became (paid) executive secretary and office manager for the Children's Bill Committee campaign, which succeeded via public referendum in 1950. Given her interests and experience, she was a logical candidate to be named in 1953 director of public relations for the Oregon Education Association, where she spent a year working with the state legislature. She joined the board of the Oregon PTA. She spoke widely, regularly, and confidently and counted among her memberships such civic groups as the American Association of University Women, the League of Women Voters, and the United Nations Association; her experience in radio had led her to membership in that industry's labor union, the American Federation of Television and Radio Artists, which provided her political entry to organized labor. Democratic party activists recruited her to run for the office of secretary of state in 1952, and her good showing there in a losing effort (it was the year of Eisenhower's landslide) marked her as a political comer. The Democrats by tradition were the minority party in Oregon, and Green was part of a younger generation's effort aimed at its revitalization. Green carried Multnomah County (the Portland area) in 1952, suggesting a base for another campaign; in 1954, at the age of forty-four, she won the seat in Congress from Oregon's Third Congressional District that she was to occupy for the next two decades, defeating Republican Tom McCall, later Oregon's governor, by almost 10,000 votes; she increased her margin to 65,000 votes in 1956 and was never again to face a serious challenge in her twenty-year career, which she ended by choice in order to retire. Like all new members, she was a face in the crowd—but, unlike the overwhelming majority, hers was a female face, and one that did not owe its success in any direct way to her being Mrs. Arthur Green in private life.

While of course she would deal with many other questions as well, "her" issue—education—was, as mentioned earlier, a traditionally "female" one that also matched her professional career; however, she had also gained some experience in the commercial world. She joined the Education and Labor Committee, which was to be her congressional "home" for the next eighteen years, eventually rising to become its second-ranking (in terms of seniority) member and the chairwoman of its Special Subcommittee on Education. Her political identity was "liberal," a contested word during the McCarthy period just ending as she entered the House of Representatives, with the base of her support coming from unions and the educational community. At the commencement exercises of the University of Alaska in 1956, she spoke favorably of a liberalism characterized by "moderation," founded on "a firm dedication to democratic and humane goals, tempered by a clear understanding of practical limitations" (Ross 1980, 66). That same year witnessed her first legislative achievement, the Library Services Act, which provided federal money for libraries in underserved rural areas. The need existed; only the money was lacking, and as the federal government had money, the answer was there. Green exhibited no philosophical reservations whatsoever about obtaining "national" money for a "local" cause. She had faced financial difficulty in her own college years and come of age during the New Deal era, when looking to Washington for various forms of financial help greatly increased. In a letter of 1957, Green outlined her philosophy: "It would be accurate to say that the issues which are closest to my heart are those which center around the education and welfare of the nation's children. Such legislative activities as federal aid to education, rural library services, and federal activity in understanding and curbing juvenile delinquency are among those which I feel to be directed toward the most crucial domestic problems of our time—the physical, mental and spiritual health of the members and constituents of the 85th Congress" (65–66).

Unsurprisingly, then, Edith Green was well positioned at the dawn of the Kennedy-Johnson era to support the general direction of the New Frontier and the Great Society departures. Furthermore, by that time she had become a member of the club on Capitol Hill; she belonged to the normal majority congressional party, represented a safe district, was expected to have many years ahead of her in her career, and was a known quantity for her work, seriousness, and reliability. An early supporter of John F. Kennedy's in Oregon in the 1960 campaign for the Democratic nomination, she gave one of the seconding speeches on his behalf at the Los Angeles convention as head of the Oregon delegation (the first woman ever chosen to lead a state's convention representatives) and was chairwoman of his unsuccessful Oregon general election campaign. With this connection and her established interests, Green was a natural sponsor of the administration's 1961 proposed Juvenile Delinquency and Youth Offenses Control Act, passed in September, a modest Great Society–type effort aimed at funneling $30 million in federal aid over the next three years to grant-applying local outfits seeking to channel disadvantaged youth toward productive futures. However, it soon became evident to Green and others in Congress that the architects of the act (especially Office of Juvenile Delinquency Director Lloyd Ohlin of the Columbia University School of Social Work) had radical possibilities in mind, such as funding outright challenges to existing social service agencies deemed ineffective, irrelevant, or worse. "What I had in mind," Green later recalled, was "a number of experimental projects, such as . . . the early identification of potential delinquents, the increased study of bio-chemical factors that may influence behavior in the adolescent stage, the anchoring of a ship near slum areas for recreation purposes and so forth. I surely wasn't thinking of . . . the 'thirty million dollar test of Ohlin's oppor-tunity theory,'" (Matusow 1984, 113). She was instrumental in preventing the expansion of the number of planning grants desired by the agency when the juvenile delinquency act was renewed in 1963 for a couple more years.

In 1961 Green had accumulated enough seniority to be chosen as chair-woman of the Special Subcommittee for Education of the House Education and Labor Committee. That same year, President Kennedy had proposed that federal aid be given to all American school districts. The issue had got-ten mileage out of the post-Sputnik hysteria along with the demographic push of the baby boomers, but the religious and school integration questions hovered over the matter: would private, religious-based schools qualify for federal aid, and would the aid be tied to integration? Edith Green had been in the middle of the creation of the National Defense Education Act in 1958, right after Sputnik, a law that provided federal aid to local school districts for specific purposes, such as foreign language instruction, laboratory sci-ence, and the development of a modern mathematics curriculum, that were deemed related to "national security." She was a logical choice to deliver an endowed lecture at the Harvard University Graduate School of Education in 1963 on "The Federal Role in Education," wherein, after sketching the long history of federal involvement in educational activities of various sorts, she specifically drew attention to her then-current efforts on behalf of the pro-posed Higher Education Facilities bill. When this law, which provided more federal money to finance buildings that the baby boomers would need as their numbers reached college age, was signed on December 17, 1963, Pres-ident Lyndon Johnson singled out Green as a key figure in the success and gave her one of the multiple pens he had used in affixing his signature to the new law. In passing during her Harvard speech, she expressed what looked like perfunctory concern about "duplication and overlapping" in federal ed-ucational research efforts (Green 1972, 21), but this, as things turned out, would be a theme she would develop in future years.

In 1965 the ancient logjam regarding federal aid to K–12 education was at last broken with Congress' enactment of the Elementary and Secondary Edu-cation Act (ESEA). The 1964 vote had produced the largest Democratic con-gressional majorities since the New Deal, and Johnson could fairly claim a real mandate for the Great Society. His education task force had worked through the summer of 1964 under the leadership of Francis Keppel, U.S. commissioner of education and former dean of the Harvard University School of Education. Edith Green participated in the committee hearings that opened on January 22nd and finished twelve days later after a parade of witnesses sang the glories of federal aid. She proposed two amendments to the bill, the first of the Green Amendments that were eventually to bedevil the Great Society shortly down the road; here, Green sought the granting of standing for local school districts to challenge court decisions that might come regarding the bill's indirect aid to parochial schools, and a revamping of the aid formula to direct it more toward poorer rather than richer states; one of her greatest hopes was that the federal government might diminish differences in educational opportunity among the states. These amendments got nowhere, but Green voted for the bill anyway, which was approved by the full committee on March 18th and then by the House of Representatives on March 26. After a perfunctory debate, overwhelming Senate approval quickly followed and Johnson staged one of his most melodramatic signing ceremonies, back in Texas near his ranch at his boyhood one-room schoolhouse.

Long identified with the issue, Green might have been expected to be as ecstatic as LBJ himself. Instead, Oregon's Mrs. Education was somewhat troubled. A Washington insider, she had become aware of the negative attitude toward state and local education officials that had pervaded the education task force; Keppel had decried them as "the feeblest bunch of second-rate, or fifth-rate, educators who combined educational incompetence with bureaucratic immovability" (Graham 1984, 63). While her residence and political activity in Oregon's capital city of Salem had hardly made her an uncritical believer in idealized notions of "local control," she had made her own career and, indeed, her second career as a politician by working with state government and educational officials for whom she most certainly did not feel contempt or disdain. On October 1st, at Purdue University, Green issued a warning that may have appeared out of sync for someone who only a few weeks before had been honored, along with seventy-five other members of Congress, for her liberal voting record at a testimonial dinner in Los Angeles. "Because of a piecemeal approach and overlapping programs," she intoned, "we may someday wake up to find a dislocated and disjointed National policy which represents neither the considered judgment of educational leaders nor the needs of our country" (Ross 1980, 130). This conservative-sounding boilerplate was followed less than two weeks later by a more extensive statement before an organization epitomizing the K–12 education "Establishment" so disdained by the Johnson administration's education task force: the National School Boards Association. Green's tone was cautionary: "Yes, it has been a productive year for educational legislation. So where do we go from here? It seems to me the [House Education and Labor] Committee would be well advised to stop, look, and listen. This country has participated in a legislative educational feast. Let the Congress and the country have time to digest it" (130). While observing, as no doubt most of her listeners knew, that she was well known as a supporter of most federal educational legislation, she insisted "that there are inherent limitations to the effectiveness of federal action in the field of action. Of the three partners, the local, the state, the federal government—the federal government is the farthest removed from the classroom where teaching and learning occur. Moreover, for the local board of education, local education is *the* problem; for the congress . . . for the Federal Government . . . it is one of many problems" (130). Anticipating the reaction of her audience, Green continued, "As a liberal, these warning signs may sound strange. Clearly the Federal Government can and should contribute much to education. But I do not want to see the congress—under pressure from every quarter—pass bills without full debate—without the most serious attention given to the relation of that program to others and the impact on our local schools and communities—which only they can really know. The success of the partnership will depend on whether a meaningful dialogue can be conducted between the partners" (130–31). Embedded in this discussion was the insinuation that the Johnson administration was rushing its bills through Congress as if the country faced the kind of national emergency it had during the First Hundred Days of Franklin D. Roosevelt's New Deal.

The centerpiece of Johnson's War on Poverty, the proposed Office of Economic Opportunity, also attracted the increasingly watchful eye of Congresswoman Green. To begin with, the danger of overselling existed; as she said to a Spokane audience on May 24, 1964, at the Gonzaga University commencement, "There is a great danger . . . that the rising tide of expectations *for* the [War on Poverty] program will expect too much, too soon" (Ross 1980, 168). Furthermore, the wagers of the new "war" seemed to be attempting to create a sort of parallel universe to the existing educational institutions, potentially crowding them out in the battle for financial support. An excellent example was the Teacher Corps, a Great Society idea that never really caught on too much at the time but that in 1965 appeared to some to have great potential (the idea would return in various guises later on, as "alternative certification" and the Teach for America program, among others). The Teacher Corps did not appeal to Congresswoman Edith Green—she viewed it as an insult to the teaching profession, a mocking of that profession's standards, and an unneeded competitor to regular teachers who would receive no special breaks, such as the taxpayer-funded tuition promised the corps' recruits (Unger 1996, 208). Green argued in a January 1966 article for *American County Government*, a publication read by local officials, that to her, at least, federal money should not mean federal control: rather, the new programs should "depend largely on the administration and critical analysis and evaluation given . . . at the local level by educators and community leaders" (quoted in Ross 1980, 131–32). And she concluded her piece with what sounded very much like a warning: "With the ever increasing effort of the Federal Government to combat the discrepancies in the American education effort, with the war on poverty, the fight against adult illiteracy, the effort to train the handicapped, the educational community must strengthen its part in this important dialog between government and educators to assure that our *regular* schools and our *regular* programs are not neglected" (Ross 1980, 131–32). She was already developing concerns that the Elementary and Secondary Education Act might create an opening for federal decision-making concerning even such fundamentals as textbook selection.

The school integration issue became tied to the question of federal funds with the passage of ESEA in 1965, and Green opposed de jure segregation of the southern sort as a matter of course, still an issue of implementation despite the fact that over a decade had passed since the U.S. Supreme Court's historic *Brown* decision of 1954. Equality before the law was important to her, though she came to the issue through the prism of gender rather than racial issues. As the Department of Health, Education, and Welfare began to threaten the cutoff of federal funds to school districts found not to be making satisfactory practice toward establishing a unitary (i.e., nonsegregated or racially identifiable) school system, Green in May 1967 called for "uniform enforcement" in all the states of such provisions (Ross 1980, 171). To many liberals, talk about "local control" of schools justifiably aroused immediate suspicion as a cover for efforts to continue resisting desegregation. Green was well-known as an advocate of equal rights for women and men; she had served on John F. Kennedy's presidential commission on the status of women, cochairing its committee on civil and political rights, and had insisted that the Great Society's Job Corps program include women as well as men. While she had, during committee hearings on the 1964 Civil Rights Act, opposed the addition of sex to the categories of forbidden grounds for discrimination, this was because she was aware that its inclusion was a tactic on the part of the prosegregationists, who hoped ultimately to diminish support for the bill by adding this potentially controversial amendment (in the end, the wording was added and the bill was enacted with Green's support). Nobody could label Edith Green an apologist for white supremacy or question her genuine commitment to equality, even when she increasingly came to identify with the forces of "local control" as opposed to increased federal power.

Especially when the 1966 congressional elections produced a strong swing (forty-seven seats gained net) toward the Republicans in the House of Representatives, Green became an important figure in putting together coalitions that would keep the Great Society going in one sense while reining in its more grandiose objectives on the other. While she could hardly be listed as an opponent of the Great Society, there were continuing signs of some skepticism on her part. On September 26, 1967, for instance, Green spoke negatively about one of the Great Society's harbingers, the juvenile delinquency bill under JFK, for which she had served as chief sponsor. Now, however, she spoke harshly of what the bill in practice had turned out to be: "I can think of no single piece of legislation that has been so disappointing to all of us. . . . If I had it to do over again I would spend $47 million on swimming pools in Washington, D.C. with more effect"(Ross 1980, 74).

The centerpiece of Great Society efforts to create new institutional structures, the Office of Economic Opportunity, found itself increasingly subject to hostility, especially from duly elected local governments. The spread of urban rioting and the attendant publicity provided by the television networks posed great threats to the OEO specifically and to the War on Poverty in general; on top of that, of course, the increased expenditures associated with the buildup of the United States' military effort in Vietnam only made Great Society program money harder to come by. LBJ, deeply committed to fighting to preserve OEO, expended much energy on its behalf throughout the year, and the struggle dragged on into the fall.

Into this thicket stepped Congresswoman Edith Green with a proposed amendment to OEO's appropriation bill for the coming year that would allow state governments to become sponsors of OEO activities and also permit local governmental officeholders to, in effect, take control of private Community Action Programs via the device of representation on their boards; many of these CAPs had become controversial and were receiving unfavorable publicity that was being used by opponents of the War on Poverty itself. Green herself was not opposed to continuing OEO at this point, as were some critics. In debate on November 7, 1967, she explained, "We are defending the right of local governments to make hard decisions on local problems. In fact, the bill demands engagement by local politicians so that they cannot avoid tough decisions on the battle lines of the war on poverty" (Ross 1980, 85). The Johnson administration publicly opposed Green's amendment, but away from the glare of the media it was coming to accept the changed political realities of the situation, accepting warnings that the amendment, or something close to it, would be a necessary price to pay to keep OEO going. Johnson faced pressure from liberals not to cave in, and became aware, as one of his aides told him, that Edith Green was now "distrusted and disliked by the liberals." Furthermore, some Republicans called it the "bossism and boll weevil" amendment, seeing it as a ploy to grant local Democratic political machines control over more federal largesse (Matusow 1984, 269). Democratic leaders in the House of Representatives, however, favored the Green Amendment; as a moderate northern Democratic member of the Education and Labor Committee put it, "I'm trying to stay in the middle—to keep Edith happy. She's vital. She can bring a lot of southerners and conservatives with her who would laugh at the rest of us" (Davies 1996, 196–97). Additionally, by the end of the year the riots had scared many local governments into viewing federal aid, OEO or not, more favorably. The final bill as enacted stated that community action groups were to be under the control of elected officials, though Green's amendment was watered down to allow the director of OEO under certain circumstances to give money to community action groups on his own volition.

By this point, Edith Green was being viewed by the administration as an

irritating force troubling the already-troubled Great Society; her early opposition to the Johnson policy on Vietnam hardly endeared her to the president, either. Increasingly it was conservatives, not liberals, and critics of the
Great Society, not supporters, who enjoyed reading her speeches and articles. *Human Events*, the very conservative Washington, D.C., weekly, enjoyed printing an article about Green in its February 2, 1968, issue, "Liberal
Democrat Scores OEO." Having the luxury of a safe congressional district
that remained safe, accumulated seniority in a still unreformed, strict seniority system, and membership in the seemingly perpetual majority party,
Green was in a strong political position, and she knew it.

She had long had a reputation for bluntness, even impatience toward political adversaries. Naturally, the lion's share of her public statements involved education, but more than ever, they revealed her split from what she
saw as the Great Society's mentality that Washington should lead the way. If
the choice were the brave new world of Great Society centralized enlightenment or the local and state education "Establishments" so disdained by the
centralizers, Green emphatically chose the latter. In congressional debate on
May 22, 1967, Green articulated traditional conservative gospel: "It seems
to me it requires an amazing among of arrogance to assume that all good
judgment and wisdom reside in Washington. I happen to believe that the
people in my state and city know a great deal more about Oregon's problems
than the Office of Education in Washington" (Ross 1980, 82). On November 16, 1967, for instance, Green spoke to the Council of Chief State School
Officers, opining that when it came to schools, "the federal government
should be the junior partner in fact as well as in platitudes and political plat-
forms" (218). A few weeks later, speaking to the Northwest Association of
Secondary and Higher Education, the congresswoman warned against "subtle forces [that] could be even more pernicious than overt attempts to impose
federal control" (218). Federal financial *assistance* was welcome, and Green
always favored including riders requiring nondiscrimination as per the categories established in the Civil Rights Act of 1964 (218).

With the 1968 election year approaching, and the rising tide of criticism
leveled against the Great Society programs in general, the Republican party
attempted to offer "constructive" alternatives, perhaps the most significant
of which came to be known as "revenue sharing," the sending of federal tax
revenues to the state governments who would then decide how to expend
them. Green became a supporter of the concept, in line with her increased
disdain for "Washington" and her sharpening criticisms of the Great Society. In an article published in 1970, she wrote, "We have to have decentral-
ization of programs. We cannot, as an education committee here in the
House, sit as a school board for every city or town in the U.S. and decide that
we, in our arrogant way, have all of the wisdom and knowledge to make the
decision for Nome, Alaska; Portland, Maine; Fresno, California; the ghettos
of Chicago; and the rural areas of South Dakota. All the studies show that

these programs aren't working. So instead of 188 programs run by the Office of Education, I favor revenue-sharing with the states or block grants with a very limited number of strings attached" (Ross 1980, 140).

The Republicans gained control of the executive branch with the election of Richard Nixon in 1968, but the Democrats still held Congress; the fight over what was left of the Great Society entered a new phase. Green's break with OEO became total. In the 1969 House Education and Labor Committee consideration of the antipoverty agency's future, Green favored extending its life by only two years, as opposed to the seven favored by OEO supporters on the committee (the eventual outcome, three, is a sign of which way the wind was blowing). On December 3rd, she denounced OEO in scathing terms, claiming that in Portland, Oregon, the local agency, besides exhibiting significant violations of conflict-of-interest laws, had been guilty of fomenting discord if not downright revolution. And Portland, she charged, was not unique: "There are hundreds of thousands of dollars unaccounted for. They have never gone to the poor" (Ross 1980, 94). She also denounced what was coming to be called "forced busing" plans aimed at increasing school integration, contending that they were unworkable in practice. Unable to alter the OEO bill in committee to her satisfaction, Green crossed a Rubicon on December 12, 1969, when she voted *against* final passage of the bill that kept OEO going for three more years. Now she was more than a critic; she was an opponent. Her criticisms of Portland's OEO did not go unnoticed back home, and the Multnomah County Democratic Party chairman, who was also a local OEO administrator, endorsed a primary challenger for Green in 1970. Green destroyed him in the primary, winning some 80 percent of the vote, and cruised to her usual landslide victory in the fall (Rosenberg, 121).

Green began gaining a new reputation as a watchdog of the public's tax dollars—a stereotypical role more commonly played by conservatives—and an opponent of "waste" and "duplication" in federal programs. Was she changing her political stripes? On February 18, 1969, in a speech to another old-line education establishment group, the American Association of School Administrators, she spoke gently of the *novus ordo seclorum*: "The federal government comes lately to the task of educating America—but with great potential for good. But may I suggest that national politics must be constantly examined and re-examined in the light of information and new experience" (Ross 1980, 219). In April 1969 she successfully offered another Green Amendment that proposed consolidating the programs of the Elementary and Secondary Education Act and the old National Defense Education Act in the direction of block grants to the states who would then decide for themselves how to divvy up the money.

Less than a year later, in a speech to the National Restaurant Association delivered on February 20, 1970, she referred with scorn to "the bureaucratic labyrinth on the Potomac" as "a recalcitrant hydra of duplication and inefficiency"; the answer proposed was for legislation "to be aimed at seeking co-ordination by state and local jurisdictions" (Ross 1980, 136). With a bow toward Dwight Eisenhower (who had warned in his 1961 farewell address about not only what he called the military-industrial complex, but also the potentially corrupting effects of federal influence on the nation's scholars via the power of money), Green offered her own new, sinister-sounding force for citizens to be worried about: the "education-poverty-industrial com-plex," defined as "people and companies devoted to reaping profit from the nation's legitimate interest in education and welfare" (136). This speech was basically recycled on several occasions over the course of the next year and so served as Edith Green's valedictory to the Great Society. *Newsweek* gave her a page to promote her concept of "The Education Complex" in Septem-ber, but the most telling locale for her views was *The Public Interest*, which in 1972 reprinted, in an unusual move for the magazine, Green's 1971 ex-tended version of the 1970 speech from *The Educational Forum*, an educa-tion Establishment journal. *The Public Interest*, founded in 1965 to promote the use of social science research in policy making, had rapidly turned into a forum dominated by deflating articles questioning at least the enthusiasms of poverty warriors and Great Society true believers; by the early 1970s, it was clearly serving as an incubator of a new political trend coming to be known as "neoconservatism," a term characterizing liberals who seemed to be hav-ing sober second thoughts while discovering new conservative instincts within themselves. Domestically speaking, at least, Green fit this bill well; as for foreign affairs, skepticism over the government's Vietnam policy could be seen as the logical extension of skepticism over its domestic policy.

Befitting her political history as a well-known liberal and longtime advo-cate of federal aid to education, she began her article, "The Educational Entrepreneur—a Portrait" by acknowledging the "Great hopes and high ideals" that lay behind the new federal efforts of the past decade. But it did not take her long to denounce the "monstrous apparatus" that had been created, the "tremendous proliferation of programs and activities . . . lead-ing to a major collapse of rational management," and the "duplication, complexity, and sheer weight of these efforts" that was "becoming unbear-able to taxpayers and officials alike" (Green 1972, 12). After some rather tedious chronicling of a couple of case studies, Green concluded that what needed to be called into question was the very structure of the new effort it-self; Otherwise, "we will be engulfed and overburdened with a runaway federal program—a diverse, overlapping, unplanned, confusing array of governmental efforts whose faults are beyond remedy and whose abuses are beyond belief" (24).

Edith Green's career in Congress was not over; she returned to her interest in gender equality, supporting the failed Equal Rights Amendment and also, given her frustration with the Equal Employment Opportunity Commis-sion's record to date, the provision in the 1972 federal education omnibus bill that came to be known as "Title IX," prohibiting gender discrimination in all programs accepting federal funds; at a popular level, it became best known for its effects on interscholastic and intercollegiate athletics (Green had been a competitive swimmer and tennis player as a young woman). In 1972 Green supported U.S. Senator Henry Jackson of Washington for the Democratic presidential nomination. Finding the Oregon delegation dominated by supporters of South Dakota U.S. Senator George McGovern, representative of what was being called the "new politics," Green complained that the Democratic party had been "taken over by the kooks" (Hartmann 1989, 80). For what turned out to be her final term (by her choice) in Congress, 1973–75, she switched from her longtime home at the Education and Labor Committee to the Appropriations Committee, the better to keep an eye on wasteful federal spending. And so it was that "Mrs. Education," back home in Oregon after retirement, came out at the conclusion of long and distinguished career as the cochair in 1976 of what must be counted as one of most utterly obscure political groupings in modern-day American history, National Democrats for Gerald Ford—no Great Society supporter he. Nor she, anymore. After retiring from Congress, she returned home to Oregon, teaching government at Portland's Western Pacific College and serving on the Oregon Board of Higher Education. She died in Portland on April 21, 1987.

DANIEL PATRICK MOYNIHAN
(1927–2003)

When New York U.S. Senator Daniel Patrick Moynihan decided not to seek another term in 2000, hence bringing his long career of public service to an effective close, a journalistic profile asked the question, "Who was Pat Moynihan?" He was often taken to be the epitome of the intellectual in politics, a breed that, at least in its liberal incarnation, was felt by many to be increasingly in short supply in the late twentieth century. A considered answer to the question might begin with the observation that Moynihan was a man who had led a number of different lives, giving him an unusually broad experience and frame of reference, most especially for a state-level politician from New York. Seen by many as a quintessential New Yorker, he, like the famous former New York City Mayor Fiorello LaGuardia, spent part of his childhood in precincts far removed from the sometimes-parochial world of Manhattan. In terms of the all-important ideological wars of American society in the late twentieth century, many of which can be traced to the debates over the Great Society, Daniel Patrick Moynihan played an especially important role. He was fundamentally in sympathy with the general aims of the Great Society, as these fit his own well-established political identity as a mainstream Democrat, which meant liberal. However, as author of what became known as "The Moynihan Report" (Moynihan 1965), which both fully endorsed "national action" by the federal government regarding the social issue of "the Negro Family," as its title had it, and yet took a comparatively "hard," "unsentimental" approach to said question based on a social scientific stance, he almost overnight became virtually a marked man, seen as a Benedict Arnold by many true believers and high idealists of the Great Society camp.

He became one of the most frequent early (and later) contributors to the highly influential quarterly *The Public Interest*, which began appearing in 1965 and whose pages were immediately and regularly filled with largely skeptical, though by no means entirely unfriendly, accounts of various Great Society programs from a "hard" social science analytical perspective. Continuing in this vein, and reflecting his background and comfort level with traditional urban, Democratic party, machine politics, he became the severest and most articulate critic of the doomed "community action" efforts that were probably the Great Society's most radical attempts to restructure power relations in local political settings around the country but especially, and somewhat ironically, in bastions of urban, Democratic party rule of the sort that had up to the mid-1960s usually been thought of as "liberal." In response to the Community Action Program slogan reflecting its hopes for constructing a new and more essential local democratic spirit, "maximum feasible participation," Moynihan coined, in a speech in upstate New York that later developed into a book, the withering, almost dismissive response, "maximum feasible misunderstanding." Here he seemed to come off as a university-trained streetwise pol who, with his experiential knowledge of the realities of both the street and of political organization, could not be taken in by the utopian parlor radicalism of professors and intellectual ivory-tower types, despite the fact that he had been a professor and most certainly was entirely deserving of the honorific "public intellectual."

Moynihan's willingness to serve in the administration of President Richard Nixon was perhaps his ultimate rebuff to the Great Society, at least as it was understood by most—yet his efforts to create, under Nixon, a "Family Assistance Plan" lent credence both to his claims that he had never at all given up his old-line, New Deal–based support for welfare state measures, and also to his ultimate political trajectory that saw him serve for many years as a Democratic U.S. senator whose voting record could not be classified as anything other than liberal, and whose last widely publicized political pronouncements constituted a heartfelt outrage at the late-1990s welfare reforms under President Clinton and the new Republican Congress. In the narrower terms of the debate over the Great Society as it unfolded, however, it is also the case that Daniel Patrick Moynihan was quite correctly categorized, along with others connected with *The Public Interest* and some additional fellow-traveling publications such as the monthly *Commentary*, as a paladin of an emerging "neoconservatism" among influential public intellectuals. Hence, whatever his view of himself and his later career, his greatest influence by far in the Great Society debate was most assuredly that of a leading critic.

Daniel Patrick Moynihan, of midwestern background, was born to a Roman Catholic, first-generation American father and a Protestant, old-stock mother in Tulsa on March 16, 1927, but was taken to New York City only a few months later when his father took a job there; he was brought up as a Catholic. A year later the family moved to a New Jersey suburb of the city, and then later to Nassau County, where they lived in comfortable circumstances and regularly spent part of their summers in Indiana with Pat's grandparents. When he was ten, however, his father abandoned the family, and uncertainty, accompanied by frequent movement (Louisville, Indiana, Westchester County, various places in Manhattan), came to characterize his childhood, along with a shortage of money at times, leading him to an extended career of shining shoes in various city locales. He eventually settled at Benjamin Franklin High School on the east side of Manhattan, graduating as class valedictorian in 1942 and gaining admittance to the tuition-free College of the City of New York (CCNY), a famous gateway for many cash-short, ambitious young people such as himself. The coming of World War II improved employment opportunities both for his mother (who opened a bar) and himself; Moynihan loaded and unloaded ship cargoes on the busy West Side piers while attending CCNY. In the spring of 1944 he joined the U.S. Navy's officer training program, which soon sent him to Middlebury College, Vermont, as a Reserve Office Training Corps student, and then in the summer of 1945 to Tufts University in Medford, Massachusetts, from which he was graduated with a degree in naval science. In the fall of 1948 he continued at Tufts, working on a master's degree and supporting regular Democratic nominee Harry Truman over Progressive candidate Henry Wallace in the presidential election. He began doctoral studies at Tufts in 1949; awarded a Fulbright fellowship in 1950, he went to London that fall to study trade unionism at the London School of Economics, remaining for three years.

Back in New York in 1953, by chance he was introduced to city Democratic politics, which in the 1950s would be characterized by the struggle between more old-fashioned "regulars" and newer, generally more affluent, less historically minded "reformers" (next to naval science, Moynihan had taken history courses the most). Moynihan joined the Tilden Democratic Club in Gramercy Park. His life experience allowed him to have a foot in each camp, but his heart was more with the oft-derided—falsely, in Moynihan's view—regulars, politicos more attuned to bread-and-butter issues than to abstractions about "clean government" and such. The regulars were also far more likely to be Roman Catholics like Moynihan than were the reformers. In 1954 he became a speechwriter/aide to Democratic gubernatorial candidate Averell Harriman, who was elected; Moynihan accompanied him to Albany and worked as an assistant to the governor's executive secretary. He married Elizabeth Brennan in May 1955; the lifelong couple had three children by 1960. In the Harriman administration, Moynihan continued to write drafts of speeches and also of reports, making a favorable impression on his superiors. In 1958, Harriman was overwhelmingly defeated in the governor's race by his fellow multimillionaire Nelson Rockefeller. Moynihan landed on his feet when he was assigned by the outgoing governor the task of writing a history of the Harriman administration (never published), which occupied him for much of the next two years, at Syracuse University, where the governor's papers had been deposited.

He also used this time to complete his doctoral dissertation in political science from Tufts, on the International Labor Organization, and, significantly, first appeared in print in the April 30, 1959, issue of Max Ascoli's *The Reporter*, a liberal political magazine, with an article on a topic that was to be of enduring interest to Moynihan: traffic safety. Most significantly, via this publication he established two important connections for his future political and intellectual activities: with Douglas Cater, who later worked in the Johnson administration, and Irving Kristol, probably the most influential editor/ founder of modest-circulation intellectual magazines in the second half of the twentieth century and a central figure in the highly influential group of writers and thinkers known as the "New York intellectuals." The article concluded with a bedrock principle that, then and always, demonstrated Moynihan's bona fides when it came to political labels: "The Federal government will have to do the job" (Hodgson 2000, 62). Moynihan was a liberal; however, he was not a stereotypical, knee-jerk one, as shown in an article published only a few weeks later, also in *The Reporter*, ridiculing the post-Sputnik hysteria and, anticipating President Eisenhower's farewell address of 1961, expressing skepticism about the "trough of Federal aid" into which the nation's scholars were beginning to be thrust (64). Irving Kristol continued to solicit Moynihan for contributions to *The Reporter*, and connected him with another New York intellectual, Nathan Glazer, with whom he collaborated in the highly influential study of continuing ethnic identity beyond the first-generation immigrants in New York City, *Beyond the Melting Pot* (1963), Moynihan writing about the Irish in New York City.

The election of fellow Irish Catholic John F. Kennedy in 1960 naturally provided Moynihan with an opportunity to make his next move, obtaining a job as assistant secretary of labor for policy planning and research in the Department of Labor under Assistant Secretary Willard Wirtz in 1961 and so moving to Washington, D.C. Though never really getting to know any of the Kennedys themselves, Moynihan did interact socially with a wide range of political, intellectual, and media types, establishing and confirming connections all the way. Very late in the Kennedy administration, Moynihan, looking for a new project, convinced Wirtz to make him secretary of a newly formed Presidential Task Force on Manpower Conservation, designed to study the question of the preparedness, physical and mental, of the rising generation for military service. On November 22, 1963, Moynihan testified on Capitol Hill on findings to date that suggested a disproportionately high failure rate of blacks on the selective service tests. The rest of the day, of course, did not proceed according to schedule.

The task force report, published on January 1, 1964, less than a week before the declaration of President Johnson's War on Poverty, claimed that a full one-third of those turning eighteen would be rejected for military service, half of these due to poor scores on mental tests. Along with other governmental departments, the Department of Labor was instructed to develop proposals for fighting the new war. Moynihan, well prepared due to his recent activities, assiduously went to work with an older, more traditional Labor Department/ New Deal tradition, jobs orientation. In the bowels of the federal bureaucracy, another orientation appeared, reflecting newer studies from the social work world of a phenomenon that became trendy in the mid-1950s, "juvenile delinquency." An expression was repeatedly used, "community action," that was to function as a benchmark of controversy for years to come. Moynihan was an immaculately conceived skeptic about the nebulous term and its bastard child, "maximum feasible participation," subjecting them to much critical commentary in his future efforts and writings. At the dawn of the War on Poverty, a centerpiece of the Great Society, Johnson's proposed Economic Opportunity Act, submitted to Congress on Moynihan's birthday, March 16th, naturally enough contained elements from both the schools of thought that had emerged in the hurried putting together of proposals in the winter of 1964. Enacted by Congress with minor changes in late August, the newly created Office of Economic Opportunity would begin the arduous task of implementing a new paradigm, along with administering more traditional approaches to combating poverty.

Very late in 1964, Moynihan began turning focused attention again to a problem of increasing national interest due to the attention paid to the civil rights movement, then cresting, and one central to his task force report: the achivement gap between blacks and whites. Moynihan initiated a study on the connection between fatherlessness in black families and the unemployment problem. Of course he profoundly knew from firsthand experience the potential negative effect of paternal abandonment on a family's financial standing. With the Civil Rights Act of 1964 in the books, what should come next in dealing with the United States' newly central race question? He was soon working on what would become known as the Moynihan Report, documenting the rapid increase in the number of fatherless black families, deemed an obvious social pathology, and the hugely disproportionate number of black women on Aid to Families with Dependent Children (AFDC, or welfare) relative to their share in the general population—even during periods when the unemployment rate for black men was falling. 1965 proved to be the pivotal year for Moynihan; in retrospect, it seemed ironic that he received an Arthur S. Flemming Award as One of the Ten Outstanding Young Men in the Federal Government in recognition of his role as "an architect of the nation's program to eradicate poverty."

In late February 1965, Moynihan appeared at a conference on poverty held at the University of California, Berkeley, striking a notably cautionary note in speaking on "Three Problems in Combating Poverty," where he noted the perhaps surprising fact that the "war" had not developed out of a social context of depression, nor was it a product of any great public

demand (Moynihan 1965, 41). Instead, it "was more of a rational than a political event," a program "developed by research and experimentation" (43).
Government officials, he argued, needed "to be candid with the public where
we feel there are gaps in our knowledge, or weaknesses in our argument"
(44). In an allusion to the Moynihan Report, he noted that careful consideration of the poverty issue was "leading us steadily towards a much more realistic view of the importance of maintaining a stable family structure at all
levels of the society," citing as an example the increased awareness of the
perversity of the old AFDC "man-in-the-house" rule that actually encouraged paternal abandonment of families. He then directly attacked some of
the forces he had been fighting within the government over the emerging antipoverty programs: "I am a little suspicious of those who are too much en-
amored of the poor. There is a long tradition in Western humanitarianism of
imputing to suffering but inanimate creatures—or social classes—a delicacy
of feeling, a heightened sensibility that unfailingly commends itself to the so-
licitude of other, more fortunate, persons who also share those qualities"
(49). Most particularly, Moynihan feared "a theme running through much
of the academic literature on community action . . . which indulges this
temptation to some considerable length" (50). The idea that "the war on
poverty can be won by welfare work" was firmly rejected: "It cannot" (52).
The trade union movement, with its emphasis, in the American tradition, on
concrete benefits and social solidarity, was recommended to the conference
attendees in Berkeley instead (41–53). In no way did Moynihan suggest that
it was inappropriate or unwise for the federally funded experimentation to
proceed, no doubt understanding that this was an utter given for his audience; rather, his message was intended to raise a point he suspected might
need to be stressed. Like his audience, Moynihan favored a federal antipoverty effort. A few months later, he was a contributor to the inaugural issue of a small-circulation quarterly edited by Nathan Glazer and Daniel Bell,
The Public Interest, a periodical destined to house much criticism of the
Great Society programs in practice. But here, Moynihan, writing on "The
Professionalization of Reform," struck an optimistic tone about the prospects
for the unfolding "war."

   Later in the spring of 1965 Moynihan completed his position paper, eventually published as *The Negro Family: The Case for National Action*. While
the civil rights revolution was real and had already succeeded mightily in
breaking down barriers, unexpectedly, the black-white gap was not narrow-
ing nearly as much as might be hoped or thought. Given rising expectations,
this would prove unacceptable if the trend continued, as Moynihan feared it
would. The problem lay in the lower-class black family where fatherlessness
was greater than ever, with massive unemployment the key historic social
indicator behind the statistic. President Kennedy's rising tide of economic
expansion was not lifting the boats of the black underclass, which was growing. No particular policy recommendations were included in the report,

though the subtitle made it obvious that action was required in the author's view. Johnson eventually read a summary of the report and determined to make it the basis of his to-be-famous commencement address delivered at Washington's historically black Howard University on June 4, 1965; Moynihan provided some assistance with the preparation of the speech, which, though of course it did not mention the report, nonetheless obviously was based on its fundamental analysis and values.

In July 1965, Daniel Patrick Moynihan tendered his resignation from the Johnson administration, as he had been induced to run for president of the City Council of New York (he and the slate he had been recruited to be a part of lost). Johnson had developed a suspicion of anyone associated with Robert F. Kennedy, Jr., who had established a New York City residence in the fall of 1964 in preparation for what would turn out to be a successful Senate candidacy two years later. Though Moynihan did not really travel in the Kennedy circles, he was associated with the "Harvards" in Johnson's mind. Now, Moynihan was a former member of the administration that had brought the world the Great Society. He still identified with its guiding principles, as shown in a campaign speech in which he called for a tremendous increase in federal spending directed toward cities. Moynihan and his slate went down by substantial margins in the September Democratic primary.

A few weeks before, syndicated newspaper columnists Rowland Evans and Robert Novak devoted their August 18th column to "The Moynihan Report," giving it its first publicity and presenting it in a way that seemed to allow for what would come to be known (from a harsh critique published in a leftist magazine by a Boston psychologist who had not read the report) as the "blaming the victim" approach to poverty. The column failed to stress Moynihan's central belief that, whatever its historical origins in slavery or institutionalized white supremacy as practiced in the United States in the century after the Civil War, unemployment, not character flaws, was what lay behind the family breakdown that was exacerbating the problem (Hodgson 2000, 114). Suddenly the report was in the public domain, being discussed in such venues as *Newsweek*.

Civil rights leaders, meeting with the president for the purpose of organizing a planned 1966 White House conference (which, when eventually held, produced nothing) in the spirit of the Howard University address, on what was to come next—"To Fulfill These Rights"—expressed their extreme unhappiness with at least their understanding of the public representation of the Moynihan Report. As things happened, the Los Angeles neighborhood known as Watts acquired its fame only a couple of weeks after the Evans and Novak column, furthering an increasingly tense atmosphere among the planners of the conference. Some leaders of the then-influential, well-connected, and wealthy mainline Protestant churches, especially in New York, who had made the civil rights movement their modern-day social gospel focus, issued public denunciations of the report that angered Moynihan, who found it hard to believe they had actually read it; their moralistic tone, on top of their intellectual speciousness, was personally irritating. Beyond that, his reputation and even his future were at stake.

Of course Moynihan had no problem with substantive, serious critiques of his work, such as that published in the liberal Roman Catholic magazine *Commonweal* by Columbia University sociology professor Herbert Gans. Nor was Gans alone; many considered and more-than-fair treatments of his work appeared, including in publications known to have a liberal orientation (Steinfels 1979, 130). But the street-violence atmosphere in the post-Watts era and beyond (several consecutive "long, hot summers" characterized by rioting and what some saw as imminent social breakdown ensued) did not lend itself to even relatively dispassionate discourse on America's "race question." As Moynihan recalled in a 1967 article in *Commentary*, a magazine published by the American Jewish Committee that was in the same orbit as *The Public Interest*, but with a far greater circulation, and that was very shortly to become a platform for critiques of "the liberal Left" and of parts of the Great Society itself, "I found myself the object of incredible accusations, some of them from academia," perpetrated by people who were practicing "the scholarship of Che Guevara." In a private letter from early 1966, Moynihan described the unfolding story as "a nightmare of misunderstanding, and misinterpretation, and misstatement" (Hodgson 2000, 118–19). This is clearly how Moynihan *felt* about his treatment.

It proved to be a determinative experience for Moynihan for the rest of the 1960s and beyond; he would have nothing to do with the "extreme" left and in fact heaped contempt on them. The fall of 1965 saw the debut of *The Public Interest*, to whose founding issue Moynihan contributed an article, and through which he became connected with people who shared his basic orientation: centrist, mainstream liberals who sought an increased federal effort to alleviate social problems, guided by careful, professional social science such as that which they practiced in their own careers. A tone of skepticism, combined with a belief in the worthiness of trying and the possibilities of government-induced improvement, characterized the publication. Moynihan obtained a sinecure at a think tank based at Wesleyan University in Connecticut from which he could get away from it all for a while, ponder the unfolding of the Great Society, rethink his positions, and produce written replies to his obtuse critics as well as articles on a variety of topics reflecting his catholic interests.

The reasonably hopeful tone of his first *Public Interest* article, about the new, professional basis of reform, was gone a year later, when Moynihan published "What Is 'Community Action'?" in the fall 1966 issue. Of all the Great Society initiatives, "none began with wider approval or larger expectation than the war on poverty" (Moynihan 1966, 3). Now, however, the war had become the first Great Society program "to become the object of controversy, conflict, and, in some measure, disappointment." Part of the explanation lay in "the way we rush into things" (3). More specifically, at the center of controversy lay the requirement of Title II of the Economic Opportunity Act for so-called community participation under the rubric "maximum feasible participation," which had produced for the program a dismaying reputation for "trouble-making" (3). This was no accident, but rather a product of design: "Many program activists assumed they were expected, even required, to *make* trouble" (4). Washington, it turned out, had wanted "a great many things that could not simultaneously be had" (4). The cycle of poverty was to be attacked via "Coordinate Community Action Programs," as Walter Heller, the chairman of the President's Council of Economic Advisors, had instructed involved cabinet members, calling in a memorandum dated December 20, 1963, for stress to be placed on local areas; local initiatives with federal government support; evaluation and coordination of existing federal, state, local, and private programs; *and* the testing and demonstration of new ones. *Twelve weeks later*, the Economic Opportunity Act was presented to Congress.

The poverty programs had been put together in these few weeks by small task forces, whose members were pragmatic, intellectual, and even skeptical, assembled under the direction of Peace Corps founder and director Sargent Shriver. Many task force members had experience with existing political machines, both pro and con. From the beginning there had been concern "that not all the jobs go to 'social workers.'" A February 23 meeting produced a draft with nearly the exact wording of Title II's section on Community Action Organization, reflecting a desire to create new structures that would see more people getting involved. What did "community action" mean to the task force, Moynihan asked. As things had turned out, the influence of an old Chicago radical, Saul Alinsky, whose book *Rules for Radicals* became a kind of cult classic, was determinative. Under the Alinsky concept, the poor, who needed power, obtained it via community organizing, "by inducing conflict," the guiding principle being "disruption." Alinsky himself had seen one of his Chicago neighborhood organizations, the Woodlawn Organization, take a leading role in harshly criticizing the administration of Mayor Richard Daley, the leader of America's urban political machine par excellence.

How politically effective had community action turned out to be in practice? Though its impact of course varied, it had, Moynihan charged, proven "unsatisfactory to almost everyone involved," most significantly in alienating many working-class groups (Moynihan 1966, 7). As an example, he cited a "bitter and disorderly protest" in the fall of 1966 over the opening of Intermediate School 201 in Harlem. With the active participation of employees of a local Community Action Program, the protesters, whose "street agitation . . . was flagrantly anti-white and anti-Semitic," demanded community control of school personnel decisions (two years later, in 1968, a celebrated, drawn-out, and extremely bitter teachers' strike would explode over the same issues in the Ocean Hill–Brownsville neighborhood of Brooklyn). The lesson to be drawn was thus: "Government intervention in social processes is risky, uncertain—and necessary. It requires enthusiasm, but also intellect, and above all it needs an appreciation of how difficult it is to change things and people" (8).

Two issues later (in the spring of 1967), Moynihan again attacked how the antipoverty program was unfolding, comparing the War on Poverty in the cities to the increasingly controversial War in Vietnam, entitling his lead "Comment" article for the issue "A Crisis of Confidence?" Federal efforts to deal with urban problems were not new in the 1960s, dating back to the 1930s and 1940s, but with the new departure of the Great Society, attention was again being paid; results, unfortunately, "have been anything but spectacular." With the continued growth of urban programs, it was more important than ever to address "the problem of objectively evaluating" them. He praised a system first ordered by President Johnson in the summer of 1965 and first employed in May 1966 (though derived from efforts by Defense Secretary Robert McNamara as far back as 1961) known as the Planning-Programming-Budgeting System (PPBS), and noted that the Office of Economic Opportunity had begun its efforts with an "attachment to research and evaluation." Head Start, the popular Great Society preschool education program established in 1965, had "begun on the basis of good research information." Early reports cast doubt on the lasting effects of the program, leading some to argue that the program should be transformed into a year-round one, something Moynihan considered well worth thinking about. But he noted that, more recently, OEO had announced an initiative— "clearly an expensive proposal"—to reduce pupil-teacher ratios in elementary schools, in spite of fifty years of research, recently reinforced by a study made by James Coleman published by the Department of Health, Education and Welfare in the summer of 1966, *Equality of Educational Opportunity*, immediately known as the "Coleman Report," showing little if any correlation between student academic achievement and class size. Limited funding, then, would be going toward hiring more college-educated schoolteachers rather than directly to the poor.

This was key to Moynihan. What did the poor really need—a strategy oriented toward the provision of services, or income? The answer was disarmingly simple: money. Moynihan cited a pilot project begun in 1961 under the auspices of President Kennedy's Committee on Juvenile Delinquency to test the social work, service delivery hypothesis—"a social scientist's dream." "But five years later," Moynihan was so bold to inquire, "what has come of it all? . . . [A]fter the expenditure of many millions of dollars, we don't seem to know any more about delinquency than when we undertook to find out about it five years ago." He admitted that, when it came to evaluating social programs, ambivalence was fundamental, since in this realm, "facts are simply not neutral—they are inescapably political," and that researchers, at least those outside of the executive branch, were "in some measures subject to constant, if subtle, pressure to produce 'positive' findings." He observed that some people expressed worry that public support for the Great Society's War on Poverty was in danger of evaporating rapidly; not so, replied Moynihan. "The American public is supporting a fantastic array of social services, and continues to do so in ever larger amounts. The issue, then, is not *whether*, but *which*" (Moynihan 1967, 8). The continued enormous expenditure on domestic programs, which long outlasted the explicit invocation of the expressions "Great Society" or "War on Poverty," bore this out.

In his last contribution to *The Public Interest* published during the Johnson administration, Daniel Patrick Moynihan again poured cold water on what was going on in the War on Poverty with his lengthy lead article, "The Crisis in Welfare," published in the winter 1968 issue. A fundamental error of the "war" had been the well-known "American fault to insist on extravagant goals—as if to set out to achieve anything less than everything suggests a lack of sincerity, manliness, or both" (Moynihan 1968, 6). Expectations had been set too high. And, returning to his point of what really ailed the poor—lack of funds—Moynihan pointed out that the United States was "the only industrial democracy in the world that does not have a family allowance" (24). Later, during the Nixon administration, which he joined at its outset as the president's assistant for urban affairs, Moynihan would try but fail to change this fact, which remained the case into the twenty-first century.

Through the workings of James Q. Wilson, a professor of government at Harvard University who had connected with him over the final publishing details of *Beyond the Melting Pot*, Moynihan obtained the post of director of the Joint Center for Urban Studies of Harvard and the Massachusetts Institute of Technology, founded in 1959 and now receiving generous funding, especially from the Ford Foundation. Living near Harvard, Moynihan socialized with James Q. Wilson and Nathan Glazer and their families. Glazer, an education and sociology professor, was an early figure at *The Public Interest* and one of the first to publicly reflect, in *Commentary*, on how the disorders of the late 1960s had caused him to become more conservative, if not altogether so. Much of Moynihan's considerable work at Harvard lay in the realm of public outreach, including weekly lunches for scholars of urban studies in residence or visiting, work on television programs, and publications designed for the educated reading public rather than for hard-core scholars, such as *The Public Interest*. He was to enjoy for the rest of his life an extraordinarily positive treatment from the mainstream press, reflecting in large measure his engaging personality, witty turn of phrase, and obvious intelligence. In the more standard academic realm, he organized a seminar on the findings of James Coleman, whose 1966 Coleman Report questioning the conventional wisdom as to actual benefits of well-meaning, good-sounding increased government spending on the education of the poor proved of greater long-lasting controversy than had Moynihan's; he coedited with Frederick Mosteller a substantial collection of the fruits of this seminar in the hefty 1972 volume *On Equality of Educational Opportunity*. The introduction to this collection, which he cowrote, reiterates the skepticism of the Coleman Report while renewing Moynihan's belief in the centrality of employment to dealing with the poverty problem: "*We recommend increased family-income and employment-training programs, together with plans for the evaluation of their long-run effects on education*" (Mosteller and Moynihan 1972, 56). Regarding the schools themselves, his boilerplate recommendation was for increased funding for experimentation, including careful analysis of their results, leavened by "patience and good sense" (64).

Moynihan continued to get around and participate in the debate about the Great Society far from the confines of Cambridge, Massachusetts. In March 1967, for instance, participating in a seminar organized by New York Governor Nelson Rockefeller called to consider alternative approaches to welfare, he spoke to the then-influential Americans for Democratic Action, an established liberal group, warning of the dangers of succumbing to the New Left and calling for collaboration with saner elements of centrist moderate-to-conservative types, including such Republicans. A few months later, in June, he spoke to the Harvard chapter of Phi Beta Kappa (the speech appeared in that organization's publication, *The American Scholar*, the following fall) on the student movement with sympathy for its quasi-religious quest for community, but more critically of the secular, liberal Establishment whose policies it was protesting. Referring specifically to foreign policy, yet making a point that could equally apply to the War on Poverty as fought so far, Moynihan stated, "Liberals have simply got to restrain their enthusiasm for civilizing others. It is their greatest weakness and ultimate arrogance. . . . We have not been able to get rid of poverty, and begin to perceive that some of our more treasured liberal reforms may have had unanticipated consequences that may even make it more difficult to do so" (Moynihan 1975, 128, 129).

Moynihan daringly responded to the only somewhat surprising, given his writings, overtures from Richard Nixon to join his new administration in 1969, where he prepared a guaranteed national income scheme that ultimately took form as the doomed Family Assistance Plan. The invitation itself is a sign of the role Moynihan was now playing in the debate over the Great Society—a founding father who, seemingly, had disinherited his own child. This was certainly not how Moynihan himself saw it, as he tried to explain on numerous occasions. In the late spring of 1967, Moynihan had delivered the Clarke A. Sanford Lectures on Local Government and Community Life at the State University Agricultural and Technical College at Delhi, New York. This apparently unpromising and obscure invitation led to Moynihan producing his most extended analysis of what he saw to be the failures of the

Great Society antipoverty program, which he wrote up in the summer of 1968 and published the following year as *Maximum Feasible Misunderstanding: Community Action in the War on Poverty*. The lectures, which he intended as a kind of obituary for much of the Great Society's more radical efforts, specifically the Community Action Programs (over 1,000 of them eventually) that had constituted the heart of the "economic opportunity" initiatives, were a historical account of Moynihan's personal experiences in the inner debates within the government over the creation of the CAPs and the "maximum feasible participation" concept, the revolution of rising and completely unrealizable expectations, and the inevitable backlash in such locales as Syracuse and Chicago Moynihan's simple, stark conclusion, the summary of his entire argument, was this: "*The government did not know what it was doing*" (Moynihan 1970, 170; italics in original). Yet it had proceeded anyway, with disastrous results.

When the book was reprinted in a paperback edition, Moynihan supplied a new introduction, dated January 11, 1970. The 1960s were now officially over, the Nixon administration was in power and seeking withdrawal from both the Vietnam War and the War on Poverty, and Moynihan was using his preface again to sum up the Great Society's contribution to the unproductive turbulence that had characterized the recent past. Explicitly invoking Robert Graves's classic twentieth-century memoir of the old, prewar English social order, *Goodbye to All That*, Moynihan bade farewell to a political era that had very suddenly and dramatically drawn to a close. Not that there was not substantial continuity: despite critics' expectations, the Nixon administration had not jettisoned the Office of Economic Opportunity (jarringly, from a twenty-first-century perspective, Moynihan observed that "Donald Rumsfeld, a liberal young Republican," had been named OEO director); even the CAPs continued, Nixon being fundamentally neutral where they were concerned. Central to this continuity was the continuing Democratic control of Congress, which persisted uninterrupted through the 1970s until the Reagan landslide of 1980 produced a GOP Senate. (OEO itself was eventually abolished in 1974.)

What, then, exactly *had* occurred that led Moynihan to say a "political era" had ended? It was the role of the intellectuals, "professors-in-government," that Moynihan stressed. The early 1960s had witnessed "a precipitous and unprecedented rise to influence of university intellectuals in the councils of government, most notably that of the national government. . . . The late 1960's was marked by an equally precipitous decline in the position of these professors" (Moynihan 1970, xxxi). Moynihan was at pains to reiterate what his text argued: social science was "getting to be more useful," and was not to be rejected at all, especially in measuring results—"But forward vision remains rather blurred" (xxix). Moynihan favored soldiering on in the effort to alleviate poverty. But, indicative of his changed position, he chose to give OEO Director Donald Rumsfeld the last word as he wrote from Washington on January 11, 1970: "Few programs were ever so unformed at birth and few were so completely and broadly defined, for good or ill, by the times in which they were implemented. Perhaps the story of Community Action must be told by a poet or mystic rather than a politician or historian" (xxxvii).

Daniel Patrick Moynihan was to lead several other lives in the decades that remained to him, as an aggressive U.S. ambassador "in opposition," as he put it, to the United Nations in the 1970s, one of the many low points in the history of that organization's relations with the United States, and of course for four terms as a U.S. senator from New York. He remained a Democrat and, in the 1990s under a Republican Congress and Democratic President Bill Clinton, he voiced a rather lonely cry against a proposed welfare-reform bill that passed by a very wide, bipartisan margin. His last public service appointment was made by President George W. Bush, to the Social Security Commission, making it nine consecutive presidents who had employed his services. He died on March 26, 2003.

APPENDIX: BRIEF BIOGRAPHIES

Abernathy, Ralph David. Born March 11, 1926, in Linden, Alabama; died April 17, 1990, at Atlanta. Son of a landowning, respected farmer, after four years of army service in World War II, Abernathy earned a bachelor's degree in mathematics at Alabama State University in Montgomery; during his college years he was ordained a Baptist minister (1948). In 1951 he earned a master's degree in sociology at Atlanta University (now Clark Atlanta University). He returned to Montgomery to assume the pastorate of the First Baptist Church, later forming a lasting partnership with Martin Luther King, Jr., especially with the Montgomery bus boycott of 1955–56. Together with King and other black ministers, he established the Atlanta-based Southern Christian Leadership Conference (SCLC); he moved to Atlanta in 1961 to become pastor of the West Hunter Street Baptist Church and also SCLC vice president. He participated in all the great civil rights marches and struggles of the 1960s, and assumed the SCLC presidency after the death of King in 1968, then leading the Poor People's Campaign march to Washington. In 1977, he resigned the SCLC presidency to return to full-time ministry. *Bibliography*: Ralph David Abernathy, *And the Walls Came Tumbling Down: An Autobiography* (New York: Harper & Row, 1989); and Adam Fairclough, *To Redeem the Soul of America: The Southern Christian Leadership Conference and Martin Luther King, Jr.* (Athens: University of Georgia Press, 1987).

Baker, Ella. Born December 16, 1903, in Norfolk, Virginia; died December 13, 1986, in New York City. Ella Jo Baker, raised in North Carolina, graduated in 1929 as class valedictorian from Shaw University in Raleigh, North Carolina, thereupon moving to New York City, where she joined various left-wing organizations aimed at bettering the conditions of blacks. From 1940 to 1946 she was a staff member for the National Association for the Advancement of Colored People (NAACP), helping organize local NAACP chapters, including in Montgomery, Alabama. In 1957, she moved to Atlanta to assist in the creation of Martin Luther King, Jr.'s new Southern Christian Leadership Conference. She promoted voter registration in the South via the Crusade for Citizenship organization. After the 1960 sit-ins by college students at the Woolworth's lunch counter in Greensboro, North Carolina, Baker helped organize a meeting for student leaders held at her alma mater, Shaw, there playing a pivotal role in getting the new Student Nonviolent Coordinating Committee (SNCC) off the ground, and retained an orientation toward grassroots organizing and activism as opposed to national-level strategies. *Bibliography*: Barbara Ransby, *Ella Baker and the Black Freedom Movement: A Radical Democratic Vision* (Chapel Hill: University of North Carolina Press, 2003); and Stokely Carmichael, *Ready for Revolution: The Life and Struggles of Stokely Carmichael (Kwame Ture)* (New York: Scribner, 2003).

Brown, H. Rap. Born October 4, 1943, in Baton Rouge, Louisiana. He was introduced to the developing civil rights movement in the early 1960s while visiting his politically active brother Ed Brown at Howard University. He worked in the Student Nonviolent Coordinating Committee, becoming chairman in 1967. He led civil rights protests in Cambridge, Maryland, long a site of SNCC activism, which led to his arrest for inciting a riot. Leaving SNCC, in 1968 he became a founder of the California-based Black Panther Party, holding the title of justice minister. In the late 1960s he became one of the public faces of the black power movement, producing a familiar quote that violence was "as American as cherry pie." In the 1970s he appeared on the Ten Most Wanted List of the Federal Bureau of Investigation and was convicted of robbery, eventually serving five years in the Attica (New York) state prison. In 1975 he embraced Islam, took the name Jamil Abdullah al-Amin, and helped establish an Islamic community in Atlanta. In 2002 he was convicted of killing a sheriff's deputy and sentenced to prison. *Bibliography*: Clayborne Carson, *In Struggle: SNCC and the Black Awakening of the 1960s* (Cambridge, MA: Harvard University Press, 1981).

Cloward, Richard. Born December 25, 1926, in Rochester, New York; died August 20, 2001, in New York City. Son of a Baptist minister, Cloward, after service in the U.S. Navy (1944–46), graduated from the University of Rochester in 1949, earned a master's degree in social work from Columbia University in 1950, and then earned a Ph.D. in sociology at Columbia in 1958. During service in the U.S. Army (1951–54), he did social work in Pennsylvania. He joined the faculty at the university's School of Social Work in 1954, serving until his death. In 1960, he coauthored, with Lloyd Ohlin, a study of juvenile delinquency that argued that inner-city delinquents acted rationally in response to the lack of available opportunities. This work led to the creation on the Lower East Side of Manhattan of Mobilization for

Youth, which influenced the early planning of the Great Society's War on Poverty. Through this work he met Frances Fox Piven, a political scientist at the City University of New York, who became his longtime collaborator as well as his wife. Cloward, a longtime professor of sociology, epitomized the politically radical professor as social activist during his long career, which was characterized by concern over poverty and inequality in the United States. *Bibliography*: Richard Cloward, *Delinquency and Opportunity; a Theory of Delinquent Gangs* (Glencoe, IL: The Free Press, 1960); and *The Politics of Turmoil; Essays on Poverty, Race, and the Urban Crisis* (New York: Pantheon, 1974).

Coleman, James. Born in Bedford, Indiana, May 12, 1926; died at Chicago, Illinois, March 25, 1995. After two years at Emory & Henry College in Virginia, he graduated from Purdue University in 1949 with a bachelor's degree in chemical engineering and earned a Ph.D. in sociology at Columbia University in 1955. A scholar at Johns Hopkins University, where he founded the Department of Social Relations (later Sociology), he returned to become University Professor of Sociology at the University of Chicago (where he had taught from 1956 to 1959) in 1973. Coleman was a pioneer researcher on educational topics, including integration and the factors accounting for student success in school. The Civil Rights Act of 1964 mandated the U.S. Commissioner of Education to conduct a study on the question of educational opportunity; in 1966, *Equality of Educational Opportunity* was published, the result of a team of investigators' work. The study, which soon became known as the "Coleman Report," provided powerful ammunition to many Great Society critics by casting doubt on the effects of per-pupil-expenditure or class size on student achievement, findings so discomforting as to be nearly unbelievable, and hence often disputed as well as ignored. The report did suggest that lower-class blacks benefited from attending integrated schools. In the 1970s, Coleman's studies suggested that pro-integration school busing programs tended to accelerate "white flight" from urban to suburban school districts. *Bibliography*: James S. Coleman et al., *Equality of Educational Opportunity*, 2 vols. (Washington, DC: U.S. Government Printing Office, 1966); and Frederick Mosteller and Daniel P. Moynihan, eds., *On Equality of Educational Opportunity: Papers Deriving from the Harvard University Faculty Seminar on the Coleman Report* (New York: Vintage, 1972).

Coles, Robert. Born in Boston, Massachusetts, October 29, 1929. Coles grew up in a household that subscribed to Dorothy Day's *The Catholic Worker*. He graduated from the Boston Latin School in 1946, proceeding to Harvard College, from which he received a bachelor's degree in English. In 1955 he earned a medical degree from the College of Physicians and Surgeons, Columbia University, eventually specializing in child psychiatry. Air

Force duty took him to Biloxi, Mississippi; he served as a research psychiatrist for the Southern Regional Council, Atlanta. He began teaching at Harvard University and eventually became professor of psychiatry and medical humanities at the Medical School there in 1977. Coles attracted widespread attention beginning in the 1960s with the publication of a series of articles in national magazines such as *The New Republic*, *Harper's*, and *The Atlantic Monthly*. Out of his work came a series of books, relating in story-like fashion the plight of children in poverty, each called *Children of Crisis*, extending into the next decade and eventually reaching five volumes. Building on the increased attention being paid to the question of poverty in the affluent United States, Coles successfully put a human face on poverty and spotlighted its effects on children. *Bibliography*: Robert Coles, *Children of Crisis*, 5 vols. (Boston: Little, Brown, 1966–77).

Hamer, Fannie Lou. Born October 16, 1917, Montgomery County, Mississippi; died on March 14, 1977, Mound Bayou, Mississippi. Hamer was the twentieth child born to Mississippi sharecroppers and received a limited formal education. In 1962, when the Student Nonviolent Coordinating Committee began organizational efforts in the Mississippi Delta region, she joined the campaign, first attempting to register to vote on August 31, 1962, and continued to work in voter registration drives with SNCC and the Southern Christian Leadership Conference. A founding member of the Mississippi Freedom Democratic Party, an alternative to the all-white state "regular" Democrats, she attended the 1964 Democratic National Convention at Atlantic City and electrified the audience and much of the nation with her televised testimony before the credentials committee describing the intimidation and repeated physical abuse, including by government authorities, leveled at her and other black Mississippians attempting to vote. She and other delegation members refused the heavy-handed compromise put forth by the party Establishment, further enshrining her as a civil rights movement heroine. She later worked in promoting cooperative farming in Sunflower County, Mississippi, her home. *Bibliography*: Kay Mills, *This Little Light of Mine; the Life of Fannie Lou Hamer* (New York: E. P. Dutton, 1993).

Heller, Walter. Born in Buffalo, New York on August 27, 1915; died on June 15, 1987 near Seattle, Washington. An economist whose career was spent at the University of Minnesota, Heller served as chairman of the Council of Economic Advisers between 1961 and 1964. A tax expert who favored reductions in marginal rates, he was also involved during the Kennedy administration in the early planning for what would become the War on Poverty. Upon LBJ's accession to the presidency, Heller informed the president of the ongoing poverty task force and got the green light from Johnson for the effort. *Bibliography*: Walter Heller, *New Dimensions of Political Economy* (Cambridge, MA: Harvard University Press, 1966).

Humphrey, Hubert. Born in Wallace, South Dakota, on May 27, 1911; died in Waverly, Minnesota, January 13, 1978. After a short career as a pharmacist in Huron, South Dakota, Hubert Horatio Humphrey, Jr., enrolled at the University of Minnesota, graduating in 1939. He was elected mayor of Minneapolis in 1945 and a U.S. senator from Minnesota on the Democratic-Farmer-Labor ticket in 1948; at the Democratic National Convention that year, he passionately and successfully spoke in favor of adding a civil rights plank to the party platform, establishing his national reputation. He was a favorite of labor unions and forcefully advocated welfare spending throughout his career, and he was known as the "Happy Warrior" due to his ebullient personality and speaking style. As Democratic party whip in the U.S. Senate from 1961 to 1964, he was involved in breaking the long-standing deadlock over meaningful civil rights legislation. Lyndon Johnson nonetheless kept him on a short leash during Humphrey's term as LBJ's vice president (1965–69). He narrowly lost the 1968 presidential election to Richard Nixon. He again was elected a senator from Minnesota in 1970 and died in office. *Bibliography*: Hubert H. Humphrey, *The Education of a Public Man: My Life and Politics* (Minneapolis: University of Minnesota Press, 1991); and Timothy N. Thurber, *The Politics of Equality: Hubert H. Humphrey and the African American Freedom Struggle* (New York: Columbia University Press, 1999).

Kennedy, Robert. Born in Boston, Massachusetts, on November 20, 1925; died in Los Angeles, California, on June 6, 1968. Robert Francis Kennedy was born into one of the United States' leading political families of the mid-twentieth century. After two years in the U.S. Navy Reserve (1944–46), he received a bachelor's degree from Harvard University in 1948 and then a law degree in 1951 at the University of Virginia. His first serious political work came on behalf of the successful 1952 Senate campaign of his brother, John F. Kennedy. He held various government legal positions in the 1950s. After serving as his brother's campaign manager in 1960, he was named by the new president as attorney general of the United States. He had an uneasy relationship at best with Lyndon B. Johnson and resigned as attorney general on September 3, 1964, in order to run for the U.S. Senate seat from New York, where he had grown up as a child. He served as a Democratic senator from New York from January 3, 1965, until his assassination on June 6, 1968. He was a supporter of various Great Society programs and, inheriting the glamour and widespread appeal of his martyred brother, came to embody the hopes of mainstream liberal activists for a continued and expanded War on Poverty, especially after he publicly criticized President Johnson's handling of the Vietnam War. His presidential candidacy was snuffed out by an assassin in the second great political murder of the turbulent year of 1968. *Bibliography*: Arthur M. Schlesinger, Jr., *Robert Kennedy and His Times*, 2 vols. (Boston: Houghton Mifflin, 1978).

Kristol, Irving. Born 1920 in New York, New York. From a poor immigrant family, Irving Kristol rose to become one of the United States' preeminent public intellectuals. He graduated from the College of the City of New York with a bachelor's degree in history in 1940. He served as a staff sergeant in the U.S. Army in Europe during World War II, after which he began an extended career in magazine editing and publishing. In 1947 he became managing editor of *Commentary*, serving until 1952; in 1953, he coedited the British publication *Encounter*, with poet Stephen Spender, until 1958; in 1959–60, he was editor of a political magazine started by Max Ascoli, *The Reporter*. He was a prolific writer of controversial essays throughout his editorial and publishing career. He was the founding coeditor, with Daniel Bell, of *The Public Interest*, an influential social science quarterly that published many hard-headed critiques of the Great Society, including articles by Daniel Patrick Moynihan, Edward Banfield, and Congresswoman Edith Green, which collectively began to create a political persuasion that came to be known as "neoconservatism," whose "godfather" Kristol was often said to be, given his editorial/publishing role. During the 1960s, Kristol was executive vice president of Basic Books in New York. From 1969 to 1988, he was professor of social thought at the Graduate School of Business, New York University, and he became a regular contributor to the *Wall Street Journal*. He later moved to Washington, D.C., to found a neoconservative quarterly devoted to foreign affairs, *The National Interest*, in 1985, serving as its publisher until 2002. *Bibliography*: Irving Kristol, *Neoconservatism: The Autobiography of an Idea* (New York: The Free Press, 1995); and Gary Dorrien, *The Neoconservative Mind: Politics, Culture, and the War of Ideology* (Philadelphia: Temple University Press, 1993).

Lindsay, John. Born on November 24, 1921, in New York City; died on December 19, 2000, at Hilton Head, South Carolina. After a preparatory school education, John Lindsay, who was from only a modestly successful family despite his unshakable image as a wealthy, white Anglo-Saxon Protestant, earned a B.A. from Yale University in 1944. He served in the U.S. Navy from 1943 to 1946 and earned a law degree from the Yale University School of Law in 1949. He was elected to the first of three consecutive terms as a Republican congressman from the Upper East Side of Manhattan in 1958. He was a strong supporter of civil rights laws and the new social initiatives promoted by Lyndon B. Johnson. He was elected mayor of New York City in 1964, where he became an articulate advocate of greatly increased welfare spending and expansion of Great Society programs; as a Republican mayor, he attracted great attention as a politically liberal leader in the cause of securing more federal money to deal with the urban crisis. He was given much credit for his active engagement, including walking the streets the evening of the assassination of Martin Luther King, Jr., with the city population during the tense late 1960s, leading to New York's avoidance of a major riot, unlike many other American cities of the era. Numerous significant labor disputes with public employees proved daunting to Lindsay's government, as did soaring crime. Narrowly reelected mayor in 1968 in a multicandidate race, Lindsay became a Democrat in 1971 and served out his term, leaving the mayoralty in 1973. His tenure as mayor was in the long term regarded as controversial on account of the city's brush with bankruptcy in the 1970s and then its revival under a very different philosophy of government in the 1990s. *Bibliography*: Vincent J. Cannato, *The Ungovernable City: John Lindsay and His Struggle to Save New York* (New York: Basic/Perseus, 2001).

Malcolm X. Born on May 19, 1925, in Omaha, Nebraska; died on February 21, 1965, at New York City. Born Malcoln Little, the man who would take the name Malcolm X upon his joining the Black Muslims (Nation of Islam) grew up in Lansing, Michigan, in foster care after his mother's mental breakdown. Despite childhood academic success, he dropped out of high school and moved to Boston, where a life of crime led to his conviction for burglary and incarceration until his parole in 1952. While in prison, he became acquainted with the teachings of Detroit religious leader Elijah Muhammad, founder of the Black Muslims. He dropped his given surname "Little," replacing it with "X" to signify his rejection of his "slave name" and the impossibility of recovering his ancestral African name. He devoted his life for the rest of the 1950s to spreading the black pride, black separatist ideology of Elijah Muhammad and was extremely successful, becoming a commanding presence and gifted communicator. A television documentary produced in 1959 by Mike Wallace for the Columbia Broadcasting System (CBS), *The Hate That Hate Produced*, greatly increased his fame, as well as that of the Black Muslims. Malcolm X's media coverage greatly increased with the rise of the 1960s civil rights movement. He acquired notoriety for suggesting that the murder of President Kennedy meant that the "chickens had come home to roost" for white America, with its violent past, and he made familiar a line, delivered often with a self-confident tone seen as threatening by many, "by any means necessary." In March 1964, having learned of a sexual scandal involving the Nation of Islam's leader, Malcolm X separated himself from the organization he had done so much to build up and began moving toward international Islam, a shift solidified by his trip to Mecca that same year that also resulted in his becoming more interested in the possibilities of integrated efforts at achieving racial and social justice. Upon formally embracing Islam in 1965, he took the name El-Hajj Malik El-Shabazz. At the Audubon Ballroom in upper Manhattan on February 21, 1965, three members of the Nation of Islam assassinated him in front of a large crowd who had come to hear him speak. Malcolm X functioned as an early "militant" alternative to Martin Luther King, Jr.'s nonviolent, integrationist message, insisting as would others later on that blacks must be willing and able to defend themselves against violence, and in death thereafter as an inspiration for black pride. *Bibliography*: Malcolm X, as told to Alex Haley, *The Autobiography of Malcolm X* (New York: Random House, 1965); and Michael Eric Dyson, *Making Malcolm: The Myth and Meaning of Malcolm X* (New York: Oxford University Press, 1995).

Moyers, Bill. Born June 5, 1934, in Hugo, Oklahoma. Moyers grew up in Marshall, Texas, and began working for the local newspaper at the age of sixteen. He studied journalism and earned a degree in divinity from Southwestern Baptist Theological Seminary, beginning his radio career in Austin, Texas, which he left to go to Washington as a special assistant to Texas Senator Lyndon B. Johnson. He served as deputy director of the Peace Corps from 1961 to 1963, and then as President Johnson's special assistant; he also functioned as LBJ's press secretary from 1965 to 1967, when he became publisher of *Newsday*, the Long Island, New York, daily newspaper. Later he worked prolifically for public television, becoming a well-known television journalist and producer—via Public Affairs Television, the company he and his wife, Judith Davidson Moyers, established in 1986—of documentaries and public affairs programs.

Newton, Huey P. Born in Monroe, Louisiana, February 17, 1942; died in Oakland, California, August 22, 1989. Newton was named for the populist demagogic governor of Louisiana, Huey Pierce Long, but as the youngest of seven children, he moved along with his family to Oakland, California, in 1945. Largely self-educated though possessing a high school diploma, Newton attended Merritt College in Oakland, earning an associate of arts degree, and then studied law at Oakland City College and the San Francisco School of Law. He met Bobby Seale, with whom in October 1966 he cofounded the Black Panther Party for Self-Defense, taking the title of minister of defense and posing for a widely reproduced photograph showing him seated in a chair with a gun in one hand and a spear in another. Newton continued to lead the Black Panthers despite his conviction in 1968 for manslaughter, a conviction later overturned but that permitted political agitation around a "Free Huey" slogan. The Black Panthers epitomized the militant, potentially violent black power alternative to mainstream civil rights activism. In 1971 he led the Panthers in a nonviolent, social services–providing direction, remaining party leader until 1973, when he fled the United States to avoid indictment for murder. In 1977 he returned and was tried twice, but neither jury returned a verdict. He earned a Ph.D. in social philosophy from the University of California, Santa Cruz, in 1980. He was shot dead by a drug dealer in 1989. *Bibliography*: David Hilliard and Lewis Cole, *This Side of Glory: The Autobiography of David Hilliard and the Story of the Black Panther Party* (Boston: Little, Brown, 1993).

Rockefeller, Nelson. Born at Bar Harbor, Maine, on July 8, 1908; died at New York, New York, on January 26, 1979. Nelson Rockefeller attended the Lincoln School in Manhattan, which was affiliated with Teacher's College, Columbia University, and then Dartmouth College, graduating in 1930 with a bachelor's degree in economics. He engaged in various business and philanthropic enterprises, entering government service in 1940 as director of the Office of Inter-American Affairs. During 1953–54 he served as undersecretary of the new Department of Health, Education, and Welfare under Oveta Culp Hobby, and then as special assistant to President Eisenhower for foreign affairs in 1954–55. In 1958 he was elected Republican governor of New York State, bucking a Democratic electoral trend that year and expending for the first of many times much money. He would be elected to three more four-year terms as governor, serving until 1973; in 1974 he took office as Vice President of the United States, serving until 1977. As New York's governor, Rockefeller came to embody liberal Republicanism, presiding over greatly increased spending (it tripled under his extended watch) and social service state programs, most especially the expansion of the State University of New York. He was a prominent supporter of civil rights and a proponent of Great Society and War on Poverty programs, and was viewed by President Johnson as an ally. If there had ever been a possibility of a Republican-led Great Society departure, only Nelson Rockefeller potentially had the status and energy to make it happen; instead, he was an increasingly marginal figure within his own party, which he never abandoned despite this. He unsuccessfully contended for the GOP presidential nomination in 1960, 1964, and 1968. *Bibliography*: Joseh Persico, *The Imperial Rockefeller* (New York: Simon & Schuster, 1982).

Rustin, Bayard. Born in West Chester, Pennsylvania, March 17, 1912; died August 23, 1987, in New York City. Rustin grew up in an atmosphere permeated by Quakerism; he became a Friend in 1936. He attended Wilberforce University and Cheyney State Teachers College before moving to New York City in 1937, where he became active in leftist circles and political movements, including pacifism. He worked as an organizer for the Fellowship of Reconciliation as its race relations secretary, traveling widely; his work was interrupted by prison time (1943–46) for refusing to submit to the draft or alternative service. In 1947 he helped organize and participate in the Journey of Reconciliation, a before-its-time dress rehearsal for the trips of the 1960s Freedom Riders, to challenge institutionalized segregation in transportation. He went to Montgomery, Alabama, in early 1956 to establish contact with the developing bus boycott movement, there meeting Martin Luther King, Jr., whom he advised on tactics and strategy, thereby establishing a lasting relationship. Rustin assisted King in organizing southern black ministers into the Southern Christian Leadership Conference. He helped organize the 1957 Prayer Pilgrimage for Freedom and its successor, the 1963 March on Washington, for which he was chief organizer. At the 1964 Democratic National Convention in Atlantic City, he unsuccessfully attempted to broker a compromise regarding the seating of the Mississippi delegation; the experience led him to write a magazine article published the following year whose title, "From Protest to Politics," summed up Rustin's continuing commitment to integration and to nonviolent social change. He became the founding president of the A. Philip Randolph Institute, funded by labor unions, in 1965 and remained its president until 1979. He continued his activism until his death. *Bibliography*: Bayard Rustin, "From Protest to Politics; the Future of the Civil Rights Movement," *Commentary* (February 1965): 25–31; and John D'Emilio, *Lost Prophet: The Life and Times of Bayard Rustin* (New York: The Free Press, 2003).

Warren, Earl. Born in Los Angeles, California, on March 19, 1891; died July 9, 1974, in Washington, D.C. Chief Justice of the United States from October 5, 1953–June 23, 1969, Warren received both undergraduate and law degrees from the University of California, Berkeley. After public legal service in Alameda County, he was elected to the first of three terms as California governor in 1943; he was the unsuccessful Republication Vice-Presidential nominee in 1948. As leader of the Supreme Court, he played a major role in fashioning the unanimous overturning of state-supported segregation laws in the historic 1954 *Brown* decision. During the Great Society era, the Warren Court continued to display an activist bent while consistently upholding civil rights laws and policies emanating from the federal government. Criticism grew, however, that the justices were legislating from the bench, and the reaction against the Great Society era led to an increased politicization of judicial appointments. *Bibliography*: Ed Cray, *Chief Justice; A Biography of Early Warren* (New York: Simon & Schuster, 1997).

Wilkins, Roger ("Roy"). Born in St. Louis, Missouri, on August 30, 1901; died September 8, 1981, in New York City. After his mother's death when he was four years old, Wilkins was sent to live with his aunt and uncle and so grew up in St. Paul, Minnesota, where he attended integrated schools and worked on the high school newspaper. While a student at the University of Minnesota, from which he graduated with a bachelor's degree in sociology in 1923, Wilkins joined a local chapter of the National Association for the Advancement of Colored People (NAACP). He took a job with a black weekly newspaper in Kansas City, where he encountered pervasive segregation, and in 1931 moved to New York City to become the editor of the NAACP's magazine, *The Crisis*, succeeding W.E.B. DuBois and serving until 1949. He promoted the NAACP's legal strategy of seeking court remedies to the injustices of legally supported segregation. In 1955 he was named executive secretary of the NAACP, and in 1965 executive director, retiring in 1977. He was a principal organizer of the 1963 March on Washington. He worked with Lyndon

Johnson and helped organize support for the 1964 Civil Rights Act. Known as a moderate and a believer in coalition building, he was a harsh, outspoken critic of the black power movement, promoting instead a continuing focus on integration. *Bibliography*: Roy Wilkins, with Tom Mathews, *Standing Fast: The Autobiography of Roy Wilkins* (New York: Viking, 1982).

Wirtz, Willard. Born March 14, 1912, in DeKalb, Illinois. He earned a bachelor's degree from Beloit College in 1933 and graduated from the Harvard University School of Law in 1937. He taught at the Northwestern University Law School from 1939 to 1942 and again, after wartime federal government service on the War Labor Board and then the National Wage Stabilization Board, from 1946 to 1954. He became associated with Democratic Governor Adlai Stevenson of Illinois, joining Stevenson's law firm, and assisted his 1956 presidential run. In 1961, President John F. Kennedy named Wirtz undersecretary of labor, and then secretary of labor in 1962, a post he held through the end of the Johnson administration in 1969. He lent his support to such Great Society initiatives as Medicaid and federal aid to education, but was especially interested in job retraining programs and fought bureaucratic wars to get these programs under the control of the Department of Labor. After government service, he practiced law in Washington. *Bibliography*: Willard Wirtz, *Labor and the Public Interest* (New York: Harper and Row, 1964).

Young, Whitney. Born in Lincoln Ridge, Kentucky, on July 31, 1921; died in Lagos, Nigeria, on March 11, 1971. Young graduated from Kentucky State Industrial College in 1941 with a B.S. degree. After returning from army service during World War II in Europe, he earned a master's degree in social work at the University of Minnesota in 1947, the same year he began working with the National Urban League in St. Paul; his master's thesis was a history of the league. In 1949 he moved to Omaha as executive secretary of the Urban League there. In 1954 he moved to Atlanta to become the dean of the Atlanta University School of Social Work. In 1961 he was named executive director of the National Urban League, a post he held until his death by drowning in 1971. He succeeded in increasing the number of Urban League chapters nationwide and especially in the South. He was one of the leaders in the organization of the 1963 March on Washington, which the Urban League cosponsored. He worked with President Lyndon B. Johnson to ensure that the 1964 Civil Rights Act was being implemented. An enthusiastic supporter of the Great Society, he called for a "domestic Marshall Plan." *Bibliography*: Whitney M. Young, *To Be Equal* (New York: McGraw-Hill, 1964); and Dennis C. Dickerson, *Militant Mediator; Whitney M. Young, Jr.* (Lexington: University Press of Kentucky, 1998).

BIBLIOGRAPHY

WORKS CITED

Alinksy, Saul. *Rules for Radicals*. New York: Random House, 1971.

Banfield, Edward C. *Government Project*. Glencoe, IL: The Free Press, 1951.

———. *The Moral Basis of a Backward Society*. Glencoe, IL: The Free Press, 1958.

———. *Political Influence*. Glencoe, IL: The Free Press, 1961.

———. *The Unheavenly City*. Boston: Little, Brown, 1970.

———. *The Unheavenly City Revisited*. Boston: Little, Brown, 1974.

———. "Welfare: A Crisis Without 'Solutions.'" *The Public Interest* 16 (Summer 1969): 80–101.

———. "Why Government Cannot Solve the Urban Problem." In *The Conscience of the City*, edited by Martin Meyerson, 141–51. New York: George Braziller, 1970.

Banfield, Edward C., and Martin Meyerson. *Politics, Planning, and the Public Interest*. Glencoe, IL: The Free Press, 1955.

Banfield, Edward C., and James Q. Wilson. *City Politics*. New York: Vintage, 1963.

Berkowitz, Edward D. *Mr. Social Security: The Life of Wilbur J. Cohen*. Lawrence: University Press of Kansas, 1995.

Bloom, Alexander, and Wini Breines. *"Takin' It to the Streets": A Sixties Reader*. New York: Oxford University Press, 1995.

Boyle, Kevin. *The UAW and the Heyday of American Liberalism, 1945–1968*. Ithaca, NY: Cornell University Press, 1995.

Buchanan, Patrick J. *Right from the Beginning*. Boston: Little, Brown, 1988.

Buckley, William F. *American Conservative Thought in the Twentieth Century: Did You Ever See a Dream Walking?* Indianapolis: Bobbs-Merrill, 1970.

———. *God and Man at Yale*. Chicago: Henry Regnery, 1951.

———. *Overdrive*. Garden City, NY: Doubleday, 1983.

———. *The Unmaking of a Mayor*. New York: Bantam, 1966.

———. *Up From Liberalism*. New York: McDowell, Obolensky, 1959.

Buckley, William F., and L. Brent Bozell. *McCarthy and His Enemies*. Chicago: Henry Regnery, 1954.

Califano, Joseph A., Jr. *Inside; A Public and Private Life*. New York: Public Affairs/ Perseus, 2004.

———. *The Triumph and Tragedy of Lyndon Johnson: The White House Years*. New York: Simon & Schuster, 1991.

Carmichael, Stokely. "The Basis of Black Power." http://lists.village.virginia.edu/ sixties/HTML_docs/Resources/Primary/Manifestoes/SNCC_black_power.html.

———. *Black Power; The Politics of Liberation*. With Charles Hamilton. 1967. Reprint, New York: Vintage, 1992.

———. *Ready for Revolution: The Life and Struggles of Stokely Carmichael (Kwame Ture)*. With Ekiwueme Michael Thelwell. New York: Scribner, 2003.

———. "Toward Black Liberation." In *Afro-American History; Primary Sources*, edited by Thomas R. Frazier, 411–21. Belmont, CA: Wadsworth, 1988.

———. "What We Want." In *The New Student Left: An Anthology*, rev. ed., edited by Mitchell Cohen and Dennis Hale, 109–20. Boston: Beacon, 1967. (Originally published in the *New York Review of Books*, September 26, 1966.)

Clark, Kenneth. *Dark Ghetto: Dilemmas of Social Power*. New York: Harper & Row, 1965.

Cohen, Adam, and Elizabeth Taylor. *American Pharaoh. Mayor Richard Daley: His Battle for Chicago and the Nation*. Boston: Little, Brown, 2000.

Cohen, Mitchell, and Dennis Hale. *The New Student Left; An Anthology*. Rev. ed. Boston: Beacon, 1967.

Cohodas, Nadine. *Strom Thurmond and the Politics of Southern Change*. New York: Simon & Schuster, 1993.

Coleman, James., et al. *Equality of Educational Opportunity*. Washington, DC: Government Printing Office, 1966.

Davies, Gareth. *From Opportunity to Entitlement: The Transformation And Decline of Great Society Liberalism*. Lawrence: University Press of Kansas, 1996.

Edwards, Lee. *Goldwater: The Man Who Made a Revolution*. Washington: Regnery, 1995.

Evans, Rowland, and Robert D. Norak. "The Moynihan Report." *Wall Street Journal*, August 18, 1965.

Fairclough, Adam. *To Redeem the Soul of America: The Southern Christian Leadership Conference and Martin Luther King, Jr.* Athens: University of Georgia Press, 1987.

Frederickson, Kari. *The Dixiecrat Revolt and the End of the Solid South, 1932–1968*. Chapel Hill: University of North Carolina Press, 2001.

Galbraith, John Kenneth. *The Affluent Society*. Boston: Houghton Mifflin, 1958.

Gans, Herbert. *The Levittowners*. New York: Pantheon, 1967.

Garrow, David J. *Bearing the Cross: Martin Luther King, Jr. and the Southern Christian Leadership Conference*. New York: William Morrow, 1986.

Glazer, Nathan, and Daniel P. Moynihan. *Beyond the Melting Pot; the Negroes, Puerto Ricans, Jews, Italians, and Irish of New York City*. Cambridge, MA: MIT Press, 1963.

Goldberg, Robert Alan. *Barry Goldwater*. New Haven, CT: Yale University Press, 1995.

Goldwater, Barry. *The Conscience of a Conservative*. Shepherdsville, KY: Victor Publishing, 1960.

———. *The Conscience of a Majority*. Englewood Cliffs, NJ: Prentice-Hall, 1970.

———. *With No Apologies*. New York: William Morrow, 1979.

Goodwin, Richard. *Remembering America: A Voice from the Sixties.* Boston: Little, Brown, 1988.

Gordon, Margaret S., ed. *Poverty in America.* Proceedings of a National Conference held at the University of California, Berkeley, February 26–28, 1965. San Francisco: Chandler Publishing, 1965.

Graham, Hugh Davis. *The Uncertain Triumph: Federal Education Policy in the Kennedy and Johnson Years.* Chapel Hill: University of North Carolina Press, 1984.

Graves, Robert. *Goodbye to All That.* 2nd rev. ed. New York: Anchor, 1957.

Green, Edith. "The Educational Entrepreneur—a Portrait." *The Public Interest* 28 (Summer 1972): 12–25.

Gutterman, Marvin E., and David Mermelstein, eds. *The Great Society Reader: The Failure of American Liberalism.* New York: Random House, 1967.

Halberstam, David. *The Children.* New York: Random House, 1998.

Harrington, Michael. *The Accidental Century.* New York: Macmillan, 1965.

———. *Fragments of the Century.* New York: Touchstone/Simon & Schuster, 1977.

———. *The New American Poverty.* New York: Holt, Rinehart, and Winston, 1984.

———. *The Other America.* New York: Macmillan, 1962.

———. "Our Fifty Million Poor." *Commentary* (July 1959): 19–27.

———. "Poverty—U.S.A." *The Catholic Worker* (June 1952).

Hartmann, Susan M. *From Margin to Mainstream: American Women and Politics Since 1960.* New York: Knopf, 1989.

Hayden, Tom. "A Letter to the New (Young) Left." In *The New Student Left; An Anthology*, rev. ed., edited by Mitchell Cohen and Dennis Hale, 2–9. Boston: Beacon, 1967.

———. *Rebellion in Newark: Official Violence and Ghetto Response.* New York: Vintage, 1967.

———. *Reunion: A Memoir.* New York: Random House, 1988.

Hayward, Steven F. *The Age of Reagan: The Fall of the Old Liberal Order, 1964–1980.* Roseville, CA: Forum/Prima, 2001.

Hodgson, Godfrey. *The Gentleman from New York: Daniel Patrick Moynihan.* New York: Houghton Mifflin, 2000.

Hulsey, Byron C. *Everett Dirksen and His Presidents: How a Senate Giant Shaped American Politics.* Lawrence: University Press of Kansas, 2000.

Isserman, Maurice. *The Other American: The Life of Michael Harrington.* New York: Public Affairs, 2000.

Johnson, Lyndon B. *The Vantage Point: Perspectives on the Presidency.* New York: Popular Library, 1971.

Judis, John B. *William F. Buckley, Jr.: Patron Saint of the Conservatives.* New York: Simon & Schuster, 1988.

Kearns, Doris. *Lyndon Johnson and the American Dream.* New York: Harper & Row, 1976.

Keats, John. *The Crack in the Picture Window.* Boston: Houghton Mifflin, 1956.

King, Martin Luther, Jr. *Stride Toward Freedom: The Montgomery Story.* New York: Harper & Brothers, 1958.

———. *Why We Can't Wait.* New York: Harper and Row, 1964.

Levy, Peter B. *The New Left and Labor in the 1960s.* Urbana: University of Illinois Press, 1994.

Lichtenstein, Nelson. *The Most Dangerous Man in Detroit: Walter Reuther and the Fate of American Labor.* New York: Basic Books, 1995.

Lokos, Lionel. *Hysteria 1964: The Fear Campaign Against Barry Goldwater.* New Rochelle, NY: Arlington House, 1967.

Macdonald, Dwight. "Our Invisible Poor." *The New Yorker* (January 19, 1963): 82–132.

Margolis, John. *The Last Innocent Year. America in 1964: The Beginning of the "Sixties."* New York: Perennial/HarperCollins, 2000.

Matusow, Allen J. *The Unraveling of America: A History of Liberalism in the 1960s.* New York: Harper & Row, 1984.

Miller, James. "The Port Huron Statement." In *Democracy Is in the Streets: From Port Huron to the Siege of Chicago.* New York: Touchstone/Simon & Schuster, 1987.

Mills, C. Wright. "Letter to the New Left." In *The New Left; A Collection of Essays,* edited by Priscilla Long, 14–25. Boston: Porter Sargent, 1969.

———. *The Power Elite.* New York: Oxford University Press, 1956.

Mosteller, Frederick, and Daniel P. Moynihan, eds. *On Equality of Educational Opportunity: Papers Deriving from the Harvard University Faculty Seminar on the Coleman Report.* New York: Vintage, 1972.

Moynihan, Daniel P. *Coping: On the Practice of Government.* New York: Vintage, 1975.

———. "A Crisis of Confidence." *The Public Interest* 7 (Spring 1967): 3–10.

———. "The Crisis in Welfare." *The Public Interest* 10 (Winter 1968): 3–29.

———. *Maximum Feasible Misunderstanding: Community Action in the War on Poverty,* paper ed. New York: The Free Press, 1970.

———. *The Negro Family: The Case for National Action.* Washington, DC: Office of Policy Planning and Research, United States Department of Labor, 1965.

———. "The President and the Negro: The Moment Lost." *Commentary* (February 1967): 31–45.

———. "The Professionalization of Reform." *The Public Interest* 1 (Fall 1965): 6–16.

———. "Three Problems in Combating Poverty." Proceedings of a National Conference held at the University of California, Berkeley, February 26–28, 1965. In *Poverty in America,* edited by Margaret S. Gordon, 41–53. San Francisco: Chandler Publishing, 1965.

———. "What is 'Community Action'?" *The Public Interest* 5 (Fall 1966): 3–8.

O'Connor, Alice. *Poverty Knowledge: Social Science, Social Policy, and the Poor in Twentieth-Century U.S. History.* Princeton, NJ: Princeton University Press, 2001.

Patterson, James T. *Grand Expectations: The United States, 1945–1971.* New York: Oxford University Press, 1996.

Public Papers of the Presidents of the United States. Lyndon B. Johnson. Washington, DC: U.S. Government Printing Office, 1965–70.

Vol. I (Nov., 1963–June 30, 1964), pub. 1965.

1965: Vol. I (Jan.–May); Book II (July–Dec.), pub. 1966.

The Report of the President's Commission on National Goals. *Goals for Americans.* Englewood Cliffs, NJ: Prentice-Hall, 1961.

Reuther, Walter. *Selected Papers.* New York: Macmillan, 1961.

Rosenberg, Maria Barovic. *Women in Politics: A Comparative Study of Congress-*

women Edith Green and Julia Butler Hansen. Ph.D. diss., University of Washington, 1973.

Ross, Naomi Veronica. *Congresswoman Edith Green on Federal Aid to Schools and Colleges.* Ed.D. diss., Pennsylvania State University, 1980.

Royko, Mike. *Boss: Richard J. Daley of Chicago.* New York: Dutton, 1971.

Schulman, Bruce J. *Lyndon B. Johnson and American Liberalism: A Brief Biography with Documents.* New York: Bedford/St. Martin's, 1995.

Sennett, Richard. "Survival of the Fattest." *New York Review of Books,* August 13, 1970.

Steinfels, Peter. *The Neoconservatives: The Men Who Are Changing America's Politics.* New York: Touchstone/Simon & Schuster, 1979.

Stossel, Scott. *Sarge: The Life and Times of Sargent Shriver.* Washington, DC: Smithsonian Books, 2004.

To Secure These Rights. President's Committee on Civil Rights. Washington, DC: Government Printing Office, 1947.

Unger, Irwin. *The Best of Intentions: The Triumphs and Failure of the Great Society Under Kennedy, Johnson, and Nixon.* New York: Doubleday, 1996.

Warren, Mervyn A. *King Came Preaching: The Pulpit Power of Dr. Martin Luther King, Jr.* Downers Grove, IL: InterVarsity, 2001.

Weintraub, Bernard. "The Brilliancy of Black." In *Smiling Through the Apocalypse: Esquire's History of the Sixties,* 669–84. New York: Dell, 1971. (Originally published in *Esquire,* January 1967.)

Wilson, James Q. "The Independent Mind of Edward Banfield." *The Public Interest* 150 (Winter 2003): 63–88.

Zelizer, Julian E. *Taxing America: Wilbur D. Mills, Congress, and the State, 1945–1975.* Cambridge: Cambridge University Press, 2000.

WORKS CONSULTED

Aaron, Henry J. *Politics and the Professors: The Great Society in Perspective.* Brookings Studies in Social Economics. Washington, DC: Brookings Institution, 1978.

"Antipoverty Programs." *Law and Contemporary Problems* 31, no. 1 (Winter 1966): 1–147.

Banfield, Edward C. *Here the People Rule: Selected Essays.* 2nd ed. Washington, DC: AEI Press, 1991.

Barone, Michael. *Our Country: The Shaping of America from Roosevelt to Reagan.* New York: The Free Press, 1990.

Blumenthal, Sidney. *The Rise of the Counter-Establishment: From Conservative Ideology to Political Power.* New York: Times Books, 1986.

Branch, Taylor. *Parting the Waters: America in the King Years, 1954–63.* New York: Touchstone/Simon & Schuster, 1988.

———. *Pillar of Fire: America in the King Years, 1963–65.* New York: Simon & Schuster, 1998.

Carson, Clayborne. *In Struggle: SNCC and the Black Awakening of the 1960s.* Cambridge, MA: Harvard University Press, 1981.

Chalmers, David. *And the Crooked Places Made Straight: The Struggle for Social Change in the 1960s.* Baltimore: Johns Hopkins University Press, 1991.

Clark, E. Culpepper. *The Schoolhouse Door: Segregation's Last Stand at the University of Alabama.* New York: Oxford University Press, 1995.

Dallek, Robert. *Flawed Giant: Lyndon Johnson and His Times, 1961–1973.* New York: Oxford University Press, 1998.

Divine, Robert A., ed. *Exploring the Johnson Years.* Austin: University of Texas Press, 1981.

Education and the Public Good. Edith Green: *The Federal Role in Education* (The Burton Lecture, 1963). Walter P. Reuther, *The Challenge to Education in a Changing World* (The Inglis Lecture). Cambridge, MA: Harvard University Press, 1964.

Farber, David. *Chicago '68.* Chicago: University of Chicago Press, 1988.

————, ed. *The Sixties: From Memory to History.* Chapel Hill: University of North Carolina Press, 1994.

Fraser, Steve, and Gary Gerstle, eds. *The Rise and Fall of the New Deal Order, 1930–1980.* Princeton, NJ: Princeton University Press, 1989.

Friedberg, Aaron L. *In the Shadow of the Garrison State: America's Anti-Statism and Its Cold War Grand Strategy.* Princeton, NJ: Princeton University Press, 2000.

Ginzberg, Eli, and Robert M. Solow, eds. *The Great Society: Lessons for the Future.* New York: Basic, 1974.

Goldfield, David R. *Black, White, and Southern: Race Relations and Southern Culture, 1940 to the Present.* Baton Rouge: Louisiana State University Press, 1990.

Gross, Bertram M., ed. *A Great Society?* New York: Basic, 1968.

Hamby, Alonzo L. *Liberalism and Its Challengers: F.D.R. to Reagan.* New York: Oxford University Press, 1985.

Haveman, Robert H. *Poverty Policy and Poverty Research: The Great Society and the Social Sciences.* Madison: University of Wisconsin Press, 1987.

Hodgson, Godfrey. *The World Turned Right Side Up: A History of the Conservative Ascendancy in America.* Boston: Houghton Mifflin, 1996.

Kaplan, Marshall, and Peggy L. Cuciti, eds. *The Great Society and Its Legacy: Twenty Years of U.S. Social Policy.* Durham: Duke University Press, 1986.

Leuchtenburg, William E. *In the Shadow of FDR: From Harry Truman to Ronald Reagan.* Ithaca, NY: Cornell University Press, 1983.

Levitan, Sar A. *The Promise of Greatness.* Cambridge, MA: Harvard University Press, 1976.

Marwick, Arthur. *The Sixties.* New York: Oxford University Press, 1998.

Nash, George H. *The Conservative Intellectual Movement in America Since 1945.* Wilmington, DE: Intercollegiate Studies Institute, 1996.

Newfield, Jack. *A Prophetic Minority.* New York: Signet, 1966.

O'Connell, Jeffrey, and Richard F. Bland. "Moynihan's Legacy." *The Public Interest* 142 (Winter 2001): 95–106.

Ogbar, Jeffrey O. G., ed. *The Civil Rights Movement.* Problems in American Civilization. Boston: Houghton Mifflin, 2003.

O'Neill, William L. *Coming Apart: An Informal History of America in the 1960's.* New York: Quadrangle, 1971.

Schoenwald, Jonathan M. *A Time for Choosing: The Rise of Modern American Conservatism.* New York: Oxford University Press, 2001.

Teaford, Jon C. *The Twentieth-Century American City: Problem, Promise, and Reality.* Baltimore: Johns Hopkins University Press, 1986.

INDEX

About the Author

LAWSON BOWLING is Associate Professor and Chairman of the Department of History at Manhattanville College.